THE TIME OF MY LIFE

After her début on the London stage before the Second World War, Joyce Grenfell never looked back. She soon made entertaining the troops her principal wartime work, at first in England and Northern Ireland and then, from early 1944, across North Africa to Malta, Southern Italy, Cairo and Baghdad. A second tour followed, taking her even further afield, to India. These tours she described as 'The Time of My Life'. Whether slumming it in appalling quarters, bathing in an inch of water, or luxuriating in the British Embassy in Cairo and dancing with the Aga Khan's playboy son, Aly Khan, Joyce finds time to write her journal and fire off letters to her husband Reggie and her closest friend, Virginia Graham, as well as to her 'Darling Ma' in America.

THE TIME OF MY LIFE begins where the bestselling DARLING MA left off – essentially a journal which she kept in the final eighteen months of the War (against the rules) while travelling thousands of miles on behalf of ENSA, Entertainments National Service Association, otherwise known as 'Every Night Something Awful'. Edited and introduced by James Roose-Evans, this once more reveals Joyce Grenfell as an enthralling and unrivalled raconteur.

**Also by the same author,
and available from Coronet:**

DARLING MA
Letters to her Mother 1932–1944

James Roose-Evans received awards on both sides of the Atlantic for his adaptation and production of *84 Charing Cross Road*, which he directed in the West End and on Broadway. He founded the Hampstead Theatre in 1959 and was its first Artistic Director until 1971, pioneering the work of new dramatists. He has directed many plays in the West End including his own adaptation of Laurie Lee's *Cider with Rosie* and, in 1988, Hugh Whitemore's *The Best of Friends*, starring Sir John Gielgud. In 1989 he directed Edwige Feuillère in Paris in the French production of this play. He has written several books on the theatre. He edited the letters of Joyce Grenfell to her mother, DARLING MA, and wrote the entertainment, *Re: Joyce!* for Maureen Lipman. His most recent book, INNER JOURNEY, OUTER JOURNEY, tells something of the journey that led him, in 1981, to become the first theatre director to be ordained as a priest.

THE TIME OF MY LIFE
MY LIFE

**Entertaining the Troops
Her Wartime Journals**

Joyce Grenfell

**Edited and Introduced by
James Roose-Evans**

CORONET BOOKS
Hodder and Stoughton

Copyright © 1989 by Reginald Grenfell and James Roose-Evans

First published in Great Britain in 1989 by Hodder and Stoughton Ltd

Coronet edition 1990

The right of Reginald Grenfell and James Roose-Evans to be identified as the authors of this work has been asserted by them in accordance with the Copyright, Designs and Patents Act 1988.

British Library C.I.P.

Grenfell, Joyce, *1910–1979*
  The time of my life: entertaining the troops 1944–45.
  1. Entertainments. Grenfell, Joyce – 1910–1979
  – Correspondence, diaries, etc
  I. Title   II. Roose-Evans, James
791'.092'4

ISBN 0-340-52813-3

Printed and bound in Great Britain for Hodder and Stoughton Paperbacks, a division of Hodder and Stoughton Ltd, Mill Road, Dunton Green, Sevenoaks, Kent TN13 2YA. (Editorial Office: 47 Bedford Square, London WC1B 3DP) by Cox and Wyman Ltd, Reading, Berks. Photoset by Rowland Phototypesetting Ltd, Bury St Edmunds, Suffolk.

This book
is
dedicated
in memory of
Viola Tunnard
as Joyce would have wished

For Darling Vole, with love. Joyce.

Contents

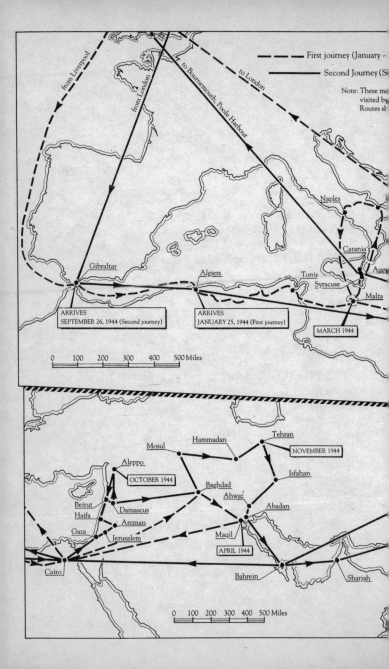

First journey (January _____

Second Journey (S_____

Note: These ma_____
visited by_____
Routes sh_____

from Liverpool

from London

to Bournemouth, Poole Harbour

to London

Naples

Catania

Augu_____

Gibraltar

Algiers

Tunis

Syracuse

Malta

ARRIVES
SEPTEMBER 26, 1944 (Second journey)

ARRIVES
JANUARY 25, 1944 (First journey)

MARCH 1944

0   100   200   300   400   500 Miles

Tehran

Hammadan

Mosul

NOVEMBER 1944

Aleppo

OCTOBER 1944

Isfahan

Beirut

Baghdad

Haifa

Damascus

Ahwaz

Abadan

Gaza

Amman

Maqil

APRIL 1944

Jerusalem

Cairo

Bahrein

Sharjah

0   100   200   300   400   500 Miles

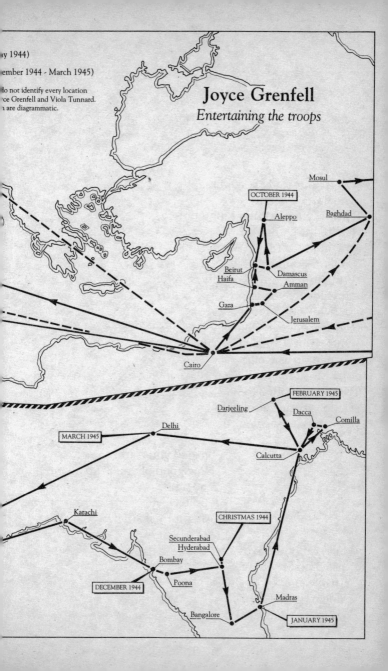

Joyce Grenfell
Entertaining the troops

...y 1944)

...ember 1944 - March 1945)

...do not identify every location
...ce Grenfell and Viola Tunnard.
...n are diagrammatic.

Mosul

OCTOBER 1944

Aleppo

Baghdad

Beirut
Haifa

Damascus
Amman

Gaza

Jerusalem

Cairo

FEBRUARY 1945

Darjeeling

Dacca

Comilla

Delhi

MARCH 1945

Calcutta

Karachi

CHRISTMAS 1944

Secunderabad
Hyderabad

Bombay

DECEMBER 1944

Poona

Madras

JANUARY 1945

Bangalore

Party

Oh Arthur, they're coming!
The party's begun –
How d'you do, Miss Montgomery,
Hello, Mr Dunn.
D'you know Major Wimble,
Sir Christopher Cook,
What fun, darling Dorothy,
How lovely you look!
Sir Wincanton Pluggley
Mrs Borridge – (Oh hell –
Oh Arthur, Cousin Caroline's
Turned up as well.)
Mrs Mostyn and Mavis,
The Vicar, John Drew.
Hello, cousin Caroline!
How nice to see you.

> So glad you could come,
> How good of you to spare
> The time
> For it's just
> An informal affair.

Hello Colonel Saxby,
Miss Bell, Mr Stone.
(Arthur look – Cousin Caroline's
Dancing alone
Without any music!)

How nice, Lady Bley,
Professor Crumb Teazle,
And how is Bombay?
Oh here's Mrs Buzbee
And Alderman Clews
(Arthur, now she is waltzing
Without any shoes.)
Mrs Biscuit, John Wilby;
(Don't look – near the door.
Oh Arthur, Cousin Caroline's
Full length on the floor.)

So glad you could come,
How good of you to spare
The time
For it's just
An informal affair.

(I'm under control now
Not making a fuss.
Let's pretend that she isn't
Related to us.)
Hello, Mrs Pomfret,
And Councillor Brice
And Dr Smith Wellerby,
And Matron – how nice.

(Oh heavens – a silence.
They're all in a ring.
Oh Arthur, Cousin Caroline
Is starting to sing!)

Joyce Grenfell
Undated

Acknowledgements

Once again, as with *Darling Ma*, I would like to thank Reggie Grenfell and Frances Campbell-Preston for their generous friendship and support over the past two years; Wendy and John Trewin, and Artemis Cooper, for their help with assembling footnotes; Catherine Treasure for again taking on the formidable task of typing; Peter Tunnard for his warmth of welcome and loan of material; Jean and Christopher Cowan of Aldeburgh for speaking so freely about Viola Tunnard and lending so much illustrative material for this book, as well as letters from Viola and Joyce; Rev. Halsey Colchester for his help and interest; John Perry who revived memories of Plato; Stephanie Darnill, the copy editor at Hodder and Stoughton, for her discernment, accuracy and diligence; the Countess of Bala for her unfailing support throughout; finally, Ion Trewin, my editor at Hodder and Stoughton, whose enthusiasm and quest for perfection, have resulted in such a splendid brace of books.

As with *Darling Ma*, so with these journals, I have tried to let Joyce's own story unfold in one flowing narrative, using an occasional letter home (to her mother or to Virginia Thesiger) to provide a variation at certain points in the story. I have not indicated by traditional dots where sentences or paragraphs have been removed, considering that a too pedantic approach would get between the reader and Joyce. For the same reason I have always tried to preserve her idiosyncratic style.

In spite of careful research, we have failed to track down all the people Joyce met on her travels. It is to be hoped that readers may be able to provide clues so that additional footnotes may be made in any future edition.

This volume carries, apart from a longer introduction, an After-word, in order to let the reader know what happened to Viola Tunnard, and it is here that I am especially grateful to Reggie Grenfell and Jean Cowan for allowing me to draw upon the letters of Joyce and Viola for this section of the tale. Lastly, my thanks to Melisa Treasure for her help with reading the proofs.

James Roose-Evans

Foreword

The Time of My Life begins where *Darling Ma*[1] left off. But instead of seeing the life of Joyce Grenfell through the letters she wrote to her mother in America, *The Time of My Life* is essentially a journal, which she kept in the last two years of the Second World War – against the rules – while travelling thousands of miles in the Middle East and in Asia entertaining the troops.

I came across these journals amongst a wealth of archive material in the study of Joyce Grenfell's Chelsea home in London while researching and writing *Re:Joyce!*, an entertainment about her life and work, starring Maureen Lipman. This opened in London just as *Darling Ma* was published and together they reminded us, nearly a decade after Joyce's death, how natural a recorder of events she was.

Darling Ma ended with Joyce and her pianist Viola Tunnard about to sail to Italy and the Middle East to entertain the troops under the auspices of ENSA (Entertainments National Service Association). With her she took, as always (it was not permitted, but she ignored this) a series of stiff red-covered exercise books with ruled lines in which to record her impressions. She was a compulsive letter writer (there are, for example, seven volumes, neatly typed, of letters to her oldest friend Virginia Thesiger, née Graham) and communicator.

It has been asked, for whom was she writing? I have

[1] Published by Hodder and Stoughton, 1988 and in Coronet paperback, 1989.

little doubt but that she was recording, perhaps not consciously at first, for posterity. One clue lies in an answer she gave to a question during a talk at the Rosehill Theatre in Yorkshire, one of the last public appearances she made before her death.

Which of the many things that have happened to me have I most enjoyed? Apart from meeting my husband, we will say. Was it the first time I appeared in print in *Punch*? Was it the first time I appeared in a column in *The Observer*? Was it the first time on the stage, TV studio, gramophone studio, film etc? *No!* It was the moment when I held in my hand the hardbacked copy of my first book, *Joyce Grenfell Requests the Pleasure*. There was something undreamed about, unsought and unplanned, and absolutely thrilling!

It may have been unsought and unplanned but I do not think it was entirely undreamed about. In any case she often adapted this speech for different situations: sometimes it was the theatre ('you and me here *now!*') and sometimes it was the medium of radio. And she was quite genuine on each occasion for she was a born performer and loved the moment of contact; but, deep down, it is clear that she wanted to be a writer. As early as 1938 we find her writing to her friend Virginia Graham:

I can observe all right. My mental picture is clear down to the mauve, pleated underneath of the mushroom picked yesterday. But when I try to write it into a story I go blank. I twist my pen, draw daisies up the margin, and go in search of an apple . . . While I'm in bed, unhampered by pen and paper I can visualise the whole thing and I laugh at the things I see. But I can't tighten it up into words.

As a writer Joyce, who was a very good amateur watercolourist, has a painterly eye for significant detail.

Often she will comment 'not beautiful but very draw-able'. She has described how, as a girl, her father taught her to look at things. Together they explored museums and galleries; looking at buildings and objects, he made her aware of the intrinsic beauty of each thing that is well made, from a key to a teapot, a bridge to a pylon. At the weekends they would explore the City. Her father knew lanes and alleys off the main thoroughfares, and often they were the only people in the empty streets, looking for special treasures, a moulding round a door, a fine fanlight, or the lettering on a tomb. They went to the National Gallery and the Tate and the Wallace Collection not once but often. Like all small children she began by seeing primary colours, until the day that her father took her to Hampton Court.

'Look at the colour in those bricks,' observed her Pa.

'It's red.'

'Have another look.'

And then, as she looked again, the solid red dissolved and now the bricks were many different colours; some were almost blue, or grey, or mauve, or pink, or sandy yellow. Only a few were brick red! It was a revelation. From that moment on she saw more than primary colours and her discovery was that the colours had been there to be found all the time.

In these journals there are many such moments of fine observation: 'It was a greyish day like dusk when all the flowers suddenly glow as if they were lit from within', or this scene observed in Darjeeling, 'Lovely design there – stone wall, stone step; warm stone colour. The children with flat little Mongolian faces, grey-beige with little slit eyes catching the light like chips of jet. Their rusty black clothes. Wish I could have drawn it.'

Her earliest efforts at writing, in a schoolroom exercise book containing the beginning of a romantic novel, were towards fiction. Only slowly did she come to see that this was not her forte. But she wrote compulsively. And during the war, especially, both in her letters to Darling

Ma, as in her ENSA journals, there is an urgency to record things exactly as they were at that moment just because there might never be another. It is significant that when she did another tour, her third, after the war, the journal, although faithfully kept, has none of the immediacy of those earlier wartime writings. This is why I have only included the final entry from that journal.

Throughout her life she kept a journal and she wrote letters. Whenever she was away she would write daily to her husband Reggie, as also to Virginia, warm and glowing letters full of detail. Here is an unpublished poem which I found among her papers, inscribed 'For R.', which sums up her very special relationship with Reggie Grenfell, and which makes more poignant her decision, recorded in these pages, after acknowledging that Reggie is lonely and missing her, to go on and do Baghdad, and so extend the tour, just because no one else would do Baghdad.

> You are secure within my love
> Unquestioned and unquestioning,
> Unchanging like the certain nursery days
> In all your ways.
>
> The presence of your love is warm
> Though there be distances between,
> No separation in my heart
> Though we're apart.
>
> Those words by careless usage are
> Grown meaningless but I would have
> Them read as if they were quite new
> For I love you.

In 1939 Joyce Grenfell was happily married, living in a cottage on the Cliveden estate, loaned to her by her aunt, Nancy Astor; actively involved with the local Women's Institute, and earning her living as a radio critic for *The*

Observer. Then, a few months before war broke out, she found herself, a complete amateur, appearing in a revue in the West End, and becoming a star overnight, hailed by all the critics as Britain's answer to Ruth Draper (a distant relation and none too pleased when Joyce became also a monologuist!). With the outbreak of war, however, theatres and places of entertainment were closed down. The infant BBC television service at Alexandra Palace ceased 'for the duration', while BBC radio broadcasting shrank to a single Home Service consisting of non-stop news and organ music by Sandy McPherson. Overnight the entire theatrical profession was out of work. George Bernard Shaw protested publicly at this 'master-stroke of unimaginative stupidity', observing that at such a time of crisis there was even greater need for entertainment to boost the morale of the nation.

The ban was lifted two weeks later, but performances were limited to the daylight hours. Joyce now found herself working in the West End, as well as helping in the canteen at the National Gallery lunchtime concerts organised by her friend, the pianist, Myra Hess, and travelling back at night by train to Cliveden. In addition, at the request of Lady Astor, who had ambivalent feelings towards Joyce's involvement with the theatre, Joyce was responsible for two wards at the Canadian Red Cross Hospital based at Cliveden, where she became a kind of welfare officer, doing odd jobs for the patients, shopping for them, writing their letters, organising tea parties, even teaching them needlework (art therapy, as such, was then unheard of) while every now and then she would organise sing-songs in the wards. It was during this period that she also did a series of troop concerts in various parts of the country. Reggie had been called up and so she lived on her own at Parr's (the cottage was so named after a former butler at Cliveden), until she had officers billeted with her.

In the weekly letters to her mother she can be seen wrestling at times with her conscience as to what was the

best form of war-work for her to engage in. Was being an
entertainer enough? she asks. Certainly Aunt Nancy did
not think so. Then on November 11th, 1939, she listened
to the Armistice Day speech made by the Queen. Her
words commemorating the dead of the First World War
made a great impact upon Joyce, as doubtless they did
upon thousands of other women throughout the Com-
monwealth, particularly the passage when the Queen
remarked:

> For twenty years we have kept this day of remem-
> brance as one to consecrate the memory of that past
> and never-to-be-forgotten sacrifice. And now the
> peace which that sacrifice made possible has been
> broken. And once again we have been forced into war.
>
> I know that you would wish me to voice, in the name
> of the women of the British Empire, our deep and
> abiding sympathy with those on whom the first cruel
> and shattering blows have fallen; the women of
> Poland. Nor do we forget the gallant womanhood of
> France, who are called on to share with us again the
> sorrows and hardships of war. War has at all times
> called for the fortitude of women. Even in other days
> when it was the affair of the fighting forces only. Now
> all this has changed. For we, no less than men, have
> real and vital work to do. To us also is given the proud
> privilege of serving our country in her hour of need.
> The call has come, and from my heart I thank you, the
> women of our great Empire, for the way in which you
> have answered it . . .
>
> Women of all lands yearn for the day when it will be
> possible to set about building a new and better world,
> where peace and goodwill shall abide. That day must
> come. We all have a part to play. I know you will not
> fail in yours. We put our trust in God who is our
> strength and refuge in all times of trouble. I pray with
> all my heart that He may bless and guide and keep you
> always.

We all have a part to play. What Joyce was not yet sure of was: what was her part? On November 23rd, 1941, we find her writing to her mother:

There's a big call for women volunteers to the forces and to industry on at the moment, and I cannot decide whether the job I'm doing at the hospital is just justifiable or whether I should leave it for something else. I do NOT want to go into uniform for a whole variety of purely selfish reasons! Mainly physical: eight in a room, rare baths, no quiet, no privacy, etc. I had enough of all that when I was at boarding school when I loved it. But now I would really hate it. But of course, if I have to, I *can*.

Finally, in 1942, she gave up her hospital welfare work and decided to make entertaining her full-time war work. She did a small hospital tour in the North of England with a variety company, followed by a ten-week tour of Northern Ireland with a troupe of straight musicians in which she was the compère and had a spot for her own songs and monologues. They were called – a little hopefully, Joyce always considered – the 'Music You Love' company, and they gave gems from the classics, ranging from 'Your Tiny Hand Is Frozen', to 'One Fine Day', and Handel's Largo.

Believing that hospital entertaining was much more her line she volunteered, in 1943, to do a ten-week tour for ENSA in Algeria, Malta, and Sicily, which turned into a five-and-a-half month tour and which was to take her as far as Persia. This first tour was followed by a second of six-and-a-half months which took her through the Middle East and out to India.

It was Noël Coward who suggested to Joyce that she should entertain the troops overseas. Earlier in 1943 Coward had undertaken to do a twelve week tour of troop and hospital concerts but he resolutely refused to have anything to do with ENSA, finding the whole concept of actors entertaining in uniform ludicrous. In his diaries he records how he never ceased to be impressed by the sheer endurance of the men, and their capacity for overcoming desolation, boredom, homesickness, pain and discomfort. He covered Algiers, Malta, Cairo, Beirut, Baghdad and Basra – many of the places Joyce was to visit. Then, when news came of the Italian surrender at the end of the first week of September, he was back in Cairo for six more hospital concerts, followed by a tour of the canal zone; then on to camps in Alexandria, and Tripoli where he found, as did Joyce, hospital wards crammed with victims of the recent Salerno landings. From Tripoli he returned to Algiers and finally back to England by way of Gibraltar, arriving at the end of October. He told Joyce that there was a lot of work to be done out there and that she ought to get out and do it. All she needed, he said, was a pianist and a piano; in this way they could be completely mobile, able to be sent to places which were not practical for ENSA to send large concert parties. As well as North Africa Coward expressed a special concern for the troops stationed in Paiforce (Persia and Iraq) whose task it was to police the Aid-to-Russia route from the Indian Ocean northwards and maintain communication and RAF bases throughout the area, and who felt forgotten since they were serving in non-combatant zones. It was in Paiforce that Joyce would score a particular personal success.

Coward, in spite of his personal dislike of the organisation, recommended her to ENSA and they suggested a six-month tour. 'Nonsense!' said Noël when she told him. 'You can't keep fresh properly for so long. Go for eight weeks.' In the end she settled for ten and ENSA agreed. Her Aunt Pauline (Spender Clay, Nancy Astor's sister-in-law) produced a pair of fur-lined boots and an inflatable cushion, both of which proved to be invaluable. At first she had hoped to travel with her friend and composer, Richard Addinsell, but his poor health prevented this. She therefore began to look around for an accompanist to go with her. In her autobiography Joyce says that the first time she met Viola Tunnard, who was to accompany her, was when she auditioned for the job at the suggestion of Walter Legge, who was in charge of concerts for ENSA, although Viola's brother Peter says that they had met long before this: 'It was really through our neighbour in Norfolk, Lady Evelyn Jones,[1] who was Reggie Grenfell's aunt; they had five daughters and lived about ten miles away and we were always meeting for picnics and parties. Joyce and Reggie were regular visitors to the Jones' home.'

Joyce describes vividly her first impressions of Viola at this audition:

On a cold grey November morning Viola arrived wearing a black fur coat with a stand-up collar and no hat. I registered a pale and drawable face, with good bones, dark hair, wide-apart brown eyes and a beguiling, shy smile. In repose her mouth went up at the corners. She was diffident about playing my kind of songs. She said she didn't suppose she'd do them the way I wanted them done. We ran through some of the numbers and I noticed she played 'ballads', such as 'Can't Help Lovin' Dat Man,' and 'The Way You Look Tonight', as well as Dick's songs, rather better than she did the jazzier ones. I sang them better, too.

'Would you like to do the tour?'

'Do you think I'd be good enough?'

'Yes, I do – I'm sure of it.'

'Well, if you're sure – I'd like to go.'

'That's fine then.'

Viola Tunnard, although seven years younger than Joyce Grenfell, became a central part of Joyce's life.

[1] Daughter of Earl Grey. Her husband, L. E. Jones, wrote *A Victorian Boyhood* and *An Edwardian Youth*.

Before this audition she had already volunteered to go overseas for ENSA. Walter Legge for whom she auditioned recalls, 'The audition lasted only five minutes. She was obviously a highly gifted musician, an able pianist and an attractive, unusual personality. My only doubt was whether this spare, almost fragile, well-educated girl was tough enough for the hardships involved in the sort of travel she declared herself willing to undertake.' Her first ENSA tour was partly as soloist and mainly as accompanist to the singers Maggie Teyte, Nancy Evans and Richard Lewis, all long accustomed to being accompanied by Gerald Moore.[1] They were delighted with Viola both as a musician and as a person. But she craved travel and so when the chance came to do a tour with Joyce she snatched it.

Viola was the eldest of three children. Born in 1916, her favourite brother Peter was born four years later, with Thomas (known as Tim) born in between, in 1918. They spent their first twenty years in Norfolk where their father was a country parson at Lexham. A great shot, fisherman and scholar, he was the traditional English country parson and much loved. Their mother had been married before, and it was she who brought the music (all three children were intensely musical) into the family. She had studied music at the Royal Academy and played the piano beautifully. Then, in 1905, she married a rich banker who, so he claimed, fell in love with her back while she was performing. He was twenty-five years older than she; their honeymoon lasted three months in Canada, where he was Director of the Canadian Pacific. They had one child, Betty. She was only thirty-two when he died, leaving a complicated will which stipulated that she would lose the greater part of his fortune if she married again. If the Tunnard children absorbed their mother's musical talents, they also benefited from their

[1] Leading 'pianoforte accompanist' from the 1930s until his retirement in 1967.

father's classical education. In her autobiography Joyce comments that she found herself often wishing she had been better educated and when she was on tour with Viola in the Middle East she relied on her to tell her about the places they visited, for there were no guide-books available then.

Viola mocked my ignorance of the ancient Greeks and Romans but allowed that I knew more music than she did. I had had seven years longer for listening, but had none of the insight into structure and musical logic that she had already acquired. When we went to concerts together after the war I learned to listen and hear in a new way, and I continue to be grateful to her for that. And for introducing me to bird-watching. Her father was also a botanist and an ornithologist.

All three children were musical, but Viola claimed that her brother Peter was more musical than she. He played both the piano and cello at school and won a scholarship to Paris to study art history. The outbreak of war put an end to his studies and when the war was over he went into the fine art business instead. Their brother, Timothy, won an organ scholarship and went up to New College, Oxford, and afterwards became a music teacher. With the money that their mother brought from her first marriage, even though considerably less than it might have been, the children were brought up in great luxury in their beautiful Regency vicarage. There were six ser-vants who lived in but eventually their mother's money ran out and the luxuries came to an end. 'Our mother pushed Viola musically' recalls Peter Tunnard, 'and often Viola was in tears.' It may well be that some of Viola's later emotional difficulties stem from her relationship with her mother. 'Ma was terrifically capable and the house was beautifully run, *but* she had these nervous breakdowns.' It was always said that she should never have been allowed to stay by her first husband's bedside throughout the year that he was dying, often screaming with the pain which no drugs could alleviate.

Viola won a scholarship to the Royal College of Music where she studied both the violin and piano (the latter under the distinguished soloist, Kathleen Long). She then did a variety of jobs until the chance came to go abroad for ENSA.

After the war she was increasingly in demand as a serious musician and came rather to resent that her name was always linked with Joyce Grenfell, as her accompanist. By then she was accompanying Peter Pears, Janet Baker, John Shirley-Quirk, Robert Tear and many more, and playing duets with Benjamin Britten. She also worked regularly at the Aldeburgh Festival. 'She would coach the most distinguished singers,' observed Walter Legge, 'with the most saintly patience.' She was so skilled that he entrusted her with playing for Herbert von Karajan's rehearsals for his operatic recordings. After the first of them, von Karajan asked Legge, 'Where did you find that girl? I'd like her for my musical staff in Salzburg. She's got rhythm, and remembers, and keeps tempo.' But Viola refused; being a perfectionist she feared that her German and Italian were not up to standard.

In her ENSA journals Joyce often refers to Viola's moods, times when Viola seemed possessed by an inner darkness and there would be no way of reaching her. Of course sometimes these moods may have been provoked by sheer despair at the pianos she was expected to play; only a musician can appreciate the torture of a piano that produces wrong notes or even no notes. At other times she may have been withdrawing from Joyce's very extrovert personality. As Peter Tunnard, with whom Viola shared a flat for twenty-five years, has remarked, 'Viola was a very private person and introverted. And she needed peace. Joyce always wanted to talk: let's do this, get our hair done, wash out our smalls – a bossy pants! Viola wanted to wander out alone, not to be talked at all the time. That was my impression.' Her moodiness went sense of humour and so were able to cope when suddenly announced as 'And now, two well-known artists, Miss Joyce Grenfell and Miss Viola Tunnard, who have been flown out especially to entertain men in bed!' to which one of the patients responded, 'Cor, they've laid that on now!'

If Joyce knew how to make her audiences laugh she had also learned something else from her experience with the wards at the Red Cross Hospital at Cliveden. 'If there is any worth in this job then it lies in making people laugh out of themselves. It means releasing them from their surroundings. *But* sometimes they don't want to be cheered up. Sometimes all they really want is to sing slow sad songs and to let them join in.' In *Re:Joyce!* I quote two incidents which reveal much about Joyce's essential quality at this period of her life and explain why the work was so deeply fulfilling for a woman who, sadly, was unable to have children. She describes in Italy a very young boy, with pale gold hair and a Devonshire accent, who lay very flat and still on his bed. He beckoned her over with his hand. 'Could you please sing a song about a mother?' She was horrified to discover she didn't know one. And then she recalled a lullaby her mother used to sing to her, 'Mighty Like A Rose':

> Sweetest li'l' feller
> Everybody knows
> Don't know what to call him
> But he's Mighty Lak' A Rose.
> Lookin' at his Mommy
> With eyes so shiny blue
> Makes you think that Heav'n
> Is comin' close to you.

The other incident quoted in *Re:Joyce!* is one evening when they had just done three concerts in the one day.

Viola finished the last concert with Dick Addinsell's

Warsaw Concerto. It was in a tent, one side rolled up,
and on the bank outside there were patients sitting and
standing in the low brilliant sunshine. At the first notes
the other patients, further away, hurried over to join
the party . . . All those young men, listening and later
singing – out of this world! I felt so remote and like all
the mothers there ever were.

What both women had to learn was how to cope with
their emotional reactions to many of the horrors they
witnessed. In Naples, March 20th, 1944, she writes: 'Oh,
God, the sights I've seen today. We haven't *touched* the
war till today. Bed after bed filled with mutilated men,
heads, faces, bodies. It's the most inhuman, ghastly,
bloody, hellish thing in the world. It was quite numbing.'
Thus, at first they were in danger of being overwhelmed
by their emotional response, 'then compassion took the
place of personal distress, and it was the presence of love,
practical and supporting,' that enabled them to continue
their work. Looking back on those tours Joyce was to
observe:

Very seldom is one called upon to do more than one
thinks possible. We did get tired, but I knew that the
spiritual source of energy was available to be drawn
upon and because there was so little time to think
about ourselves, we were able to carry on working for
longer than we might have done under less challeng-
ing circumstances. We grew working muscles and
learned techniques that allowed us to be spontaneous
and ready to improvise. Noël had been wrong about
not staying fresh for more than eight weeks. The
rewards were more than enough to keep us going.

The rewards were indeed unforgettable. As she
observes in these journals, 'The all high in success is,
"When are you coming again?" Take all the orchids, all
the telegrams, all the press notices, and give me that,

accompanied by that absolute genuine eagerness of the British soldier away from home! Golly me.'

There are two versions of her ENSA journals. The first which I came across is typed, and in the top left-hand corner, in Joyce's handwriting is the inscription, 'For darling Vole with love', and so I have dedicated this volume to the memory of Viola Tunnard as Joyce would obviously have wished. It is from this typescript that she drew material for her autobiography. Later when I discovered her original handwritten journal I found a number of passages excised from the typescript.

It is rare that Joyce speaks of herself, and of her own moments of lowness or depression, and yet for us, now, reading at this distance of time, it is these moments of vulnerability that provide important clues. She always seemed so resilient, so cheerful, so dependable, but these moments point to the importance in her life of her religious faith, as a Christian Scientist, a faith in which she had been brought up by both parents but which she was to re-discover on a deeper level as an adult. Christian Science believes that each individual must become 'Unselfed', that is, become more spirit, more God. As Joyce herself once said, 'I think what I am doing is *losing* Joyce Grenfell, and finding out the person God made. The older you get the more you realise that happiness is losing your false sense of what you are, your *false self*. What was that lovely quotation from Goethe? "Become what you are!" Well, that interpreted, means become what your true potential is, your spiritual wholeness.' So many people today, in social services and in public services, offer the minimum; they do the minimum that is required of them and hold back upon any further personal involvement or identification with their work. Joyce saw it otherwise: 'I do not believe anyone is any good without heart – you've got to mind about things.' It is a question of caring. 'This hospital business demands a hell of a lot of one. One must be on one's toes, unselfed. And how.'

On her return from the first ENSA tour she notes in her journal: 'It is good to feel stretched and to know that the job has been truly done. I've learnt a lot from it. Some of it has been good for the work; all of it good for the soul.' Joyce enjoyed success and her circus horse instinct, as she used to describe it, also enjoyed being centre-stage; but she knew at the same time that for every outer journey there is an inner journey, and without that inner journey, without that daily work and discipline upon the soul, or psyche, the outer journey will be impaired. In her crowded life, both at the professional and the personal levels, her hour a day for reading and prayer was crucial. In the very last letter which she wrote to Virginia Thesiger from hospital, a month before she died, she observed, 'I am not interested in the pursuit of happiness, but only in the discovery of joy. The one thing I am truly grateful for is the sense of God's Love I find everywhere.'

'What shall the theatre do if there is a Second World War?' was the question asked one Sunday morning in St John's Wood, London, in the summer of 1938, by four key figures in the British theatre: Leslie Henson, Owen Nares and Godfrey Tearle, actors; and Basil Dean, producer and director. Since Dean had had some experience in the First World War of organising entertainments for the troops, it was agreed that he should write a paper setting out the ideas of the group and arrange for this to be circulated among Members of Parliament and other groups. This document, entitled *The Theatre in Emergency*, and dated April 1st, 1939, began: 'The hysterical assumption that in the next war all theatrical entertainments will close down for good may be dismissed at once. The civil population will turn to entertainment for relief from their anxieties.' The initial response from the War Office was not encouraging, however, and so Dean decided to approach the Navy and Army and Air Force Institutes (NAAFI) suggesting that as they already provided food and drink to the Services, they should also sponsor the provision of entertainment. To this they agreed. Dean and his cohorts, with Sir Seymour Hicks as Chairman, began by calling their embryonic organisation ANSA (Actors National Service Association) but Leslie Henson shrewdly observed that if they called themselves ANSA they would only be accused of knowing all the answers! So it was changed to Entertainments National Service Association (ENSA).

With the outbreak of war, the Theatre Royal, Drury Lane became the headquarters of ENSA, with Dean in charge. To his credit the service which he envisaged was radically different from anything known in Britain before or anywhere else, and it soon came to be copied by other countries. Unfortunately, with such a fledgling organisation, there was no system of communication between ENSA and the Army, Air Force, or the War Office. The latter, obsessed by the need for security, understandably, was reluctant to provide ENSA with any information as to where troops were stationed. As a result, in the early days, concert parties would arrive at a camp only to find the unit had been moved to some unknown destination. In the meantime, in the first months of the war, ENSA was so overwhelmed by requests for entertainment that, in no time at all, it began to attract headlines which were to dog it throughout the war: CHAOS IN FRANCE, ENSA WASTE AND MUDDLE, SHOW CHAOS, and so on. There were indeed many examples of muddle, inefficiency and sheer incompetence, as Joyce Grenfell, Noël Coward, Jack Hawkins, and many others have testified. 'The general view among the men,' records Joyce, 'is that they get too much mediocre entertainment.' It used to be joked that above the entrance to the ENSA headquarters at Drury Lane there should be written the words: 'Abandon hope all ye who ENSA here!'

Another problem that bedevilled ENSA was the fact that by the close of 1941 there was an increasing shortage of professional artists, most of whom had been called up for military service. The root of the trouble lay in the fact that the government had no over-all plan for mobilising the resources of the entertainment industry. The call-up for military service had drained away the best of the younger talent, and when theatres and music halls were permitted to re-open, the commercial managements and agents began to view with alarm the inroads that ENSA was making upon available talent, making them reluctant to part with artists for ENSA.

ENSA's activities in the Middle East began in 1940. During the period of the great blitzes and raids on London, the troops overseas became increasingly worried about their homes and womenfolk and children. Their general feeling of neglect was intensified by the heavy delay in mails (as Joyce observes in these journals); some letters taking as long as three months to arrive, and others not arriving at all. Disturbed by the lack of news the men began to lose heart. It is easy, therefore, to appreciate the intense boost to their morale when artists such as Noël Coward, Joyce Grenfell, Viola Tunnard, and others began to arrive, bringing first-hand reports and reassurances, and, above all, by their presence, showing that someone cared. As one army bulletin sent from Deir ez Zor, east of Aleppo, in the middle of the Syrian desert, was to report:

> For two years there were no ENSA shows here for the men of the Persia and Iraq Command (Paiforce) and never once did any star appear north of Baghdad, and then Joyce Grenfell came out. She toured the whole command, visited every unit, no matter how long it took her to get there, or how small the unit. She sang to audiences of two signalmen whose nearest neighbour was two hundred miles away, gave informal shows, chatted to the men, went to hospitals, in some of the hottest places, little mud stations and all.

It is no wonder that she was loved and cheered by so many of the troops.

Back home at Drury Lane, Basil Dean had to deal with some 50,000 applications, mostly from amateurs. ENSA auditioned some 14,000 and offered engagements to 800. Much of the criticism of ENSA stemmed from the fact, as Richard Fawkes observes in *Fighting for a Laugh*[1] that it became too big. Basil Dean was forced into having to choose between quality and high standards, and meeting all the demands made upon ENSA. He chose the latter and so, inevitably, failed. There just was not enough talent to meet such a demand and so he had to fall back on second-rate artists, some of whom Joyce Grenfell describes in these journals. Such artists, if they can even be called that, attracted the anger and scorn of the troops, and this in turn rebounded upon Dean. Added to this was the fact that many top artists, like Noël Coward, refused to have anything to do with ENSA, and made their own arrangements to entertain the troops. The reception that shows received also depended very much upon the attitude of the local commanding officer and how efficient or otherwise he chose to be. Again Joyce is fiercely scathing wherever she finds ineptitude and inefficiency.

The entertainment and welfare officers we had to work with were a rum lot. Rum is the right word. I am not in sympathy with drunks, and rarely in my experience does drink bring out the best in people. Coping with those who had taken enough to slow up their thinking and blur their speech brought out intolerance in me. There is no boredom like the boredom of trying to get through to a sozzled entertainment officer who was not interested in what he was supposed to be doing in the way of organising our shows, and only wanted to be left undisturbed by a big bossy outsider like me who demanded action. I don't get angry very easily, but when there was plenty of time to plan for us,

[1] Macdonald and Jane's, London, 1978.

and (recurring worry) our piano, and nothing had been done, I did get tetchy. Viola said I was worth watching when I became what she called 'altesian'. This was a word she made up from the French *altesse*. It seems that I got more and more dignified, taller and more distant. I never entirely lost my cool, but I made it clear that I was not pleased. It usually worked. But only after a great deal of emphasising and the use of plain language.

By the time that Joyce came to tour for ENSA it had its own military style uniform known as Basil Dress (which produced further attacks on Dean who was accused of trying to run a private army). Joyce and Viola, like many artists, preferred not to wear it except as a means of saving their own clothes during the long tours, knowing that the men preferred to see them in civilian clothing. 'I must say I hate the uniform. I loathe wearing it.' One of the few West End managements to send shows out to the troops was Binkie Beaumont, head of H. M. Tennent, the most powerful management in London. Under his banner stars such as John Gielgud, Edith Evans, Beatrice Lillie, Michael Wilding, Elizabeth Welch, and many more, were sent out. One such company included Vivien Leigh, Beatrice Lillie, Dorothy Dickson and Leslie Henson, who played Gibraltar and North Africa, in an entertainment called *Spring Party*. The company travelled everywhere by air, from Gibraltar along the North African coast to Cairo, Ismailia and Suez. These rough flights over the desert often tried the nerves. On one journey, the port engine of the Dakota began to splutter and finally gave out altogether. One of the girls became hysterical.

'This is frightful. What will happen if we crash?' To which Bea Lillie replied, 'Two minutes' silence in the Ivy, dear!'[1]

---

[1] The Ivy off Charing Cross Road, then the top theatrical restaurant in London, made frequent appearances in Joyce's letters to her mother.

It was while Joyce was on tour in India, during her second tour for ENSA, that she received a cable from Noël Coward: 'DEFINITELY PLANNING REVUE TO OPEN MAY OR JUNE 1945 WOULD LIKE YOU HOME AS SOON AS POSSIBLE'. She cabled back that she was due home in the middle of March, was that soon enough? He said it would be and so she began to make notes for new material, in particular a sketch about an ENSA girl returning from doing an overseas job of entertaining the troops. The revue was called *Sigh No More*. In the end she had only two sketches in it and two songs, one which she wrote especially for this revue with Richard Addinsell, and which remained the one of which she was always proudest: 'Oh, Mr du Maurier.' The show itself was not a success. Joyce was given star billing along with Cyril Ritchard (who had been the star of the very first show she had appeared in, *The Little Revue*), Madge Elliot, and Graham Payn, with Mantovani and his Orchestra. *The Times* regarded it as a light, easy, amusing entertainment but 'disconcertingly without the impress of a definite style' and this in spite of its having been written, composed and directed by Noël Coward. In all the notices Joyce scores again and again: 'Miss Grenfell is in her best form'; 'The real honours of the evening go to Joyce Grenfell'; 'the show really belongs to Miss Joyce Grenfell'; 'the outstanding success is that of Joyce Grenfell'; 'It is not until Joyce Grenfell knocks us all sideways with "Travelling Broadens the Mind"[1] and Graham Payn puts over the hit number of the evening, "Matelot", that the show begins to sizzle'; 'the real hit of the evening was scored by Miss Joyce Grenfell in her monologue describing a girl's tour of the Forces in Italy and the Middle East'; while Harold Hobson declared, 'If there were no Grenfell the applause would not be excessive for Coward.'

As Lesley Blanch wrote in a major article about Joyce Grenfell for *The Leader*: 'However varied the finer shades

[1] See page 377.

of carping displayed by critics reviewing Noël Coward's new show, *Sigh No More*, all were united in their praise of Joyce Grenfell. She was, they said, the pièce de résistance; she stole the show.'

And as J. C. Trewin wrote in *Punch*:

Her ear for the shades of accent is as accurate as that of Shaw's Higgins, and she is devastating both in her own monologue as the too-sweet singer of Tulse Hill back from years of warbling 'Ave Maria' to the troops abroad ('I do all Deanna Durbin's numbers'), and as the terrible schoolgirl of Mr. Coward's song, who, quitting dumps so dull and heavy, obeys orders to sigh no more, lift up her heart, keep her chin up, and come smiling through.

After *Sigh No More* closed in the early spring of 1946 Joyce flew to America to visit her mother for the first time in nine years. Since her mother's last visit to England Joyce had gone on the stage, appeared in four London revues, been overseas for two tours of hospitals and camps, made brief appearances in several films and done a great deal of broadcasting. It was while she was in America that she received a cable from Reggie: 'CLEM SAYS GEORGE WISHES TO GIVE YOU THREE QUARTER LENGTH ROBE. REGGIE'. She guessed that Clem must be Mr Attlee, the Prime Minister, and that George was probably King George, but what on earth was a three-quarter length robe? She cabled back: 'MYSTIFIED PLEASE ELUCIDATE'. By return came Reggie's reply: 'TIMES CROSSWORD SILLY'. Of course! Three-quarters of the word 'robe' is OBE. She was being honoured for her work in hospitals and camps.

'Looking back on those tours,' Joyce was later to observe, 'I now see them (although I did not realise it then) as the time of my life. I was learning to do my job under the most demanding conditions I was ever likely to meet; I was seeing the world, and getting an opportunity as never before or since of doing what seemed to be useful work that stretched me to the full. The warmth of the welcome and the affectionate farewells when we left each new place might have turned our heads, but, in all honesty, Viola and I were both so grateful to be allowed to do the job that we were slightly awed by it and that kept us humble.'

JAMES ROOSE-EVANS

FIRST TOUR

---◆---

JANUARY–APRIL 1944

January 1944

After waiting, ready to fly with all papers in order, since December 24th last, Viola Tunnard and I have started for the Middle East by sea. It has been a long wait and a rather bitter one because ENSA has done so *very* poorly and wasted so much time when we might have been singing in the hospitals.

I have written an angry, but oh so dignified letter to silly Basil Dean. It won't do any good but has shifted some of the weight off my bosom. I could dwell on the whole dreary business at length but it is so boring and wretched so I won't. Anyway here we are. D19 is a cruising liner and we have got large cabins to ourselves on C deck. Steward a gasbag who enjoys horrors ('Hope this trip is better than the last. Dive-bombed we was'), name of Cameron. At the port Viola and I sat in an RASC lorry marked 'Civs.' for forty minutes. I ate a meat paste sandwich bought on the platform. Knitted-vest in texture, nil in taste. We watched lorries coming and going. One was marked 'Maureen Higginson' in an elementary hand, chalked up. And her friend Lilian Hackinbush had signed below. To the docks under escort of a nice paste-faced private who took our arms and encouraged generally. Thank goodness our luggage is so compact and light. Only forty-four lbs allowed for air and we decided to stick to that in case we are lucky and get passages home that way.

[1] The former P & O liner, ss *Strathmore*.

Three days later: The Capt in a pep talk has told us no one may keep a diary so I must abandon this and stick to personal anecdotes. Very sad; I had looked forward to recording events. However, they would probably make dull reading – meals, miles round the deck, reading, conversation, canteen perks.

Some of the young Red Crossers have combined with a group of young men to dance reels and Viola sits for hours noisily pounding that beast of a piano in the second-class recreation room. It is a pretty sight to see *les anglais avec leur figures si triste et leur derrières si gai* galumphing in rhythmless cavorts. They grow pink and glisten and it is good clean fun and exactly like the Folk Dance Fest in Bertie's *Little Revue*.[1] I suppose I'm a beast to find them so diverting. The thing is that the English ought never, or seldom, be allowed to get carried away by another nation's natural expression. The Scot who organises these orgies is neat and bouncy and makes a good job of the thing. But these others are like enormous Great Dane puppies, out of control and sudden in their movements. It's the same when the English get 'hot' or Spanish or Russian. I suppose their lack of self-consciousness is rather disarming. Anyway the eightsomes were very enjoyable to the dancers; and to me. I shall attend again.

The Two Leslies[2] and Viola and I did a show for the second and third class one evening. A rather frightening element of wild civilian seamen had fussed me a bit, but it all turned out happily, with the British Navy outweighing any subversive moods. The Two Ls were broad and competent and the audience loved it, the dirtier the better. My gentle little offerings were alright and I think they liked the contrast. Poor Viola had the big piano again which broke her heart. There is no middle C, no A,

---

[1] Herbert (Bertie) Farjeon: librettist of *The Little Revue*, in which Joyce made her sensational debut in 1939.

[2] Music hall act: Leslie Sarony, who also wrote songs, and Leslie Holmes.

no notes at all in the last two octaves to the right, and C
sharp is an interesting combination *chord* of C sharp and
A flat! I made some Free French sing 'Parlez moi
d'Amour' with me and we finished with open-throated
renderings of 'Shenandoah', 'Loch Lomond' and 'Daisy
Daisy'. Oh yes, and 'Danny Boy', and 'All Through the
Night'.

Back to the lounge afterwards for some orange drinks
and Viola played to us, starting with some ephemeral
tinklings of her own devising, and passing through
Chopin, for the Poles, and finishing on Bach. She has got
the real thing, I think. Temperament too. I'm afraid we'll
get very few chances for her to play properly, for I gather
the pianos out there are beyond hope. My ego is rather
'minuscule' just now. When I hear the great roars from
the boys at the really rather horrifying jokes told by Leslie
Sarony I wonder if I was an ass to try and do this job in my
own quiet way? I think it will be alright. It always has
been. Oh, God, I'm so glad that my dearest Dick[1] isn't
here because it would be quite beyond him and we'd both
be abysmal. Apart from the health thing there is the
question, a continual one too, of service. I do believe in
this and I do try to do something for it. But Dick lets all his
agonising doubts get between him and the job and that's
no good. Out here, away from the London values, the
thing seems pretty clear to me. It's a job like any other,
and prestige, professionalism, and 'my rights' are
vanished. We really are servants to do a job and to do it
with our hearts and humbly. I want to keep this clear in
my mind.

I washed Maud[2] last night and she is a row of neat little
curls today.

---

[1] Richard Addinsell: composer of the *Warsaw Concerto* and many of
Joyce Grenfell's songs.
[2] 'Maud' was Joyce's nickname for her hair. As she got older so her
forehead was furrowed by wrinkles and she began to arrange curls over
her forehead in the manner of Princess Maud, grand-daughter of
Queen Victoria.

Sunday, January 16th, 1944   On board D19

I write in abysmal glooms for absolutely no reason. Do
hope I'm not psychic and all the loved ones are dead at
home. Suddenly feel as if I can't do the job any more,
which being interpreted probably means tiredness. But I
don't quite feel that either. For first time have definitely
low view of self: which makes a change and is a jolt. Viola
gave me to think a bit and in a nice way. For many years
I've more or less succeeded in keeping too many feelings
out of things but just now I seem to be all feel and it's no
fun – What's more it's stupid. It's pretty hard I find *not* to
leap into the centre of the picture. I don't mean to; don't
plan it but lo! suddenly I'm there, unthinkingly. Partly
it's more restful than sluggish churnings all round and
that's when I do it awarely. But more often than not it has
happened and I've not known about it till I start reviewing the evening or luncheon or tea party and find I've
been talking an awful lot (sometimes quite well, I admit),
and I'm beginning to find I do it too often, and it's a bit of
a worry. In all honesty I enjoy it *when* I'm good but, also
honestly, I don't do it in *order* to be the centre. That just
happens incidentally. But if it is growing on me, and I *stop*
noticing it then it's time I coped. Tonight, 7.15 p.m.
I feel a fair beast; I also feel far off and unworthy and
sorry for myself and all together bloody. I'd like to go to
bed with a bottle and a good cry but instead the ADC has
asked me to perform after dinner for them. Ha-ha –
Pagliacci, that's me.

Tuesday, January 25th, 1944   Algiers

I write from an ENSA hostel that smacks oh so strongly of
the whole bloody organisation in that it is *la vie com-
munale*, beds half an inch off the floor, wickerwork to sit
on in the dining-cum-sitting room and institutionally
bare. But with a difference. *Ici on a une matronne française.*

She is pure golfing Lossiemouth to look at and wears khaki battledress. She is sandy and talks from one side of her mouth in hesitant English with a strong Comédie Française accent. I like her. She is nice to Viola and me because we are *des très grandes artistes de Londres*! Our bedroom has three Naafi beds in it, is twenty feet high with a tiled floor – icicle designs in pink-brown, olive-green and white. We are provided with a 'commode', a tin marked 'Litter' and two chairs. There is a grey marble basin with one cold tap. For some reason I am reminded of Katherine Mansfield's letters from the South of France. That air of brilliant light, cold wind and her despondency? My low moment on arrival soon went, for Viola and I got the giggles over the sun-trap dining-sitting room which is semi-circular in shape, the bow being all windows. At the top and bottom of these windows are panels of coloured glass – the colours powerful, the panes uncompromisingly square. The in-between panes are frosted, all but one or two, so that the Mediterranean, which lies immediately below, is totally invisible. It seems a pity. The colour scheme in the sun-trap is a nice, bright orange. Bunting is pinned to the glass doors with drawing-pins top and bottom, allowing for some fluting, and then a piece of bright blue paper-tape tied around makes for variety. There were plates of oranges, still with their leaves on, and a mound of great fat grapefruits. At tea Madame brought in a red market-gardener's basket full of tangerines. I ate half one with Viola and immediately all the Christmasses in the world swep' over me. Goodness.

Leaving the ship took far too long and was very exhausting. We breakfasted at eight, having seen the white city of Algiers brilliant in a sort of frosty sun across the bay. Rather exciting.

The ENSA Lieutenant had spots on his neck, not his own teeth and no personality. He seemed, like all ENSA personnel, to exude inefficiency and a dampness. The welfare officer shook us rather. She looked so exactly right for what I've always thought a Madame of a brothel should look like that I could hardly credit her. The rouge, a strong carmine, the lipstick put on with a hit or miss technique and the rusty black dress and coat were all in the picture. But she spoke good English and drove with Viola and me to the hostel which is at Point Pescade, about five miles out to the left. I asked the matron if the house was flats, for the stairs seemed to be outside the front door, but she said, but no, it is *'une maison particu-laire'*, which was an understatement. After very good coffee with bread and a sort of guava jelly we left a newly arrived ENSA sextet from the Dutch ship and the Leslies and went for a walk. The hills rise up at once from the coast road and we went up a little lane with high walled villas on either side. Through a paling gate we saw a tree covered in lemons, della Robbia and lovely against the pale blue sky. Geraniums seem to like the thin red soil and they grew in great hedges, deep scarlet, cyclamen pink and white. Almond trees are *out*. As we climbed we picked wild iris, wild marigold (tiny and yellow), a bean flower, white with a feathery mimosa-y leaf, bee orchid, a little yellow furled flower that a French gardener told us was vinaigrette, a sort of giant stitchwort growing over a hedge like a great vine. We walked for two hours. Then baths. This was a major operation. Two Arabs carried buckets of scalding water to the grey marble built-in baths and we ran the cold tap till the temperature suited our toes. Viola and I shared the water. Delicious supper. The ENSA chairs were uncompromisingly hard so I blew up my air cushion for Viola's use and sat on my baby pillow myself.

On our walk we saw an Arab wearing a hairnet.

Thursday, January 27th, 1944   The Hotel Victoria,
Algiers

Viola and I moved here yesterday when the Town Major gave us permission to do so, via ENSA. Nigel Patrick,[1] who has taken over ENSA here after doing the Canal Zone, pays a little attention to us, mainly because of the KRRC[2] link, I think. We have a room on the third floor, No. 26, with two very comfy beds, stone floors, three windows and two balconies and running water, cold only. It seems that is universal in Algiers. Even the Alletti, *the* hotel, has hot water for one hour a day only – no fuel. The beds, after the ENSA ones, were Beautyrest-V-Spring all in one. No hot water bottle shook me a little, but a pair of golf socks and my fur coat on the bed got me off to sleep and I awoke much too hot.

This morning, another perfect one, we breakfasted at the Officers' Transit. Rather nice early in the day before the smells start. It is a filthy city. Little Arab boys from about seven to twelve sit waiting to shine your shoes all along the way. From No. 26 Viola and I can see the sea at the end of the Rue Colbert. The grape bloom look is on everything at 8 a.m. Walked to the fruit market. A heavenly sight to our London eyes. Stalls piled high with oranges and lemons and tangerines; strange vegetables, salads, roots, bundles of herbs – rosemary. Branches of dried dates. Little dead birds lying sadly on slabs – thrushes? They look like it. Can't think they are worth eating, so tiny and sad. I bought a basket and two kilos of oranges and tangerines. Back at the Victoria, there was a note from Roger Makins who is Harold Macmillan's

---

[1] Nigel Patrick: West End and film actor who starred in the original cast of *George and Margaret*, a long running comedy at the Wyndham's Theatre.
[2] King's Royal Rifle Corps, which Reggie joined when passed fit for military service in 1940.

counsellor here.[1] He asked me to stay up at the British
Resident Minister's house. I wrote back saying I'd love to
but that I couldn't leave Viola and perfectly understood if
he couldn't take us both. He at once sent back another
note, by a Mercury with a Lancashire accent on a motor-
bike, to say he'd love to have us both. We move there
tomorrow. No time to pack today as we were working in
the afternoon and dining out in the evening.

Viola and I changed into tidy clothes and had an early
lunch at the officers' mess. Our ENSA car was at the door
at 1.40 and we set off to do our first hospital, Q4, a great
sprawl of a place a few miles out, high on a hill. Once it
had been a moderate sized orphanage. Now it is an
encampment with a nearby almshouse thrown in. There
were lots of up patients in blue hanging about the entrance when we arrived. So like Taplow[2] somehow – I
liked it and felt right at once. But the men are entirely
different. They have been through it and they are simpler
(in the right way), more appreciative, more sensitive. I
struck a group of Welshmen first, one of whom didn't
like the idea of 'gels bein' out 'ere with all the dangers'.
However he said it was 'alright' to see us all the same.
Needless to say dear ENSA had done the minimum of
advance work and no one was expecting us.

Friday, January 28th, 1944   Villa Desjoyeux, Algiers

Roger's car fetched us at 10.30 this morning. Mrs Dupree
met us up [at] the Villa Desjoyeux. She is wife of a
Secretary and is helping Roger run the house pro tem. He

---

[1] Roger Makins, later 1st Baron Sherfield (1964). At that time he was
Assistant to Harold Macmillan, then Minister Resident at Allied Forces
HQ, Algiers. John Wyndham was Macmillan's PA, and the three men
shared the requisitioned Villa Desjoyeux. Joyce and Viola were invited
to stay by Makins, an old friend of Reggie Grenfell.
[2] The nursing staff of the Canadian Red Cross Hospital at Cliveden were
housed in Taplow Lodge.

is here with Duff Cooper.[1] We unpacked and washed. John Perry[2] is here with a huge Great Dane called Plato belonging to his General Mason-MacFarlane who is in Italy. Perry flew with Plato from Gib[raltar] yesterday and now awaits an air priority onwards to join the General. A hundred and fifty lbs of Great Dane is a lot of pounds and priorities aren't easy. Perry and I agreed it would be convenient to lose Plato but on the other hand it would probably cost Perry his job to do so. Viola and I went back to Q4 today and did three more wards.

While she was playing a Chopin waltz I noticed a one-armed sailor humming it with her and afterwards asked him if he liked music. 'I used to play,' he said and all I had time to say was 'Bad luck' before I sang again. Poor devil; he looked *so* low. But I discovered later he is going home any day now and doesn't yet know it so I hope that helps a bit. A tough little Cockney with a leg off sang loudly in this ward. He had the word Mother tattooed across the back of his left hand in very crude childish handwriting.

Better hospitality today.

Met a nice sister called 'Toby' who nursed Esmond Knight[3] when he was blinded in Iceland two years ago.

[1] Duff Cooper, later 1st Viscount Norwich, had been appointed British Representative to the French Committee of Liberation in Algiers, and went on to become Ambassador in Paris. His wife Lady Diana, née Manners, was best known for her role in Max Reinhardt's production of *The Miracle*, which ran from 1923–8.

[2] John Perry: partner to Binkie Beaumont of H. M. Tennent, the most powerful theatre management in the West End for many years. After the war Perry managed the Lyric Theatre, Hammersmith, for H. M. Tennent, where Joyce was subsequently to appear. At the time of his meeting with Joyce in Algiers he was PA to Mason-MacFarlane, Governor of Gibraltar. In 1944 Mason-MacFarlane was sent to Naples to try to help put the country on its feet. He left Perry in Gibraltar, telling him to follow on with his great Dane, Plato. Everyone on the plane assumed that the passenger travelling under the name of Plato was, in fact, Winston Churchill!

[3] Esmond Knight: actor who could play Shakespeare and musicals. While serving in *HMS Prince of Wales* in 1941 he was blinded in the action against the *Bismarck*. He partially recovered his sight and continued to act until his death, while filming, in 1986.

She minds for her patients. I do like that. Two nice nurses
called Dunbar and Bembridge are to look after us tomorrow when we dine in the sisters' mess before going to the
officers' social afterwards.

This job is *so* rewarding. Gosh, I'm glad I came.
Though I sometimes wonder if one hour's escape is much
of a help to the boys. I like to think it is. [Tommy] Trinder[1]
was a big success when he went to Q4. They loved him
and Nigel Patrick says he was very good in the wards.

A huge great guardsman who has just lost a leg sang
'Swing Low, Sweet Chariot' in a beautiful bass voice for
us in one ward. And in another a sentimental Scot gave
'Smiling Through' with terrific feeling, pianissimo and
long pauses and all the applause-catching tricks, and
they loved it. It *was* good too. He had no voice but he
knew how to cope with good slop. The mini-piano has
developed a pedal squeak. Italian prisoners carried it
from ward to ward for us. They were voluble and very
slow.

Night drops like a blind here. There's a tiny new moon.
It's clear and exciting weather. A postcard sunset
tonight.

Oh, John Perry *has* lost Plato. We got in at 11.30 and he
is still out searching, whistling and I daresay praying for
him.

I write this in a room with a carpet, curtains and a
bedside lamp. My bottle is filled, and jonquils and mimosa scent the room.

Saturday, January 29th, 1944   Villa Desjoyeux, Algiers

My room has three enormous windows, two of them face
the bay, way below us. I think San Francisco must be a
little like this. A band of orange light woke me this
morning and I saw the sun rise behind a faint line of
mountains miles away across the bay. Algiers, below,

[1] Tommy Trinder: top music hall comedian, who later made the successful transition to television.

was wreathed in wisps of mist and looked like a dream city. From the bathroom window all you see is a giant magnolia tree, each sculptured brown-backed leaf pointing [to] the Eton-blue sky. Outlines are so sharp here.

Plato came home at 4 a.m. and scared the daylights out of the Arab who sleeps in a tent just outside the front door! I missed all the excitement, slept on like a log.

For an hour the city has been lost in a sudden mist but is coming through again now. Viola is practising. Rolling arpeggios are filling the air, a Hoover is humming upstairs, and I feel lovely and relaxed.

We have decided that we can't go on combining social life with the Job. At any rate not every night. I sang solidly for three hours yesterday and talked most of the night and it won't do. The job must come first, dammit.

Sunday, January 30th, 1944   Villa Desjoyeux, Algiers

Two letters yesterday, one from Gin[1] and one from Dick. Funny how exciting it is to see familiar writing in a strange place. Dick says no theatre to move *Alice*[2] to so she'll probably stay on at the Scala for a bit. Gin writes gaily of nothing. She pens a really pretty letter, she really does.

Yesterday was a mighty long day. About 12.30, with much ceremony, the French *femme de chambre* prepared a bath for us in Harold Macmillan's bathroom – the only one that marches at the moment. The approach is through the best bedroom (Harold's) and the oyster satin bed, chiffon curtains and general Curzon-Street air seems very wrong for the rugged grandeur of our Resident Minister. The bath, alas, was tepid. However, we each dipped in it and felt the better for being wet all over and I warmed myself afterwards by sitting stark naked on

[1] Virginia Thesiger (née Graham): Joyce's oldest and closest friend.
[2] *Alice in Wonderland* and *Alice Through the Looking-Glass*, opened at the Scala Theatre in Charlotte Street on December 24th, 1943; adapted by Clemence Dane; music by Richard Addinsell.

the windowsill while the sun beat comfortingly down my spine. Viola and I lunched in alone off cutlets and fresh green peas, followed by sliced peaches. We were waited on by *three* Grenadiers!

Out to No. 94 [altered from Q4] hospital again at 2. We gave our first programme in Ward 7, Officers' Surgical, housed in what had been a poor law institute. About sixteen beds. Heavenly audience. We did everything in the repertoire that we can't do for troops – Viola played beautifully. I did five monologues and sang most of Gin's sillies[1] as well as all Dick's songs. We could happily have stayed in there for the rest of the afternoon but we were expected up on a medical ward at 3 and didn't get there until 3.20 as it was. A man called Gilliland is in Simon Phipps's[2] regiment. Goodness, they were a nice crowd. Horses.[3] While Viola is playing I can watch them and it is good to see the 'ironing out' her music does for them. Or the release it seems to bring. With the officers I find a reluctance to give in to emotion. They prefer the gay stuff. With the men it is exactly the opposite. They like to wallow and it is our sadder numbers they like the best. Lots of sentiment. Dick suggested that I should do 'Mighty Like a Rose' and yesterday for the first time, I did. They loved it, too.

[1] Virginia Thesiger wrote verses and songs, one of which, with words by Harry Graham (her father) and set to music by Virginia, was sung by Joyce in *Light and Shade*, a Herbert Farjeon revue, written with assistance from Eleanor Farjeon, music by Clifton Parker, and presented at the Ambassador's Theatre, 1942. The words were as follows:

> Weep not for little Leonie
> Abducted – Abducted – by a French Marquis
> Though loss of honour was a wrench
> Just think how it
> Just think how it
> Just think how it improved her French!

[2] Simon Phipps (cousin to Joyce) joined Coldstream Guards in 1940; he was made Captain in 1944; ordained 1950; consecrated Bishop of Lincoln, 1974.

[3] 'Horses' – see also her expression 'Pegasi' (p. 167) – meaning the audience so responsive it felt like galloping, taking off.

We had tea in the sisters' mess, uncared-for and ignored. Ah me; manners. I suppose it's the old trouble – no one's job, so no one does it. But it is rather bad, I think. After tea we did a medical officers' ward, mainly naval. Nice, but somehow surgical is always more receptive than medical.

In a ward full of Merchant Navy toughs I saw a pretty sight. Viola was playing a Chopin waltz. On his bed at the back of the room lay a young man with very blue eyes. He had a little bunch, about six, I suppose, of those little furled yellow flowers that grow wild all over the place here – vinaigrette? – and he twirled it in his fingers as he listened to the music. It spun into a yellow blur as he turned it in the sun.

I saw a Canadian private who used to be at No. 5 at home.[1]

We supped with the sisters. No one was detailed to look after us, matron took no trouble at all, and by golly I was really rather irritated. We had to walk into the dining room and find our own seats and no one took any interest of any sort. Finally Toby, the sister who nursed Esmond Knight, came away from her table and joined us at an empty one at the end of the hall. The matron sat alone at her table watching the whole thing and doing nothing. The revealing thing was her entire volte-face later when I'd performed in the officers' mess and it occurred to her that perhaps I wasn't just another ENSA. She came up and said how sad she'd been that she hadn't been able to have me to dine at her table for supper but that as we were late she had had to begin, etc.; she invented, rather feebly, that she'd told some sister to put us at her table and look after us. But I'm afraid these well meaning meanderings didn't fool us. It's really rather awful to be made much of because someone discovers that perhaps after all one isn't just another old ENSA!

But it really was horses in the mess. Terrific! And I

---

[1] One of Joyce's wards at the Canadian Red Cross Hospital at Cliveden.

couldn't have felt less like it when I began. We'd already
done four programmes and I was all in. What's more, the
atmosphere had seemed so very unsympathetic. But I
was wrong. They were wonderful. The officers' mess is
housed in two large brown tents – marquees. We danced
in one, on a cement floor, so that the sound of scraping
feet nearly beat the three-piece orchestra. Next door was
the bar and anteroom. Our transport was ordered for 10
and at 10.30 we managed to get away and by this time I
craved only bed. It was a lovely night, newish moon,
stars and cold. The taxi ENSA sent for us had a broken
window so that we had plenty of night air on our perilous
descent from the heights down to the villa. Viola says the
drinks were powerful and alarming! Bed was very
pleasant.

I write this in the garden in blazing June sunshine. I'm
appalled at my inadequate wardrobe. The furs are going
to be a bore from now on; my one pink silk will be
working overtime and all our shoes will wear out in an
instant on the rocky roads. Oh dear!

If only we can keep up as we go along. I think we must
be wise about limiting our performances. Three a day is
plenty, if we do them properly. The mess president,
admittedly in his cups by the time he spoke, said we'd
done a unique job in the hospital and thanked us from the
whole staff for the time we'd spent there. Which was very
nice.

I'm wearing trousers to save my suit, but I'll have to do
a quick calculation when I see Roger's face when he sees
them today. I know I'm the wrong shape but they do save
skirts and stockings. I'm wearing a pair of bright salmon
pink cotton ones. They lack charm but are practically
thick and serviceable. Must now write to my Ma.

Extra thought. On our way up from tea to do the
second officers' ward we popped into Ward 1, where
we'd given our first concert two days earlier, just to see
our old friends. They were very welcoming and as we
were leaving one of them said: 'Joe didn't do his Popeye

for you larst time you was here. He does it good. Go on,
Joe.' So Joe, lying flat on his back with his leg strung up to
the ceiling, called for a sailor's cap, put it on sideways,
removed *all* his teeth, and squashed his face up into a
perfect Popeye. Applause all round. Lovely.

Monday, January 31st, 1944   Villa Desjoyeux, Algiers

Yesterday was one of the most perfect I have ever known.
Usually days are good because of some personal reason –
you are with someone, under special circumstances; or
you are in a mood. Yesterday was a slice out of time and
for none of the usual reasons. The day was Sunday and it
began with the breakfast, egg and bacon, toast, and
orange. Then, while Viola did some chores and later
practised, I sat in the garden and wrote to Mummy and
an airgraph to Dick and in this journal. June weather. At
12 Roger came back from his office, and we three set out
in the Minister's car with a picnic lunch to go to Tipaza to
see the Roman ruins. It was as pretty a day as I have ever
seen. The light here probably gets hard and blatant, but
yesterday it was gentle and delicate. Sunday has a quality
all over the world. Boys gather on corners over bicycles
even in Arab villages, and towards evening family
groups took the air in leisurely walks. We drove west
along the coast road with the Mediterranean on our right,
smooth as silk and aquamarine in colour. The clash of
baby blue sky with greeny blue sea is delicious out here.
Bougainvillaea is beginning, geraniums rioted in every
garden; I saw my first *growing* grapefruit. That little
furled yellow flower we saw the evening we arrived
grows everywhere. It must be of the freesia family, I
think. Roger says it is called *la fleur Anglaise* here. There is
pinky purple campion, wild marigold, thistle with a
dazzling green and white leaf (rather Mexican somehow), broom, gorse, and great candelabra-like asphodel,
not pink nor white nor mauve but all three, luminescent,

with a faint stripe down each transparent petal and a waxy grey stem and leaves. Roger stopped Corporal Chew a few miles short of Tipaza and we climbed through some barbed wire down a slope towards the sea to have our lunch. I never saw such a spot. To our left, far enough away to be comfortable and not menacing, was a mountain, hazy in the sun, pinky brown. Below was a gold red rocky strip curving into a little bay and filling our eyes was the incredible, pale aquamarine sea. The field of young wheat was shimmering green around us and goldfinches sang in olive trees. There wasn't a breath of wind. We could hear water splashing in the little bay, and when I stood up I saw a naked boy of about fourteen bathing from the red rocks. He was white in the sun. Another, wearing a faded blue shirt, watched him from the beach. Two little Arabs in pale grey cotton clothes collected firewood and sang a falling tune over and over again as they moved very slowly among the scrub. Greece must be like this, I think. It was the loveliest sight and feeling I have ever known. We ate our lunch and luxuriated in the beauty about us.

Later, Corporal Chew, who is stiff as a ramrod with cleanliness and discipline and who comes from the North of England, drove us on to Tipaza itself. We parked the car at the ruin and walked through the gardens to see the Roman remains. Fountains, a theatre, an aqueduct, beautiful in their severity even in ruins. Their feeling for proportion is exact and that is why your eye is rested. I hadn't been prepared for the magic of the wide red-gold stone pavement, mosaic inlaid, open to the skies now, on the edge of the cliff. The villas are outlined quite clearly. What a city it must have been! I remember getting a flash of excitement about this sort of thing when Elliott[1] read me his poem about Baalbek and told me his emotions on seeing it against the lilac mountains of Syria. I had the same breathtaking awe yesterday. I do wish I was edu-

---

[1] Joyce's friend Elliott Coleman, American poet and professor.

cated and knew about these things. Without knowledge I can experience the wonder; with it it must be five hundred times more thrilling. Roger [Makins] helped. We walked for an hour or so among the ruins. A grey herb – marjoram? – (someone later told me it might be absinthe; I don't know) grows all over the hills there and the effect is lovely. Pale greeny blue sea, an undine colour, pale chalky blue sky, reddy-gold rocks and ruins, pale grey marjoram in great clumps, olives, juniper. To complete the scene we came on a black Arab shepherd with a flock of multi-coloured sheep. There were spotted lambs in spaniel colours! Their ears are petal-shaped and hang down rather mournfully.

We came back to the car down a path edged with flowering rosemary. Golly, what a place. My tear duct had to be carefully disciplined all day. I have never seen such beauty in my life.

From Tipaza we drove home by way of the Tombeau de la Chrétienne, a sandy-stone beehive high on a hill with views on all sides. It is still a mystery but probably dates to the same time as the Pyramids. We sat on some rocks out of the wind and looked down on to the completely flat and well-cultivated valley running for fifty miles or more below. The Atlas Mountains rose austerely as a background. The French seem to be good agricultural colonists. I've seen aerial photographs of farmland in Ohio reproduced smack across two pages of *Life*, a quilt of various textures. This was like that. If we hadn't been to Tipaza first, this might have knocked my breath away. As it was it left me fairly cold. The hand of modern man was too visible. We picked armfuls of broom and an enormous asphodel and brought them back to the villa. Here Roger left us to recover and get ready for dinner while he went to work and to two cocktail parties before coming to collect us for dinner. We were clean and tidy in our blacks for we were going to the Duff Coopers and were alarmed at the thought, though hopeful of amusement.

We had a very pleasant evening. Diana had a head and didn't dine but joined us afterwards. Dinner was terrific. I sat next to Duff Cooper and observed with interest the rows of knives and forks and the clusters of wine glasses. The menu was gala peacetime banquet style. Tomato soup, thick and delicious. A large lifelike fish came next with its mouth full of flowers! Geraniums. Leaves made a verdant nest and it seemed a shame to spoil the picture. Then croûtons – no, bouche – then hot ham with fresh peas, and finally, oh joy! caramel ice cream under a film of spun sugar like all the birthday treats that ever were. I pined wistfully for a second go but didn't get it. There was quite a variety of wines, brandy and cigars. I found Duff Cooper quite easy. We talked of theatres, Deirdre and Rupert,[1] the difficulty of reading war books, and I watched with interest that he drank five full-sized (bigger than the rest of us) glasses of Algerian red wine. When I turned to Roger who was on the other side, I listened in, at the same time, to Martha Hemingway[2] doing an enjoyable 'you-make-me-shy' act with Duff Cooper. I took against her then and there but envied her divine hair, the soft yet upturning duck's tail variety, fresh as a boy's and infinitely more becoming. She is a US war correspondent and wore khaki. I hear her say: 'Ernest wears – because of his work –' (What in heaven's name can it be other than writing?) 'a beard and it's snow white. He is a literate who cannot stand the company of other literates.' Duff Cooper said he was the same way. Then she got on to Seymour Berry[3] and destroyed him.

[1] Rupert Hart-Davis: publisher, friend of Joyce and Reggie. Deirdre – his sister.
[2] Martha Gellhorn: then married to the American novelist Ernest Hemingway.
[3] Seymour Berry: Major, City of London Yeomanry; served North Africa and Italy, mentioned in dispatches. MP for Hitchin, 1941–5; succeeded his father as 2nd Viscount Camrose and became chairman of the *Daily Telegraph*. Married the Hon. Joan Yarde-Buller, whose first husband was Prince Aly Khan, in 1986.

And to Archie Crabbe and destroyed him. And to Basil Dufferin[1] and left a *little* of him alive. I thought her affected, surface bright and worthless. But after dinner, when we were girls together, she let down and the glimpses of reality were more encouraging. But there is a type of American new-intellectual who buzzes with know-all earnestness that I find rings hollow. She is obviously capable; I wonder how she writes. Diana joined us after dinner looking lovely. She was dressed in the colours of our Grecian day – palest aquamarine blue, rather a Greek drapery sort of tea gown with a transparent cellophane belt studded with gold stars. Her hair is still that faint dust gold and she looks like a goddess, *still*.

I had to perform. They were nice and easy. I am to go again! Ah me, parlour tricks are an entrée, there's no question of that. Useful kind of guest. We got home about 12. Too late.

This morning is colder and windier. While I've been sitting out here in the sun the Dutch-Cockney cook came out to show me what he called a 'curious kind of rose'. Very waxy white it was, with a spray of pine to set it off. It looked more like a small camellia than anything. It was, in fact, a carved turnip! Delighted at having fooled me, he returned to his kitchen.

Mail has just come! Two airgraphs and two air letters from Reggie and an airgraph from my Pa. Reggie's last air letter dated 24th – *very* quick. Must answer him at once.

[1] Basil Dufferin: 4th Marquess of Dufferin and Ava, killed in action 1945.

February 1944

Remembered nice piece of dialogue at the Duff Coopers' on Sunday.

Martha Hemingway:	Where is Noël?
Joyce:	Oh, he's in South Africa.
M.H.:	But what in heaven's name *is* there in South Africa?
Lady Diana:	Smuts.

We went to Hospital No. 95. Incredible place, ex-boys' school, miles and miles of it, vaulted, monastic, cool in summer and cold right now. 2500 there. Far grimmer than 94. How lucky the boys were at Taplow – air, light, space, newness and even gaiety. In the first ward (we did all orthopaedics yesterday) there were two of the illest men I have ever seen, I think. Just skulls but with living wide, very clear eyes. It was a huge ward and difficult to know where to put the piano. We put it in the centre in the end which meant that I had to keep spinning round as I sang. I tried a monologue, but it was no good in there – too big, too decentralised. While I was walking around talking before we began I said to the illest of the two very ill ones that I hoped he'd excuse my back when I had to turn it on him and he said he would if I'd excuse him for not being shaved. Oh, gosh.

Thursday, February 3rd, 1944   Villa Desjoyeux, Algiers

One of the very ill men in the first ward we did on Monday died that night. I wish I could tell his family how he smiled and even sang with us the day before he died. Tuesday was the hardest day we've done so far because of the tents. The courtyards of 95 have enormous dark brown marquees in them holding about sixty beds. They are narrow, ill-lit and their acoustic properties are exactly nil. However, the need for entertainment in these surroundings was obvious, and it turned out that no one ever does sing in the tents, so we said we'd go. I tried standing in the middle, walking up and down, standing at one end. It was equally bad wherever we went, but even so the programme was welcomed and we got them singing FF [fortissimo] for ages. Such nice sisters in both tents. One, Barr, with a face like a friendly balloon, egg-shaped, had been torpedoed coming out – I think they both had, now I come to think of it. The very matter of fact account the pretty little Scots sister gave of it over our tea and egg sandwiches was the more sensational because of its understatement.

'We held hands in the water,' she said, and, 'Oh, it *does* feel funny when a depth-charge goes off and you're floating about near by.'

The final concert that day was in a much smaller, square, whitewashed ward with about sixteen beds in it. Lovely for sound. Lots of eye patients, including a completely blinded boy who was being taken care of by a couple of pals with all the tenderness of mothers. When I sang a funny song or did a monologue their eyes were all on him to see if he was amused. They were happy when he was and exchanged looks. He was shy and completely unadjusted still to this new blank in his life. As if he was better invisible somehow, he kept turning up his coat collar and sinking into it. But he sang with us; and he cried a little. It was the gentleness of his two friends and their concern and solicitude that moved me so much.

This was a particularly good concert. We went on for
about one and a half hours. An ex-jockey from the North
told me his pal was a good singer and we got the pal to
perform. He gave us a heavenly song called the 'Blaydon
Races', verse after verse, in a true horn of a voice, full of
rough rhythm and vitality. He'd got his ward mates
trained to the chorus and they did their stuff admirably.
The sister, between looking after a blood transfusion in a
corner bed, came over and sang 'Just a Song at Twilight'
and 'I'll Walk Beside You' to roars of applause. Another
sister asked me if I'd go along to a nearby eye ward,
where a man had asked if I'd come to see him. He, too,
has lost both eyes. Comes from Reading. A very tall,
particularly good-looking man. He has reached the
accepting stage and had a look of strange radiance. Sister
told me he was always cheerful and his courage hadn't
once given out. His wife, at home, doesn't know about
him yet.

Friday, February 4th, 1944   Villa Desjoyeux, Algiers

Spending morning in bed. Just about as tired as I ever
thought I could be. I find that my slipshod lesson-reading
and slack practice of cs[1] won't do out here. Constant hard
work is required. I did some yesterday morning and it
helped me get through a very tough day when I felt like
plain hell.

Dine Duff Coopers. Dull evening. Poor Diana has a
hard row to hoe with these tick-off dinners. Eve Curie,[2]

---

[1] cs: Christian Science. Each day a practising Christian Scientist will 'do
the lesson'. These lesson-sermons are daily readings from the Bible plus
extracts from Mrs Mary Baker Eddy's major work, *Science and Health,
Key to the Scriptures* and are published in *The Christian Science Quarterly.*
'Doing the lesson' takes about an hour a day.

[2] Eve Curie: the first woman war correspondent to report on the desert
war, described in *A Journey Among Warriors*. She was the daughter of
Marie and Pierre Curie.

in French ATS [Auxiliary Territorial Service] uniform, looked much abler and nicer than *en grand tenue* as I'd last seen her at the Biddles. But she, like the inflated but not great, gave herself away by not bothering with anyone except the important. An unattractive trait. I could barely extract civilities from her when we stood together before dinner waiting for the doll-pretty (very) Princess de Merode to arrive. She was twenty-five minutes late but being very ançien régime and of such high family she didn't find it necessary to apologise. Her emeralds were plentiful. Her smooth, rather bulging brow was good. So was her complexion. She wore black with, I'll bet, an American uplift brassière under it, her little rounded bosoms pointing east and west in true Hollywood style. She has baby blue eyes and very good teeth. I have no idea what she is like, but Roger is against her. General de la Tour de Tassigny[1] kept calling her Petite Madame which was dainty but rang hollow. She smiled often but not with her eyes. A dull evening. Duff Cooper thought so too. His jaws were bulging with ill-suppressed yawns. Virginia Cowles[2] in a pale yellow angora sweater set and pearls (Smith, Bryn Mawr, or Bennington) was talking with a man called Chapin.[3] I've no ideas about them at all.

Yesterday, Thursday, Hospital 96. Grim approach along filthy dockland. Grey and rain. Arab town of Maison Carre. Felt exceptionally low and incapable. No one to meet us. Telephoning finally produced a grinning warrant officer of kindliness but no brain. The piano hadn't arrived. However it finally came and we did a gentle little programme in the officers' ward, where it went very nicely in a quiet way. I felt remote,

---

[1] Joyce must have misheard: General de Lattre de Tassigny commanded the Free French land forces in North Africa. Eve Curie was his assistant.
[2] Virginia Cowles: war correspondent and assistant to the American Ambassador in London 1942–3. Married Aidan Crawley; originally a Labour MP, who later changed allegiance and became a Tory MP.
[3] Selden Chapin: US chargé d'affaires.

under-waterish. Couldn't get through. Just tired, I think. Ophthalmic ward rather quiet too but accepted with pleasure.

Tea with assistant matron, Miss Gratton, in little cream-washed wooden hut, nasturtium picture calendar, bowl of oranges, local rugs and very good sandwiches of date and cheese. A corner of England; safe and secure. Two nice women, worthy, narrow, kind and capable.

It was outskirts of Tunbridge Wells, shopping at D. H. Evans, with dress circle seats at the matinée, gift shops, 'the Queen', and rigid little social codes all concentrated into essence form.

Last night, after dinner here with Harold Macmillan, John Wyndham,[1] Roger, Colonel Richardson of 95, John Addis,[2] Viola and I went to do a show for Allied officers in Algiers, run by the Americans. I co-starred with Trinder, on way home from Italy, in terrific Palladium form. Filthy but funny. Wonderful bicycle act – the Romanos. Was rather apprehensive but all was well. Very well.

Saturday, February 5th, 1944   Villa Desjoyeux, Algiers

Harold [Macmillan] is a revelation to me. At home I would, having only *looked* at him, have said he was worthy and dull; without humour and heavy. Can it be the Algerian air or was I always wrong? He turns out to be a character of charm, understanding, wit, kindliness and an endearing small-boy type. Last night he told us about an official morning call he went to pay on de Gaulle. As it was no distance to the de Gaulle villa Harold, in his old grey flannel suit, walked down the hill. When he entered

---

[1] John Wyndham: wealthy aristocrat, Macmillan's PA, and eventually his private secretary during his years as Prime Minister. He was created Lord Egremont.
[2] John Addis: former Third Secretary, Foreign Office, served with Allied Force HQ (Mediterranean) 1942–44.

the gates a fanfare of soprano French bugles blew at him. Rather surprised, he looked around to see who it was for and then realised it honoured him. He was interesting about de Gaulle. Says the reason Winston and F.D.R.[1] don't like him is that he is very nearly the same calibre as themselves and they resent it. Undoubtedly a really big man, H. says. He is sensitive and devout (very) and completely soaked in the tragedy of France. He cannot forget for an instant. Unlike Giraud[2] who is the light-weight type and can be gay as a butterfly at dinners and fêtes while his wife and daughters languish in German hands. He says de Gaulle is very like a Highlander – single-minded, melancholy, sentimental, slow to move but powerful; with a deep fire and strong wit. I'd like to meet him, I must say.

Diana and Duff Cooper lunched here yesterday. He, very ambassadorial in a stiff collar. There was an enor-mous black felt foreign office hat in the hall when I went down, and I wondered whose it could be, picturing a giant. But it was the little man's. Diana looked a dream in a bottle-green sweater, dark skirt and a soft lemon yellow handkerchief tied over [her] head like [a] peasant child. How decorative she is. And alive too. I used to think her eyes were without feeling but she seems very warm and approachable now. I expect I was without understand-ing. I'm continually having to revise my views on people and things. I used to be so certain I was right.

This hospital business demands a hell of a lot. One must be on one's toes, unselfed – and how. I am begin-ning to learn a bit about it, I think. When you go into a ward and begin the programme, you can sense the

[1] Franklin D. Roosevelt was nearing the end of his third term as American President, and would be elected for an unprecedented fourth term.
[2] General Henri Giraud. He had five stars on his sleeve where de Gaulle only had two, and the Americans were backing him as leader of the Free French in North Africa – but de Gaulle's grip on the leadership of Free France proved immovable.

degree of acceptance available. Even when it is small it is
always worth giving everything one's got because there
are always some it reaches and that justifies the effort. I
find it very interesting to watch the shyness and intro-
vertedness giving way to relaxed acceptance and count it
a real victory when, in the end, everyone is drawn into
the circle. At home I think I used rather to resent the
occasional smart alick one found in a ward, who seemed
to set the pace and hold a gangster sway over the others
by virtue of his bullying big-noise stuff. This type usually
answers back or comments derogatorily under his
breath. Very non-co-operative and very putting off to
me. But at last I think I know a little about him. He is
self-conscious and possibly nervous; anyway he is the
inferiority complex boy who must attract attention. If,
and I think I mostly can now, if I can ignore him and keep
on as if I hadn't noticed his distant rumblings, I can
almost always win him in the end. It's happened three
times on this trip so far. And in all three instances the
menace, having broken down and joined in with the
others, has come up after and thanked me specially for
the show. *Very* rewarding. It's a question of letting good
flow through one, I think. Of standing aside and letting
God be expressed. Oh, it is a good job and I'm humbly
grateful to be able to do it.

Viola and I dined with Jock Whitney[1] in General Baker's villa very near this one. It is comfortable and pretty
and we had a delicious dinner. Paul Warburg, Freddie's[2]
brother, called for us, and I must say he is as full of charm
and gaiety as Freddie; and that says a-plenty. I felt kin to
him at once. He is Jewish and clever and kind and
generous and human and quick and of wide intelligence.
There is a generosity of heart in a good Jew that is

[1] Jock Whitney: Captain, American Air Force Combat Intelligence
Division.
[2] Fredric Warburg: publisher, gave his name to the house of Secker and
Warburg.

unequalled anywhere. Paul has Freddie's unexpected vocabulary, extravagant and, to me, enjoyable. The dinner party was a little stuffy somehow. Jock had Eve Curie, who doesn't grow any cosier. She gives herself away I think in her undisguised lack of interest in any but the important. She seems without heart. She has no light touch, no humour. And what has she to be so very pleased with herself about except the happy accident of being her mother's daughter? Virginia Cowles, in another angora sweater, was there, looking lots cosier than Curie, but I didn't have a chance to get to know her any better. There was a pompous little US Colonel of the Don Ameche type, only without moustaches, called Glavin. His marble eyes were glazed with self-confidence and self-pleasure. Curiously he was at Balliol for three years, which fitted uneasily into the picture somehow. His chosen costume for dinner was a complete riding outfit.[1] Glavin missed much of Paul's teasing and answered each little try-on with unsmiling earnestness. If it had been possible for him to unfrock Paul I think he would have done so with relish. General Tupper? was courteous and old world and I didn't get to grips with him; nor with Air Commodore Pankhurst who sat on my left. Paul wondered how he dared fly, wearing his ears so wide and low. 'You'd think,' he said, 'they'd be an awful drag on the take-off.' Paul and Viola and I had enjoyable giggles on an oyster satin sofa, away from it all. Pity Jock hadn't made it just a foursome, Paul, Viola, he and me. We would have had a lovely time. As it was, Curie loaded the boat a bit and Glavin, horsing it with miniature solemnity, held things back. Jock, who is shy and unsure, felt his hosting rather a lot. I'm afraid we were a little unhelpful on our oyster satin sofa.

Viola found a Lincolnshire soldier from near her home in the really enormous orthopaedic ward we did

[1] Edward Glavin, born New York, 1902, was a career soldier in the US Army. He had been a mature student at Balliol, 1931–3.

yesterday afternoon. He was so delighted to see her and told her to be *sure* to say that everything was beautiful and safe out here so's not to let them worry at home.

In the last ward we did yesterday, also ortho but mercifully lots smaller, there was a French soldier who has lain in bed for five months. I sang *'Parlez-moi d'Amour'* for him and his sad brown eyes smiled at me. He speaks no English but has a local friend, *un petit gamin de douze ans*, who comes to see him. People are nice to each other.

96 is a less happy place than 95. I wonder what accounts for it? We saw far more suffering at 95 and yet the spirit of the place shone out. It is huge, dark, cold, bare and forlorn – physically. But there is an atmosphere of good that must do a lot of healing, I think. Perhaps I'm not quite fair to 96, but the warm interest in the welfare of the men doesn't seem to be there.

Sunday, February 6th, 1944   Villa Desjoyeux, Algiers

Our third day at 96 was best of all. Two medical wards in big Nissen huts.

Viola and I dined *en famille* with Harold, Roger, John. And after dinner Viola played for an hour or more. Heavenly it was. Before dinner we had baths and dramas. Mine was the piratical occupation of the minister's marble tub by young Mr Addis, after I'd painstakingly run that bloody old geyser for myself. He is the twelfth child of an eleventh child and the uncle of twenty-five assorted nephews and nieces, so that may account for his being *'mal élevé'*. Viola took the Heath Robinson[1] garden hose and played it on the other bathroom from the washbasin geyser next door. And when she'd acquired a deep enough bath turned off the tap but forgot

[1] A favourite phrase: Heath Robinson (1872–1944), the cartoonist caricatured machinery; thus the phrase 'Heath Robinson contraption' was born.

the hose would still be full of water, and allowed it to
flood the passage and half her room. She and Madame
Seguey bailed at it with a face sponge and cloth for at least
twenty minutes while I idly sat by and laughed. The
stream got out of hand at one moment and the sound of
lapping waters was really quite sensational.

Tuesday, February 8th, 1944   Villa Desjoyeux, Algiers

Our much looked forward to day of rest was good. It
began with rain, merged into a sort of April uncertainty.
We had to wait an hour, while a crisis was coped with by
Harold and Roger, standing patiently on the doorstep
ready to go and never going. But finally we left at about
ten to one and made for the Forêt de Bainein, not very far
out of Algiers, high up, with pines and the sea view. We
found a clearing in the sun and ate hard-boiled eggs, ham
and pork sandwiches, tangerines and cheese. Harold in a
1910 cap, worn centrally and high. He was far off in a
ministerial trance for a while, but afterwards, as we
walked through the forest, he approached the earth
again and was very companionable. He has a strange
way of pouring out but *seeming* not to absorb. But it is
only an illusion, for he does absorb too; but unobserv-
edly. The trees in the forest were sparse, small, and
mainly pine. Very little undergrowth. But the total effect
was light and pine smelling. A little pale starry sort of
crocus up there. Or scylla? Mauve. We walked for an
hour and came upon our dear Ambler sitting with his
back to a cork tree facing the sea miles below, having
walked all the way, at least eleven miles. He was reading
and eating his sandwiches, so insular, Preston and nice.
When we rejoined Corporal Chew at the car we planned
a detouring return through lovely undulating farmland.
Now and then we stopped and picked flowers. Roger
spotted a spread of mauve iris stylosa and, later on, I
found a clover field with tall yellow jonquils standing in

it, so we stopped again. They smelt intoxicating. The Minister and Roger both bent down to pick. Viola and I went mad over all the little wild flowers – marigolds, white camomile, daisies, wild orchid, brown and green, yellow vinaigrette, anchusa (that scratches dreadfully to pick) and a sort of purple valerian, only coarser and thicker. We loaded the car and moved on, eating chocolate and dazedly seeing all the lovely sights we passed. The mixture of spring and autumn is a bit queer. Fig trees are white and leafless now; wonderful bones – lovely designs. And then the ash trees are unpleating their sticky leaves, almonds are frothing pink and some large plane-tree types are still hung with dead leaves, gold in the sun. Eucalyptus is a repeat pattern of blue-grey-green that isn't sad. The pearly trunks are good in sun or rain. I suppose it is the quality of light that turns the naked little leafless grey trees into misty undersea coral fans. While the grass is still new and green and the earth newly turned dark terracotta it is all exciting and alive. I imagine it dwindles to a uniform dust colour later on.

I am writing this in bed, where I've just had breakfast. Viola has just called me to look at a nursery school of small French children playing action songs in the sloping garden of a nearby convent. Through the morning air we could hear their piping voices singing '*Savez-vous planter des choux*' and could see them doing all the movements with clumsy grace. Some non-co-operative members of the class were hopscotching on the outskirts. A nun passed by, black and square. The young teacher moved on into a new song, involving clapped hands, deep bows and a finale – hands high above the head, mouvementé, with the fingers wide, waving from the wrist. The class followed her, just off the beat, very earnest and endearing in their artlessness. The whole scene took me back to those books of French nursery rhymes we used to have, illustrated with pictures exactly like this.

Yesterday we went to 99, about twenty-five miles out along a dead straight road with the mountains on the right and plains in between with dull little red-roofed villas on the left, and beyond, hidden, the sea. We had been into Algiers in the morning for our final tetanus injection (harmless) and noted Gert and Dais[1] at the Alletti and lunched at the Oasis with dear Ambler. It was 1.30 when we set off with our French *philosophe*. Hunched at his wheel gloomily saying he didn't *crois* that his *auto* would make the incline to Rivet, where we are due on Thurs. He could, however, manoeuvre the route to Alma where the general part of 99 is housed. (The TB and orthopaedics are up at Rivet.) Usual unheralded ENSA arrival. Oh dear God, how trying it is! And such a waste of time and energy. The main thing, though, is that it doesn't affect the concerts. We gave three beauts yesterday. Nice Sister-in-C. called Johnston. *Good* piano. The place is very isolated and we were made very welcome. The last show of the day was in a tent, dark and brown, with about thirty beds. The cement floor helped the sound a lot. In our free for all at the end we had many volunteers – a Welsh hymn-singer, an Irish slow-style tenor, crooners two a penny, and – *nouveauté* – a tap dancer. His health seemed unimpaired by a spirited buck and wing. (His friends had said, 'Gi'us a bit a tap', so he said he would. 'Shall I fetch me tap boots?' he asked me and off he hared to his ward, returning in a pair of bright brown boots fitted with metal taps. He was rather good.) 'Get Butch to sing for you,' they said. So we did – rather tremolo it was but much appreciated. A very long Canadian with a really charming bass voice sang 'Home on the Range' and was cheered for it. Viola rounded off a heavenly hour and a half with Warsaw, listened to in very affecting reverent silence. I *wish* Dick could see their faces. The all-high in success is: 'When are you coming again?' Take all the orchids, all the telegrams, all the press notices, and give me that, accompanied by that

---

[1] Gert and Daisy: a Cockney double act performed by Elsie and Doris Waters, sisters of the actor Jack Warner.

absolutely genuine eagerness of the British soldier away
from home! Golly me.

Thursday, February 10th, 1944   Villa Desjoyeux, Algiers

My birthday,[1] and the sun is shining in a cloudless blue
sky. Viola brought me a bunch of nasturtiums with
a single white narcissus for smelling. And a leaf
full of oranges she'd picked in the garden. It is Harold
Macmillan's birthday too. He is fifty. He and John
and Miss Campbell are off home by plane today, so
I'm quickly sending a letter to Reggie and one to Dick
by them.

On Tuesday evening Viola finished the last concert
with Warsaw. It was in a tent, one side rolled up and on
the bank outside there were patients sitting and standing
in the low brilliant sunlight. At the first notes of Warsaw,
wandering patients further away hurried in to the party.
It was magic – a Pied Piper tune. The verdict was
'Smashing'. A high tribute.

Halsey[2] arrived from Philipville, 350 miles, to see me,
having driven all day in a jeep. Roger had said he could
dine in here and he came about 7.30, very tired and dirty
and very sweet and pleased to see me. I was delighted to
see him and to find him looking so very well and brown
and in such good heart. He loves the SAS [Special Air
Service] and is genuinely longing to do his first job. (They
drop them behind the enemy's lines to do special jobs.
Oh!)

When I look at very young creatures like him and Denis

---

[1] Her thirty-fourth.
[2] Halsey Colchester: of East Anglian origin; when in London would stay
with Richard Addinsell or Clemence Dane. After the Army he joined
the Foreign Office, but took early retirement in order to become
ordained. Married and has five children.

Baggallay and Jakie,[1] all so perfect in their way, full of expectancy and gaiety and life, I can't bear this bloody war. Better to kill them, though, than maim them. Seeing these young soldiers, armless, legless, eyeless, lying in the hospitals for months – not that for the others – death isn't *half* as bad.

Diana Cooper, Peter Loxley,[2] Roger, Harold, Viola, Halsey and I for dinner. Nice and cosy. Halsey dazed by carpets, lights, fire, flowers and Diana. He showed me his proudly won wings and after dinner I sewed them on for him. We saw him off in day-white moonlight. His jeep hadn't turned up so he started to walk. What a night it was! The stars are bigger and whiter here. The shadows of the palm trees lay immediately below them in still, starlike patterns. I shivered with the beauty of it.

Friday, February 11th, 1944   Villa Desjoyeux, Algiers

Yesterday was a lovely birthday. Sun all day. There was a muddle about transport to 99 at Rivet, but finally a *'joli garçon'* in a plaid *tailleur* fetched us in the ENSA wagon, piano lashed to the back. On our way down from the heights up here to the coast road we had an acute angled bend to negotiate, and couldn't do it in one movement. So, with our front wheels resting on the eight-inch cement parapet of a very deep cliff drop, we prepared to reverse in order to take the corner. Instead of putting the car into reverse, our French boy slipped it into third and stepped on the accelerator! By some miracle we didn't hurtle over the cliff – he braked in time. He, Viola and I were white as lilies, and it was the nearest thing I have

---

[1] Jakie: John Jacob Astor, fourth son of Waldorf and Nancy Astor. Followed his mother as MP for Plymouth.

[2] Peter Loxley: private secretary to Rab Butler, and a great friend of Chips Channon. He died in a plane crash on his way to the Yalta Conference in February 1945.

ever been through. His Gallic shrug and *'on ne sait jamais quand un accident arrive'* were cold comfort. A little later, as some colour returned to his cheeks, he said, *'Et c'est tout fini dans un instant.'* Poor creature. I've been going over this experience all last night and feel far worse about it now than I did then. Delayed reaction. It really was very horrid.

The drive to Rivet is, once past 96, on a dead straight road clear across the completely flat valley. But after the village of Rivet the road winds up the mountain 1000 feet to the hospital. Wonderful views at each bend with the sea showing more and more, thirty miles away, the higher we went. A nice atmosphere at this hospital. Matron, Miss Glenesk, very co-operative, and it does help so much. A big job to do there. All chest wounds, TB, and orthopaedics. We did three shows before tea. Then Halsey and Tom Curteis arrived in Harold's jeep and had tea with us in the sisters' mess and came with us to do our last show of the day. Some up-patients (ORs) and orderlies gathered below in the garden and we had a fine time. General Gammell's[1] very attractive son in the KRRCS there. Just lost his foot. He is twenty-three. Halsey was very sweet and it helped having him there because he is gay and quick and laughs. I did *so* want it to be a good concert and it was. A very quiet one but it rang a bell. And then we drove home in the jeep. It was entirely open to the elements, the canvas canopy tied down here and there with string. I had the front seat. Viola had my air cushion on the floor at the back with Tom Curteis. There was a flamboyant sunset spreading itself among the mountains and flooding the whole valley with a thick pink haze. I have never seen mountains go *literally* purple before – off postcards, that is. These did. A sort of grape purple. By some trick of atmosphere the valley held its pink mist even when the sun had gone. Only for an

---

[1] Lieutenant-General Sir James Gammell: chief of staff to General Eisenhower, Supreme Allied Commander in North Africa.

instant but it was very thrilling. Our eye took in about fifty miles to the west – fifty miles of dead flat plain, all cultivated in farmland; etched in plough, frothed in orchard, green in early vegetables. The soil is dark Devon red. The mountains rise along the side. The sea lies north, a narrow mist of silver last night. Halsey drove, his beret well on, his eyes expertly spotting the holes in the road and avoiding them. He was so thoughtful and kind. I dined with him when we got back, at a tiny little French box called 'Les Hurlevants'. We shared a corner table – they were all partitioned off – with a voluble French couple, so it didn't matter what we said. Delicious food, particularly the omelette; we sat on and talked. After dinner we drove up towards the Forêt de Bainein to see the view down to the sea in the moonlight.

If I had a son I'd like him to be like Halsey, and particularly as he is going to be.

Saturday, February 12th, 1944   Villa Desjoyeux, Algiers

After a sensational moonlit night, yesterday was cold and grey. November in Norfolk. To 99 at Rivet with the '*joli garçon*' at the wheel again. But cautious this time. I've come to the conclusion that it is the matron who sets the atmosphere in hospitals. Miss Glenesk is the best I've seen so far. She is the right age (fifty?), energetic, kind, wise, with the welfare of the patients first in her thinking. She runs Alma as well as Rivet; they are twenty miles apart, so it must be a big task. Young Gammell says that of all the hospitals he's been in since he was first wounded, and they've been many, Rivet is easily the best. Everyone likes it there. Being so isolated has its advantages. The people there fuse into a unit; in this case very happily. 94 was ill-assorted, 95 very well-knit, 96 uninspired, 99, Alma, good. 99, Rivet, excellent. John Gammell says that he'll never forget matron's goodness to him the night he arrived. He'd been twenty-four hours in the hospital train from Philipville. The ambulance had to detour twenty miles to drop another patient down at Alma before climbing the mountain to Rivet. It had no springs, and his newly amputated leg was giving him the worst hell he'd had since he was hit. The driver missed the hospital turning, how I can't imagine, and drove two miles too far to the shrine on the summit, had to turn round and discover the right road. By this time Gammell was in the depths of agony and misery. When he finally got in, it was matron who looked after him. None of your distant grandeur there, he said. She did the job herself. He was grateful.

Rivet was built by the French as a TB sanatorium and never completed or occupied. It is a vast white modern block, three storeys high, glass both sides so that the sun from the south floods the balconies that way and the incredible panoramic view fills every window on the other. We did two long, narrow balcony wards yesterday, both facing the view. Singing was easy there for some reason. I would never have expected to find a room 200 feet by 8 ideal for sound, but it was. I stood facing the view, bang in the middle of this corridor and the beds on either side were crowded with up patients as well as bed patients. As I sang I saw the weather doing theatrical things fifty miles away. A rain storm like a white ghost blew slowly along the coastline, clearly outlined. Bits of Algiers would suddenly burn white in a corner of sunlight. A rainbow arched incompletely over the plain to the east while I was singing 'Nothing New', and it moved me so much that I had a couple of the boys wiping their eyes at the end of the song. I know they didn't mind. I hadn't intended it. This business of staying three days in one hospital is dead right. The boys get to know you and follow you from ward to ward. Word seems to circulate, bush wireless technique, that you are OK and you find a confidential welcome everywhere. We had really good singing in East A. They listened in holy silence. I was able to sing yesterday. It is a good feeling.

The first ward we did on the first day sent a message to

ask me to come and see them again, and when I did a very shy boy called Scott gave me a mat with a regimental crest on that he'd worked. The KOSB [King's Own Scottish Borderers] badge on a strawberry pink linen square. Beautifully done. I was touched. I really must learn the 'Ave Maria'! It gets asked for every time.

When we got back about 6.30 (only two shows yesterday), there was an enormous gerbe of frothing mimosa for me from Halsey. He arrived soon afterwards and took a bath in Harold Macmillan's bathroom, while Viola and I tried out the newly fixed geyser in the other one. Viola didn't manipulate it as successfully as I did and had a tepid bath. But I managed a boiler. We were told by Diana to dress for Teddy Philips's party so I wore my grey lace and wished I hadn't, for his seaside villa at Point Pescade had no carpets, and a howling wind was blowing. It was a strange party, and never quite jelled. Roger, Viola, Halsey and I arrived about 8.30 and there were a few cold people huddling in a deep religious silence before a picturesque log fire that didn't do a thing to warm the huge room. The flowers were lovely. Great branches of mimosa and a scented white shrub with glossy dark green leaves. We found a cosy corner with a couple of big straw-filled mattresses for sofas, and there I spent the whole evening with a naval Captain Miller snuggling on one side and Halsey on the other. It was a question of snuggle or freeze. I never once removed my coat. Delicious food – tomato soup, scrambled eggs, baked potatoes, cold ham, compôts d'orange. An Austrian private, mysteriously dressed as a soldier in His Majesty's Forces, Africa Star and all, played and sang very attractively on the guitar. And a singer from Martinique with black pinpoint eyes and a letter-box mouth was finally and with great difficulty persuaded to perform.

Poor Halsey revealed that he had to drive all through the night back to Philipville with an important dispatch. I gave him Dick's sweater and we sneaked a Cornish pastie from the feast to put in his pocket, and at 11.20 he went

off, looking very young and rather sleepy with his hair
slightly up at the back where he'd leaned against the wall
on our straw palliasse. Back here about 12 and Viola
played for an hour or so. It was doing Roger a lot of good.
I came up about 1.30. A wild wind was roaring in the
palm tree outside my window. It was a very beautiful
ice-cold blue and grey night. At Teddy Philips's villa the
sea was spraying the windows. The garden with a vast
white boned tree in it, the sea hurtling foam at the back –
all like a set for a ballet – lit with a pale blue light,
mysterious and exciting.

Letter to Virginia Thesiger

1944 J. Grenfell,
Officer i/c Entertainments
RASC (ENSA) Dept NSE
Sunday, Feb. 13th, 1944   c/o HQ BNAF

Dearest Gin,
Two letters from you – the second came in yesterday.
Surface mail, too, so it really isn't too bad at all. (Dated
Jan 24th, it was). Life is very full and I'm, off the record,
very tired. Thirty-nine concerts of an hour each in fifteen
days! But there is so much to do and when you pass a
ward and they yell out: 'Ain't you coming in here?' you
just have to go on. We average three a day.

   Staying here with Roger Makins has made the whole
difference. We've had hot bottles, meals in, and carpets
and warmth – all the things you don't find in this town.
Working at this pressure these comforts have made a lot
of difference. Tomorrow, though, we get off on our one
or two night stands, which will be different to say the
least. The trimmings – tea and good transport, billets, etc
– do help *so* much to the final entertainment. I know now

why the big stars have stooges to fend for them and clear the way for them. It leaves you free to 'give your all'! I mean it quite seriously as a matter of fact.

ENSA out here is better than at home; but even so it is a poor thing. However, Nigel Patrick – remember him in *George and Margaret*? – has taken over here and really has its interests at heart and knows how to cope with the players, so all is in good hands. And by dint of hard work I've made them understand that I'm not just a fuss-pot but anxious to do the job really well. They now see I mean it and take me seriously as a worker and not just a London film star flitting by on a lady-bountiful tour! These hospitals are *the* jobs to do. It's so *needed* and (sh-sh) I can do it.

I think I'll get less tired as I go on. At the moment I'm sort of whacked and that's because we've had to do a certain amount of social life as well and that involves sparkling, and really you can't do both. I'm OK, though. I miss you all in bad patches and get awful waves of homesickness, but truth to tell I'm so busy I don't get time to think much. And I'm so b——y lucky to be here doing this job and seeing this beautiful country, and being full of fruit and sun (and soon, I gather, *snows*!). We finish with the N. African Continent about the end of the month, then Malta, Sicily and sunny Italy.

Hilda[1] has just sent me a mysteriously arrived letter from Cairo addressed c/o Brit. Embassy and written in Baghdad. She says *please* go on to Baghdad and round there because they are *so* far off and feel so forgotten and have, some of 'em, been out there for four and five years. So I'm now seriously toying with the notion. That means staying out another month, which makes the return about May 1st. If we *do* Baghdad it means a quick shopping trip in Cairo to buy a cotton or two, as we're all equipped for the early weather here. I don't know.

[1] Hilda Grenfell: Reggie's stepmother, daughter of General the Right Hon. Sir N. G. Lyttelton.

As I write, Viola is playing Chopin for Roger and it's high time we both went to bed, as it's 11 p.m. and we leave at 8 a.m. for a 175 mile drive up mountains. I don't look forward to it – hairpin bends.

. . . Much love, darling. Go on writing, please.

Tuesday, February 15th, 1944   At 31st General Hospital,
Algeria

Last day at Rivet very rewarding. We finished with Viola playing solos in the officers' ward. Very nice. When I got back I telephoned Halsey to see if he'd had a ghastly trip in the storm and found to my horror he hadn't arrived. We heard there was snow on the mountains and my heart sank. A very naked little jeep with Halsey and his driver in it might slip off a precipice any time. I did feel worried. Our near miss cliffdrop on Thursday had shaken me a bit more than I'd thought and it linked up unpleasantly with Halsey's non-arrival at his camp. When I rang up on Sunday morning they said the MPS hadn't any reports of any accident between Philipville and Algiers, so that was something. But it was still very mysterious and I couldn't get it out of my head. I buried the boy six times, visited him in wards, saw him lying dead in a gorge – oh, a dozen beastly visions. Roger took Viola and me to the Forêt de Bainein again. We found a bank in the sun among little spindly firs, out of the wind and delicious, and there we ate eggs, ham sandwiches, oranges, cheese and chocolate. And then I slept. I was rather badly in need of an iron out, and lying there in the warmth I was able to sort things out a bit and felt a lot better when we walked up to the point to see the view. Packing, letters, dinner quietly with Roger.

Viola, in a gauche, funny mood but one could visibly see her struggling to get through it. She played for Roger. I wish she could get the demon out of her soul. It seems to

have taken control of her now and then like the evil spirit
in the Bible. She gets noisy and out of tune, and it makes
her miserable. You can see it happening.

It was sad to leave Roger and the villa. Rain was
teeming down on us as we drove away with '*Joli Garçon*'
(Grassin by name) at the wheel, 8 a.m. Mrs Lawrence,
ENSA welfare, who is nice and of an attractive plumpness
with brain and heart, came with us. The car was comfy
and undraughty. We went through, rolling farmland,
lovely green and springlike. Oranges like pictures in a
Caldecott[1] book I had as a child. Great patches of eucalyptus trees. Pink almond frothing in red-earth fields.
Very wet and liquid in colouring. Good. Then we de-
scended a huge gorge. I dislike it. Very forbidding and
lowering and endless with hairpin bends. I grew to
loathe that darned little Z sign – every few yards, it
seemed to me. We got into strange waste country with
sparse firs and grey hummocky hills. Italian prisoners
working on the road called for cigarettes but we hadn't
any. Rain stopped. We got to a high, dry T. S. Eliot-y bit
of rock and found a petrol refuelling depot all by itself,
miles from anywhere. There we filled up and talked to
the little group who ran it, and the eager way they
clustered around the car was *very* touching and showed
their homesickness. They thought we were French at first
and wouldn't come near! Then I called out, 'Hello' and
they rushed us. We ate lunch a bit further on. I cursed
myself for not thinking of eating it with the petrol men. I
picked a huge orchid at the first place we spent a penny
(cultivated country and damp and green) and at the
second I found some rosemary in full flower – big light
blue flowers. *Lovely*. We climbed by beastly zigs and zags
on the plateau. To me it *was* the Russian steppes. Miles
and miles of it streaked in snow, bare, ugly – miles and

---

[1] Randolph Caldecott (1846–86): English artist, whose illustrations for
children's books were acclaimed on both sides of the Atlantic, thus
appealing to Joyce's Anglo-American parents.

miles on each side. We passed shepherds in dun-coloured rags among dun-coloured sheep and goats on dun-coloured fields. Little black goats now and then. Pretty as pictures. Arabs selling eggs all along the road. Then it snowed and blew and the car petered out. '*Joli Garçon*' shrugged and gave up – his soft Fedora at an angle, pale grey suede gloves eloquent on his waving hands. While we sat and waited for a car to pass, we saw a thrilling sight. The snow was thick and there was silence except for the wind. Out of the swishing pale greyness of the storm there suddenly happened a long line of black galloping Arab ponies, kicking their heels and tossing their heads in some strange equine delight. They moved on in an instant, like a frieze – a grey wash drawing. One of the magic moments. They were soon gone.

'*Joli Garçon*', idly turned on the engine and tried again. It worked. We were OK and came on. Tea at Setif with Colonel Vandenbergh, welfare officer for all N. Africa. Pleased with himself but the right man for it, I think. Keen and clever and kind. Said Noël had done best job of all out here. We moved on about 3.30, all the better for our cuppa.

Large black crows. Snow in streaks. Arabs in sweeping grey folds, heads down to the wind. A very old Citroën with at least ten Arabs in it hurtling down the road. Ice on the road. I didn't relax for one second all the way. It's very silly and I'm a fool.

Arrived at No. 31 about 5. *Miles* from anywhere – bleak, remote, treeless. The unit here for a year. Very, very cold. Was glad of Aunt P's boots and me furs. 3000 feet up, I believe.

Knowing Halsey was alright – he'd had his suitcase stolen, met important colleagues, so hadn't returned with dispatch, etc., etc. Finally travelled back on Sunday – knowing Halsey OK gave me a further span of fifty years!

Thursday, February 17th, 1944   At 100th Hospital,
                                              Philipville

We worked hard at 31. And they looked after us beautifully. The home sister, in her khaki battledress, led a
procession of three Italian prisoners each morning with
our delicious and miraculously hot breakfasts. The
second evening we had a singsong in the sisters' mess.
Some local vocalists from a nearish-by (thirty-five miles)
unit had come over to have their weekly choir practice
and they joined in with us. I drank too much hot tea and
after I'd been in bed for an hour or so I got a distinct call. I
lay and argued it out, but it was no use. Going fifty yards
in a nightgown under a fur coat and with boots on
through deep mud and falling snow is no fun. Nor is
washing in a freezing hut with mud everywhere! And *we*
only had it for two days! The girls have been there for a
year. And while they do complain – and why not? – they
are so good and cheerful about it and I take my hat off to
them. Mud is a depressant. Pale grey, liquid mud.

We drove through deep snow to Constantine. Very
good driver from Manchester. Staff car. Drifts. Might
have been Northamptonshire. No view. Poplars. Arabs
huddling. Very cold. Constantine hidden in snowstorm.
Then on to Philipville. Sun out suddenly. The street
scenes – snowballing – in brilliant colours like a Dutch
picture. British soldiers throwing snowballs from high
roof of HQ down on to the passers-by. Gay feeling. No
time to see old part of city.

Long, slow drive, dangerous road. Viola slept on my
lap. I wasn't sleepy somehow. Then we gradually de-
scended and it grew green again. Driving rain and wind.
The road to this hospital along the sea – angry and
frightening. Where 31 had mud, 100 has sand and wind
and rain. We are beautifully cared for and sleeping in part
of the sisters' sickbay Nissen.

Hospital life starts *very* early. Boots on cement can't be
slept through either. There is a canary belonging to a sick

sister singing its fool head off. I think the sun is coming
out!

It did come out. However today, as I lie in bed in the
Nissen, is loud with rain on the roof. Yesterday was a
very, very good day. Captain Hayes fetched us just
before 11. The little mini-piano we have with us had
spent the night in this hut, and Viola played it for about
twenty minutes. Fat loosening chords and liberating
runs.

The patients here iller than 31. Good atmosphere
everywhere. This is a huge sprawling Nissen hut camp,
built on a steepish sandhill just above the sea. Behind it
rises a scrubby mountain or two. Halsey's camp is only a
mile up behind the hospital. He came down in a jeep to
take Viola and me to lunch in Philipville – 'L'Allemande'.
Very pleasant light meal – soup, poached eggs, peas and
bacon and fruit. He has been offered an Intelligence job
and at the same time hears his lot may go home. Difficult
for him to decide, I expect; but I think the Intelligence job
so much the best idea.

We finished our third concert about 4.30 and had a
lovely tea up here with the sister who is looking after us.
Then Viola went off to try the piano for our show that
evening and I went off to pay a visit in the privy marked
'Sister Only' that sits in a place by itself near this hut.
When I emerged, pretending that I hadn't been anywhere but for a stroll, there was a group of patients
hanging about the door to [the] Ward 31 hut next to ours.
They asked me to come in and 'sing us a song' so, rather
hesitantly, as I'd been at it all day and there was more to
come at 9 p.m., I went in. And of course sang. For half an
hour. They were angels. Tiny ward of about twelve beds.
It was beginning to get evening-y and they wanted to be
sentimental so we wallowed – 'You'll Never Know', 'All

the Things', 'White Cliffs', etc. Rather a flattering incident unfurled about 4.30 as I was on my way back here
from the last ward. An up-patient in a blue and white
striped pyjama top, standing outside the huge orthopaedic Hut H, called out 'Hi, Joyce,' so I said 'Hi' back
and he said, 'Come on over, Joyce' so I said, 'I'm coming
to you tomorrow,' and he said, 'No, come on now,
Joyce.' So I left Viola and Captain Hayes and went across
the sand to Hut H. When I got within twenty feet of the
man, he dived inside the ward and I heard him say over
his shoulder to the awaiting public within: 'It's okay,
she's alright.' Oh, did I glow? And I've been glowing a
whole lot here because everyone is so very nice to us. We
dined with matron last night and came back to our hut
immediately to change for the show we were putting on
for the unit in the recreation hall. Viola wore her red and
I, bravely, for it means removing *all* my underclothes
except me pants, my grey lace. It was a cold night too.
The show was in one of those big Nissens and they are
perfect for sound. Apprehension is a spur, I think, for I
was very definitely uneasy before we began. It went
beautifully. As well as anything I have *ever* done. Attentive silence, warmth, quick responses. Thoroughly enjoyable to do; and I think that must have communicated. It
was very best possible Windsor Greys! The colonel made
a wonderful speech. Oh!

This morning the day sister who has just refilled my
bottle told me that it was the best show they have ever
had; that everyone in the unit is saying so. The CSM
[Company Sergeant Major] last night, said the same. In
fact it went Big! Which is lovely and I'm humbly grateful.
Viola had a more than reasonable piano and they *loved*
her. I wish Reggie and Dick could have been flies on the
wall last night. It was OK.

For some unknown reason, unless tiredness, Viola was
very uncertain yesterday morning and I couldn't get
together with her during the show. She is a strange girl.
It's perfectly genuine temperament I think. But she must

learn to beat it. This is a piece of work like any other and a technique can and must be developed to get one through on the days when inspiration won't. I'm so fond of her and can't bear it when she gets taken hold of.

Monday, February 21st, 1944   Bône

ENSA hostel. Bône. You reach it down a very narrow alley and it is four doors from a very notorious brothel. Large *Out of Bounds* signs are chalked all over it and a posse of Army police guards its approaches after dusk. Join ENSA and Learn About Life!

Two ward shows a.m. Officers' ward after lunch. Did a solid hour and they were a very good audience. John Bingham,[1] a major, came over to see me for tea from his camp twenty miles away. He looks older, not very happy. Family gossip. He is intelligent and amusing. Think he may have been glad to talk a bit. I am a useful piece of blotting paper out here, I find!

One hour's necessary sleep when J.B. had gone. Then, in Victor's[2] Alice Blue, with Viola to Halsey's camp. Descent from transport down a series of steep banks and steps in total darkness hand-led by Halsey through the usual rain. Then a very small and deliciously warm Nissen; tiny with a bar. Huge fire blazing with cork tree logs. White walls, very little light except the fire, rush matting. Good. The pirates in the SAS fuse far better than those polyglot doctors. The Nissen about twenty-five feet long. Painted battleship grey (because only paint available), both ends red brick, unplastered. Long line of wood tables piled with baskets of tangerines and lit with naked candles on cigarette tin lids for holders. No other light. Local Arab pottery – rough reddish browns and

---

[1] John Bingham: brother of George Charles Patrick, Lord Bingham, who later became 6th Earl of Lucan.
[2] Victor Stiebel: who designed Joyce's dresses, and close friend of Richard Addinsell.

yellows and faded greens. Bottles of red wine catching
sudden light. About thirty of us altogether. I sat next to
Toby Millbank[1] and Halsey in the centre, backs to a big
stove. Wonderful food. Soup, macaroni, chicken, pan-
cakes filled with pineapple jam, and toasted cheese. Poor
Halsey suffering in case (a) they didn't take to me, (b) I
didn't take to them, (c) we both failed to appreciate the
good qualities he knew we both possessed! But all was
well. After dinner we moved back to the first Nissen. Five
Italian prisoners had, when we arrived, made the perilous descent from the PU[2] with our beastly little mini-
piano. Their swearing was fully justified. It must have
been decidedly trying – black, wet, steep and heavy! I did
a short programme of songs and monologues. The penny
dropped slowly, but it usually got there, and the laughs,
though late, were loud and deep. Poor Halsey suffered
again here. But by keeping off the subtleties and making
it all fairly gay I think a happy time was had. And I
managed to squeeze in 'Skylark' specially for Halsey.
Again scene lovely on eye. All those very fit, rather
young men, in the strong firelight listening and later
singing – out of the world. I felt so remote and like all the
mothers there ever were! War distils so much that is
good. Or is that untrue? Is it, perhaps, that war throws
the good qualities into clearer focus?

Don't feel SAS right place for Halsey. He is no pirate.

We left 100 yesterday a.m. Sunday. Rain as usual. I
packed early and then went to see some of the patients in
orthopaedic H and 31. Big evacuation on and of course
they all hope it's home, which it will be for many. And
that is going to be hellish hard; the adjusting. Many of
them were already rolled in blankets and their stretchers
in lines at the foot of their beds. Papworth, the little
Cockney with a real clown's face – deep mouth lines, 'See
yer by Eros – Piccadilly, at the Peace Parade.'

---

[1] Toby Millbank: 2nd in command of battalion.
[2] A Land Rover-type vehicle for Personal Use.

I lunched Halsey at the officers' club. Delicious food. Two omelettes! – ham first and then jam and burning rum! With escallopes de veau in the middle. He drove me to the hostel in his jeep. It's on the edge of the Kasbar and very squalid to get at. But it's quite alright inside. A high block of primitive flats. The usual bareness and cold. My room, 17, is said to be the best. An oil stove did take some of the chill off, I think. Two French windows giving on to a badly bombed site and roofs. Rather Parisian. Someone had put flowers – carnations, mimosa, roses, marigolds. I was on the fifth floor so it took him a minute to get down to the street. Then he looked up and waved as he walked down the Marseillaisian alley past the brothel. *Hated* to see him go. However I'm sure that all is well with him and that's alright.

Unpacked and then sank into very springy bed under me furs and slept like a dead thing. The ENSA officer here has just put up his third pip and when Viola went to report to him after she'd left me at the officers' club she found him very drunk. He was blind by the time he finally remembered to come and see me here. A revolting sort of little third-rate rat – common with good teeth and short bristly hair at the back. Full of himself but making no sort of sense. Called me 'darling' and 'Joyce' and tried to make a good impression but I was duchessy and wasn't having any. He is the sort of little bounced-up ENSA that I have no patience with. If he isn't entirely different today I shall refuse to see him while I'm here. There's no need to. I can do the job far better if he isn't around. He makes me feel sick. After trying to penetrate his boring skull with some sense I gave up, and Viola and Halsey and I went for a walk. We found some lonely RAF boys who were just longing to talk, so we all had a gossip in the '*place*' where all Bône was taking its Sabbatical walk. They were so nice – all of 'em. There's a sort of technique in coping with the casual conversation in the street. You see them looking at you and thinking you are – you must be – English? And they essay a hello. The next move is to say 'hello' back quickly and follow it up with something about only having been over a short time and that home is still OK, etc. By then they are relieved and happy and crowd around, and you exchange where you are from and you say what you are doing here and it's all made easy. Homesickness *is* a dread disease. And Englishmen are very homey. From the '*place*' we went on and found a sort of open market-place with a view of snow-topped mountains at the back, the sunset sky filled with flying *storks*! Then on down a side street and I ask a passing lance corporal with Jersey on his battledress if he knows where the English church is and it seems we are almost at it, so we go on and then we turn a corner and a roar of deep masculine singing ('Rock of Ages') is pouring out of a little whitewashed church packed solid with troops. The padre comes down the aisle and welcomes us in; soldiers are acting as vergers; there is an atmosphere of friendly ease. After singing another hymn, the service starts. Padre is a cross between Edward Everett Horton[1] and Bobbie[2] doing his curate. But he is sincere and they like him. The hymns are numerous, the prayer very simple. We sign the 'fellowship' book that is passed around the congregation.

Back to the hostel for 7.30 supper to find the delectable ENSA officer now weaving and making no sort of sense. He had, I gathered from an overheard conversation from the little ENSAs at the next table, been very rude and familiar with the girls. *In vino veritas.* Bah. Went to bed at 9 and spent a goodish night, although I can't stretch out in this bed as the army blankets aren't long enough to cover both ends if I do. Did a spectacular wash standing in a bucket of hot water and using the basin as well. The

[1] Edward Everett Horton: American actor 'with inimitable crooked smile and diffident manner' (Leslie Halliwell). Films included *Top Hat* and *Lost Horizon.*
[2] Bobbie Shaw: Nancy Astor's son by her first marriage to Robert Gould Shaw. See *Darling Ma* for descriptions of house parties and games at Cliveden: 'Bobbie (Shaw) was his same old curate and he made a speech that was quite funny and, I'm glad to say, clean.'

other ENSA move off today, poor things. It must be tough to be an unimportant little unit out here. Nobody cares, it seems.

Friday, February 25th, 1944   Tunis

My ma's birthday. I send her waves of birthday thoughts and love.

We are in Tunis. Long day's drive yesterday, 290 miles. Was depressed by the battlefields. Open Salisbury Plain stuff; miles and miles of it, bare and unrelenting and as ghostly as Glencoe. Three dead tanks in profile on the skyline. Many rusty ruins in the ditches. How hellish it must have been. We picked up a lieutenant of about forty, a re-made sergeant-major or I'll eat my bonnet, who had broken down and had to get to Tunis by nightfall. Verbose, solid; I daresay very worthy and, I'm afraid, very English in the worst, insular, unimaginative way possible. I see no future when I meet men like him. No integrity, no feelings. A get-what-you-can and be-damned-to-the-rest type. He was probably a good sergeant-major. He makes a pathetic figure.

We are at the Majestic Hotel, an officers' transit mess. Viola and I have a double bedroom with a rose trellising wallpaper in the main part, and, in the window alcove, a riot of yellow nasturtiums on a grey ground. The window is a patchwork of wooden crates and paper! One pane remains. The room is, in consequence, dark. There is a bathroom with HOT water. We bathed before dinner. There is one sheet on each bed and two indescribably unappetising blankets, deep un-original grey, with stains. We recoiled. But there is, to balance it, a deep and quite clean carpet. Bizarre.

Majestic once must have had a glory. It is now dimmed. The dining room is huge and white, checked cloths, earthenware, discoloured knives and forks. Good food last night but breakfast today uneatable. Tea tasting

of all the unwashed pots in the world and old tea leaves.
Cups bitten off all round the edge. In this land of fruit, no
fruit.

Tuesday, February 29th, 1944   Tunis

We rose at 7 to catch plane for Malta, Saturday a.m., but
at airport discovered it wasn't in, so we returned anti-
climaxically, to the Majestic. Viola played piano at Opera
House all a.m.; I sat in sun on terrace writing long letter to
Joyce Carey[1] about this project. Lunch, then drive to
Hammamet. Day had turned grey and hot and dusty and
I felt very low indeed. And far from home. Hammamet a
lovely little place once visited by the wicked Windsors.
Tiny crescent beach, pale silver sand and white houses
and a gently lapping green sea.

Dined Majestic, Viola and me, very tired and dull.
Night before had been made hideous by drunken naval
officers in room next to ours. Forte party at 2 a.m. Second
night almost as bad. Down to airport 8 a.m. Sunday.
Breakfast in shed – slabs of sandwiches, coffee in pottery
cups, bowls of boiled sweets. Pilots, ground crew, pass-
engers in transit all standing at the bar there. Like a play.
Some left-wing affair, with a message, put on at the
Mercury Theatre[2] and much praised by *Time and Tide*.
Very peculiar. Our first flight! In a DC 3. Lorry backed up
against her first and baggage taken on. Then, as a very
young American called out our names, we made the
steep steps into the aircraft. Viola and I sat in Seats 2 and 3
on the left side. Slightly dented tin seats, Mae West, belt
and strap. About seventeen of us. I was next to a kindly
Jewish captain who took an interest in us and helped.
During flight Viola and I in turns sat up in front with the

[1] Joyce Carey: actress, daughter of Lilian Braithwaite, and a member of
the Noël Coward inner circle of friends.
[2] Mercury Theatre: small, but important, avant-garde theatre in London
in the 1930s.

driver. Nice young Australian pilot. My sensations very slightly disappointing. The movies, blast them, take the edge off all experiences it seems to me. But the first second of being airborne rather magic even so. We flew at about 3000 feet. The sea like that crumply silk people bring back from India. Over a few little clouds, like an orchard. Then Malta below us like a cream-edged cake. All the cities clearly outlined, the huge churches and tiny fields. All warm cream colour except for the little fields. Very attractive. S/M Guinea met us. Nice and kindly if a trifle pleased with himself. To Metropole Hotel in Sliema. Badly blitzed. Our room, 7, is yellow walled, rugs and stone floor. Bathroom off but wc a long way down passage. Tiresome 'This and That' company here. Also 'Snapshots'. Tommy Dale and wife came in to visit us and we unpacked, and they stayed and *stayed*. Kindly meant, however.

Nigel Patrick, now a major, turned up in afternoon and we spent it driving with him, Guinea and Miss Hunt, Welfare, to far side of island to see hospital where we play this week. Tea with kind little Matron Perry. Corner of home! Fires, cretonnes, goldfish, china cups, *bread and butter*! Nigel's eyes popped.

March 1944

No. 90 is a huge permanent building and less easy to
work in because the wards are so vast. We lunched with
Matron Perry in the sisters' mess on Monday and did
three huge wards. The orthopaedics very ill and quiet but
it went well and they loved it. I had an inspiration and
said don't clap. Little cockney boy, Powell, lost both legs.
Italy. Flung by blast into a ditch where he lay for four
days before they found him. Frostbite. He said: 'I speckt
there's a lot of chaps worse off'n me,' and later, 'It's
alright if you don't let yerself think.' OH. Yesterday we
went for fifteen minutes up to the five-bed TB ward,
where I sang a few songs. Matron told me afterwards
they have, all five of them, only four or five months more.
But they were all planning for the future.

Miss Perry, the matron, forty-eightish, small, flat
figure. Goodness beams from her. Without any powder
or lipstick, no meat, no hot drinks, no smoking. An
eccentric but very noble little figure with a kindly little
rather 'elfin' face! Beautiful manners, thoughtfulness,
heart. Strength of character. Must have been very pretty;
long dimples. Very quiet but authoritative. I suspect her
of being one of the great people. She has the withdrawn
look of inner certainty.

Camels have padded spaniel feet. Oranges in Malta
cost 8d off barrows and 4d in shops. Bizarre. Still no mail.

Later, same day: I write in bed, beautifully clean after an all-over wash in one inch of hot water. Viola has gone to see 'Blimp' with Mr Stone of Barclay's Bank who eats here.[1] I hadn't the strength. We had a *very* good day. Two rather difficult wards in the main building – long and full of illish patients. But we did an hour in each and they wanted more. Hard work it was but lovely too. Did officers' ward last thing this evening. Very self-conscious somehow but they warmed eventually. I determined that they should! They wanted to enjoy themselves and were held back by British reserve. However I broke it down and a very good time had by all. Viola in specially good form and in very good looks too. I venture to think she grows a *little* bit in self-confidence? I grow fond of her and her funny gaucheries. She is so very young at twenty-seven.

A Miss Kay Warren rang me up on Monday and said she'd heard I was here and she and her sister were keen on the theatre and they lived at Imdina which was near No. 90 and if we'd nothing better to do and would like to see the old walled city, would we lunch with her before the shows on Wednesday. So we did. She and her sister middle-aged spinsters. She of the grey flannel suit, red felt hat and matching carnation school. So 1920 some-how. I think the sister (Ella?) is older but downtrodden. Kay has the 'flare'. I feel that is what they've established – Kay has the flare. They got to Noël when he was here and clearly worship him. They live for the theatre and do lots of amateur things here. Their club premises were de-stroyed in the siege, and today – two years after – the workmen had dug through the debris and found Kay Warren's fiddle quite untouched in its case. And a tin box containing all their stage curtains, intact. Viola and I met Miss Warren in the square at Imdina at 12 and walked around the little very old walled city. Fascinating cream stone again. We saw a woodcarver at work in his shop.

---

[1] *The Life and Death of Colonel Blimp*: 1943 film, written, produced and directed by Michael Powell and Emeric Pressburger.

An immense white moustache he had – a sort of bonhomie film type. Rosy cheeks, white hair, linen over-
all and his tiny box of a shop, hanging with cut-out
designs, and filled with logs from which he would make
boxes and dolphins and candlesticks. Imdina very baro-
que and very beautiful. We went into a house built in the
bastion belonging to people called – Hervey? Harding? –
to see the view from their roof. Mrs H. was busy watching a cake full of three eggs so couldn't concentrate on us,
I'm glad to say. We climbed up to her roof and saw all of
Malta lying around us. What a view – tiny green fields, all
the cities clear in the distance. The sea all around. Some
clouds about helped. Such an extraordinary house. The
hall living room so English. Flowers, gardening gloves,
Country Life, an old hat, sporting prints and a plate or
two. Miss Warren and sister live with their mother in a
grim thin house on the other side of the walled city –
which is, I suppose about 200 yards square; or little more.
Mrs Warren is what is known as failing – about seventy-
five. She is handsome and well boned and sits in an
armchair being called Mummy and forgetting things
now. The 'girls' are like something out of a rather clever
and sinister novel. They aren't old yet and they feel
rather young but don't look it. Very spread and inclined
to puffiness. They probably don't drink but they look a
bit as if they did. Sad Sandwich Bay faces; good sorts;
lively; oh *sad*. We had a good lunch in old Mrs Warren's
bedroom. The house is nondescript and not their own.
English owners, brass warming pans, prints again, a
Cozy stove. After lunch I rang up Miss Perry, the matron
at 90, to ask if I could bring Miss W. to the final show of
the day, and did the call from Miss Ella (?) Warren's
bedroom. It was like moving day. All her suits and
dresses were hanging outside the cupboard. Bed unmade. Piles of underwear, scarves, stockings and a hat
on the dressing table, on mantelpiece, etc. It was like a set
for a rather squalid play. I took to Miss Ella who is, I
think, downtrodden by Kay. It was Ella who wanted to

hear me but Miss Kay who came. And I thought Kay was a bully to her. She, Ella, was rather inarticulate and apologising. They have lived in Malta for twenty years and are like those English people we met in Belgium in 1929 when we went to Coq for a holiday. I asked them if they liked living as they did in Antwerp. 'Well, you see, we've got our bridge club and our tennis club and really we hardly notice the Belgians at all.' For Belgians read Maltese in the Warrens' case.

(As I write, 'Land of My Fathers' comes walloping upstairs via the Re-diffusion radio system. It is St David's Day. Two of the Welsh patients in the hospital wore enormous daffodils in his honour and we had a Welsh song to celebrate.)

Before we went on to the hospital we stopped in with Miss Warren to see the Baroness Inguanez d'Amicos, who is the leading light in Maltese aristocracy – First Family. She lives in an immense old house with eight maids. Most of it is hideous but her little sitting room is hung with rush matting (to warm the stone walls?) panelled in dark beams. White Wedgewood all around the dado. Lovely doors with metal decorations. A white parakeet. She was like my grandmother Phipps but even tinier. Very attractive and very English. Under a long Paisley *coat* with fur collar, very à la Queen Mary, she wore a spencer fastened at the neck with a diamond horseshoe brooch. Pearls and diamond earrings. About seventy-five I believe she is. Her maid looking like an Italian peasant I had pasted in the lid of my nursery music box. She wore a bright red cotton frock to her ankles and a 1910 apron. Bare legs and sort of espadrilles. I wish we'd had more time to visit the house. Struck me as being a little too glossily Victorian but the main body of extreme age and symmetry.

I like Malta. The delicate little carriages with their tassel-edged square roofs. The pale colours. We've passed a curving crescenty piece of street every day on our way to No. 90. It's near the public washing place, and women were kneeling at the great stone trough when we passed today. There are two framed shrines in niches nearby, let in the wall and lit up as we come home in the dark. By day there are always women and children sitting about in the sun, and their gay clothes of faded cottons are like the best sort of watercolours.

Went to see little Powell today. He's moved into the main ward and is next to a boy who lives only ten minutes' walk from his home at the Elephant and Castle. Mutual satisfaction. There was a very large tough-looking Cockney in the last ward we did yesterday. 'Where are you from?' he asked me, and I said, 'Kensington, up Knightsbridge way.' 'I know it,' he said. 'I've had me barrer all up and down there – Oxford Street, Tottenham Court Road – all over the West End!' He has promised to let me have strawberries cheap off his barrow if we ever meet up again in London after the war. He was a huge man, with a dark skin and an inclination to drop off to sleep all the time! But he said he'd quite liked the show.

I've written letters to the wives, mothers, and a sweetheart, of four of the very ill boys in the big orthopaedic ward we did on Monday. Went in to tell them I'd got it done, this evening.

Friday, March 3rd, 1944   Malta

Daddy's birthday. Wish I could get some news from home. No mail for what feels like ages but is in reality only just over a week, I believe.

Yesterday Viola and I were fetched here by Sgt Nithsdale, RAF, and taken to the convalescent depot on the far side of the island beyond St Paul's Bay. It was a stormy day – the sea an inky blue with crests. Pumpkins on roof tops to ripen as we went into country districts. Banana tree in flower. Nithsdale, who has big ears, is intelligent

and kind and knows about the island. Hope to go sightseeing with him on Saturday. Drive home along coast
road past all the scenes of the siege and air battles. It must
have been living hell, those seven months. Simmonds,
who drove back with us, says he'll never forget the day
the Spitfires flew in and they knew the tide would turn.
Viola and I went to see 'This and That' at a nearish-by
barracks. It was better than I'd expected but very ENSA –
good to look at, with slick production and attractive
clothes. *No* talent. That was the real trouble. I got very
tired of my hard chair but had the company's eye on me
and I had to be an alert audience.

Saturday, March 4th, 1944   Malta

Another specially good day. Sightseeing all a.m. with Sgt
Nithsdale in Valetta. As exhausting as such things always are. The library, palace and Cathedral of St John.
Absolutely stunned by the interior of the Cathedral. Such
richness. Remote from God, of course, but magnificently
dramatic. All carved stone, too, and not the plaster one at
first assumed it to be. Flower stalls on streets a joy,
specially the one on the corner of the Cathedral – *very*
dark stocks, purple almost *port* colour, deep blue
hyacinths, marigolds, carnations, white narcissus. Quite
enchanting. By the time we arrived at the hospital ship
Maine at 12.15 I was ready to drop. Nice Surgeon-
Commander Ford met us – rowed over in a little local
boat, very gay in colours, very dippy too, manned by a
Maltese who faces the way he is rowing. Such a naval
welcome. All the senior officers on deck to greet us.
Every detail thought out. We inspected both wards
where we were to sing. They ran the width of the ship, all
white, with cots secured to the floor in several rows.
Flags were hung at the end where they planned for us to
work. We were there to decide just where to put the

piano. Then up to the Surgeon-Commander's cabin for a wash, change into tidy shoes from our sightseeing slip-slops, and then lunch – with the ship's captain and Ford. A nice Maltese sailor servant. Good food, after which we were organised to rest up in the captain's cabin. As Viola says, we were treated half like very precious racehorses and half orders-is-orders! I lay full-length on the bunk and Viola curled in a big chair. The first show was like all first shows at the awful hour of 2.15, rather sleepy. I couldn't get through me tubes. And it was bad for sound – low and broken up by pillars. It went alright but not nearly such fun as the second show on the lower deck. Lots of officers at this one; it was enjoyably easy. Only snag today was the S-Commander organising us away from the wards each time. However I lurked a good deal as usual and it was worth doing. Tea in Ford's cabin. French, Dutch and Jugo-slavs aboard. Lots of Londoners as usual, then back to Metropole, where we took a bath – big Saturday event here. It was very tepid and in a very small bath, but we both got wet all over and felt lovely. Took advantage of tepid water, too, and did some washing of our smalls. Then into our best blacks, me smelling pretty of 'White Lilac', to the *Maine* again – crossing the water in moonlight this time. Ford came out and met us again which was specially nice. Drinks in the ward room to meet what he called 'the Boys'. Very gay it was and we sang a little bit and they buzzed around very warmingly. Then a gong went or a whistle blew or something and it was clearly their dinner time so the S-Comm and a very nice Lieut called Ryan who is a king anaesthetist from London took us off to the Union Club in Glenna for our dinner. Very pleasant too. Today was one of the special days. The sun shone, we met endless nice and attractive people, we did the job *well* and I go to bed now feeling very nice. Lovely letters from Reggie – Feb. 12th, and Gin, Feb. 14th. Ryan was particularly nice and sensitive. One of the people who Mind about Things. He was good on the job we're doing and seemed to get the point. Oh dear, Reggie says to come home after Italy and I don't quite know what to do but I have a hunch about doing Baghdad.

Sunday, March 5th, 1944   Malta

Today is Halsey's birthday; also David Astor's.[1] We woke up to a downpour and it kept on all morning. We braved it about 10.30 and went to Valetta on foot, the rain driving at our backs, down our legs, and down my neck. The cars here are camouflaged cream with black lines to look like the local stone walls. Crossed the 1½d ferry. Oh, it was wet. We finally reached the English Cathedral as the service ended. Very empty and sort of dim. As the procession processed down the aisle the clergyman did a sort of double take at me, stepped out of his line and advanced on me to say he must thank me for making him laugh so much in 1939 at the Little Theatre! He was very flattering; sad to learn we were moving tomorrow. Said he'd heard great things of us from 90; ex-Navy. Gave up his comfy living and lovely rectory in Surrey to come out here again in the Malta blitz. Later learned his name was Stephens. He is about seventy. He is much loved by sailors everywhere. Wish I'd been able to do a show for him.

At the Customs House steps we were met by the two ENSA Sergeants Nithsdale and Guinea and driven off to the gardens of the Governor's Palace, and the Catacombs (St Agatha's) at Imtarfa and finally home through the country part. The guide at the catacombs was equipped with some interesting English. Referring to the rabbit warren of incredible little cells he said, 'She home from the Phoenicians, in them day. See bed wid stone pillow.– one for de farder one for de mudder and one for de bebbe.

---

[1] David Astor: second son of Waldorf and Nancy Astor, he became editor of *The Observer*.

She made with sandstones.' The catacombs are horrible but remarkable. The Phoenicians must have been a pigmy race. The place is good as new, made 2000 years BC. Little cabins with bed niches, grinding stones, a prison with a huge stone door swung on hinges. All very terrifying.

Monday, March 6th, 1944   Malta

We got up at 7.30 and finished our packing, breakfasted and out to the airport. High wind blowing. Don't think Viola fancied it. Lots of people waiting to fly. We were weighed and my stuff weighs 69 lbs which is awful. Can't think how it has grown to such a size. Sure it was OK at home. Or maybe the scales are wrong? We weren't able to leave this morning. Too many priorities in front of us. Very lowering. We watched the plane take off and then sadly returned to the Metropole. Anti-climax. I write in our bedroom, bed still unmade, rather dusty, cold. Wastepaper basket full of all our old bits of packing papers and orange peel from the orange I ate last night. We've got to hang about all day in case there is an unexpected plane. Bah.

Tuesday, March 7th, 1944   In Sicily, Grand Italia Hotel,
Catania

Yesterday turned out rather pleasantly. I spent rest of morning writing to Winifred[1] and two airgraphs; to Myra[2] and Pa. After lunch to the movies with Viola, see rotten picture about Edison, thinly disguised as Spencer Tracy.[3] Had nine letters – two from Reggie, one from Pa, two from Gin, one from Ma, and three from Dick! In both

---

[1] The writer, Clemence Dane, whose real name was Winifred Ashton.
[2] Myra Hess: pianist and close friend.
[3] *Edison the Man*: released 1940.

his letters Reggie says please come home after Italy. I'm afraid he is a bit lonely. But I think I *ought* to do Baghdad – everything points to it. It will only take three more weeks and I gather they really do feel let down out there as no one ever seems to get that far. Met Miss Russell, YWCA, here tonight who said *please* go to Baghdad. And on the airport this morning when I told Wally Crisham and Toti[1] that I was going there they said: 'They asked us to go there but we couldn't face it. Baghdad is the End, my dear.' So I *must* go. Dick writes very gaily. Noël has asked him to do music for *Blithe Spirit* which is *wonderful*. Dick says he is going to write it down at Appleshaw[2] which may be a very good idea. He sounds better. One letter, his last, was written from Fife, Scotland, where he was staying seven days with Victor on his leave.

Gin says raids horrid. So does Dick. But Reggie seems to try to minimise for me but says all windows in Kingston House N.[3] have gone, so one must have been very close. *Hell.* St Jas. district too I gather; and near Gin.

After tea Viola and I called on Princess Poutiatine-Tabour, friend of Colonel Mayne at No. 100 hospital. She turned out to be largeish and blonde, White Russian, lived Paris, about thirty-eight, mad about ballet and trained in the old school. She teaches it now in Malta just to keep busy. She was sad somehow, living in a rented flat with lace curtains in the *doorways*, orange cotton chair and sofa covers, many photographs and lots of flowers in little vases. A piano covered in a brocade cover, tray with glasses, picture of her mother, Russian Princess, and some ballet stills. Also a pile of songs – Ivor's and Noël's and Tree's and 'I'll Walk Beside You' all muddled up with Tchaikovsky painfully copied out by hand and 'Waltz Gems'. We talked of the ballet at home and she told us of

---

[1] Walter Crisham: actor and dancer; Hermione Baddeley, popularly known as Toti, who starred in *The Little Revue*, in which Joyce made her first professional appearance.

[2] Appleshaw: Richard Addinsell's parents' home in the country.

[3] In SW1 London, the flat of Joyce's aunt, Mrs Spender-Clay.

her pet pupil, daughter of a petty officer in the RN, called Maureen Clarke, who has gone home to join the Sadlers Wells Company and make a career. She is only sixteen now and has danced since she was six. Clearly the Princess loves the child as her own and misses her. The poorly written letters from London were brought out and read to us and all Maureen Clarke's virtues for the ballet were extolled. We have promised to look her up when we get home. The Princess's husband came in later, a little-ish man with whom she didn't seem to bother much. She was emotional and carried away by her contact with anyone who knew about ballet, and Viola does. Then I sang and she was warm and enthusiastic and begged for more and more. All the time conversation was being interrupted by a particularly charmless little white terrier of a very bloated appearance who is the blotting paper of her affections – like Lady Mount Temple's[1] poor pekes! Just as we were preparing to go she asked us if we would please try to get some very special medicine for her when we go to Italy. She wrote down the name and particulars and handed it discreetly to me saying, 'It's for the dog.' This morning when I came down there was a note for me on the table telling me just how urgent the medicine was. It is, I think, a worm powder and is vital to the dog before it can be operated on for cataract, poor beast. She wrote: 'It will be a real *charity* from your part if you will get me that medicine' and then goes on to explain about it and ends, 'Please forgive me for the bother I am giving you but in wartime, one feels so helpless on that rock!'[2] So as soon as we can, Viola and I must try and locate this medicine and get it, somehow, back to 'that rock'. It is rather awful to see anyone so lost as she is, fastening her affections on this dog and killing time by teaching local Maltese to dance. It's a marking time business and she looks unhappy in a rather philosophical Russian way.

[1] The second wife of Wilfred Ashley, 1st Lord Mount Temple, Tory MP and father of Edwina Mountbatten.
[2] 'That rock' – presumably she meant Malta.

There is no doubt – they have got charm, the Russians. Viola and I dined in and later went out walking in the very cold moonlight with 'Chic' Sale, the US naval engineer, and Majors MacEwen and Johnson of the US Air Corps, down to the Regent Dance Hall. ('Select Dancing for Officers and Civilians Only'.) Here, in a great cold barn of an upstairs hall, we danced to a Maltese band playing strictly to the dots in a ruthless rhythm, each item announced by an electric sign standing on the piano. 'Foxtrot', it said, in yellow, and 'Old Fash. Waltz' in white. 'Tango' was red. Some of our friends of the *Maine* were there, and in the Excuse Me dance I was bewildered by a long stag line, like a Long Island belle, and only whirled a couple of steps before I was cut in on! How bad it is to be so spoilt! I enjoyed it a lot. I must confess that competition was *not* keen. A Maltese siren in a pink knit sweater and uplift brassière with all of forty-five summers to her name, and some good honest, mostly square-shaped, WRNS [Women's Royal Naval Service] were me rivals! And a handful of dangerous floozies who looked a little sad, waiting about in bare legs. It was over at 10.30 and we all went down to the bar below which was just closing and had five minutes with Viola on a hideous piano and a great many naval gents and us singing FFF together. Back at the Metropole, Chic urged us to go and sit by his fire, but wisely I said no; they stayed up till 2.30 a.m., so I'm glad I didn't. Chic is 6 ft 4 in and dark and handsome. He doesn't look very well and is probably a weak character but he has charm. From Tennessee or Kentucky or sumpin'. At the Regent Dance Hall he said he wished he could talk to me as I was the first person he'd seen in a long while he felt he could talk to. He is all self-knotted up inside and wants a lot of encouraging and confidence giving. Bit neurotic I think maybe.

We left Malta at 10.45 after waiting in the airport far too long in a very beastly wind. Saw Isobel Catto there. She is YWCA in Cairo and has been visiting Italy and Malta and Sicily. Saw, too, Lady Limerick, who is Red Cross and

who has been doing the same. We heard that Leslie
Henson's party was due to arrive and I hoped they would
just before we left and they did.[1] With exactly five
minutes to spare. Wally was first off the plane, hatless in
his old camel-hair, greeting me with cries of 'Darling' and
lots of bonhomie. Toti emerged next, looking fright-
eningly bloated and half-dopey. Not attractive. Miss
Prudence Hyman,[2] wearing her hair in a string net, told
Viola we'd love Catania as we'd be *so* comfily cared for.
Leslie, suddenly, was very small and looked rather old in
a mac and a felt hat worn too low because of the wind. I
was glad, in a collector's item and un-Christian way, to
lay an eye on them but not sorry to have to move on quite
soon. The flight to Catania took one hr ten mins and was
decidedly bumpy.

The hotel here is frigid but otherwise comfortable. Our
officer is a one pip lieut called Compton Wilkins, who is a
wary one with a juvenile's face. Ex-actor. He knew
nothing of my job and was furious that I hadn't arrived
the day I was due – Sunday. We got over that quite soon
and I made it clear to him what I wanted. He is quite nice;
too young but that'll get well quite soon now. Had my
hair washed at the nearest coiffeur by a twelve-year-old
boy who joyfully tried to rub all my hair off, I rather
think. But very thorough. His father did the *mis en plis*
with flourishes and got busy waving my back hair which
is never any good, but with no Italian I had to resign
myself to it.

At 6.30 Lt Col Curteis came to fetch Viola and me to an
Italian cocktail party given by the Prince Borghese in his
palace here. Very ornate, style Rothschild, but effective
after the squalor of bomb-emptied Malta and the peeling
richnesses of the ministerial villa in Algiers. The Prince a
pale, shy little man with an honest face. His guests a
mixture of chic Romans, the women in black, musical

[1] Leslie Henson: actor, recognised by his bulging eyes. Toured for ENSA
throughout the war.
[2] Prudence Hyman: dancer who appeared in West End revues.

comedy soldiers in baby blue with brick-wall patterned patches of medals on their unmilitary bosoms. We came in for much staring. A bore of a young nobleman fed me endless little sweet cakes of delicious novelty and kissed my hand too often. Del Monte. Very extraordinary party. The Italians and Sicilians on their guard, the English being remote and talking deliberately poor French to get along! The aristocratic face has a familiar stamp, usually not a very strong face. Lots of it there tonight. I was cold and wore my red suit with a clean white shirt. Thank *heaven* I brought my furs. Cold sandwiches for supper at the officers' club. Hot coffee, later, at the YWCA.

On the airport today I met Brig de la Bere (sp?) who is welfare in Malta. He said he'd heard such glowing things of us. That the men's letters, after our shows, were all high praise. That my singing a French song to a French sailor on the *Maine* had impressed all! That I'd done the best job ever done on the island!! I nearly cried.

I write this in the bed lately occupied by Leslie Henson. It is very comfy. I've killed two whopping mosquitoes, though how they lived so long in this frigid air beats me. The film unit (ENSA) are running *very loud* talkies downstairs. I had two more letters from Reggie today, one from Pa, one from Gin.

Wednesday, March 8th, 1944   Sicily

No clear picture of Sicily yet. The cold in our hotel eats into the bones and freezes all sensibilities.

Thursday, March 9th, 1944   Sicily

Worked at No. 66 General Hospital. Cheerful little matron called Hallowes. Three shows, and the middle one, surgical, absolutely the best ever, I think. They were all front-line casualties and all at the top of their form in spite of wounds. Like a West End audience!

Last night Raphael de la Torre[1] took Viola and me to the Opera. He is a sergeant-major, ex-actor, half French, half Spanish, but completely English too! Very tall and thin and a long dark face. The Opera House is large and well shaped. Style Rothschild again. Very gilt and red velveted and lit with hundreds of round white lamps. Painted ceiling in clean colours. Very gay on the eye. The singers were local and poor except for Scarpia (it was *Tosca*), who was sung by Viviani who was *rather* good. In comparison anyway. The Opera is run here by army welfare and the house was packed out, mostly with us, but they had sold some seats in the upper galleries to the Sicilians for half price. We began with 'the King' and then the galleries – mostly students – demanded their National Anthem and there was much yelling and disconcern in the orchestra, and finally the welfare major and his interpreter came on to the stage and said that if they wanted to hear the opera they must shut up or go. So they shut up. I think his words were fortified by the appearance of our soldiery at the entrances.

Viola and I went for a gentle stroll down the main street yesterday morning and we saw a market in progress. There was a well-dressed gigolo sort of man selling bath towels in an hysterical and dramatic manner surrounded by a crowd. His face was familiar – as a type – and I suddenly realised he was of the kind that became gangsters in America. I believe seventy per cent of the gangsters there originated here. I can quite believe it.

Viola has been bitten on her face by three mosquitoes; or by one mosquito three times. We do keep having such bloody pianos for her. She is very good about it but it must be hell. The *Quiet Weekend*[2] company is due here

---

[1] Raf de la Torre: stage and radio actor.
[2] *Quiet Weekend*: domestic comedy by Esther McCracken, ran for 1059 performances at the Wyndhams Theatre.

today. The '*on dit*' is that Peggy Scott[1] has gone home or has broken her leg, which sounds awful. And Leslie Henson keeps losing members of his company by the way. Gavin Gordon[2] is in hospital here with a boil on his nose, pore thing; and David Hutcheson[3] is in hospital in Italy with *frostbite* caught when the company got snow-bound for two days.

My room here has three huge, red-brown doors with heavily carved frames and tops – sunflowers, poppies, tulips and writhing leaves. The walls are pale green and there is a painted ceiling with an octagonal dome including views and a circular centrepiece of a naked gal in a mauve skirt fondling a swan. It is cold. My window gives on to the Via Etna. Etna itself ought to be visible from Catania but isn't, so far, on account of cloud. The waiter here does a lovely neat job in peeling an orange for one. With great agility he knifes off the peel and slices the fruit into juicy little rounds, covers them with sugar, and presto! So good, too.

Monday, March 13th, 1944   Bari, Italy

We flew here yesterday from Catania. Viola and I sat up in front with the driver – us, from California. We had apprehended a rough passage, but it wasn't, though we met rain. Exciting to find Italy below us; little hill-towns looking very fairy-tale-ish high on peaks. Orchards frothing in white blossom. And occasionally bright pink. White farms. Dark brown earth, green cornland, yellow mustard. A flock of minute white sheep. Army lorries bowling along a shiny strip of wet road – straight as a

---

[1] Margaretta (Peggy) Scott: actress, whose films had included *Things to Come* (1937).
[2] Gavin Gordon: actor, singer and composer.
[3] David Hutcheson: West End actor, who had appeared with Margaretta Scott in the 1942 film *Sabotage at Sea*.

string. Mussolini built, along Roman lines? The sea a miracle of blue-green.

Sicily was too hurried. We arrived on Tuesday and left on Sunday and did six shows at 66 and seven at 33 and saw *Tosca*, went to the Borghese cocktail party, *Quiet Weekend* on Saturday night, and took a swift look at the Greek theatre at Syracuse. I stood on the apron stage and looked up at the huge circular auditorium in whitened stone and tried to imagine what it must have been like. It was sunny and I got out of the wind. Viola, who was chasing a long green lizard up the mounting seats, said she could hear every word I said when I spoke in ordinary conversational tones. Wild flowers springing up through the stone seats – antirrhinum, yellow geum, a blue sort of pea, daisies. We drove down to Syracuse on Friday, with an Italian chauffeur called Enrico in the ENSA Fiat – very comfy. Attractive smallish agricultural country between Catania and Syracuse. Orchards, no vineyards. Very squalid little towns. We passed an isolated radiolocation site and on an impulse I suggested we stop and talk to the crew. They were in the charge of a Glasgow sergeant with the most charming manners. He offered us tea and produced two chairs for us to sit on and we all talked of home. The tea took ages to boil and we had it from enormous tin mugs. All the men were wearing what appeared to be tortoiseshell rings with tiny photographs of their wives or girlfriends framed in them and dusted at the edge with gilt. Seems to be a fashion. Saw more of this in the hospital later. We stayed at the camp for about forty minutes and it was so friendly and cosy. Just ten or twelve men, miles from anywhere. The sergeant showed me some pictures of his seven children. He was only about thirty years old.

Hospital 33 was the best we've met yet. The Glasgow sergeant told me he'd been there thirty-two days with something and that 'the sisters were a great crowd and the matron a real lady – *grand*' – he said. He was right. The impact of the happy atmosphere of the unit met us at once. Matron – tall, a *little* toothy, with a comforting certainty and kindliness about her. Big with red-gold hair and I felt safe at once. Her sisters like her. I imagine she is wise and understanding. The colonel came to meet us – name of Arthur – neat with white hair. On the spot. We did seven shows while we were out there – all good. The hospital took a real interest and co-operated. We had tightly packed audiences and some grand singing. Friday night Viola and I stayed at the officers' club, Villa Poleti. There was a dance afterwards but I was beaten and couldn't make it. Viola and I had a disturbed night at the Villa Poleti – following festivities of the dance. Much door rattling and even balcony climbing. However we remained unharmed. Woke to idyllic morning. From our balcony we saw the bougainvillaea tree in full bloom and beyond, the strange *cavernous* gardens by the sea, still and very blue. It was *hot* in the sun. Divine. Our last show at 33 on Saturday afternoon was in the officers' mess and nursing sisters and doctors came too. It was fun. So easy and they laughed so freely. I loved it. Afterwards the colonel started to thank me and I tried to stop him but he said he must because it had been so lovely. He said that each morning matron brings him a report on the condition of the patients and that morning *all* the patients we'd played to the day before were more cheerful, had slept better and *were* better. He said 'this is no coincidence'. Oh, dear God – what a thing!

The *Quiet Weekend* company, 'Direct from Wyndhams Theatre, London', arrived in Catania on Thursday. How nice to see real actors after ENSA! It was very refreshing. When we saw the play on Saturday night at the San Giorgio Theatre I realised what a first-class job it was doing. It is so remote from war, so sane, so cosy, so very homesick-inducing; but that isn't a bad thing out here, I think. The house was jammed with soldiers and a very few nurses. They adore it – all the silly little domestic details of Marjorie's housekeeping were so reminiscent of home. I'm sure half of them had forgotten how things

used to be. The all importance of whether her bramble
jelly had set or not; the continual trouble with the plumbing, etc. – they relished it all. Peggy Scott hasn't broken
her leg. She's got a film contract instead! All this company have the right idea about working out here and are
doing a really good job. They feel as I do about bloody old
ENSA too. Bobbie Harris[1] is with them and talked to me
about doing poetry for the troops. I expect there is a
minority public for it, but I don't know how it is to be
done, quite. He struck me as nice, ravaged and intelligent.

The ENSA officer for Bari was in Catania and I took
badly agin' him. Bloated with a weedy great black moustache. A bully and common and, like most of them –
drinks too much. How can ENSA do a good job when it is,
for the best part, run by a set of shoddy fifth-rate drunks?
A good organiser, ruthless, heartless, is drinking far too
much and has that dead look about the eyes – at twenty-
seven. Golly! He *is* efficient though. Friend of Binkie's
and says he will be working for him after the war. I can
quite see it. Raphael de la Torre, on the other hand, is
more real, better brained and with integrity. But he will
get less far, in the worldly sense. He talked at length to
Viola about a play he's done from the French, *Le Bon Roi
Dagobert*. Sounds rather attractive.

We are staying in the Imperiale Hotel on the sea front.
It might just as well be Worthing. We arrived in rain; it
continues and there is something blowing like mad called
the Bourra? Borra? Bura? Anyway it is a horror. Typical of
ENSA – there was no one to meet us at Bari but the RAF
very kindly sent us in one of its cars straight to the hotel,
where I met Lieut Marshall, who runs it (it is an officers'
club) and he said we were expected and showed us to a
very nice corner room complete with private bath. The
plumbing is a little curious but the bath was hot today

---

[1] Robert Harris: actor at the Old Vic and in West End. He led the
company at the Stratford Memorial Theatre in 1946.

and the beds are delicious. The window won't quite close and it is hellish cold in here right now, as I write on my unmade bed, wearing me fur coat and a rug in an attempt to keep the least bit warm. Downstairs there are desks and chairs but conversation is quite unavoidable and I have had to retire here in desperation. Viola is practising in the tea-lounge! Lady Freyberg[1] is here running a New Zealand club and she is dining with us tonight. Last night Viola and I were writing on either side of a desk in the hall when two officers invited us to join them for drinks. My heart fell but they looked lonesome so we said yes.

Toc H[2] men and girls here last night. WAAFs [Women's Auxiliary Air Force] too. The ENSA officer i/c in Fraser Green's absence is called Pelster, Lieut. He is squat, pale, with glasses and an ex-Paramount [Films] man. He doesn't begin to know what it's all about. Over nasty tea and against the deafening accompaniment of the hotel band, I tried to tell him what I was trying to do. I do not think it penetrated at all – but I hope for the best. We got to 98 today. The colonel is the late colonel from 33 – I come full of messages for him from everyone there. I rang him up last night to pave the way a little and he sounded nice.

I'm very bewildered about what to do concerning Baghdad. We can't begin to scratch the surface here in a week. Still no word from London. I begin to think we should remain here for a month instead of trying to get that far. Poor Viola had a horrid come-over about her brother Peter last night. He is Scots Guards and we heard they had had a bad time. Oh, I do hope he is all right. She

---

[1] Wife of General Bernard Freyberg, VC, who had commanded the New Zealand forces in 1941 in a valiant although ultimately unsuccessful rearguard when the Germans invaded Crete. She was the daughter of Sir Herbert Jekyll.
[2] Toc H: A Christian Fellowship founded in 1915 by Rev. Tubby Clayton. One of its most famous padres was known as Woodbine Willie, so named because he gave free Woodbine cigarettes to the troops in trenches out at the Front.

minds so much about him. I think they must be very close to each other. She quotes him a lot. He sounds gay and attractive. Viola looked very pretty last night.

Our Milanese chauffeur in Sicily, Enrico, took suddenly and passionately to me and when I said goodbye to him at the airfield yesterday morning his eyes filled with tears and his lips quivered and he pressed my hand in a great dramatic gesture and I felt like a player in a big scene.

Tuesday, March 14th, 1944   Bari, Italy

The matron at 98 is elderly and I suspect quite dead inside. Her assistant has an unfortunate complexion of the greasy, open-pored sort. She is, or must be, full of guts, for she escaped from the Far East in a series of awful adventures and is now here doing her job with the air of a rather tiresome prefect. I wonder if lack of imagination helps? I should guess that neither has an atom. They have no inkling of what we are trying to do, and don't appear to care. The colonel – Mackinnon – is a rugged Scot who has probably got far too much to do. His first appearance didn't encourage me. After 33 where both Colonel Arthur and Miss Robertson co-operated so well and we did a fairly thorough job, the going is decidedly uphill. Thought the sisters looked a little grim too – and suspicious. Dear God, how I hate suspicious women. It's all rather like 94 was, and I must keep at it or get low again. *Still* no word from Algiers or London, and Pelster at the ENSA office is wonderfully slow and dull and lazy and, I suspect, useless.

Viola and I went down to the Garrison Theatre this morning. The ENSA office is there. Chaotic – run by some sloppy young sergeants in an indescribable confusion. Transport problems, and the other artists, visiting entertainment officers – all happening at once. I don't believe that a single thing I said to Pelster got through at all. Ah me.

Yesterday was hard going. We lunched with matron in the sisters' mess as usual. It's housed in a great semi-finished stucco block so echoey that the least conversation is exhausting in it, for it bounces off every surface and pummels you back. Her room is very comfy and gay with four budgerigars in two cages – communicating gates! – snaps of godchildren and nieces and nephews, some blossom in local and rather attractive earthenware pitchers. Palest pinky-white wall, apple-green paint and this awful echo. Art shop pictures, collected in Sicily, all around the walls – 'That's Taormina' – 'That's Vesuvius' – 'That's a field full of Sicilian flowers'. A ghastly statuette, all pout and pinafore, of a three-year-old child in plaster. A doggy calendar of course – Aberdeen. A big radio, an electric kettle – all the comforts of the home. But perhaps I'm wrong? Maybe she has a heart and does mind? She seems *so* dead somehow. She was very nice to us and laughed at my jokes; but I rather wonder if her work matters any more?

The last show was in the facial mac[1] ward and Captain Battle, i/c the ward, turned out to know my stuff and was very friendly and obviously cared that his patients should have fun. Our piano was beyond praying for and out of tune. My posters have been left behind in Sicily. *Dear* ENSA!

Last night Barbara Freyberg came to dine with me, wearing khaki with NZ on her shoulders. She is here running welfare for NZ troops. She looks very unchanged but is rather '*émue*' I think, and no blame to her for, on top of Pamela Mackenna's death, her son Paul[2] was missing.

---

[1] 'Facial mac' – phrase inspired by the brilliant facial surgery done at East Grinstead by Sir Archibald McIndoe, the plastic surgeon. One of his most famous cases, described by Joyce in *Darling Ma*, was the young pilot, Richard Hillary.
[2] Paul Freyberg escaped from prisoner-of-war camp. He succeeded his father as Baron Freyberg in 1963.

But she thinks he is all right after all. We talked of Enid,[1] Lady Colefax,[2] Diana and Duff Cooper, Olga Lynn,[3] and the Otleys. I came over dead about 9.30 and thought that if I didn't go to bed I'd scream.

Wednesday, March 15th – The Ides Of   Bari, Italy

Oh, good, good, good. Peter Tunnard is all right! He rang up the Naples office (ENSA) two days ago and asked for Viola. She is out walking with Dan Kelly and has had two very bad days of worry, saying little, looking strained. And now I can't wait to tell her. I've looked for her all over the town but failed to find her. Anyway *the* thing is that she is going to be so happy to know. I did some thinking in the night, having got myself all complicated and wrong in the past two days. Just a bad unreal patch. My reward is this Peter news and running into Ben Schomperlen[4] and Alva Honey from No. 5 Canadian. And getting a straight answer from Major Mellor of ENSA (Naples) to my question of whether we ought to stay on in Italy or go on to Baghdad and he says definitely go on to Baghdad. So that is settled and I felt happy inside about it because my hunch was that it was the right thing to do.

Yesterday was rather hellish somehow. We took a brief little walk in Bari between showers, and it was grim, squalid, poor and depressing. We looked so obviously

---

[1] Enid Lawson: wife of the Hon. Edward Frederick Lawson, son of Lord Burnham; he was general manager of the *Daily Telegraph*. They lived at Hall Farm, Beaconsfield, near Joyce and Reggie.
[2] Sybil Colefax: a famous interior decorator and wife of Sir Arthur, an eminent lawyer. With Lady Cunard one of the two leading hostesses of literary and political London.
[3] Olga Lynn: contralto singer who appeared in several Ivor Novello shows.
[4] Ben Schomperlen: doctor at the Canadian Red Cross Hospital at Cliveden.

English and everyone spoke to us and it was touching and good. At the ENSA office we drew some money and inspected the huge Garrison Theatre, ex-Opera House. Flamboyant and on the grand scale. Wonderful acoustics. While Viola did some necessary work on the minipiano we were to use, I sang from the stage, and it was so well built that even my mouse sounds bounced off in the right places.

Thursday, March 16th, 1944   Bari, Italy

Rather took to Mellor in the office today. Large and North Country but with a heart, I think. I do not believe anyone is any good without heart – no matter who or what they are doing. You've got to mind about things. He is quite clear about the Baghdad plan and says we are really badly needed there and that we would do a good job here but that there are others doing it and no one is doing it out there. So that is my answer. The present plan is to move to Naples on Sunday and do a week there. Viola will see Peter and as it is all organised there we must do it, and then we are to fly via Malta to Cairo on the 26–27th and then on.

This hotel is full of officers of all the Allied nations but mainly British and Canadian and after dark they get going in rather an alarming way. I suppose it is understandable; only I'd rather not be in it! The sodden male is an un-charming being. I feel that we are wrong to be here at those moments and that we are seeing things we oughtn't to see. That is why I was glad to get upstairs early last night. After we'd been asleep for about an hour a party began in the room over ours, and it was so spectacularly noisy that I can only suppose they were hurling each other from great heights at frequent intervals! There was apparently much movement of furniture. And it sounded as if they had de-tiled the bathroom and were tossing the tiles about. Now and then there was singing. There *must* have been casualties. Never heard such a noise.

Unlike our worrying nights in Tunis and Syracuse we felt a certain security, for our door really did lock this time.

Friday, March 17th – St Patrick's Day   Bari, Italy

On Wednesday, Pelster of ENSA, in response to questions – for he never volunteers information, I've discovered – told me he'd arranged for us to go out to No. 5 Canadian General near Andrea and that they would send transport for us at 10.45 – and for our piano. We stood in the hall, waiting, and lo, a high dust-coloured vehicle drove up and out of it got Anna Millar[1] and Staff Chipman. I was *so* glad to see Anna – we embraced warmly and I introduced Viola and we all piled in and drove off along the most inferior roads all the thirty-five miles. Anna, Viola and I sat on the centre seat which is mysteriously constructed so that the two outsiders fall off into a narrow space between where the seat ends and the car's sides. I was the middle one, so didn't suffer but Viola was continually slipping, so was Anna. We got to the camp about 12.30, having talked all the way above the roar of the engine which appeared to be right inside the car with us. Rather exhausting.

The camp is on the side of a hill with little pine trees between the sisters' tents which looked pretty and will be useful later on. The wards are all tents and yesterday the approach was entirely through a sea of deep mud so we were courteously escorted everywhere by jeep, Chipman at the wheel. Anna gave us lunch with the rain beating on the canvas. But it was a good lunch and stood up well to compare with the Lucullan feasts we used to have in the

[1] Anna Millar: Staff Sister on Ward 11 at the Canadian Red Cross Hospital at Cliveden.

sisters' mess at Taplow. We ended with squares of chocolate cake in a pool of delicious syrup. I saw *so* many old
friends.

Saturday, March 18th, 1944   Bari, Italy

Never seems any time to write in this book. Yesterday
morning the front hall was made different by the appearance of Diana Gould[1], newly arrived by boat with the
Merry Widow company from Cairo. Madge and Cyril[2] are
to follow by air. Diana, looking marble-eyed and alarmingly à la Medusa, in a tweed suit and paisley shirt and
headscarf together with pearls and a winged diamond
pin, told me in fine ringing tones of the hellish night she
had had to endure in an Italian doss house. 'Jesus,
darling,' she said, which I found unattractive to start
with, 'no one minds roughing it, but to pig it is madly
unnecessary and it was *the* squalor of *all* time. No sheets,
tins to drink from, not a drop of hot water – fleas and lice
and an unending smell of rotting apples. Just hideous
hell, darling, and I'm not going to stand it.' Nor do I think
she can have, for within a few hours of her arrival she had
rounded up the Town Major's aide and got organising to
such an extent that she had notes flying around to all her
friends. So clever, I thought. She discovered that Nick
Villiers and Dick Westmacott were here and they in turn
discovered, through her, that I am here, and so further
notes were dispatched and I've been bidden to dine, but
can't, mercifully, for they are all too young for me, as I'm
rightly and properly dining with a Brigadier of my own
generation.

 Yesterday was spent at the NZ hospital here, No. 3. We
did four shows all in orthopaedic and amputation wards.

---

[1] Diana Gould: actress and dancer, later married to Yehudi Menuhin.
[2] Madge Elliott and Cyril Ritchard: played Sonia and Prince Danilo in
The Merry Widow on this tour. Ritchard starred in *The Little Revue* in
which Joyce made her first appearance on the professional stage.

In the evening we dined with Lady Freyberg at her NZ officers' convalescent club here. Big stars to meet us – a general, a brigadier, the matron in chief, two colonels, but the only name that remains with me is Kendrick; he is head of the NZ medical division. Attractive and on the spot. General Sergesson Brooks was there when we arrived and wants me to do Red X shows for him in Naples next week. After supper, which was delicious and began with hot oysters in baked potatoes! – Viola and I did a show. I think we had about 120 there. It went *smoothly*. Viola played well and they loved her. And at the end we were each given a basket of flowers, mine all blues and mostly hyacinths, and Viola's red and white, mostly stocks.

Cocoa followed and I unwisely had three full cups and was on the run *all* night.

I wish I knew how to keep the feelings I feel here while I'm working. I'm a bit tired now and then, but there is such a buoyant, spiritual, selfless feeling in it all that carries me through on wings and I am *so* grateful about it. It is the most wonderful sight and sensation in the world to watch an audience relax and abandon themselves to listening and enjoying it.

ENSA will never get right so long as it employs lumps of flesh like Fraser Green to run a huge district like this one. Any organisation that has been needed for our pro-gramme this week has happened only because I've slog-ged round in person to get it all cut and dried. It's the muddliest office of them all – with the eternal exception of Drury Lane, where a permanent chaos reigns and the *bon mot* (Diana Gould's I think), 'Abandon hope all ye who ENSA here', is indeed a truth.

This morning Viola and I went along to see what was happening about our departure tomorrow, and F. Green lying back in his chair never moved, knew nothing and looked thoroughly unappetising. A white blob of a face with a growth of undisciplined hair bursting from his upper lip. There is *no* quality there. Ah *me*.

Sunday, March 19th, 1944   Naples

We flew here this morning from Bari. Good going, few
bumps in spite of the pilot warning us we might meet
many over the mountains. They lay below us, cleanly cut
and covered with snow. A little alarming if you let the
distance between them and you get at you at all. I write in
the window of my balcony bedroom in the ENSA hostel,
Parco Margherita, halfway up the hill, with the bay to my
left. The sun is shining and it is *almost* warm; windy
though. I can hear a bird, probably singing from a cage.
Every vehicle in Naples seems to have to pass by here,
and they all change gear right under this block of apart-
ments. The hill winds steeply, zigzagging up to the top.
It's rather fun to watch a truckload of Negro troops, all
standing, rising by invisible means along the parapet to
my right. I have hopes of the ENSA office here. It is, on the
surface, anyway, efficient. John Wigram is in charge of
what the rather cissy Lieut who welcomed us calls 'Rowt-
ing'. Major Mellor is nice too and escorted us to this
rather scrappy billet where we share a very small room
with no hanging space and inadequate comfort. But it
must do, I suppose, unless Roger, who is here till tomorrow, can magic Harold Caccia[1] into doing anything for
us? Roger won't be in till after five today, and we have no
telephone here. However I have left a message for him
and given him *our* address. This hostel is full of other
ENSAs including The Aspidistras[2] with whom I played in
Diversion in 1940. They are playing in a small variety
company and clearly find it all a little depressing, for
there is no one of their class in the show and it is pretty

---

[1] Harold Caccia: at this time Vice-President, Political Section, Allied
Control Commission, Italy. Later British Ambassador to Austria,
United States; Head of the Diplomatic Service. Created Lord Caccia of
Abernant, 1965.
[2] The Aspidistras (Elsie French and her husband John Mott): described
as 'a vocal entertainment' toured for ENSA for nine months in Africa and
Italy.

feeble. There is a straight play company here. The Aspidistras told me they were doing the *Barretts of Wimpole
Street*[1] but looking at them during lunch I completely
failed to cast it from their very mixed throng. There is a
Billie Burke-ish[2] blonde of very uncertain age; a plain
spinster type (for character?). A pretty girl – very – and
some ill-assorted rather pansy young men. Everyone
here wears khaki except us and for the most part they
look rather well in it. It is compulsory for them if they go
forward at all and most of these, I gather, have or will
soon. In all honesty I don't in the least want to go forward
but if I have to I will! Elsie French tells me that Inga
Anderson,[3] covered in regimental insignia, is up there.
Far, far more frightening than the battle, I should think!
There was a picture of her in yesterday's *Union Jack*,
pointing at her arm sewn like a button queen with
divisional signs and us wings, etc. etc. I admire her guts
but not her act or her appearance.

Still no word here from Peter Tunnard. Viola's just
gone out to find a telephone so that she can get on to him
if possible. I'm afraid he must have gone back into the
line because it is unlikely he wouldn't have left messages
otherwise. Oh dear.

I have had a grand batch of mail today. Reggie still
hopes I'll come home from here, but I can't. I do feel a bit
worn but it's only a question of five more weeks and I'm
sure I must. He sounds well. Dick says he looks well.
Victor says Linklater's play[4] is terrible, terrible, terrible,

---

[1] Successful 1930 play by Rudolf Besier about the difficult courtship of
Elizabeth Barrett and Robert Browning. Twice filmed.

[2] Billie Burke: American actress; best known for dithery matron roles in
many Hollywood films, including *The Wizard of Oz*. Married Florenz
Ziegfeld Jnr.

[3] Inga Anderson: Canadian singer and cabaret artist, used to decorate
the sleeves of her ENSA uniform with badges from the units she
entertained.

[4] *Crisis in Heaven*, by Eric Linklater, was directed by John Gielgud at the
Lyric Theatre in 1944 with Dorothy Dickson as Helen of Troy. It was not
a great success.

with Dorothy Dickson in a Marshall and Snelgrove number, of turquoise chiffon! He and Dick saw it in Edinburgh on their way south after Victor's leave, spent in
simplicity in a white house on a hill in Fife. Reggie has at
last heard from me, so that's a comfort. They all came at
once.

Later: The Billie Burke blonde is Mary Glynne, widow
of Dennis Neilson-Terry[1] and the 'character' is Fay
Compton's sister![2] It's a mixed rep. co. and they are
doing *Rope*, *Blithe Spirit*, and a two-handed psychological
piece called *Jealousy*[3]. Apart from *B.S.* I can't say I think
their choice very good for the boys.

Roger failed to get the message I left for him. We spent
the afternoon and evening in our little room resting and
writing and trying to catch up on ourselves. Supper was
at 8.30 and we are sitting at a table with Elsie French and
John Mott – The Aspidistras.

After supper we all climbed up on the roof to see
Vesuvius in eruption. A lovely and alarming sight. The
night was cloudless, a shooting star, no wind. The volcano was hurtling fire and we could see the molten lava
spreading down the sides. The sound of the grumbling
hit us out of rhythm with the sight. John Mott says it
hasn't erupted for four years and that this is supposed to
be a very bad go and they have evacuated some of the
mountain villages. Golly, I wouldn't stay long with that
red-hot stuff pouring down the hillside. It travels at five
miles an hour which is faster than walking pace. It was
strangely exciting and rather beautiful to see the
eruption.

---

[1] Dennis Neilson-Terry: son of Fred Terry, and a cousin of John
Gielgud.
[2] Viola Compton, Fay's eldest sister (the writer Compton Mackenzie
was their brother).
[3] *Rope*, famous psychological thriller by Patrick Hamilton, subsequently
made into a film by Alfred Hitchcock. *Blithe Spirit*, Noël Coward's 1941
play. *Jealousy*, French play by Louis Verneuil, English version by
Eugene Walter.

Monday, March 20th, 1944   Naples

Oh God, the sights I've seen today. We haven't *touched* the war till today. Bed after bed filled with mutilated men, heads, faces, bodies. It's the most inhuman, ghastly, bloody, hellish thing in the world. I couldn't think or work or even feel in the end. It was quite numbing. The first ward (it was at 65) was a huge surgical full of casts, pulleys, and very sick men. All the time we were playing there were sisters doing dressings, patients feeding from tubes, orderlies bringing people in from the theatres and newly arrived from the line. About half the room was too ill to listen or care; the others lay and took it in with their eyes. It was no fun to see the suffering going on in there. I struggled to get a clear mind and do the job and eventually I think I did. But it was an experience I don't often wish to witness. But far the illest people I've seen as yet. The nurses are at it every minute and seem so calm and encouraging. I take my hat off to them. It's a terrific job and they are doing it beautifully here.

There is a head and face surgery team at this hospital which means they get the full burden of all such cases. We did three shows, three of the most extraordinary I ever hope to do. A blinded Scotch boy called Dan – still dazed by his wounds and in a sort of awful gaiety. Their tenderness to each other is heartbreaking. In two wards patients were out of their minds and struggling, and in both cases there was a fellow patient, now convalescent, holding the sick man down gently and patiently, watching him all the time. And a bad face case who was also shellshocked had a friend to see him and he just sat and held his hand in silence. The warmth of human contact and the restoring confidence of a friend must help at a time like this. I *must* forget all this or I shan't be any good but in another way I must remember it for the effort I, as an individual, must make to see that there are never any more wars. If the striking miners and factory workers could be in one of those wards for an hour and see those boys they'd never strike again.

A baby soldier from Devon asked me if I could sing any song at all about a mother! He was so ill and so weak and I longed to hand him over then and there to the mother whom he is longing so for at this moment.

I have *got* to get it all clear in my mind or I'll be no good at all and that's what I'm here for. Viola and I have decided, and I know we are right, that we are not such value in these very acute wards as we can be when these same creatures have reached the boring and convalescent stage. Here they are too ill to know or care – except the very few and they will soon *be* convalescent in N. Africa or Sicily or somewhere further back. I'm glad now we made the decision to go to Paiforce next week, because we shall be of more use there. The nurses here, 65, are welcoming and friendly, but even so I feel that we are more of a nuisance than a value here. They are *so* busy and so admirable in their apparent inexhaustibleness. It must be awful to be in a ward and watch your friends suffer so; and die. I must stop this. It's *no good*.

Dined with Harold Caccia at the Brigeta officers' mess. After dinner Harold Caccia and his American opposite number Sam Reber drove me halfway up Vesuvius to see the lava coming down. We went in their jeep with one Tchaikovsky at the wheel, US Army. Harold asked him when he first arrived if he was related to the composer and he replied, only distantly as he was from the Polish branch. He comes from Buffalo NY and drives with respect and skill. The eruptions were continuous from the volcano and as we got along the *autostrada* there was an endless Derby Day stream of traffic, *all* American!, going and coming from the spectacle. The track up to the mountain was nothing more than a track but the jeep made it. It was icy cold but we reached a good view and the hot air blowing off the flow met our faces. Very queer and not a little frightening to see this moving wall of red-hot molten rock travelling slowly down the hillside.

It made a hissing noise. We were still three-quarters of a mile away. The eruptions were almost continuous above us. A great firework display – star fountains of red light, fans of hurtling fire. Most extraordinary. By that evening the flow on the west side had reached a village and since has covered it. Ghastly. The whole sight was evil but rather beautiful like an old picture painted on glass.

Peter[1] and Viola had a cosy evening. She finds him dreadfully changed by the experiences he's had to face in this bloody war. They have had such losses and he has watched so many of his friends killed.

Thursday, March 23rd, 1944   Naples

We woke up to find a Vesuvius smoke fog over Naples. Peter fetched us in the ENSA transport and drove to the officers' club and left our overnight bags before going to look around a bit. I still have no clear picture of Naples as a city. It has charm. It is filthy. It must have been gay. There is something very comforting to the eye in seeing shop windows full again. And full of real things, lovely gloves and stockings and chocolates and silks and heavenly little pâtisseries. We bought gloves – black suede, and then had hot chocolate and sweet cakes in a coffee house. It had begun to rain so we sat on and it was restful and pleasant.

Miss Rogers of the British Red Cross met us at Sorrento. She used to be on the Bucks British Red Cross at High Wycombe and we used to correspond about my liaising with the Canadian Red Cross at No. 5,[2] petrol issues, etc. Viola and I were shown into the royal suite where Queen Alexandra once stayed. It is frescoed in

[1] Peter Tunnard had gone out to the Middle East in January 1942 as a lieutenant, later a captain, in the Scots Guards. When he met Viola and Joyce in 1944 he had landed in Anzio, in a new brigade, having recovered from a wound in hospital. They arrived in Sorrento a few days later, during the eruption of Vesuvius.
[2] Ward No. 5, Canadian Red Cross Hospital, Cliveden.

blue-grey and a diamond-shaped panel edged in bronze brown and filled with white blossom. Freehand painting. Some German crests are over the door and window to commemorate a Kronprinzian visit. The British Red Cross haven't laid their touch anywhere except to improve the comfort. Tin mugs for cleaning the teeth from in the bathroom. Marked with a red cross. And on the beds gay turquoise-blue eiderdowns – *linen* covered. A fire was lit for us as we arrived and it was very cosy and unlike ENSA. A light by the bed to read by! We hadn't got any dressing-gowns with us as we'd brought the minimum of luggage, but Miss Lyons the QM produced identical royal blue flannel numbers from her stores. These are miracles of warmth and comfort but as ill-fitting as possible. Lolloping Peter Pan collars, a most interesting general cut, and then a brown bone button at the neck and a couple of ends to tie one in by. They are marked BRC but were made by the San Mateo Chapter of the American Red Cross in California, USA. The kindly ladies who ran 'em up must have cut them out first with a knife and fork. Viola and I laughed at ourselves in them till we cried.

Tuesday evening we did a show here for the officers. First I took a hot bath in the side of the hotel where we aren't sleeping, so it meant going over fully dressed with towel and sponge bag in hand. Mysteriously there was plenty of scalding water but not a drip of cold, and as I was a little late I had to plunge bravely into the hot. It was *very* hot and it set up a strange thudding throughout my system but I bore it valiantly and washed hard. At dinner I sat next to an enormous and attractive man called Bonham-Carter – cousin of Cressida and those.[1] We did the show in the long room alternately used as a dance hall on Fridays and a church on Sundays. It is frescoed in rather elaborate terracotta designs in the Morris manner but without his taste. As nasty a room for sound as ever I

[1] Desmond Bonham-Carter (knighted 1969) 6ft 7ins tall and served with Royal Tank Regiment; was a director of Unilever, 1953–68.

have sung in, for it resounded like a swimming pool and you couldn't do a thing about it. Poor Viola had a bloody piano. Very loud and with no possibility of keeping it from barking, try as she did. I felt so out of form that I had to pull myself together with a wrench. It went alright but I know when I'm right and I wasn't that night. Simon Phipps was there, and Ronnie Rowe, Ruby Peto's son Tim, Jonathan Blow. All very young, all Guardees. After the show we went, in the inevitable jeep, to the 2nd Scots Guards mess for a drink. Simon is a nice creature, very civilised and rather sensitive. He wore a white sheepskin jacket and a beret, and looked rather chic and bizarre. He wears his beret very central. We didn't stay very late as we were all tired. A goodish night only, as Vesuvius pooped off at intervals and shook doors and windows and worried us. I kept thinking it was guns and their thunder.

Breakfast in our room. It was pouring with rain; we abandoned all hope of getting over to Positano, then the sun came out and we sat in the courtyard talking to our friends before setting off for Naples at 11.30. There was – there always is – transport trouble and poor Peter T. was all over Sorrento seeking something to get us away. He finally produced a desert car that looked a little doubtful but we piled in, me in comfort in front, Viola and Peter to bounce on cushions and a coat on a springless seat at the back. Our driver was a charming Scot from Edinburgh who had sprung direct from under an engine he was mending and came as he was in his overalls. We talked of the beauties of this part of Italy and he asked me what I did, so I told him. There was quite a long pause after this as we negotiated the hairpin coast road, and he whistled as we missed cars whizzing in the opposite direction. Then he suddenly said: 'If it wouldn't be nosey, what *do* you sing?' So I told him that and he said, 'Fancy.' Near Castellammare we suddenly stopped and the car failed to move again. So we got out. By this time the endless great belched-out clouds from Vesu were piling up into a great pall and it looked very menacing. The thrusts were so powerful that a great puff would blow straight up several thousand feet. Tightly curled grey stuff that then frothed into grey-white cauliflower clouds. Sometimes the grey ones arrived a pinky colour. Their swirling was beautiful in the sun that had now come out. Viola and I watched this while Peter sought transport again and finally stopped a Scots Guards lorry with three Guardsmen in it wearing those silly down-the-nose peaked caps. We piled in again and rattled along on an iron edge till I nearly cried out from the jarring. It felt as if my bosom was being beaten. Suddenly Peter stopped the lorry and leapt out. We'd arrived at the local general's HQ and Peter knew his ADC and could, maybe, get us some transport that wasn't all iron edges. Viola and I sat on our edges and listened while the Scots driver gave some pithy advice to a convalescent fellow Guardsman who had wandered down from a nearby hospital to talk to our friends. He told him to get an appendix, mebbe, or else a nasty cold, because if he came back he'd only get put on sergeants' mess fatigues, see if he didn't!

Peter emerged from the house with all arranged. First, we were to lunch there with the general, as the hospital we were due to entertain had been evacuated because of Vesuvius! Secondly the general forbade us to go on that road at all as he wished it kept clear for the speedy evacuation of any civilians who were in the line of the descending lava. (All day after this we heard wild rumours about the speed of the lava – a wall varying from ten feet to forty feet in height according to account.)

Peter Tunnard is much more composed than I'd imagined. He is clever, I think; much more mature than Viola and more worldly. He has an avid interest in people, mostly people older than himself. Those weeks in Anzio haunt him. For the first two days – nearly three days – since he saw Viola he was quite different from anything she had ever remembered at home and it worried her. He was quiet and didn't respond and one felt he was full of dread. But yesterday afternoon and last night in the restaurant kitchen he suddenly thawed and giggled and came to life. He and Viola have a very attractive affection and slightly respectful attitude to each other. He walked home with me and talked so fondly of her. That's a relationship I've always missed with Tommy.[1]

Slept like a log last night. No more Vesuvius crumps to suck open our door. But it was pouring with rain when we got up. It took over an hour to get through to ENSA to see if they had laid on 59 hospital as I'd asked them to do yesterday. They had not. It was too late to do it today and so I suggested we try and do the convalescent depot here and the ENSA Ingram fell on it; too lazy to cope with anything. Arranged to have transport here at 4.30 to take us back to Naples. Very cold morning. Miss Rodgers lit her fire for us and we sat by it. Then Viola went down to the horrid piano where Peter and Tim Peto and I joined her a little later and we had a walk through the village where Viola got the worm powders for the Russian Princess in Malta and we bought some chocolates for Miss Rodgers and ate some cakes in the pâtisserie – sponge, like Granny's used to be, with white icing. *Wonderful.*

We went into a church with a remarkable and pagan crypt where parishioners pray to St Anthony and other saints and pin photographs of their loved ones on a panel so that the saint shouldn't make a mistake, and if it is a prayer for a sick person the actual member or part of the body that needs healing is represented in silver cardboard just to make it quite clear in Heaven. Whole cupboards, glass fronted, filled with cardboard legs, hands, arms, and, I swear, some kidneys! Many of the Catholic churches here are beautiful. All are remote from God.

Early tea in Miss Rodgers's room while we watched with concern the advance of a heavy dark brown Vesuvius

[1] Tommy Phipps: Joyce's younger brother.

fog coming at us over the bay. Our transport was an hour late by which time an officer patient, just returned from Naples, advised us strongly not to try to make the journey this evening. It was getting dusk and the ash fog was choking and very thick. So here we *still* are. We plan to leave at 8 in the morning. Viola has gone with Peter over to dine with friends of his at Positano.

Saturday, March 25th, 1944   Naples

Back in Naples again. When we woke up and looked out of our Queen Alexandrine windows to the sea, a most fantastic pink pall lay over the water, its edges lifting slightly in the wind. It advanced and receded and was very horrid. All the cliffs of Sorrento were right under the layers of dust and the olive trees and roofs and orange groves were all uniformly powdered. When we got into the hotel we felt filthy and both washed all over and put on clean clothes before going out to Caserta No. 2. Again they sent a three-tonner for us which is quite mad and wastes petrol quite unnecessarily. Oh, the discomfort of it! We both sat in front with the Italian driver and were frozen and jolted all the way.

Specially nice matron at No. 2. Miss Mitchell. Gay and quite giggly. She advised us to concentrate entirely on Ward B, a huge surgical – orthopaedic, mainly in cradles, etc. – for it had over a hundred beds in it, all in bays off a central corridor. So we did three shows, one between each bay. ENSA, dear ENSA, had omitted to send our piano with us so we had a delay while an upright was borrowed from an NZ unit nearby. Maddening. The concerts were rather good. The two days' enforced rest at Sorrento had done us a lot of good and I felt in fine strong voice! It was a strange place to work in. Having to hand out to an audience on two sides divided by a wall is a bit of an effort. I ended by singing each song completely twice over, once on each side of the dividing wall. One patient, lying on his stomach, could only just see me so I had to get right into a corner so that he could peer with at least one eye! They were a very nice lot. Pretty ill still, but all of them knowing their fighting is over and most of them not unpleased about it. How I sympathise. Lots of them will get home as soon as they are able to travel. There was a definite need for us there. Wish we could have stayed longer.

Good day at 67. Special unit again, rather like 33. Happy atmosphere and the patients, most of whom are en route for home, in very good heart. We did three shows in big wards. Very kind entertainments officer, name of Colonel Brindle, who not only knew but cared! Nice change. Posters do help. The new ones aren't as nice as the Malta ones. They are yellow with my name in large letters four inches high and Viola's underneath in two-inch ones. The whole is about fourteen inch by eight inch, I should think. Colonel Brindle had them up in the wards when we arrived after lunch. Matron is new, Miss Price, and I liked her a lot. Middle-aged and comfy with a wild rolling eye and a sense of humour. Vitality and a heart. Her room blessedly free from the wee doggie atmosphere they so often have.

Hear we aren't flying tomorrow but Monday. So rang up Harold Caccia to see if he could arrange for us to visit Herculaneum tomorrow, and Roger answered the telephone! Arrived today from Algiers. His movements have been incredibly rapid since last Monday. Flew Cairo Monday, from Cairo to Algiers Friday, Algiers here today. He came in to see us this evening and we meet tomorrow.

John Perry at dinner. I like him. His new play, from Kate O'Brien's *Last of Summer*[1], is coming on next month with Fay Compton and Jill Furse.

[1] Kate O'Brien: Irish novelist. *The Last of Summer* opened at the Phoenix Theatre on June 7th, directed by John Gielgud. Jill Furse was not, however, in it. It was not a great success. Perry had earlier collaborated with M. J. Farrell (the nom-de-plume of Molly Keane, the novelist) on several successful plays, among them *Spring Meeting*, *Treasure Hunt*, *Dazzling Prospect*, all directed by John Gielgud.

Sunday, March 26th, 1944   Naples

Lunch at Harold's [Macmillan] villa. Lovely position on
the sea with the Bay of Naples to our left and Vesuvius,
now powdered with grey ash and still blowing deep grey
cauliflower smoke, slightly more central. But a ghastly
modern villa, very ill-planned. All the rooms leading off
into the next one. So cold and bare and no trees in the
garden for necessary summer shade. Bitterly cold there
today in this fierce wind. John Wyndham[1] in top form at
lunch. Over the dining-room table hung a yellow glass
Venetian candelabra of peculiar unpleasance. Roger remarked that it must have taken quite a blower to achieve
one of the curving arms and he supposed he'd had a
small boy to jump on his stomach to emit the final blow.
His account of the St James's bomb was picturesque and
macabre. 'A man in the street nearby was knocked into
the air only to fall into an EWS [Emergency Water Supply]
tank where he was drowned. Rather funny.' John says
the street near Wilton's oyster bar and Spinks was littered
with a confusion of medals and shellfish. The Brownriggs
who live over the PO came down to see a friend off in a car
and when they got to the street the car was bent in two
and the chauffeur was in it but there wasn't a sign of his
head. He went on untiringly. Harold rather tired at first
but a plate full of pasta and some Lachrimae Christi made
him better and he was in fine form too. After lunch he
read to us from Boswell's *Life of Johnson*. Particularly
about Papists, for he says these Latin countries awaken
all John Wyndham's Protestantism and he wanted Johnson's views on the subject.

About 2.30 Roger, John, Viola and I set off in a staff car
to see Herculaneum. Harold preferred a walk. How
lovely the Roman ruins are. So perfect. I'd no idea of their
delicate decoration. Completely Empire. Terracotta with

[1] John Wyndham: after Macmillan's retirement as Prime Minister in
1963, he returned full-time to the family estate at Petworth and wrote an
engaging memoir, *Wyndham and Children First*.

white designs, black with gold. Little pictures – frescoes. A chaffinch, a long-tailed blackbird. Flowers. Diana's pagan chapel, all mosaics in brillant colours and shells around the alcove altar. Quite enchanting. Two bronze candlesticks of exquisite craftsmanship. The baths with their fluted ribbed roof like a Nissen hut. The décor is so nineteenth century that I was puzzled. John said, 'Chester Terrace, Regent's Park', which was indeed true. Roger explained. Pompeii and Herculaneum both came to light about the end of the eighteenth century and those lovely designs must have been much publicised for they were in constant use in the Empire period. The urn, the swag, the fluted column. Our guide, in spats and with four large buttons on the belt at the back of his ample overcoat, had little but interesting English. 'Look at de bart', he commanded. 'Look at the cek – slize cut off. Look at the lavatrine in de kitchen.' This last seemed a very insanitary idea but was indeed true. 'Look at de wood steps – char'.' Now and then he would use some rolling French. 'Look at le charrdin – fleurres.' The charred steps mounted to a top storey. The villas at Herculaneum were rich but the rooms were delightfully liveable in; not too big. Indeed proportion was perfect, seems to me. Wish Daddy could have seen it. Maybe he has. I must ask him. I wonder what the secret is that has kept the colours so clear? What is in the pigment; the terracotta is a lovely soft warm colour and there was a little blue left – a wonderful lucent colour.

There was a real beast of an east wind blowing all the time we were there but the sun was out. About us Vesuvius was hurtling out curly grey smoke and I'm afraid poor Sorrento must still be in its pall.

We dined with Roger and Harold at the Brigeta mess. All Naples's lights had failed when we arrived, and we ate by candlelight; naked ones standing in saucers. As pretty a form of illumination as ever was. Viola, at the other end of the table, against a white wall, looked quite lovely. She had on a black dress and her hair and eyes

were extra dark, but the candles lit two little flares in her
eyes and made her skin look alabaster.

Monday, March 27th, 1944   Malta in transit to Cairo

At Malta now. It looked lovely as ever in the evening
light, goldy cream and very clean. Funny to be back
again. We are in the room above the one we had last time,
18. The waiter, who has a sad sardonic face, seemed
pleased to see us again. We went to deliver the worm
powders to Princess Poutiatine and were ecstatically
welcomed with extravagant Russian gestures. And then,
at 7, sat down to tea, from a thermos! with pink and gold
china from Czechoslovakia. We were all rather dazed
with tiredness, us by flying and the Princess by giving all
to her ballet classes from 2 to 6, solid. So we soon left and
returned to the hotel for a very good supper. The apparent sanity and cleanliness of Malta *is* refreshing after
Italy. Early to bed where I now write in a coma of
sleepiness.

Tuesday, March 28th, 1944   El Adem, in the desert

We left Malta at 7.30. A lovely calm morning. One of the
doctors from 90 was at the airport escorting a patient with
a mastoid who is going to Cairo to be operated on. He
was carried in on a stretcher and strung up near the front.
Thank goodness it was smooth the whole four hours. It
was extremely cold at times and those little tin dents that
they provide for seats don't yield in any way. I had the air
cushion Aunt Phyllis gave me in the small of the back and
my baby cushion behind my head; brownie over the
knees shared with Viola, and froze. At moments the heat
came on and merely reddened one's face. The ill man
seemed to sleep most of the way. I expect they'd given
him something. I ate an orange; ate a biscuit and some

choc with Viola. Read more of *Howards End* by E. M. Forster which has been on the go since Sicily I think, and which I admire and don't quite understand. He has such vitality and lots of wit and yet the whole jells into very little. I must get hold of *Passage to India* now. Colonel Maxwell, who is legal, sixty, and shaped like a toy teddy bear, failed to settle once. He stamped, he stretched, he stood, he sat, he mooned, he stood again. Ad nauseam. Viola had an informative Australian pilot on her right and gleaned bits of flying data in between the tapestried pages of *Orlando* [Virginia Woolf].

The first glimpse of the desert is exactly as the glorious technicolour films had said it was. Dusty brown sand in endless stretches with very slight descents, scrub bushes, a thin track here and there. As we got near to El Adem there were occasional trucks beetling along the tracks. And then we came down. A few tented camps bending under the wind and the hangar and some huts and that is all. Wonderful kindness met us. We were taken to the transit mess and given drinks (on the house) and then lunch. The officer in command came to meet us; a lesser one showed Viola and me to the ladies, kept under lock and key, and a good quarter of a mile's drive from the transit mess! I was very glad to see it.

At lunch they announced that it wasn't a bit sure whether we could proceed as there was no visibility at our destination. They'd had a terrific sand and wind storm here yesterday and it was still hovering in Cairo. Oh dear. The pilot said he'd know for sure at 3, till then we'd better wait around. At 3 we heard that conditions were still unsure so the pilot decided to stay overnight. Colonel Duckett, whom I met on Malta airfield seeing Isobel Catto off three weeks ago, knew the colonel i/c Tobruk and telephoned him, with the result that he sent a car and the brigadier, Viola and I, went with him to sightsee. What a godforsaken country this is! It is flat, brown, with a little rank greenery blowing, blowing, blowing. We saw some bright yellow daisies and a couple

of brave mallows leaning in the wind. And then the tins.
Millions, I think, literally millions of empty petrol tins.
They lie all over the place and bear witness, when they
are filed in rows, to a past camp. Whole houses are built
of them. I suppose they are cemented together? We
passed a camp made entirely of petrol tin huts. Dozens of
abandoned army vehicles – German and ours – turning a
thick rust red in the weather. Going down the slight hill
to Tobruk there was a large war cemetery on the right of
the road and I wondered if it was there that Walter Leigh[1]
is buried. Coming back, we stopped and I looked but
couldn't find anything. Most of the graves are simply
marked with a regulation white wooden cross, but here
and there either a unit or a loving family through a
present unit has erected an awful ornate marble tomb. I
suppose it is a comforter. How much better I feel it would
be to let the whole place crumble and get blown over. It's
a hell of a place and a War Graves Commission merely
turning it into another Etaples, as they undoubtedly will,
is a mockery. When we are all out of this piece of Libya it
would be as well to leave no mark. The men who died
here are in someone's memory and the graves won't help
anyone.

We drove through Tobruk and it was a nightmare of
ruins. Not a single whole building – a dead town – many
of the shambles barbed-wired off as they are possibly
mined still. A few Sudanese troops, decorative in their
khaki turbans with a sudden rush of black feather to the
side. A few English soldiers. We had tea with Colonel
Rutherford in his mess and fair paralysed the other
officers by our unexpected presence! Good tea and toast.
The colonel a little shy and unable to eat his toast as his
teeth were upstairs where he'd broken them! A very Irish

[1] Walter Leigh: composer, worked first for the Festival Theatre, Cambridge. Composed *Agincourt Overture* and well-known *Concertino for
Harpsichord*, incidental music for plays, pantomimes, comic opera and
revue, including Farjeon's. Killed in action, Libya, July 1942, aged
thirty-seven.

major, a jovial padre with 'good m.c. and a groggy knee from footer'; a brave young captain from St John's Wood who sat between us and talked quite comfily. There were various others who looked at us and then away again in an unflattering hurry. Tobruk is a beast of a place and these poor wretches are there for months on end. It is all so unlovely, *nothing* to rejoice the eye anywhere. Except at night. The sky here tonight was of a clarity and brilliance I've never seen before. The moon is still new enough to be delicate and the stars were white and more twinkly than we've seen them in Malta, Sicily or Italy.

Viola and I are being housed in the transit mess dining room, magically transformed into a girls' dorm. We share it with a nice quiet Parisienne de Gaullist who has no English and who is also in transit. She is more modest than either of us and undresses and washes under the jacket of her boy's striped pyjamas. She is rather silent but suffers for La France and is rather touching somehow. She, like me, has washed all over in the little basin provided for us together with tin jugs of hot water. The co here, Womersley, has taken such trouble to make us comfy; blankets for rugs on the floor, oranges in our room, hot cocoa, a big mirror, an oil stove – all the comforts of the home down to a roll of soft white w.c. paper. He is one of Whitney Straight's[1] people. Very nice and gentle and so thoughtful. Viola and I did a twenty-minute programme at the movie house on the station. Audience of 700, they tell me. I was alarmed, tired and rather grubby, but it went all right. Bad for sound, alas, and my voice was a bit creaky. Oh dear. However it did go well, and they were very enthusiastic. This is such a dreary place and they have it so long at a time. Yesterday's storm blew off the roofs of the officers' quarters and

[1] Whitney Straight: American-born, but long resident in Britain. Professional racing driver before the war, he turned to flying, served in the Auxiliary Air Force (MC; DFC) and after the war became chief executive of British Overseas Airways Corporation.

the hangar and the Irish major at tea today said that he thought about 300 tents had been lost in the district.

Thursday, March 30th, 1944   Cairo. British Embassy

Viola and I keep catching each other's eye at the improbability of this whole trip. Monday Naples, Tuesday Malta, Wednesday Cairo. And now we are at the British Embassy with Uncle Miles[1] in a comfort I'd long since forgotten. We left El Adem at 8 yesterday. Smooth trip all the way except just before landing. Seeing the battlefields below us; all the famous places – mere handfuls of huts – and Hell Fire Corner and Mersa Matruh. Extraordinary to fly over those miles of sand and to think of all that must haunt them now. The sea was a heavenly greeny-blue with white frilled edges on our left. There was a slight dust rising when we landed at Cairo West about 11 and I thought how awful a real one must be. We queued up with everyone for checking-in and security, and I thought it might be a good plan to ring up the British Embassy to see if Uncle Miles really was expecting us and so I did and he was. There wasn't any transport though, so we had to ride in to Cairo, twenty miles off, by truck. I went in front with a sweet little Geordie driver who was thick with rich Tyneside and gave me information all the way. The petrol fumes were a bit much but I made it. We passed the Pyramids. 'They're all right in the distance,' said the Geordie, 'but they're only a heap of stones when you see them properly.' He had strong views on music. 'Nothing serious.' When we got here it was five to one and the ADCs met us and helped us into the house with our luggage, suddenly looking even more dusty and

[1] Miles Lampson: 'Uncle M.'; created Lord Killearn the previous year. Spent ten years as British ambassador to Egypt. His first wife Rachel (who died in 1930) was the sister of Joyce's father; his second wife Jacqueline was the daughter of a distinguished Italian physician with a Harley Street practice.

shabby than usual. We were both feeling hot, too, in our flying wool wear, and I was very dirty. 'There is a big luncheon party,' said Glynne Bernard, RAF ADC. 'Lots of tapestry ladies and a bishop or two.' So we hurried upstairs and found these two lovely rooms facing the Nile with a balcony and chairs and cushions and a table in it – and each with our own bathroom. A housekeeper with keys jangling at her wrist came to help us and I dreaded the chaos she'd find in my bags but had to abandon them to her. We powdered our noses and just had time to register the comfort and quiet and were downstairs in time to greet Uncle Miles and meet the tapestry ladies and both bishops.

Viola and I spent the afternoon yesterday in sorting ourselves. Miss Tee [the housekeeper] had unpacked us all over the room and removed all our dirty clothes. It's *lovely* to be looked after. Viola fell into bed and slept like a child. I washed my hair and rinsed it with limes and then sat about trying to dry it. Then I wrote to Reggie from a chaise-longue covered in pink and white toile de Jouy.

Friday, March 31st, 1944   Cairo

Never seems to be time to write in this book and yet I've idled in the past two days as I haven't for weeks. Atrophisation of the brain and another beastly cold and I'm furious.

Back to Wednesday. I took *the* most wonderful bath full of green good smell and hot and deep. And then I spent a full hour in getting dressed and doing my face and hair in a warm room at a mirror with lights! Luxury . . . We were to dress for dinner which shook us a little. I put on my old grey lace and Hilda's pearl and gold stars and used some Mary Chess 'White Lilac' again and felt very festive. Dinner quietly at 8.15 with Uncle Miles, Norman Smith, and Viola. And then to the Opera House to see Emlyn Williams, Adrienne Allen, Eliot Makeham, etc., in *Night*

Must Fall.[1] (They are here for a brief season.) We went in the ambassadorial car and had escorts at either end with a distinctive tootle on the horn to clear the way for us. Two Union Jacks, one on each front mudguard. A rifleman sergeant on the box with guns. The car sailed by on satin.[2] Attentive fezzed gents at the theatre and a smooth passage to the box where we could easily have sat twelve but were in fact four. The house is, or it was, for the Empress Eugenie, and is rather disarming. After Naples it didn't even dint my impression except that I knew it was clean and good for sound. The house was sold out and very attentive. The play done with a real flourish and finish and doing the job one hundred per cent, to divert and make us forget outside things. It's a horrid play but brilliant, and Emlyn's performance is terrific – if now and then too much of a good thing. I can look and listen at and to Kathleen Harrison[3] till the cows come home. She is a joy. Her hands – full of washing and chores and kindnesses, hanging over her stomach with the elbows pressed to her side. And the bird movements of her incredible Cockney head. She stole the whole of *Flare Path* last week, I hear.

Yesterday, Thursday, was lovely and sunny and cloudless and usual, I daresay, but to us it was a 'nice change'. Breakfast wheeled in by Miss Tee on two trolleys – bananas and fresh eggs and coffee in silver pots. And a paper. And Miss Tee whipping our clothes away for washings and pressings and asking what we'd wear today.

[1] *Night Must Fall*: a thriller by Emlyn Williams, first produced at the Duchess Theatre in 1935, ran for over a year. Adrienne Allen married the actor Raymond Massey.
[2] It was said in Cairo that Sir Miles was always trying to outdo King Farouk in the number of escorts and outriders who accompanied the Ambassadorial car.
[3] Kathleen Harrison: actress distinguished for her Cockney characterisations notably Mrs Watty in *The Corn is Green*, Mrs Miller in *Flare Path* and Violet in *The Winslow Boy*. Also a popular film and radio actress (*The Huggetts*).

Down to the ENSA office in an ENSA car complete with fez'd gent at the wheel who was at our disposal for the day. Greatrex Newman[1] very welcoming and nice and *looks* as if he knew what it was all about but one can't count on it. Wants us to go to the Persian Gulf and will enquire into details for itinerary today. He was helpful and courteous and made sense. His account of the behaviour of Harry Roy[2] and his Boys out here made Viola and me feel (literally) sick. Of course he is scum; but it's not right that he should be allowed to get away with gangster ways in the middle of a war and I hope he gets what is due to him. Viola and I then collected some money and went shopping. The prices scared us a bit. Corsets at £6, worth £1. Material for cotton frocks at 7/6d a yard and worth 1 shilling. At first glance the shops looked heavenly – ribbon counters bright with swags of all colours, cosmetic counters bottling in all directions, stockings, gloves, bags, belts. But when you looked closely the stuff was cheap and mostly nasty. But I did get some grosgrain ribbon with body to it for my old black shoes. We came back to lunch very dazed and almost hot.

I am haunted by those hospitals in Italy, those awful roads, the conditions under which the sisters lived at Bône, the gnawing discomfort of the soldiers living beside their tanks on the Caserta road, etc, etc. While I sat in Uncle Miles's box at the races today I kept having views of the past two months, of home even. It was so green and easy and idle and enjoyable because I merely sat in a cool shady box and watched it unroll. No struggling for

[1] Greatrex ('Rex') Newman: producer of the Fol-de-Rols and other concert parties, and for many years a brilliant contributor to many of London's lighter entertainments. A member of the inaugural committee of ENSA, he was a recognised authority with this type of entertainment, and always popular with the troops. In July 1941 he was put in charge of the Overseas Section of ENSA. When Newman arrived in Cairo at the beginning of 1943, reports Basil Dean, the backlog of lost opportunities was formidable. Another black spot was Baghdad. He was one of the best people ENSA had.

[2] Harry Roy: dance band leader.

seats, cars, no dust. Oh Privilege, Oh Eternal First Class, Oh Red Carpets! I must admit I love it all for a change. But as a life – no.

I dined with Jeffery Amherst[1] at the Mohammed Aly Club.[2] Very nice it was too – good simple food, peaceful London club atmosphere, only better lit and more comfortable. I made rather a spectacular entrance wearing my old black suit, for my knickers fell off in the entrance hall! I was wearing my best Aunt Nancy ones of pink georgette and real lace, pre-war Paris, and they are far lovelier than any of the exterior clothes I've got. They didn't come right off but just frothed about and below the knees.

Jeffery is a very pleasant companion and asks *all* the right questions. How bad for me but how enjoyable. We just sat on and talked and talked. He says Cairo is a malicious place and he goes out very little but lives five miles away with a little garden and thus he keeps his sanity.

Viola was taken to a Moslem wedding by the two ADCS and loved it, though they said it was disappointing. She said it was very Birmingham and no one *talked*. They just waited, covered with ill-set diamonds, for something to happen, and a mezzo-soprano costing £150 a night sang with a range of six notes for well on an hour!

[1] Jeffery Amherst, 5th Earl, with Coldstream Guards in both wars. Commercial air pilot before the war, external relations manager for British European Airways after.
[2] Cairo's grandest, most luxurious private club, boasting a casino and excellent restaurant.

April 1944

How we do get about. By civil aviation this time. We were quite empty so Viola and I each had a chance to lie full length. We flew over Palestine and it looked lovely and green and ordered. Then, out of nowhere we came to Habbaniya, which is a completely new settlement made from nothing in 1934, watered by the Tigris and full of trees, birds, jackals and the RAF. It's a surprising place – so entire and self-contained and stuck suddenly in the desert. We were taken to the officers' club in a staff car where we tried to do something to ourselves after the journey. We were, for the first time, wearing the ENSA uniform, as unbecoming a little outfit as ever you could see. Khaki drill cut out with a knife and fork and built in twenty-four hours by a Cairo tailor. Considering the breakneck speed in which he did the job it's really a remarkable fit, but there its virtues end. It is stiff, hideous in colour and too big on the bottom and too tight on the chest. And the hat! It's a kind of jockey cap and doesn't do a thing for either of us. Indeed I carried mine all the way and wore a scarf instead. The rather surprising pinky-beige silk shirts are very good and they fit, which makes a difference. We didn't wear the issue sandals, beige suede with wedge soles. They look very nice but are mighty hard on my feet. I must say I hate the uniform and loathe wearing it. Except as a saving for our own clothes I see no virtue in it and shan't dream of wearing it here.

After lunch we boarded a twenty-year-old aircraft with great box kite wings with wires and flopped over to Baghdad in peril of our lives. I never saw such an old Heath Robinson contraption. The seats were simply two wooden boards and the windows opened and shut as the mood took them. We clumsied down and arrived in Baghdad thirty-five minutes after rising from Habbaniya and it was only just in time for me. It was bumpy and hot, and rough riding was never one of my pleasures. Poor Viola has a streaming cold and feels like a beetle. We were met at the airport by a Captain Holt with such an exaggerated accent, ecktually, that I thought he must be putting it on. But no. He is brother to Paul Holt of the *Express*. He sprang a lot of arrangements at me and called me his sweet before five minutes were up, but I was controlled and didn't say anything though Viola was seething and wanted me to altesse a bit. Too tired, to tell the truth. We are staying at the YWCA and it is very nice indeed, bang on the edge of the Tigris, now rushing by in spring flood from the melting snows.

I have a big double room with a very fancy ceiling made of mirror chips, and green and yellow glass, all fused into a small and large star pattern of unequalled hideosity. The electric fan like a plane propellor whizzes from a many-rayed mirror sunburst. Otherwise the room is just green-walled with yellow curtains and the bed is good. As soon as I had unpacked I flopped on to it and slept gratefully.

Stewart Perowne[1] came by to see me about 7, glad as I was to meet again, and then Holt, all manner and flourish, brought Whittle the ENSA office man along to take us out to dine at his mess. I can't quite make out what Holt's connection with ENSA can be. Publicity? He is a newspaper man and not quite unpleased with himself. His

[1] Stewart Perowne: 3rd son of the Bishop of Worcester, orientalist; served in the British Embassy in Beirut in the 1940s. Wrote many books on Oriental and historical subjects. Briefly married to Freya Stark. His father conducted the marriage service for Joyce and Reggie. Died 1989.

accent is so extraordinary – super Western Brothers[1] cum
Sid Field[2] in his 'I beeg your pardom' manner. Whittle is a
dear little man with a round red face and two gleaming
rather far-apart front teeth. (He has others but these catch
the eye.) From Sussex with a voice like a coster, he has the
service part of ENSA at heart, really cares about the men.
Some of them have been here for five years! They keep
the supplies going through to Russia non-stop in the
incredible heat that beats down here a little later on. He
says they have long since got over the dancing girl stage
and are settled down to look for something more lasting
and with quality in their entertainment. He walked us
home across the Tigris bridge about 9 last night. Very
lovely, even though, as he said, it reminded him of
Battersea! There were all nationalities in the streets. A
blaze of light everywhere and very little smell. It *looks*
clean. Quite a lot of rather sober English faces, indrawn.
Oh, I do pray we can do a good job here. It looks to me as
if hospitals may be quite a lot less important here than
they were in the other places. All the men are homesick
even if they aren't ill otherwise.

Tuesday, April 4th, 1944   Baghdad

I slept so beautifully and for eight solid hours. I was
called at 6.45 with *two* cups of tea by a maid in a white
bandana. It was my first night in a hairnet and I rather
enjoyed it. In fact I enjoyed the whole dreamless undisturbed span of sleep and woke up to find I can't have
moved at all for my hair is entirely unruffled. I needed
that night.

Cairo was a change but it was also hard work. Viola's

---

[1] Western Brothers: Kenneth and George (actually cousins) wore white
ties and tails, monocles and white carnations, and sang topical 'Old
School Tie' and 'Hello Cads' songs at the piano.
[2] Sid Field: comedian. Joyce and Reggie had adored his first West End
appearance in 1943 at the Prince of Wales Theatre in *Strike a New Note*.

cold was a bit thick so she abandoned the Rifle Brigade party, but I went off to it with Arnold Wrigglesworth, and Graham Lampson[1] and found it fun. A large house belonging to two Greek sisters, I think. Very Green Street, Park Lane, as opposed to Pont Street or Cadogan Gardens. Everyone looking well-fed and coiffed and fresh and all, of course, in evening dress. The party began with a pianist playing for dancing and the room was emptyish and cool while people ate in adjoining rooms. Arnold and I were full of good Embassy dinner so we danced. And then Aly and Joan arrived and I danced with Aly.[2] An American hot swing band succeeded the sergeant pianist, which was in my view a pity. Aly wanted 'Let's Get Lost' and 'Skylark' because I'd sung it the night before – and no one knew either! I didn't stay very late and got a lift home with the Alys in their mile-long car driven by him at a fantastic speed. There was nothing to do but abandon oneself to the speed, and pray.

There was the usual ENSA muddle about our departure on Monday. First of all the RAF tried to tell them that the only plane to these parts went on Saturday, but Uncle M. did some magic and we were booked for Monday instead which did allow us to complete our holiday as planned. I rang up the ENSA office to clarify details on Sunday morning and found that Rex Newman was out, so left messages for him to get in touch with me. Which he never received and never had been out. However, in the end, we had to bustle into our uniforms, and carry our coats down to the BOAC office to be weighed. And that made us keep Jeffery Amherst waiting half an hour, for he'd come to pick us up to take us out to lunch at his little house five miles out at one o'clock. He lives in a semi-

---

[1] Graham Lampson: elder son of the British ambassador.
[2] The Prince Aly Khan: heir of the Aga Khan. An officer in the British Army. Married first the Hon. Joan Yarde-Buller, daughter of Lord Churston. Divorced 1949, when he married the film star Rita Hayworth.

detached villa with a slip of garden out in an Americanish suburb. His gardener, aged twelve, let us into the garden, his houseboy aged seventeen waited on us. The décor in the house is lamentably German. A hideous snowscape with iron trees and a frozen stream – six feet by four. Too big. And a modernistic chandelier consisting of shallow green saucers upheld by chrome branches bursting from a brown wood stem. It was a relaxed and happy party and after lunch we all slept after Jeff had read us an amusing letter from Noël and given me another from Lynn Fontanne[1] to read aloud. We drove back to the Embassy about 6.30. Strong, low light. The Nile barges with great masts moored to a bank en route. The graceful walk of girls in black veils. Sunday equipages. Many large, low, pre-war cars full of rich young locals coming in from the clubs. A girl in a pink cotton frock with a white jug on her head.

That evening there was packing and my nails and a letter to Reggie to go before we left next day (in the bag). Then at nine, Uncle M., Graham, Arnold, Viola and I drove a few hundred yards 'to the Ades'[2] for their large party in honours jointly of Uncle M. and Princess Shiv. – something, who has had five husbands and is about seventy.[3] She wore mauve and blue organza with paillettes and a whacking great diamond necklace. Hair straight as a Dolly Sister's,[4] iron grey, but busy at the ends. Curious sight. I didn't realise she was really royal so didn't curtsey, which was a pity. The house was

[1] Lynn Fontanne: British-born actress, but long resident in America. With her husband Alfred Lunt an enduring theatrical partnership on both sides of the Atlantic.
[2] One of Cairo's great Jewish families; Emile Ades, a gambling companion to King Farouk.
[3] Actually Princess Shevekiar, whose first husband was Prince Faud (before he became the first King of Egypt). Immensely rich, she entertained on a lavish scale.
[4] The Dolly Sisters: Jenny and Rosie (actually twins). Starred in 1918 film, *The Million Dollar Dollies*; Betty Grable and June Haver portrayed them in a 1946 film.

hideous, style Rothschild again only about thirty years younger than usual. Very old rose and gold with lampshades that defy description – taffeta, shot at that, lace, tulle, silver threaded, mauve, rose and blue. Tasselled, puckered, tuckered and flounced. I wore my old grey lace, Viola her dark red. We stood about for an hour or so with drinks, waiting for Prince Paul of Greece, who wandered in about 10 or after.[1] I was by this time hollow with hunger. Jeffery's lunch had long since vanished. Then there was dancing. I started off with Jo who doesn't do much but wander and pump, then to look at the baccarat room where Aly was taking a hand. Uncle Miles, Peter Stirling,[2] who is a wild gambler and the most popular figure in Cairo, and the Princess, etc., etc., were all playing. I watched it all, bewildered, then Aly took me off to dance. And I did so for most of the evening, ending cheek to cheek in the most intime way . . . Very good American band, not hot or swing, and an RAF four-piece kept the music going all the time. Very good too. I left about 1.30 knowing I must get up at 5.

Cairo was fun. I enjoyed all its comfort and escapism and my whirl with Aly. But I'm glad to be out here back on the job again. We are going to be kept very busy and start off with a hospital here today. As I'd rather thought, we shall not be doing only hospitals out here. There aren't enough to warrant it but there are dozens of isolated units all over the desert who need it badly.

I'm very annoyed with Warren in Cairo, who never saw me, for he told them I'd be here for six weeks and I can't stay any longer than three because of Reggie. I *must* go back this time. They have arranged for us to go by flying boat from Basra direct back to Cairo on the 23rd.

[1] Paul of Greece: Crown Prince and like his father, King George II, in enforced exile.
[2] Peter Stirling: a few years older than his more famous brother David who served with the First Special Air Service (SAS) Regiment. Peter was a senior member of the Cairo Embassy staff.

Delicious day with a breeze. Viola practised on the lovely piano in the King Feisal Theatre where we play one night next week. Holt has interviewed us both and the brigadier wants lots of publicity because it builds up interest for the men. Viola didn't see it at first and I was rather horrid to her about it which I hated. But it's not a question of self-publicity here; it's the job of giving them some sort of interest and excitement.

Wednesday, April 5th, 1944   Baghdad

Out to No. 25 General Hospital about 4.30 very dazed from an afternoon sleep. I wore Victor [Steibel's] Alice Blue and felt very well dressed except that its lines force me to breathe in eternally or show my tummy.

Stewart Perowne fetched us at the YW at 6.45 to take us to dine at the racecourse with the racecourse owner, a character of the locality. It was a cool evening with a breeze. We had collected Stewart's secretary Miss Flanagan, a papist, and we drove over the desert to the grandstand where the party was being held. Not a big nor a chic affair but friendly. Some English wives in rather tired coats and with sad hair were drinking with the various service officers, mostly quite senior. A blank-eyed general called Bromilow. We talked of sticking the pig, his dog and the horse world. One of the Iraqi guests, deep in his cups, gave him a mare last night – 'Best blood in the country the fella tells me. Legs go out all over the place, but I mustn't notice that because she's the best breedin' blood in the country.' He was enchanted. There were three full-size, whole sheep lying on enormous dishes, roasted as they were. I object to eating recognisable mutton. Champagne was also served. I sipped some and found it very heavy and sweet. There were toasts – our host, the race committee and then the local King, and, proposed by our host, 'The King of England, George the Fifth,' which was a little out of date perhaps. However his English didn't exist so we hid our pleasure at this slip and more drink was circulated. It wasn't a very subtle or gracious party but it had a certain crude joviality. We left about 9 to attend a reception honouring the Lebanese who are delegating here in gratitude for the Iraqi attitude during the recent troubles. As we drove out to the Town Hall all the lights in Baghdad went out and we arrived in darkness. Matches were being lit and we saw flash glimpses of sheiks in Arab head-dresses, dark faces, English uniforms. Carefully feeling our way in case there might be a step, we reached the ballroom. It seemed to be enormous and the band was rendering a very slow waltz as if it was in sympathy with the dark. Presently the lights came on and we found ourselves in a huge room, new and clean, but with a depressingly familiar look to it. It came to me – the Portman Rooms, Baker Street, at home! There were a great many men, white too mainly, and a smattering of women, mostly English. Diplomatic wives, ministry officials. A brother of Quintin Hogg's,[1] Harold Freise Pennyfather, Tom Moray of the British Council. A few couples danced but there was a solid body of men at one end of the room just standing. Was amused by the bead habit. They carry a short string of beads to fiddle with while they talk. It can't be said to have been a gay or glamorous party but as a slice of Iraqi high life it had its interest. With some difficulty we got Stewart to take us home. Viola was feeling awful, and still is, which is bad. The doctor is coming to see her this morning. We are due to move tonight to Kirkuk. Hope she is going to be able to. What I have seen of Baghdad I like. It seems much more genuine than Cairo or Naples or Algiers or Tunis. And thank goodness the anti-malaria and anti-VD campaign hasn't covered the walls with slogans about keeping clean because lice like dirt and dirt brings typhus.

[1] William Hogg, a diplomat, was the younger brother of Quintin Hogg, politician and lawyer who, like his father, Lord Hailsham, became Lord Chancellor. After disclaiming peerage in 1963 he was created a life peer and took the title Lord Hailsham of St Marylebone.

N. Africa was full of this; so was Naples – or was it Bari.
'Get the Mepacrin habit.' 'There is VD here – look out!'
and, I think it was outside the approaches to either Bône
or Tunis, a huge poster recounting the troubles to be met
within the town. All manner of diseases. I daresay it was
a necessary evil but it made grim reading. 'Swat that Fly.'
'No staying for 5 miles, malarial district.'

Thursday, April 6th, 1944   In the train from Baghdad to
Kirkuk

I write in a first-class sleeper that is very mouvementé
indeed and with an action that is new to me. As well as
shaking we are swaying too, and rocking. I've got a pink
voile shirt, made from a remnant by Mrs Woolgar as a
help against the heat, and it is hanging on a hook over the
seat. The electric fan is causing it to shimmer and the
train's motion is making it swing like a mad thing. I give
the ENSA office at Baghdad full marks for looking after us.
Or rather I give Bill Whittle full marks plus. They have
sent blankets, sheets and pillows for our use and a
sergeant to look after us and both B.W. and Pennington
came down to see us off. Stewart lent us the first secretary's icebox and packed it with orange drinks in ice,
and Miss Wilson of the YW sent us away with sandwiches. It's an ordinary carriage and might be in any
country except that the seats are leather and the Royal
Iraqi's or Iraq Railway's monogram is frosted on to the
windows. A bearer who speaks English has made up the
beds and brought us glasses for our drinks. We boarded
at 7.40 from Baghdad North and the usual interested
Arabs had a stare at us. I have just been to the lavatory
and found it well observed by the ticket-collector and two
pals who are sitting in a cupboard the same size as the lav
and facing it. There was no paper so I came back to get
some from my case. When I returned there was a roll of
snowy white tissue! Presto.

Saturday, April 8th, 1944   In the train from Kirkuk to
                                                          Khanakin

We spent a dozing night in the train coming to Kirkuk.
The attendant called us with sticky glasses of hot and
very sweet tea at 6. It had taken us twelve hours to come
120 miles! Captain Moss, Brigade welfare officer, met us
and drove us to the Iraq Petroleum Co.'s guest house
where we were to stay. He had laid on *all* the wrong sort
of programmes and we had to reorganise everything. Oh
so *wearing*. I suppose it's nobody's fault – we aren't the
usual ENSAS and they don't quite know what to do with
us. It always works out all right but needs so much
explaining and getting done. Ah me. He had arranged for
us to go to No. 28 General Hospital in the morning at 11.
We had breakfast in the luxurious guest house, grapefruit, scrambled eggs, and then lay on our Beautirest beds
under the best Witney blankets and slept for an hour.
Then baths and at 10.45 Captain Moss reappeared and
had cancelled the Naafi Canteen and the Soldiers' United
Service Club in favour of an isolated gunsite twenty-five
miles off and a show in the Iraq Petroleum Company hall
to the English residents and any soldiers who wanted to
come.

We set off to go to the Dibiss camp. It was hottish and
rather sultry. The road was straight and flat but as we got
there it suddenly curved and dipped and rose again and
we found ourselves at a bend in a wide and fierce river
with cliffs. A fort, standing high on a little hill. We did the
show out of doors with Viola playing the piano perched
up on the truck that had brought it and me standing
below in the sun. Blinding it was, but it was either me or
the audience and it made more sense the way we did it.
They sat on forms and petrol tins and we had about sixty
or seventy, I think. That was our first out of door show.
It's a bit tough on the voice but I must say I loved it. They
all looked so fit and brown and were so *very* nice.

Tea at Brigade HQ above the oil refinery. Then to the

Iraq Petroleum Company hall for Viola to try the piano, borrowed for the occasion from a resident. We found a major there just about to give a gramophone recital of Stainer's 'Crucifixion' to an audience of soldiers and a few English residents, so she only had time to touch it. We then walked back through the compound to the guest house and found it hard to locate. The whole place is laid out like a garden suburb. You might be in Greenwich, Conn., or Hampstead. Bungalows artlessly sitting in little gardens with a few eucalyptus trees and some Persian lilacs and what appears to be a sort of birch. Social life flourishes among the oil company personnel and Captain Moss says they have been very generous to the troops, running dances for them and inviting them to use their pool and letting them come to whist drives, etc. In return the Army gives them seats for shows but never enough, so last night's concert was a gesture of thanks to them.

The show was a wow. About 150 and almost all on comfy chairs and sofas. *Reasonable* piano – no more. They loved the music, they laughed at the monologues and got all the points without me having to prod. *Good.* I did 'Local Library' for the first time for ages. Viola did Albéniz, Chopin, Rachmaninoff, Moeran, Bach and Warsaw. Celia's brother,[1] who is a captain in the Brigade came to see me and said it was lovely to come to a show with quality in it after all the ENSA stuff they get out here. That was the general view. Of course our audience was a special one even though it was half troops, for these were troops who knew the sort of thing they had come to hear. Preaching to the converted in fact. But as such they have very little of their own sort of thing and I was glad we could give some of it.

Viola went into one of her blank moods last night

---

[1] Celia Johnson: actress, married to Peter Fleming, author and journalist (on *The Times*); she would make a lasting reputation after the war in the film *Brief Encounter* opposite Trevor Howard. Her brother, John Johnson, became a leading London literary agent.

and was walled off from all contact which was very depressing. Tired, I think, and still jangled by the beastly piano she'd had all day. I failed to get through at all, and only made things worse by trying to. Miserable business.

We caught this train at 7.30 a.m. in a daze of sleep and breakfast. We are bowling slowly along flat Iraqi country. It is more fertile than I'd expected. There is quite a lot of wheat struggling through the pale earth. We stop every few miles and are magnets for all the Kurdish village life who rush for the train and stand and stare at it and us and each other. The villages lie a little behind the railway lines, mud-pie houses patted smooth. Some have storks' nests on the roof and the storks look outsize perched up there on the little dolls' houses below. The children are gay and giggly and wear rags with red predominating. There is a swashbuckling dash about the men who all carry daggers in the odd twisted scarves they use as belts. These look about six yards long and are twisted till they are hard and then turned and looped into three or four rows. The little girls have a Kate Greenaway look – rush of tousled curls to the front. We are fascinated by it all – the shaggy dog sheep with very long limp petal ears and a bouncy gambol. The donkeys, specially the baby donks, with large heads and silly little legs. These come in black more often than not and are enchanting. This is Old Testament country and just about the same as it must have been then, I suppose. No wonder, given the inclination, the prophets had visitations. There is nothing to distract the eye and no visible fleshpots to indulge the body. Only the coming and going of weather and the sun and moon.

In her articulate way Viola has indicated regret for the dudgeon she returned with yesterday. My foolish disquiet made me feel limp as a string – that and the long day. I don't understand her distrust of genuine motive – it's as if she'd been hard done by and was now alert for it to happen again. I am so fond of her and these pointless inner wars sadden me badly. There just isn't any method of getting through to her when they get a hold.

Easter Sunday, April 9th, 1944   Iraq Petroleum Company,
Khanakin

Today I write in an English garden on a hanky lawn edged with pansies. There are thick patches of stocks, marigolds, carnations – mostly dark clove ones – nasturtiums, poppies and tobacco plant. At this moment the air is loud with the cries of eight Kurds and Arabs delivering an air-cooling machine from a truck. The agitation and fuss, the encouraging heave-ho's and the heavy breathings take on a ritualistic tone. My view is that it can't be as difficult as all that. But they are loving it and groaning and calling out and shifting along the little path. We are staying with Mr Dix, manager of the refinery. He is a very nice, large, plump man. I think he is 'philosophe'. He is also kind and hospitable and has a heavenly garden and a bungalow full of lovely things and blessedly cool and uncrammed at the same time. We got in to Khanakin about 3.30 having changed up the line. It was hot and dusty and our eyes felt ashy. In the second train our considerate sergeant made himself scarce in an adjoining carriage so that both Viola and I could lie out full length and sleep. The leather seats were hot and sticky, but a breeze cooled the air. Flies were our worst nuisance. I sought sanctuary from mine behind my bandana which I spread over my face and bare arms. It was stifling under there but preferable, far, to flies landing on my nose, lips and the lobes of my ears.

We were met at the station by a nice bronzed Captain Morgan in KD [khaki drill] shorts and a crash helmet, for he'd biked over twenty-five miles to meet us. He led us three or four miles out of the station across rolling bare land, past some mud villages till we came to and crossed a bright river cutting into the earth. We followed it and

came to the Iraq Petroleum Company refinery perched
on a rise of land overlooking the river with mountains
rising behind it twenty miles away or more. Strange bare
mountains, puckered up in the sun. They do get snow,
though. But this is said to be the second hottest place in
the world and it can go to 127 in the shade.

We were stopped at the high wire gate in the wire fence
that surrounds this place, and having identified
ourselves were allowed in and driven to the guest house
bungalow that lies next door to Mr Dix's own. It is a
four-bedroomed bungalow with a dining room in the
middle, porched, and window netted, cool and shady
and facing on to another little English garden – antir-
rhinums, palest yellow and coral asters, mignonette,
more stocks, larkspur and petunia. Mulberries, oleanders and Persian lilac trees shade it deliciously. After that
gritty journey it was Paradise. We were shown a room
each, opening out from each other and a bathroom each.
Cream walls, books, roses, and blue linen curtains patterned with snowdrops! Mr Dix met us and made us
welcome. We unpacked and washed and then went
across the garden to his bungalow for tea. Silver on a tray,
linen, lettuce, savoury sandwiches and an egg sponge
cake of incredible lightness topped with lemon icing.
Colonel O'Ryan from a local ccs [Church of Christian
Science] was there. We sat in cool comfort and sipped our
tea in perfect ease. Mrs Dix is back in England now living
near Guildford, I think. We asked how he liked giving
hospitality to ENSAS and he admitted it had surprised him
rather!

Mr Dix is mad about flowers, and his garden. He
determined to grow a dahlia and has done so in a pot,
only it's outdone itself and is five feet high with two
pillar-box red flowers suddenly at the top.

Monday, April 10th, 1944   Back at the YWCA in Baghdad

Yesterday began freshly with a breeze and some clouds, more decorative than functional. But at 3.30 as we drove on our way to do a couple of shows twenty-five miles off at Kiel Ribat, we ran slap into a sort of cloudburst. We were sitting in the back of a station wagon all teed up in our tidiest and when the rain started I suggested to the sergeant, who rides in front, that we might close his window. But our Ghurka, all smiles, said there wasn't a window. Nor there was. The rain turned to hail and it uncompromisingly aimed itself at us. Finally we cowered under an army blanket like a couple of old Arabs and got there fairly dry. The sun was full out when we arrived. Captain Morgan, who is 6th Div. welfare officer, met us with the RSM [Regimental Sergeant Major] and took us to a tent to leave our coats. The show was held out of doors with some canvas screens put up to back us and the men all sitting on forms or in deck chairs. We did the first show for Sergeants and Other Ranks and they were a heavenly audience. I could underplay everything and they got it. It *was* a treat. If only Viola had had a decent piano. We had a beauty all right – B flat playing no less than two notes simultaneously when struck. It was, of course, quite out of tune.

Tuesday, April 11th, 1944   Baghdad

Much restored after a night of almost solid sleep, disturbed twice but briefly by all the dogs in Baghdad doing a concentrated yelling job. I'm in a different room this time, facing the Tigris. There are two beds in it, and so Viola, who dressed in her inner room next door, came in to sleep. We were in bed and asleep by 10. The simplicity of this friendly place with its school beds (but comfortable) and the flowers everywhere welcomed us very warmly. Miss Wilson made the right noises at us and made us feel glad to be back.

Thursday, April 13th, 1944   Baghdad

Yesterday was the first really idle day I've spent for weeks and it was very good. I got up about 10, which is reasonably late here as we are called at 6.30, and have breakfast an hour later. Then I sat in the garden and manicured my nails, and read *Orlando*. The first time I read *Orlando* I was so fascinated by it that I swallowed it whole at a sitting. That was in Northern Ireland two years ago on that funny tour.[1] I'm enjoying it more this time by taking it slowly, stitch by stitch. Viola practised on the good piano at the King Feisal Hall all morning.

Did the Lancer Camp last night. Big hall with about 450 men in it. The piano was an improvement on our recent ones but Viola found its action uncomfortable and was unhappy on it. However the show went away like a dream. I wasn't dead sure of it though, until halfway through – which is as well, I daresay. Out here in Paiforce I've taken to giving all my most sophisticated stuff, and miraculously it works. Last night I did all Gin's songs and 'Schoolgirl' and they went. It made it rather an effort as Viola only played once, but we did eighty minutes and got enormously encouraging applause and calls and whistles at the end. No one offered us a drink or food – it being nobody's job to do so, for the Lancer Camp Hall isn't regimental but open to all troops to whom tickets have been allocated. A public hall, in fact. Rather sad really, as there was a fine opportunity of meeting some of them who'd loved the programme. So to bed. Where neither Viola or I could get to sleep. I'd gotten all the eyeblack into my eye when I tried to take it off, and then I was spinning as I do after a big show and beating like a

---

[1] Described in *Darling Ma*.

tattoo all through. The dogs were at it again and the frogs. It was very lowering. I got up and washed all over in cold water, which was a help, and I ultimately fell into a troubled sleep dreaming about domestic chores at home.

About 5 a great banging took place in an effort to waken someone somewhere – hoarse cries and loud knocks. And the dear dogs took up the theme and embroidered. I am dazed and my eyes feel like cinders. Ah me.

Three letters from Reggie yesterday. He says the raids aren't half as bad as we hear they are. I wonder!

Friday, April 14th, 1944   Kut. Chez Williams[1]

Oh the desert! Oh the desert in heat! Oh the desert in heat and wind and dust! Viola and I with Sgt Holding and an Indian driver left YW yesterday at 9.30 to drive across the wasteland to Kut, where we were to give a show. We took with us an armed Indian escort (4) in a truck and made off with oranges and water bottles and our suitcases. It was blowing really hard when we started – a hot destructive blast. But it wasn't too bad till we were halfway across the desert and then it began. We shut the windows and stifled. We opened cracks and choked. It was unpleasant and relentless. We took three and a half hours and we were met by the Town Major in a jeep on the outskirts of Kut, come out to look for us, which was welcoming of him.

But I do not like dust storms. Very depressing and poor for the morale. Felt far away from home and sanity and safety. Rather Maughamish and frightening.

We gave a show in the local NAAFI at 8 o'clock to the only English troops there – about eighty. Very informal

---

[1] Mr Williams worked in the local irrigation works; his wife was European; Joyce wondered perhaps Polish or Austrian.

sort of evening with them at tables and us in the middle. Many Cockneys and all of them nice. A simpler audience than we've had lately, but friendly and willing and ready to enjoy itself. After we'd done the programme we went on for a further half hour or more doing songs people asked for. A Palestine Jew attached to the unit sang a solo and then did a duet with me. He was small, handsome and well built. His voice was powerful and so was the garlic he had supped on. I got a strong blast with every note, for he sang *at* me when we dueted. It was a cosy evening and the fact that we made it so very informal went down well. 'Wish we had your sort here more often,' one of them said. And another gave me the all-high tribute of the understating Londoner: 'It was quite nice.'

Kut is, as Wally Crisham would say: 'The End'. It is 115 miles from anywhere and when you get there it's nothing. The Tigris allows a little greenery to spring up. And that is all.

Saturday, April 15th, 1944   Baghdad

The drive back from Kut next day was even dustier than in the dust storm, but it was cooler and the sky was blue. The dust seemed to beat up through the floor. We were both covered in it and the Indian driver's hair turned white under it during the trip. We had huge thick-skinned Palestine oranges and water bottles.

Mirages – of endless blue lakes mostly. Mosquito hawks, like large swallows flying about us, cutting the air in swift dives. A picture postcard scene of a camel train, far on the horizon. At first blurred and elongated by the heat into an unrecognisable but moving fence. Then it broke into proper shape as we got a little nearer and there were many young camels at the back trying to keep up. I'd no idea how vast the desert was; nor how grim. When the car stopped – to allow our dear escort to catch up with us – I got out and stood on the road – which isn't a road really, merely the repeatedly used track turned by employment into a road. Cracked pale sand-coloured dust. Not a stone. The eye craves a height to lift it from the uneventful horizon. The constant lake mirages with floating islands were sinister. Fortunately our armed escort wasn't called upon to go into action. But there have been sniping Bedouins along that road. Back at the YW Joan Wilson met us with the rumour that the Canadians had taken Calais.[1] The invasion was on? My heart sank like lead. Will we get home? Has Reggie gone overseas? Oh golly. I lay in two inches of water, hand-carried by the bath boy, and soaped the dust off in a worried frame of mind. Further enquiries from Stewart revealed that the rumour is from an Axis source so it may be completely false. On the other hand the invasion will start soon, I suppose – if it hasn't already. Visions of being stuck in Cairo, or worse, in Algiers. Second thoughts: prefer Algiers.

Packing, tea, and farewell Baghdad. Liked being there so much. Viola in very low mood. No news from Peter again and no news of Italian war. I had letters Pa and Gin.

We left in a flourish of goodbyes from the YW with me dispensing signed pictures in a rather filmy way! Mary, the maid, tried to refuse our tips, which makes a change. She looked after us so well.

Our train attendant knocked on our door last night and asked for 'a aspirine'. He took two of Viola's and has beamed ever since. Have a hunch he thinks they are some magic dope and his faith has freshened him up no end!

[1] This indeed was only a rumour, although a strong one. The invasion of France was not launched until June 6th.

Monday, April 17th, 1944   Air Port Hotel, Maqil

Colonel Upton and Captain McCollin met us at Maqil. We at once noticed how much hotter it is down here. Many oleanders in riot all along the way to this hotel. It is a large de luxe hotel, modern, rather startling in these surroundings. We have got No. 4, a not very big double room, but adequate. The programme laid out for us this week will take some doing. Two shows a day and all biggish ones and even three for next Thursday. As they had arranged for us to rest Sunday before we were tired, I suggested we swap Thursday programme to Sunday and get a rest Thursday when we will have earned it. Idled the whole of Saturday, unpacking and mending and washing and sleeping in a hot daze. Show for a Royal Engineer unit in the evening in a huge workshop they'd turned into a theatre. There was a gala boxing match on in Maqil and we were unadvertised so our audience wasn't as big as it would ordinarily have been, but it was fun and they loved it. I wore green and white butterflies, now on its very last legs. Very sad. It is miles too big for me at the top, I just have no bosom at all which is horrid. Wonder if I'll be a very gaunt old Grenfell as I go on. I've mended that dress till it won't take any more weight of mending. It's the same with the grey lace my Ma sent me. I've almost rewoven it with darning. Both those dresses have been useful to the limits.

Our room very hot when we got in but with the fan switched a bit faster and the stillness of bed, soon asleep. There were noisy come-to-bedders in the corridors and a plane left at 6, otherwise all was peaceful. The plane was parked just outside our window and when it revved up felt as if it might shake the building.

Yesterday was Sunday. Long restful morning in bed. Breakfast brought in by a sloe-eyed Iraqi in a white coat who arranged the tray on a stool from the bathroom and unfolded our napkins and spread them over us before leaving. I washed my bedroom slippers because they'd got so dirty in the train. They are made of towelling with loofah soles. Hate not having 'em to wear, for one of my fastidiosities is walking without shoes. They will be dry soon.

Bill Whittle travelled down on the mail train from Baghdad and got in yesterday morning with letters for us.

Further cuttings from the local press, all in extravagant praise which is comforting. Letters from Reggie, Gin, Dick and Captain Hayes of No. 100 hospital near Philipville thanking us for our stay there. Reggie's was old – early March. He likes his new job. Gin writing graphically of a hellish night, March 14th, when she and To[1] and Bebe and Ben[2] put out incendiaries and were amazed at the efficiency of the stirrup pump. It really does its job, Gin says, surprised. Dick sounds busy and well and full of ideas. When I get letters from home I get a great wave of longing to see them all. Still no news of the invasion. Oh, I do hope we get back first. I do, I do.

Lunched yesterday at the Officers' Club with Bill Whittle at Shaiba. We discussed wisdom of sending so much entertainment out regardless of quality. It is often army welfare's fault for demanding so much. They order eight parties for Paiforce, say, and twenty cinema units without qualifying that there must be talent. Seems to me that Drury Lane should cut down its parties by fifty per cent, weed out the talent, discard the heavyweights, re-assemble its cuties, and *try* to deliver a little quality entertainment instead of so much poor stuff. The general view among the men out here is that they get too much mediocre entertainment. If they all saw one really good, well produced, talented show per month, it would be far better than boring them with rotten goods twice a month. As it is, they are getting blasé and it's a

[1] Tony: husband of Virginia ('Gin') Thesiger.
[2] Ben Lyon and Bebe Daniels: husband and wife who broadcast regularly (*Life With the Lyons*), having settled in England after careers in films in America.

very good thing. From the future point of view the theatre business is being let down by this continual lowering of standards. Bill says that ninety per cent of the comics who come out use star material swiped from Max Miller and Trinder or Sid Field. And swiped shamelessly. They even come into the ENSA office in Baghdad and ask for records of Monsewer Eddie Gray[1] so they can copy. It makes him sick. All the girls sing the same songs in the 'style of' someone – never as themselves. We have heard very good accounts of a party called 'Thirty men and a girl', which is really the Royal Artillery band, all professionals, and an attractive young soprano called Elizabeth Perry who does the routine songs – 'I'll See You Again', 'Ave Maria', 'Bless This House', etc., etc., but with charm. It seems the British soldier prefers something it already knows to anything unknown. Or that is the view. I have proved it differently, for my programme is, in the main, all new to them, and they do like it.

We were welcomed at 61 by the matron, Miss Cowan. We arrived as a storm broke. Lightning was on Hollywood lines. The whole place lit for twenty seconds at a time in great white and blue flashes. Then rain in egg-sized drops, and wind. We were shown Miss Cowan's collection of animals. 'I collect all little animals,' she said, 'wooden ones, brass or china. This is a carved ivory camel, but it's not very good. My Indian bull is beautiful work, though.' There was a drawing of Snow White picked out with silver paint that caught the light. 'Isn't it clever? See? I had it passé-partood by the therapy boys here.' There were dogs and horses and a pink china duck with cotton wool stuck in its tail for the dressing table. And a collection of revolting little three-ply figures – gnomes, peacocks and a witch. 'I got them for tuppence

[1] Eddie Gray: red-nosed comedian with false moustache, billed as 'Monsewer' because he talked in a mixture of Cockney English and 'fractured' French. Began at the age of nine as a straight juggler. Appeared with members of the Crazy Gang on and off, and then from 1956 to 1962 with them at the Victoria Palace, London.

each at Wimbledon and had them coloured out here.'
You never saw such bric-à-brac. And she was pleased as
punch with it all. A very nasty little wooden owl was
produced, with large yellow glass eyes. Her mascot. It
had been over the highest pass in the world, she told us.
She'd given it to a friend to take there for her! She was
mad as a hatter with flashing little black eyes and thick
little legs in white cotton stockings. We dressed in her
bedroom, all the trunks, tables and cupboards raised
from the floor on rocks. To sweep under? As against
flood? Don't know. Driving to the hall in a high gale we
got lost in the compound. She and the colonel, who had
come to fetch us in our car, got out and were buffeted in
the wind and tried to find the way. That was mad too.
Not to find their own hall in their own compound. At one
moment Miss Cowan was in front of the car, running,
with the wind blowing her along. A stocky little white
figure with her veil standing off her head like a kite.

At the hall we had the elements to compete with.
Windows rattled and were beaten by sand and at moments I was inaudible. *Another* barking piano and Viola
played a Nocturne of Chopin on it and found A sharp
wasn't there at all, so it made a very interesting pattern
with gaps. The hall was very long and narrow. An
underground tunnel and the audience didn't start till
halfway down it which was so unnecessary and made my
job twice as hard. And the front three rows of benches
were filled with non-English-speaking Italian POWs and
Palestinian Jewish patients! Not a help really. I hated that
show even though it went well as far as they were
concerned. But the endless wind and noise and the
distance between the front row and the stage and the
heat and that bloody piano got me down, I'm ashamed to
say. When it was over we found a young scorpion in the
lid of the piano. Happy thought. And Bill Whittle revealed that while I'd been singing a mouse had walked
across my feet and I hadn't even seen it!

The bath was full of sand when I'd finished with it last

night. That wind is still blowing and it is very hot too. Our room is covered with fine white dust. We are in great luxe here, but I wonder just how bloody it is if you are a private in a tent with no fan, no adjacent bathroom, no spring mattress and three years' gap between you and Muswell Hill or Tyneside. I can see that heat and dust and wind can make one very gritty and cross. I must take a pull. I must also get up. It is 10 a.m. and Whittle comes for us at 11.

Tuesday, April 18th, 1944   Maqil

To the locals, this weather is cool and springlike. To me it is hot. HOT. Breakfast in bed and slow idling and getting up. The fan whirring above us. Bill Whittle fetched us and we went to the Naafi in search of shampoos and talcum. Then, to the YWCA. Set well on the river's edge with lovely big cool rooms very attractively furnished. Like Heals. Natural wood chairs skilfully made, again in Palestine, with low swung string seats. Gay plain coloured cushions. Flowers everywhere – nasturtium, roses, larkspur and marigolds. Miss Ford running it. Good looking in the rather pale noble looks people's mothers had in faded photographs. South African. Feels she isn't doing a real job out here and wants to get to China or Italy or, later, to Greece. We took tea here and were shown over the house, now pretty full with ENSAS. She says they have been well-behaved on the whole. Bill lunched with us at the airport hotel. The food is very good. Somehow I would never have planned hot thick soup for a hot thick day, but it came and we had it and it was just right. After lunch, bedders. I lay on mine in Reggie's old black and white spotted dressing-gown which is very old and thin and silky and comfy. Mended and did my nails and then fell off to sleep. We were due at No. 29 Hospital at 5.30 and had to force ourselves awake. Took a cool sponge down and put on Alice Blue. Viola said I was very altessian in my dark red head scarf but it was only sleep and the aloofness that induces. Did one of our best shows at 29 in a large, dark, cool ward with air conditioning in it. They had put chairs all down the middle and these were full up of patients and there were many doctors and sisters and hospital staff sitting on beds and standing at the back. Another brute of a piano – a barker with several ivories gone – so Viola couldn't do solos and even found it almost impossible to keep it quiet enough for me. I kept edging further and further away. They were a very good audience.

Back to the hotel again about 6.45, and we took a stroll in the garden before early supper and changing for the second show – RAF Basra. The garden was lit by some lamps over the swimming pool. It was being cleaned out, and half a dozen voluble Arabs were sweeping it out and enjoying the damp. One of them left his job suddenly, and climbed out on to the lawn above the pool, where he went into a series of praying gestures directed, as far as we could see, at the electronic light hanging on a rose trellis and now buzzing with night flies and mosquitoes. He went down on his knees and touched his forehead to the earth about eight times, got an itch which interested him and caused a pause, and then went back to work, picking his teeth.

The RAF sent a staff car and two sergeants for us. Bill Whittle followed in our yellow car with Indian driver. A perfect little theatre with a ramp and easy chairs for all. The RAF always do themselves properly, and quite rightly. We arranged the piano – not too bad either – in front of the deep maroon velvet tabs, and it made an intimate setting. Viola wore her pink dress with square neck and long sleeves and looked *lovely* – pale and distant and very attractive. It is impossible to tell her so, though, for it maddens her to be told she is in good looks. I was in the old grey lace again. Ah me. The show moved along on magic wheels and was a riot. Viola played Liszt concert study and Claire de Lune and a couple of Chopins and they were as still as mice and wanted more. It was Windsor-greys-Pegasi-winged-Arabs and Derby winners all in one! We did an hour and thirty minutes and could have gone on for at least half an hour more but Bill, worrying in the wings, kept saying, 'You'll kill yourself', so we came to a finish with a lovely communal effort on Swanee River. They sang beautifully. No roaring. Phrasing and feeling and mood. We went to the officers' mess for sandwiches and drinks. It was like an Aldwych farce set, baronial in style with panels and royal portraits and shadow chintz and heavy Kidderminster on the floor. A very nice lot of officers but, my golly, shy. Silence would have followed silence if Viola and I hadn't burbled on to try and ease it. We are bidden to their dance on Thursday, but it's our day off and I'm not sure. Particularly as we heard at the YW that they had said we'd be there and would perform! This before they'd asked us, which is a queer way of doing things. Bed was wonderful!

Bill Whittle thinks I should do music hall. 'Wish I could manage you. You'd do Moss Empires and with a twenty-minute spot you'd tear the place up.' A new thought with which I am intrigued. If I can handle these biggish crowds out here, could I cope with a tough cross section of Birmingham, say, or Leeds or Newcastle? I am tempted to try it, I must say. Aubrey Blackburn[1] thought of it once before, but I wasn't sure. With this experience out here I'd be willing to give it a chance for a short tour somewhere. For a moment or two last night Bill convinced me I could. I wonder. I wonder. Goodness. I wonder. Bill is a nice creature. He looks like a chubby boy scout with a country boy's face. In his KD shorts he is brisk and looks so clean. He is fundamentally kind and wins me by his heart. He is also tops at his job and if I had a manager, ever, I'd like to have Bill. He is running us beautifully, and of course it makes the whole difference

---

[1] Aubrey Blackburn: Joyce's theatrical agent. After the war Joyce toured all these cities as well as America and Australia, sometimes playing in theatres that seated 4,500!

to the job to be looked after, advance publicity done and all the petty boggles cleared up for one. I do hope his Doreen is good enough for him.

Wednesday, April 19th, 1944 Maqil

We left here yesterday after early lunch to go up the river to Khorrmanshah naval base. Slight muddle over launches on the Navy's part, so the RAF, whose jetty we should have left from, still warmed by the show the night before, laid on their own special and took us up. *Very* hot day, I don't care what the locals say. On the river it was pleasant because of the breeze we made with our speed. And the speed made a wash that swept over the decks now and then and soaked us quite nicely.

The Navy at Khorrmanshah consists of a well meaning but very third rate little group of officers. The accents varied from undisguised Stepney to Purser's Putney. Their minds went with their accents, and we were clearly a disappointment to them, for we weren't the ENSA girls they are used to, and they couldn't make out just *what* we were. The show was exactly as I had expected it would be: 'jolly' and about as subtle as a straight from the right. They were ready to enjoy themselves and to be noisy, so we passed up all our nicest numbers and threw them popular stuff, and they loved it. Never seen ABS in tropical kit before and it is very endearing – a lot of little sailor boys in white shorts and clean white socks. At tea saw through window a group of four on punishment drill; offence: the drink. They were at the double and it was very hot. One rather portly one, naked to his KD shorts, was a bit older than the others and of course ought to have known better but evidently hadn't. He lolloped round the square with his cap on the very back of his head and his heart full of seething fury. He was just that much slower than the other three and that much angrier. We were, fortunately, invisible behind our mosquito-netted window. He was like Sidney Howard[1] twenty years ago. And *very* funny. The Lieut. Commander was shy to a point of inarticulateness. We were finally fixed up in a room belonging to one Lieut Higgenson who was apparently away. The beds had one sheet on them each, which was curious. It was very hot and an ugly storm rose up and there was revelry among the officers who retired late and with singing. Some of them had playfully fixed up a booby trap of petrol tins tied to a rope intended to trip up the security officer on his rounds. And it did, successfully, and with much noise. One of the bloodiest nights I ever hope to endure.

After the show the matron from No. 32 CGH came up onto the stage and asked me if there was a chance of me coming to their hospital fifteen minutes down the river. Of course I said yes, for Viola and I are for hospitals, first and foremost, and were horrified to find that we hadn't been routed there. So at 9.30 today we set off in the captain's launch and went to No. 32 where we did a 10 a.m. show in a ward full of bed patients. Lovely it was too, in spite of the hour and Viola having only a field harmonium to play on. It was the pedalling sort that packs into a box and you pick it up and walk off with it! Colonel Walton, very verbose; but nice and kind and fond of his wife and two small sons. We saw polyfotos by the sheet and I am going to ring Mrs Walton up when I get home. Matron friendly. Miss Gibb. After the broadness of the Navy I found the gentler quickness of the martial sick very restoring.

We set off in the captain's launch about 11 and it was delicious. The storm still around, and the sky grey and no air. But we made a little breeze and Viola and I, supported on white linen cushions, lay back and watched the pale water-coloured riverside pass us by. Silver green-grey palms. Dhows of light dust coloured wood. Native

[1] Sidney Howard: American dramatist; in this country he is best known for his play, *The Silver Cord* (1926) and *The Late Christopher Bean* (from the French).

children bathing naked. Coffee bodies. Occasional pastel colours. A woman in a black abba fetching the unappetising water of the river in an emerald green pottery ewer. Rugs in all purple pinks and reds drying across the boom of a big sailing barge. Pale yellow rags on a little boy. A pink cap on his sister. Blue overalls. A faded mauve nightshirt on an Arab squatting on the bank. Little shallow canoes, fishing. Grey tern flying beside us. Big black and white crows ludicrously perched on top of an oleander. Pink and white oleanders. About 12 we passed by a speed boat and hailed. Offered and accepted a quicker lift for we were going to be late for our YWCA lunch with Miss Ford. Lovely swift speed in the Chriscraft. I abandoned Maud to the winds and arrived ironed out but tousled. Very rejuvenating all that air and gentle landscape and soft colours.

I really hated last night. We were expected to be ENSA girls – Good Sorts, drinkers and Cheerio types and that is a part I can't play. Ah me. And the heavy thunder and the squirmy little officers getting tighter and tighter in ghastly determination.

We return to our room at the Air Port Hotel with relief. Whisked out the Lux, whitened my shoes, pinned up Maud and now am on the bed.

Thursday, April 20th, 1944   Maqil

Last night's show was one of the really terrific ones. We did two and it was very close and stuffy and I only half felt like doing it. But when I got on to the rather nice stage of the Maqil Port Club Hall I was suddenly on my toes and loved it. Smallish house first time – 150 or so? And 6.30 is a dull hour. But they were very quiet and attentive and having a pleasant time. We supped with Captain McCollin and Colonel Upton and the padre – whose name was, inappropriately, Beer – in between performances. I had hoped the second house would be nice.

Several new friends were coming and I hoped it would go well; it did. 550 there and they responded to the merest flicker of an eyelash. I had that wild and dangerous sensation of *knowing* I could do what I liked with them. It's a rare feeling. The first time I ever felt it was that first performance at the Little in 1939. That pre first night charity dress rehearsal – Wed. April 17th, 1939.[1] I'd never had any audience before in my life and there it was and I rode it like a dream horse, in perfect free rhythms. It's an awe-inspiring feeling and intoxicating. But not to be trusted. You can't count on it for an instant. Next time will be different. It always is. I do feel so light and neat-minded sometimes and then it works. It comes through unimpeded by me and I feel remote as a leaf on a tree while it goes on. It only works *when* I can get to the side of it and let it happen. It was good last night, rounded and pointed and well timed. Viola played with the same completeness. We must have found it in the air. She was articulate and it was really lovely. No fighting for it either. A show like that slips off one without strain. You can't let go for an instant and the on-the-toes part is urgent but it's not a quarter as tiring as the usual *worked* show.

Afterwards there was a great deal of applause and whistling and they just sat on wanting more, but it was time to stop. Lots of nice things said, but my favourite came from an elderly colonel, who has lived here for twenty-four years. I apologised for not having the fans turning because they interfered with the sound and he said: 'It didn't matter for you had all the cool greenness of England in your voice.' Supper at Brigade HQ mess with Colonel Upton. Quiet, pleasant and cool, with eggs and bacon and long drinks of grapefruit squash, iced. Bed about 12.30 and we couldn't sleep at all. Too spinning. And there was noise in the hotel. A light fused somewhere and was mended by about six natives at the tops of

[1] Joyce's first appearance on stage when she was an overnight sensation.

their voices at 3.30 a.m. Viola, lying in bed, looking gazelles, just said, 'I don't understand ignorance. I just don't understand it.'

Bill Whittle was so pleased about last night and beamed all over. He is a nice little man.

Friday, April 21st, 1944   Maqil

Yesterday was our day off. And very welcome. Lay abed all morning. Viola bathed in the hotel pool and said it was very lovely. Had it to herself. Dinner about 8.15 with Lt Commander Stoy and Bill Whittle. We decided to wear day dresses to the RAF dance, as our stage longs are getting so much hard wear. Stoy is fat and kind and easy. Took very much to Viola and paid attentions all evening. He is regular Navy; simple and straightforward. Dance rather pleasant. Cool evening, garden lit with coloured lights. Stuck for too long with a man called Sullivan newly posted to that unit.

Pleasant party. Bill brought me home about 11.30. Left Viola centre of admiring circle, looking radiant and very attractive in her cream dress.

Saturday, April 22nd, 1944   Maqil

Brigadier Clark told us about a Londoner in his unit who asked if he could have a word with him concerning a cable he'd just had from home. It read: 'Son born both doing well love Mary.' The brigadier said how splendid, and the private said it wasn't, because he hadn't been home for two years. 'Oh,' invented the brigadier wildly, 'perhaps the cable has been a long time coming?' The man wasn't to be comforted and went away very low. Sometime later he came rushing back with a letter in his hand: 'I've got a letter from my wife, sir, and it's all right, it's not her it's my mother. She's a widow. Must have been playing around with some man.' He was fully comforted and indeed delighted. So was the brigadier.

We dined with him in his mess over at Shaiba last night after doing a show there. Bill Whittle estimated we had 800 in there. It felt huge, I must say, and scared me a bit, but they were good and quiet if not particularly subtle.

Colonel Hinchcliffe and Colonel Upton came over to see us. Very easy supper afterwards in the Brigade mess with drinks first in the anteroom. Bill Whittle is so tactful and takes himself to the side when he thinks we ought to be left to the nobs. Viola and I are now doing the programme almost entirely for Bill's benefit. He *owns* us and is so proud and anxious that we want to go well for his sake! It is very good for us. He is watching everything and looks after us like a mother – my chair, glass of water, book for the American ma; Viola's piano in right place. Lights, our dressing-room amenities. And of course his advance publicity helps like anything. It will be a hard fall from all this care and attention to carrying our own bags at Paddington! Will we ever have control enough not to keep on saying, 'When we were in Paiforce' – ?

Décor in messes out here have a touching nostalgia in that most of them have a hunting picture hung up somewhere as a sort of link with home. A symbol of England. Though I doubt if one per cent of the members have ever been on a horse. The officers' club at Shaiba had a series of hunting pictures, all with titles. 'Gone Away', 'The Meet', 'The Fall', etc., etc. The mess at the RAF Maqil was panelled three-quarters of the way up the wall, dark painted panels, and hung just too high to be seen are a series of good Medici reproductions of Dutch pictures, all familiar. Not content with this effort there is a further series of pin-up girls, culled from *Esquire* and the *Tatler*, thumb-tacked along the panelling in strange contrast to the serene exteriors of the Netherland homes above. The girls are beautiful, base and bare, and come in glorious Technicolor. Her Majesty the Queen in a tiara worn low over the brow in style 1929 looks a little left behind. I've noticed Cecil's lovely photograph of the Queen in several messes out here. The crinoline one done at Buck House.[1] At the end of our show I always sing The King because it's too silly to have sung all evening on the stage and then suddenly *not* to sing The King, and I've noticed that only a few of the men, usually, sing with me. Brigadier Clark last night said that lots of his men don't know the words. He is having them taught it! 'None of us know the words but the Argentines, the Armenians and the Greeks.' I expect that's true of the non-Aryan refugees at home now too. I always thought soldiers didn't sing it as a principle. That they only stood at attention in silence.

Sunday, April 23rd, 1944　　　In the Ensign aircraft from
　　　　　　　　　　　　　　　　Maqil to Cairo

I write just after leaving Habbaniyah where we paused for refuelling and cups of tea. This craft is a good deal more comfy than anything we've been in before. Viola and I are alone in the front cabin with a choice of six armchairs, all of which go up or down by lever to your whim. We are each in window seats. I have the lake below me and she has the river and a distant view of the station – like a perfect toy model complete with little sponge trees dipped in green ink. (The altitude is having a prolific effect on my pen. It is gushing at an alarming rate.)

Yesterday was the last day of our tour in Paiforce. Felt rather dim all day. Stye on my eye and a preference for the long lie beat me. Viola shopped with Whittle all morning and we lunched together at the Air Port Hotel.

---

[1] Cecil Beaton photographed the Queen in 1939. As Hugo Vickers, his biographer, relates, the King and Queen chose one for a Christmas card which they sent to every serving man in the British armed forces.

Stoy, Viola's Navy follower, came to the hotel for a final look and took tea with us. She is in fine form and feels wonderful in the heat. Coolers on the brow and concern when I get a little (rarely) silent! I'm very fond of her.

Had two shows to do last night over at Shaiba again. First one at 6.30 to a lot of mixed Royal Engineers and Royal Army Ordnance Corps. Large bare hall but good for sound. Hellish piano so had to do whole show. It went a treat which surprised me and only goes to prove that if one will let things happen they will do so naturally. Particularly good, long-drawn-out applause at the end. Nice show. Was suddenly on my toes. Quick supper in officers' mess then on to do second show in another hall nearby. As we drew near heard the unencouraging sounds of beery song and my heart sank. Hunch was right. Turned out to be RA battalion in transit and some mug had issued their beer *before* the show instead of after it. There had been trouble about a lot of IORS [Iraq Other Ranks] who got in the hall and had to be ousted and the beery British fought each other just for the hell of it. *Not* a good start. They were in a strange mood of darned cussedness. Just chippy. Not at me, not at the beer, but at the world. We started the show. They listened to 'I'm Going', and applause was coupled into whistles and remarks. Did a little backchat and suggested quiet. But it was no good. They didn't want to hear – couldn't listen. No animosity in it against me. They appeared to quite like me! But they couldn't take in anything. Did all my slop songs in an effort to soothe the savage breast, and they sat pretty quietly but were incapable of actually hearing what I did. Most extraordinary thing I ever met. It didn't upset me but it got me angry and I determined not to be beaten. In the end I only did thirty minutes and they were miserable for everyone – mostly the officers and poor Bill. Curiously enough it didn't get me down. It wasn't in the least personal. Took a poor view, as did Bill and Viola, of the officers who had absolutely no courage or control over their men. A give-away of their weakness. Mob rule is an ugly thing. So many of the officers out here strike me as being very weedy and inadequate. Last night's performance was a revelation. Lamentable. The officers of the regular battalion here (Garrison) were not to blame. These were not their men. They suffered horribly, poor things. So did Viola. Saw her saucer eyes looking up at me over the piano in horror and distress. It was a pity, the whole thing. In the end, after the men had gone I did twenty minutes for the officers only, which was a help to take the taste out of all our mouths. Sad to have such a thing happen on our very last night. Can truly say it's the only bad audience we ever had. And again, in justification to us, it wasn't personal. They were merely agin the government and too full of beer and being browned off. One man called out, 'You're not bad', which I took to be kindly intended. Poor Bill, he was white with fury. It made me a little sick but on the whole I felt fairly remote, which was lucky.

We aim at Cairo today and then go home. It has been a most lovely three and a half months, and I have enjoyed it to the full. Having Viola has been so right and such fun. We seem to have done just the right length. Confess to feeling a little jaded now but not too bad. Last night's unfortunate show was our 155th. I've done three broadcasts and several impromptus as well. Had meant to write new material, get ideas for songs, write poetry, etc., but somehow there hasn't been time for any of it, though I've made notes for poems.

It is good to feel stretched and to know that the job has been truly done. I've learned a lot from it. Some of it has been good for the work; all of it good for the soul. Home will be mighty nice and unpacking bliss.

Tuesday, April 25th, 1944   British Embassy, Cairo

The Embassy house is full of General Smuts[1] and the comings and goings of the Greek royalty.[2] Jan Smuts, the young son, is fed to the teeth with them, is allergic to the Greeks, he said. No room here, alas, for Viola who is at the Metropolitan Hotel where ENSA holds some rooms. She says it is quite alright but I shall miss her badly. Cairo is a bit on top of me today. Our passage is delayed and there is much tension about things in general because of the invasion. No bags going. No one leaving England. No ships – that is the gossip. Have a hunch we may get to Algeria and just kick our heels there. Oh, dear. Reggie seems to be receding further and further from me. I hate it.

We got here on Sunday. There was a khamsin [oppressive Egyptian wind] blowing and no sun. Depressing and very hot.

Next day off to cash some money, find out about our movements. When I got in before lunch an enormous armful of flowers was brought to my room by one of the fancy dress slaves. I couldn't believe it. There were six dozen roses, six dozen delphiniums, and six dozen carnations. I counted them just to see! And a card from Aly [Khan] saying he was glad I was back and we must meet soon.

Glynne Bernard asked me who had sent the flowers – all packages arrive through the ADCs' room so they miss nothing! When I told him he remembered that there had been calls for me from Aly all Sunday and he'd forgotten to tell me. And after lunch he rang up. If it wasn't so uncomplimentary to be liked by him I'd enjoy the whole

---

[1] Jan Christiaan Smuts: South African statesman, philosopher and soldier who fought British during Boer War but became a strong believer in British Empire.

[2] On the previous day, British troops had put down a mutiny among left-wing members of the Greek armed forces. King George and his entourage had flown out from London.

thing but as it is I've no wish to be just one hundred in a hundred and thousandth icing. Being weighed by the pound has never flattered me. I like the little man and am amused by his fierce oriental goings-on. But it's no good and as I'm quite unprepared to go his way I might just as well stop before it gets difficult. He wanted me to go dancing with him last night – if it wouldn't bore me. Just for an hour or so.

His technique is perfect. The simple humility and nonchalance. But I have spent an entire evening dancing with Aly and the fox-trot has quite a different meaning under his guidance. No. I stalled and he said he'd ring up in the morning but he didn't. My ego is disappointed, I own. But common sense is telling me it is all for the best. I suppose having been married for so long and never to have had the fun of just beaux accounts for the girlish pleasure I've taken in this little pursuit. I've loved it. Specially that armful of flowers. A vulgar display but very delicious.

Viola says she's half on Aly's side for finding me a good thing and half furious that he dares! She is a joy to me. There have been moments when she exasperates me too; but these are few and pale in the pleasure I get from her company and attractive mind. It was a stroke of luck having her on the job. Last night when I dressed for dinner I went to my red hair-pin box and a note fell out. It was this poem from Viola.

J.G.

Swift horses leaping, dusk in snow,
Mountains in a rosy pool,
Swinging blossom against the sky –
You have sung with your head as high
As theirs – and moved with laughing grace
Through men and donkeys, your heart beat
A silver tune which bore us far
Up the shining path of a Morning Star.

It made me cry with pleasure. I remember those horses, Setif in February, and that sunset in the valley out of Algiers – all of it. How darling of her to think of those things.

The next day a huge grand dinner party for Smuts and the Crown Prince and Princess of Greece. After dinner there was a rush and a flurry and I went off with H.E. to a gala film leaving the dinner party to Smuts. No time to do more than watch the great man so far. His appearance is enchanting – so pink and white and fresh and compact and alert. He is a really big person – it rays out from him. Always encouraged by the wideness of heart in a man of his calibre who takes trouble and apparent pleasure in everyone. Smuts *is* interested. He is bright as a bird and one feels the springs of his resistance are in excellent working order. He is a strong but welcoming personality. Doesn't overpower but sweetens the atmosphere. And his essential integrity shines out. A few days before he left the Union he walked up Table Mountain. I believe he is seventy-two.[1]

I write on my brass bed with evening falling like a curtain as it does here. Viola is out dancing. Peter Tunnard and Tim Lindsay Peto both have scarlet fever which is a very good thing, keeps them out of the front line. Viola is relieved. I feel a long way from home out here, I do, I do.

Thursday, April 27th, 1944

Saw Aly in Groppi[2] who asked me to dine or lunch tomorrow. Fenced a bit. Would love to go but don't want the effort of coping which proves something uncommendable in my character. It's time I went home. The

---

[1] Joyce was nearly right: Smuts was born in 1870. The Smuts had left South Africa ('the Union') on April 21st and arrived in England on April 28th to see Churchill.
[2] Smart cafe; Groppi was a Swiss who introduced ice-cream to Egypt.

RAF think it might be quite soon now but probably not before Friday. Am really rather horrified at myself out here. I feel far off and unreal and half of me, the worser half, loves the life of luxury and ease and escapism while the other half is feebly battling against it because it has so little in common with what we are pleased to call reality. Privilege is mighty nice for them as have it. Smooth passages ought to leave room for construction but I'm not sure it doesn't paralyse the intentions. I'm glad we're working again today, even though the forty-five mile drive down to the hospital promises to be unpleasantly hot.

Friday, April 28th, 1944

It was! The road seemed to go on for ever and I was shaken till I felt like screaming. The quarter-master is entertainments officer at No. 27 and a sillier man couldn't be found anywhere. Nothing was laid on. My head reels as I think back to the number of times we've arrived at a hospital and had to start the whole thing from scratch, explaining what we do, what we want, and why we don't want to do it in the up-patients dining hall but in a ward instead because we are there to cater first and foremost for *bed patients.* It is an exhausting feature of the job and if ever the ENSA office took the trouble to pave the way it would never be necessary. In Paiforce all was smooth. But nowhere else. To be quite fair Nigel Patrick did cotton on in Algiers and in the end things were ironed out there.

Saturday, April 29th, 1944

Viola low again. I can't make out quite why. Can't bear to see her face go all miserable. I think it's only a mood that battens down on her, but it seems to have power and hurts her. She came to lunch and was better after it, I think. She's had these sort of come-overs two or three times and there is no apparent cause though of course there must be something to account for it. I'm so fond of the creature and can't bear it when her eyes get big and bright with un-allowed tears and she can't speak. I always feel someone must have done her down at some time or another. She's inclined to expect the worst too soon. Wish I could help.

. . . And now I'm on my bed having slept for an hour. Miss Tee comes to say bath is drawn and what will I wear. Gosh, it will be strange to get back to the usual life. Can't wait to see Reggie. Funny thing the way I long for him more and more as a lasting, enduring, darling and real person. He's the lynchpin in my life all right. I am one of the lucky ones.

May 1944

If only we could leave this place. I'm having far too much fun here. All my days to myself and far too much time to indulge. Everything is out of proportion in this climate and conditions warp all views. I despise myself to my depths. I suppose it's because I'm quite unused to attention that when it comes it takes me breath away a bit. Most girls have their whirls at eighteen or so. I never did and now I don't quite get it. Bad at doing things lightly and I'm muddled and unhappy and long to get away home. Still no planes coming in or going out. It's eight days now since we came to Cairo. It looked as if we would get off tonight but a khamsin blew all yesterday and nothing was able to land.

On Friday dined with large party including Joan and Aly Khan. Viola played, I did some monologues and sang, and later we turned on the gramophone and all danced on the balcony. It was cool out there and starry. Long session with the follower in which I tried to make myself clear. Can't deny I'm not enjoying it. Whirls are fun and the ego swells visibly. But it's all out of proportion and as such wrong. *It* thinks this is *the* great thing; even took *it*self to really believe it. Suppose *it* never had the chance with that upbringing and limitless resources. Entirely despise character and cruelty and goings-on, but I *like* the creature and can see there has been something there that might once have amounted to something. But swamped with self and indulgence and piracy. Hasn't any idea about reality. Can't fathom me but intrigued by what *it* can't understand. Lives entirely in the minute, completely selfishly without a thought for anyone else. Or am I wrong? Next morning dozens of heavenly roses. Can't deny I don't enjoy the whole thing. Must tell Reggie. But it is all wrong even so and I'm surprised at myself for getting so swep' up. Things seem to matter so little out here. Vision gets blurred by the sun and it is all so easy and wallowing and far, far away and I feel adrift and very odd.

On Saturday morning to the Gezira Sporting Club for lunch with Joan and Aly. People swimming in the pool, dripping out to the buffet and then eating large salady meals at little tables under the striped awning. *So* hot. Talked to a local called Sadik[1] who played the local game of compliments with a fine flowing hand. Of course one atmosphere breeds another. *Chez moi* I have none of this sort of success but it seems to be in the air out here. Have had more attention in this past week than in all my days put together. It seems to be involuntary too for I don't really want it though to be honest can't say I'm not loving it too. Mixty-Maxty.

At a party that evening, dancing. The garden lit by the beams thrown from the verandah, and the night-scented stock, tobacco plant, and heaven knows what, all made the whole thing quite lovely. No use pretending I didn't love it all – the dancing, the cool ease of it, the flowers, the food, the music and, above all, the attention. Is this wrong? I realise it is purely human, purely temporary, and wholly a frill. But is it wrong? . . . It is all a long play, beautifully set and lit and produced with the silk skill of a perfect conjuror. And never real. From a conceited point of view I resent being one of many, just another in the line. But this is wrong too. If one is to play this worthless game it must be done with legerdemain, light as a feather. I'm not good at this. Some of me gets lost in the

---

[1] Ahmed Bey Sadik: sequestrator of German property in Egypt.

process. It's time I went home to sanity, I know that. Daresay, humanly speaking, an outing like this does a gel good so long as no one gets hurt; and that is important. Reggie wouldn't mind because I am so un-involved in it but there are other facets and I wonder. Conscience weighs a lot with me, and that's to be praised I daresay. Bed at 4 a.m.

Yesterday was Sunday. Very hot with no sun and a wind blowing like a furnace blast. Took myself off stealthily to church. First time since early January. As always happens the lesson might have been personally selected for me. The burden was: *do not indulge*, and I made a lot of resolves which pray God I can see through . . .

Oh, Lord. Glynne has just telephoned to say that Movements have rung him up with the disastrous news that we can't move from here till Wednesday evening at the earliest. This is now Monday morning, I am low as possible about it. Keep thinking though that my Ma once said we couldn't make progress until one had improved or healed one's present situation. There must be something in that I think. Have just written to my follower to say best not to meet again because I can't do these things lightly, bits of me get left and it's no good, no good at all. He won't understand and will be more injured than hurt I'm afraid but I can't keep up and it's getting to be too conspicuous and difficult. I've enjoyed it wildly! like living a play.

Mercifully no part of my heart is even touched but before it could be is the moment to say stop. Hope it is all an illusion on his part. Hate hurting. Don't *think* it's possible in this case but since writing that note I feel better inside and I'm sure it's right. However, that is my view. His may be less simple. I'm fond of the creature but everything he believes, does and stands for is foreign to my nature therefore it's no good and must stop.

Saturday, May 6th, 1944

Still here in Cairo. Still waiting for a plane. Still feeling wrong and muddled and far off and still aching for home and safety. This day by day wait is very soul destroying. Doesn't allow me to get down to any work. Trouble with Cairo is that there is far too much time for everything. Far too much comfort and ease too. I'm dissolving visibly. Getting thinner too and less and less real. It would be good to go. No one is clear about the situation. Priorities are vague. Planes do go now and then but naturally important service personnel are taken off first. I am hardly of vital necessity to the war effort. Yesterday was told cable has gone to the Foreign Office to get a clarification on the situation of poor unimportant civilians such as us. If we knew for sure we were not allowed to move for such and such a time then we could plan to get to Syria or Palestine or some such to do some further work. But this day-by-day hanging on is very trying.

It's been a very gay week. Out to every meal, dancing, driving, drinks (orange juice by the gallon), and flowers and food and great fun. Am ashamed of my feebleness. Need hardly say I haven't abided by my note to Aly. Which is self-indulgent and highly despicable of me. I have no defence to offer. Admit all scorn. I put it down, rather drearily, to exhaustion – the war, the climactic conditions and too much time and the sudden recognition of a certain emptiness in my life. All completely human reasons and not very worthy. Attention is dazzling and affection is warming. My head stays clear and I sleep like a log, don't think poetically, have none of that alarming double clarity that I sometimes get (see Robert Graves's 'Lost Love'), nor do I moon. At least not at night or alone. It can all be analysed beyond circumstance and an away-from-home loneliness, that is, on my side. I'm less sure of the other. *Its* extreme loneliness is one of the most complete I've ever seen. Miles off. That is *its* un-European side, which predominates. Can say nothing but good of *it*s gentle bewildered attitude to me. Hope, like all *it*s attacks, this leaves no mark. Hardly think it is likely but this is supposed to be different. Wonder why I always think I know all the answers. Could hardly know less.

Goodness, I didn't know unhappiness could be so over-whelming. Nor loneliness so agonising. Find I mind dreadfully. The whole thing is quite under my skin and I ache for all I have lost. But now after five weeks groping and bewilderment I see a balance and possibility and am adjusting.

Wednesday, May 17th, 1944. Rogation Day

6.45 a.m. fly from Cairo in bomber. Glynne and Aly see us off. Felt panicky in plane, hot, miserable, hell. Tunis at 3 p.m. Casa Blanca 10 p.m. Slept most of day. Viola angelic to me. So muddled.

Thursday, May 18th, 1944.   Flat 8, 70 Ennismore Gardens,
Ascension Day   London, SW7

Arrived England. Delay while we were cleared through. London about 12.30 looking very drear, and *oh*, the cold. Can't say in the least glad to be back. In fact miserable and lost and cold through and through. Which is bloody of me but there it is. Reggie came for lunch looking well. Aunt Pauline buzzing. Flat very small and our room in a chaos at once. Claustrophobic egotism smote me. I'm no good yet. Saw my Pa, then Colonel Grenfell. Tea with Dick [Addinsell] where he was especially understanding and helped a lot. Dined in with Reggie. Would so like to be glad to be back but can't yet.

INTERMISSION

LONDON, SUMMER 1944

It was to take Joyce several weeks to recover from the enormous demands of the tour, as well as from the trauma of her own emotions. On May 20th she goes to report to Basil Dean at ENSA Headquarters in Drury Lane – 'Took against him for he really doesn't care, and can't listen.' She spends much time catching up with old friends, frequently at the Ivy. May 22nd she records lunching with Joyce Carey, 'and talked too much. On to Winifred [Clemence Dane] at 4 where I sat for the picture, and talked too much again. I'm like a record that's on the repeat stop. Dined with Gin and Tony [Thesiger] and had a quiet cozy time. Didn't talk quite *so* much. Wonder when I'll unspin. Very dizzy and a bit miserable.'

Music was always important to Joyce in her life. 'The more I hear music,' she once wrote, 'the more I know it is nearest to the Spirit, the essence of things, of all the arts, evidence of things not seen or heard, but of that unchanging, limitless life of spiritual being that no war or misery of uncertainty and fear can ever touch.' And so, at a concert given on May 24th by her friend the pianist, Myra Hess, 'I sat alone in a box and got ironed out deliciously; am beginning to register a little.' Throughout this time it is quite clear that such close friends as Myra Hess, Dick Addinsell ('he is very good for me. I was low as a rug and inclined to cry'), Virginia Thesiger, Cynthia Wedderburn, Joyce Carey and others, all helped in her 'rehabilitation'. What Reggie thought we are not told. His patience, his deep love for her and his gentleman-like reserve were indeed her linchpin.

Shortly after D. Day she goes to stay in Berkshire with Cynthia Wedderburn. 'Entire morning in bed. Cynthia came and talked to me and we gossiped happily. I'm minding the whole business far too much. It must be dealt with. I miss so much.'

On June 12th she discusses with ENSA doing a second tour in September, which will include India. It is the time of the doodle bugs and night raids on London. She hates it all. 'I'm really cowardly and mind a lot. Keep wishing I were elsewhere. Reggie unmoved which is a good thing.' On July 7th she goes with Viola to do some shows for hospitals in Southampton and at once feels better. 'Those two days at work were mighty good. I thrive on work!' They do further concerts at Windsor, Kingston, and at East Grinstead. In one chronic ward she asks an old man if he would like a few songs and he replies that he hates music, then retires under the bedclothes where he remains until she has finished singing!

She lunches at the Ivy, dines with Reggie at the Ritz, goes to the theatre and movies, visits friends. There is also the housework, mending, shopping, cooking – but she hates ironing, 'I'm a bad ironer' – writes new sketches, broadcasts, tries out new songs with Dick Addinsell, and writes new radio pieces for Stephen Potter.[1] She reads Noël Coward's *Middle East Diary* – 'of great interest to me as it is the same route as mine. But it isn't very literary or otherwise worth reading. He emerges hardworking but too grand.'

Then on Sunday, August 20th she goes to see Noël Coward at his house in Gerald Road, Chelsea. 'He wants me to go into a new revue, next January! *Very* pleased indeed to be asked. Wants me to sing and do monologues. Must get back from India in time.'

[1] Stephen Potter: writer and BBC producer. Joyce appeared in his *How* programmes.

Reggie is now stationed in Oxford but has days off. She reads Gin's copy of *Lady Chatterley's Lover* and discovers that 'it is good and not a bit *News of the World*.' Finally, on September 27th, she and Viola set off on what is to prove their longest tour of all.

Joyce Grenfell and Viola Tunnard arriving ('again', notes Joyce) at Baghdad, 1944. They lost count of the number of flights they made during their 1944–5 ENSA tours.

Their arrival, as reported by Paiforce's own newspaper, *Trunk Call*.

TRUNK CALL, 8th November, 1944

5

GLAD TO BE BACK IN PAIFORCE

-- SAYS JOYCE GRENFELL

Left:—Joyce smilingly greets Paiforce and "Trunk Call" cameraman as she steps off the plane.

Below:— Snapped later with her accompli hed pianist Viola Tunnard

SMILING radiantly and looking extremely charming, Joyce Grenfell, vocalist star, stepped out of a plane last Monday to greet Paiforce for the second time. She was accompanied by her pianist, Viola Tunnard, also smiling happily.

Since this popular couple were last in the Command, Joyce Grenfell has sent more than one welcome message to Paiforce—a broadcast and through Trunk Call.

Here is a special one she gave to Trunk Call's representative who interviewed her soon after her return :

"Surprising as it may seem, we are very pleased to be back in Paiforce again.

"We looked out of the 'plane window and recognised several of the places we'd seen last time.

"I have been broadcasting quite a lot since I was here, and I sent one or two messages to this Command which I hope you got.

When people at home ask me what Paiforce is like, I tell them that the scenery I saw was a little arid's !

"I gather that the part I'm going to see first this time Iran, has a few more ups and downs in it . . . .

"Since I started these tours I've certainly seen the world—and some of it must be pretty tough to live in. I am lost in admiration for the way you all stick it' out—grumbling a bit which is good for the soul, but remaining the nicest audiences we've found.

"Looking forward to seeing you."

HOSPITAL CALL FIRST

The new tour opened at a hospital in the Baghdad area with an impromptu recital. Joyce Grenfell sang songs of England, Ireland Scotland and Wales to an audience who raised the roof.

Melody was punctuated by humour, in the form of character sketches. Fifty minutes of the most complete entertainment might easily, if the audience had had its way, have become five hours.

On their way to Paiforce from England, they did a brief Syria and Palestine tour.

To Joyce
Grenfell &
Viola Tunnard
with Peter *illegible*
apologies &
best wishes!

A caricature of Joyce and Viola in performance — from *Trunk Call*.

In Baghdad again, 1944.

The camera was never far away. Here Joyce and Viola in Mrs Denham-White's garden in Calcutta, early 1945.

AIR RAID SHELT
IN BASEMENT.

Top left and right: Two shots of Joyce on what she called the Hospital Tour. Here, says the official ENSA caption, she is 'photographed while entertaining wounded soldiers at a New Zealand-run hospital somewhere in Egypt' in 1945.

Left: Earlier in the Hospital Tour she sings in an unidentified ward.

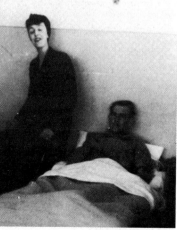

Sightseeing was always on the agenda. *Above:* Joyce and Viola with Tim Lindsay Peto in Beirut in 1944. *Left and below:* in Aleppo, Syria.

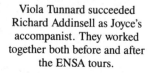

Viola Tunnard succeeded
Richard Addinsell as Joyce's
accompanist. They worked
together both before and after
the ENSA tours.

OUR ARTIST'S SKETCHES OF SOME OF THE ARTISTS
APPEARING AT THE PICCADILLY THEATRE, LONDON.

After the final ENSA concert it was back to London and Noël
Coward's 1945 revue, *Sigh No More*.

SECOND TOUR

SEPTEMBER 1944–MARCH 1945

September 1944

Second tour began on September 26th. We thought in our sweet innocence that things would be different this time; that because we'd said we were ready to leave on the 20th we would leave on the 20th. But no. The Priority Board saw no reason why I should have a seat. That was before the Adj General Adam and Brig Morgan said their say, whatever it was. From that instant things happened, and we left Paddington carrying little white cardboard lunch boxes at 11.15 on Tuesday morning. Viola and I sat in a carriage with a major general and his Brig. By spy work I read his label upside down and it said Chappell. Later learned the Brig was called McCallum. Both were friendly and we shared my *Times*. The BOAC kept us fed with constant sandwiches all across Europe and North Africa. White cardboard boxes were taken on at all stops and were ingeniously packed with snacks, getting better as we approached the land of promise. We had an hour at Gib and were driven to a hotel to wash and feed. The wash was difficult as the water was salt! Down at Algiers for lunch and it was hot. It was a day like our magic one there last January – the sea that clear cool aquamarine and the sky clashing with it. Faint haze.

The train ride through Berkshire all along the river between Reading and Didcot was a long pleasure on the eye. The beeches just starting to turn; little patches of yellow and orange. May trees scarlet with haws and the grass still green and pleasant. The sluggish Thames lay smooth and blue, reflecting the sky, and gardens grew with marigolds and first Michaelmas daisies. Some orchards still had apples. On a white cliff cutting I saw a sudden blue of little harebells, pale as a breath blowing in the wind. I saw it all with a dazzling clarity and loved it looking like that for our last day there. Going away has been different this time. Better war news, some sun and less blackout and people look lots comfier.

At Cairo we were met by a nice smiling lance corporal with a note from Walter Moyne[1] saying we were staying with him and he hoped we weren't too tired and that we were to order any food we wanted and sleep as late as we could. Fine. His house is in Zemalich, – 4 Shariah Gamalaya. I am in a French-boudoir-style room with a fantastic tin and china chandelier built around a white bird with a carnation in its mouth. The whole is elaborately strewn with garlands of gilt leaves and five candle lights rather unnaturally pierce the foliage to justify the whole thing. There are French prints, *18ème siècle*, still marked with sales stickers plum in the middle of the glass and there is a characterless white cupid on the mantelpiece with a stamp sticker on its arm, marked at far too many piastres. Next door is a bathroom with bidet and wc off it, behind Turkish towelling curtains. It is perhaps twenty feet square, mirrored and marbled and lit inadequately by a lot of discreet bulbs in unexpected places. Last night I ran the water for twenty minutes and finally succeeded in collecting about an inch and a half, for it is a square pool approached by two descending steps. It measures six by eight foot! Viola is in a less ornate room across the hall. Her chandelier has nursery-rhyme figures eternally going round it.

We got up at 5 and were lent a car to take us to the ENSA office. Kindly welcome from Rex Newman with lots of

---

[1] Walter Edward Guinness, 1st Baron Moyne: wealthy friend of Churchill; Minister Resident in Cairo since January 1944. Murdered in Cairo by the Stern Gang, a Jewish terrorist group, November 1944.

concrete plans already afoot. We got to Jerusalem Monday. Air. He is having an eight-seater bus converted into a carry-all for our piano, bags and selves and this will follow or take us everywhere in the Command. There was money to be collected and uniforms to be measured for and we got in about 7. By this time the night had dropped suddenly as it does here and the moon was white and egg-shaped and the stars closer to the earth than at home.

———◆———

Letter to Virginia Thesiger

Saturday, September 30th, 1944   Cairo

. . . We've lunched with pals and last night one of my Coptic admirers took us dining on a roof under a great white moon with stars and a faint breeze and fed us nectar, and then swept us along in a Lincoln Zephyr through brilliantly lit streets to the new open-air dance place Anzona, where we swung in delight to a good band wearing white, and were given bracelets of wonderful jasmine strung on cotton and smelling of heaven. Today we lunched *en famille* with Walter, and tonight we are being fêted by a sweet Copt who Cares and are first dining at his flat and then friends are coming in and I *suspect* I might be asked to sing.

In between times Viola and I have worked like beavers on new songs and are getting a fine smoothness over the routines. And we've slept and eaten, and now, at last, for the first time since we left here last May, I really do feel ready and capable of doing the job. It's a lovely feeling. Between you'n me I've felt awful these past months, sort of grey inside and I think I rather dreaded doing it all again for a great many reasons, but now I'm laying ghosts

and getting rest and time to sort out and I do believe it's
going to be OK.

-------◆-------

Saturday, September 30th, 1944   Cairo

Wrote letters and in this book all afternoon yesterday and
about 5.30 Viola and I went into the bare balcony room
opening off mine and worked with the piano for an hour
and a half. The echo was alarming and the piano barked,
out of tune too. However, good work was done, I think,
and I felt lots better. My voice is still sort of hazy – partly
lack of practice and partly heat, I think.

October 1944

We flew up here this morning in the C. in C.'s private plane.

I write from a Naafi bed in the officers' club at Gaza now. Tel Aviv is simply Golders Green by the sea. The troops adore it for its Brighton quality and after the deserts of Iraq I daresay a pavement and a sea front, together with lots of competing shops, has a strong appeal. Only the sea attracted me at Tel Aviv. The inmates are of all nations, but to hear German talked loudly is strange on the war-tuned ear. The drive down to Gaza was through unexciting landscape except when the sea came into vivid view on our right as it did at intervals. Not many flowers now. Datura bushes, bougainvillaea, mauve morning glory trailing over hedges and porches and in a front yard in Tel Aviv I saw hibiscus. Being back Abroad again wipes out all the in-between-part and the familiar funny discomforts are taken more or less for granted. All plumbing ceased this evening. We knew that little weakness before – Algiers, Italy, Malta and Baghdad each put on a sample for us.

Wynne Rushton, who was ENSA billeting officer in Cairo last time, has coped well and remembered my plea to get to the really out-of-the-way places. ENSA has laid on a large Naafi bus capable of seating eighteen people but, having removed some of the benches, it now holds our piano – quite a good one too. Viola is delighted. We plan to hang all our dresses from the rod at the back of the bus and that will save continual packing and unpacking which is the part of this job that kills one, particularly as we are doing mostly one-night stands. The sergeant i/c is called Simpson. Looks nice in spite of being entirely without teeth for the moment. Our driver is said to be very uncouth, name of Tooth. It all links up somehow in a dental surrealist way – toothless Thimpthon and Driver Tooth.

Wynne Rushton with his eternal rosy baby's face and feminine features is enthusiastic to the point of hysteria. He went into the subject of Lily Pons's[1] visit to the Command, under American auspices and said *how* disgraceful it was that our stars *wouldn't* come out. He has so much to say and is so thrilled with it all that the effort of emitting sounds articulately often ends in a complete break in the voice and a strange yodelling is the result. I sit fascinated while his intense enthusiasm is communicated by a sort of fake anger. Viola gets awful inner giggles and has to turn it into a cough for cover. He is conscious of being county – of Norfolk – and is always asking me if I know Lord Whichit or Princess Such As – who *was* Mary Glubb. Our arrival in the C. in C.'s private plane has given him enormous pleasure and 'frankly, Miss Grenfell', he said, 'I shall use it for you.' In horror I tried to make it clear that such a thing was not to be done but he said I could trust him to be discreet. Heavens. I tremble.

We first saw our bus at Tel Aviv and it wasn't for some time that I deciphered the large red-and-white poster on the windscreen, for it was only visible upside down from the inside of the bus, and when I did I blushed to see our names in five-inch letters. We must, I suppose, travel so identified for the rest of this phase.

After a typical cup of Naafi tea – dark with beige-coloured milk – Viola and I wandered in search of the

---

[1] Lily Pons: opera singer of French birth; made some films in Hollywood from mid-1930s.

beach. 'Officers' Lido is good,' the proprietor had told us. I haven't got a bathing suit but I thought a pair of fairly opaque lock-knit knickers and a bandana skilfully tied around my chest would do. However when we finally reached the beach it was entirely covered by swarms of all-sized high-legged and incredibly speedy crabs. We took against bathing after this and sat on a marooned raft gazing at the sunset over the sea. Washing in a tin saucer-sized basin requires talent but I have it and made a complete toilet before supper. The club was quite active. Three girls in civilian clothes, six or seven rather nondescript officers. We ate our meal, and then went for a gentle stroll under the moon. It was hot and still. The breeze doesn't rise in the evening here as it does in Cairo. I must say I will always have a very special feeling for C., but I don't think Samson missed much by being eyeless in Gaza.[1] It is remarkably unremarkable.

Wednesday, October 4th, 1944   In the bus

I'm going to try and write in the bus but I don't somehow think it will work. No, it won't!

Friday, October 6th, 1944   King David Hotel, Jerusalem

No time, ever, to write in here and there is so much I want to put down. We started work on Tuesday, 3rd October. No. 91 Gen. Hosp. at Gaza. It was enjoyable to do the job again and Viola and I were as one that afternoon. It was quick, finished, with a good line and shape to it. On to Rafah Ordnance Camp. Its immensity alarmed me a little till I discovered that the English there were quite few. We drove to our tent and found it beautifully laid on with

---

[1] 'Eyeless in Gaza': a phrase from John Milton's poem, 'Samson Agonistes'.

blue rugs over rush matting, chest of drawers, dressing-table and even a jam jar full of flowers. Dinner in officers' mess eaten on a long narrow verandah watching the stars come out and listening to a small regimental dance band, on loan from Haifa for six days, playing for our entertainment. Lights failed but it was really rather lovelier in the starlight. We did a show in the Naafi theatre. About 150 there. Long red and white dress. Very hot. Lights of a blinding brilliance. I have drunk more lemon squash in the past few days than I'd drunk in a whole summer at home. And the comforting thing is that one doesn't have to keep popping into the lav. I suppose the heat mops it all up. We managed to break away about 10.30 but the evening only began then for the officers who sang and played in the open air for about two hours more – far too near our tent too. We met great kindness at Rafah – breakfast in bed. Colonel Provan, Australian, came to bid us goodbye about 7.30 a.m. Tent life is of necessity a little public. Sgt Simpson brought the bus up to get us away about 9 and we did a long dull drive to Asluj for lunch. Tommy Tooth, our driver, may be a rough diamond but he handles that b————y old bus with great smoothness. Viola and I each occupy a double seat on either side of the thing. At least Viola spent most of this trip playing the piano at the back.

Asluj is a very small camp on the road to Egypt. It has repair shops and petrol and a Naafi. Two lieuts in glasses run it – names of Llewellyn and Duffield. We ate with them in their tiny little chapel-shaped mess, white-washed and cool. Don't understand why all army food is the same slightly orange colour. We had Welsh rabbit and veg. under an orange-coloured sauce and our tinned peaches were, of course, the same unnatural colour. A huge brown tin teapot was brought in by a young Geordie who is batman to the two lieuts. We did the show in the Naafi and our audience kept increasing as a convoy came in and, after feeding, joined us. Nice time. After a hurried cuppa we set off again in the bus to go a further forty-five miles across the Sinai desert to play to a CMP [Corps of Military Police] post miles from anywhere. We didn't pass a living soul the whole way and only saw the buildings of a Palestinian police post sticking to a small hill. A sort of stage-tradition Sgt, name of Hoare, met us at Abu Aweigla. His deportment and physique were terrific. The little stone mess had gay, if faded, curtains in local red flowered cotton. A tiny little circular bar stood in a cupboard-like room off this and when we arrived the men were having their evening beer, so I suggested they bring their drinks in with them and we'd make it a party. We were about twenty-seven and the atmosphere was perfect from the word go. After I'd done about an hour and a half and Viola had played Warsaw (beautifully) we paused for sandwiches and I was given some very gaseous lemonade that blew me up. Noël's 'London Pride' goes over well. It has even more meaning out here and we've worked it up into quite a spectacular number with me speaking the middle part against the piano! There was a lot of nose blowing at the end of it which amazed me. Goodness me, they were an attractive lot. Ages varying from about twenty-two to forty-five, I should think. Family men. All looking wonderful with sunburn. A small sandy Scot in odd tennis shoes took a time-exposure picture of us standing under the naked light by the bar. He was advised, encouraged and criticised articulately on all sides and I found my smile widening into an uncontrolled grin as the interminable twenty seconds went on. After our sandwiches we sang some more. A young boy with thick fair hair called me to sing the 'Ave Maria'. I explained that it needed a real singer and he said, 'Oh, go on, have a whack at it. That song's a killer-diller.' An unusual description of the work. We have got a copy of the 'Ave Maria' and as we get asked for it every single time I really think perhaps I'd better learn it. I'll never be able to do it well. It was hard to tear ourselves away from there. It had looked so nice – rather like that evening we had with Halsey in Philipville

– the sunburned faces in a dim light and at every one of the six windows black Arab faces peering through the cracks in bewildered fascination. This post had a radio and knew some of the recent songs but had missed the horrors of 'Mairzy doats'[1] till one of 'em half remembered it and asked me to do it.

The drive back across the desert in moonlight was mighty long and I've seldom been more tired. Long day – drive from Gaza to Asluj, then the show there; drive on to the CMP post – a very long (but good) session there and finally the drive back to Asluj where they were accommodating us. One's body is a bore at times and mine got so pins-and-needly and stiff in the bus trying to sleep. Pillow behind the head – ? propped against window – ? on the back of the seat in front? None of it was comfy. Our beds at Asluj were two Naafi armchairs let down to their full length and made up with sheets and a blanket. They were in the room marked 'Ladies' used by ATS in transit. Pale green modernistic wall wash and the usual hunting scene or coaching exterior in the picture line. We had running water in a washroom next door but the lav was away and as it was very unfragrant I was glad. Oh, how I do like plumbing. Our night wasn't too bad because we were beaten and could have slept anywhere I think. Flies woke me up.

And now we are in Jerusalem. Hard to take it in. Here we sit in twin beds on the second floor of the King David Hotel with the sun pouring in on us and church bells clanging far too often. Viola is deep in the *Palestine Post*. We are both full of breakfast and are due to sightsee with Henry Hunloke[2] in one hour's time. We came through the desert to Beersheba where Viola indulged in a whim and bought a huge watermelon, then on through Hedron

---

[1] Nonsense song which begins 'Mairzy doats and dozy doats . . .' ie: 'Mares eat oats and does eat oats'!

[2] Henry Hunloke: Lt. Col., Royal Wiltshire Regiment (twice mentioned in despatches); Unionist MP for West Derbyshire, but resigned his seat later in 1944.

and Bethlehem to here. The watermelon refreshed us all at first, but even two slices each, carved out with skill by Viola with my knife, made almost no impression on its huge bulk and it became a dripping difficulty for the rest of the trip. The country, getting nearer Jerusalem, grows lovelier. Rather like Algeria and the South of France. Little mountains, cultivated dips, square houses that camouflage clear into the landscape. It is too late for most flowers but there are still bougainvillaeas and the morning glory, and in Gethsemane we saw a wall covered in passion flowers. These little mountainy hills look like oyster shells from the air; ribbed.

It is difficult to capture any feeling of the New Testament here. The whole thing is overlaid with a thick crust of Catholicism and the walling up of relics. I've seldom felt further from God. Yet, at Gethsemane, looking at the city wall, I did have a faint memory of how it must have looked. Wynne Rushton took us sight seeing and knows his stuff backwards and is enthusiastic. But he is also a rabid RC and we had to look at every holy stone and rock and believe all the unauthentic rumours of just where Jesus had stood, knelt, wept and cried and thought.[1] Poor Jesus – how very bewildered he'd be to see it all and how much he'd wonder what it was all in aid of. We visited a convent under which once stood the forum of the palace where Jesus was accused. I took in exactly nothing but was conscious of museum feet and eyes and a pining for rest. We saw the church of the Holy Sepulchre and were unmoved. But I thought the Greek silver was lovely – Byzantine. We walked up the market. *Very* colourful! And it was hot and flies flew and I think an Arab spat at my leg. It *could* have been a bird but I think it

---

[1] George Bernard Shaw, writing to Dame Laurentia McLachlan, OSB, of Stanbrook Abbey, from the Holy Land, observed, 'This, the guides tell us, is the stable in the inn. This is the carpenter's shop. This is the upper chamber where the Last Supper was served. You know that they are romancing – there is not a scrap of evidence . . . Your faith and your tourist's observation jostle one another in the queerest fashion.'

was an Arab. I've only got the fuzziest impression of the Holy City. The Gate Beautiful in the old wall remains clear and is beautiful and I liked the bare simplicity of St Anne's church but back at the King David Hotel I was too full of incense and the awfulness of the wicked Roman and Greek nonsense to love any of it.

Saturday, October 7th, 1944 King David Hotel, Jerusalem

Yesterday a.m. to Bethlehem. All that you can't start to feel in Jerusalem you do feel in Bethlehem. The great square, solid, lovely church of the Nativity with its simple lines – good. The Greek Orthodox lamps and little bits and pieces can't disturb the wonder of the twelfth century building. A Christian Arab guide dressed like a college student pointed out the bells 'you hear on the war-liss'. There was some black and white etched sort of wall décor in a faint floral swag design that took my eye. And a small two-way staircase with very open ironwork that was satisfying. In Bethlehem the married women still wear the Crusader head-dress, white cotton over some sort of raised foundation. Most becoming. And many of the people have blue eyes – come down from those days? French and British ancestry? I loved Bethlehem – it is free and open and very sweet.

To No. 16 Gen. Hosp. after lunch. Two TB wards. It was good. Hard work in the first one for sound as there were constant alcoves and pillars and one was continually having to move so that they could all see and hear – if possible. Hosps. are my dish all right. I really do know how to do this part of the job, I think. But if only there were more *time*. We could have spent the whole day in each ward talking – telling them about home. One man, from Edinburgh, asked about food. I said it was better there, much. Which is true. He asked me if I was saying so to comfort him – 'propaganda?' or if it was really true? They are wary out here and worried too. Many of the

men I sang to yesterday have less than a year to live. They
have all been told. No sign of depression, only a rather
agonising wideness and clarity of eye that unbuttoned
me. A young sailor, a Geordie, sat cross-legged on his
bed leaning forward so's not to miss a trick and when he
laughed he slapped himself and rocked. Another got
such giggles at 'Ernie' that he pulled the sheets over his
head to control himself. A surging of feeling pours over
me about the whole thing and I wish I knew and could do
more. The way they thank one afterwards is undoing.
Scotch scones for tea and a visit to a nice depressed Welsh
officer from Bangor who said he'd listened in to me. In
the last ward, lit by the low sun and therefore lovely to
look at, with the men lying and sprawling on red-
blanketed beds in a white ward, zinnias burning in bowls
at intervals and a dusty green of olive trees seen through
the window – in the last ward there was a very young
Indian lying alone in a little room at the end. He made a
beautiful design – lying on a very white bed hung with
snowy mosquito curtains, his lovely face and long boy's
arms dark in contrast. He smiled a gentle smile and spoke
in perfect English to say it had been 'so nice'.

We spent half an hour flat on our backs back at the King
David before dressing to dine with General McConnel
and do a show for him in his new house. Here was
modern architecture with grace and distinction. You
could have put eighteenth-century stuff in it, modern
chintzes, china – anything. Because it is of its kind
absolutely first class. I did about an hour for them – all the
heads of depts there. It went smoothly. Pegasi[1] in fact.
But I was whacked at the end. It looks as if Air Commodore Coleman, AOC here, is going to lay on some air
transport for us which will ease our one-night stands
with 300-mile jolts in the bus considerably.

[1] Pegasus, the winged horse. Joyce is here using it as an apt image of
'taking off' in performance, those rare occasions when an actor's
performance really soars, arising from a strange mixture of chemistry
between audience and actor. (See also pp. 14, 130, 204.)

Sunday, October 8th, 1944   Philadelphia Hotel, Amman

The bedroom from which I write is especially pleasing to
me. It is small, cream walled, with two white iron beds
topped with white lace canopies from which fall the
mosquito nets, now looped back as the season is over. On
each bed there is a scarlet blanket and mine has a huge
orange lion, fierce with stripes – and a King George V
face, and Viola's has a tiger. They are wonderfully out of
keeping with everything. Outside our window is an
enormous Greek amphitheatre rising in the sun. Last
night I sat on the front porch taking tea while Viola, who
is a more energetic type, climbed up to the top of the
theatre to see what she could see. Four little Arab boys
met her near the top and called her 'General'. It's nice to
think our ENSA uniforms can cause even such an illusion.
The boys sat on a Greek seat and one of them sang
a funny almost European tune. Way down below on
my porch I could hear every sound with incredible
clearness.

Yesterday we left Jerusalem in a little plane called a
Proctor. That's the nearest thing to flying oneself I've
ever done. Tiny little machine. Just Viola and me and
W/C Harris who drove. He took us over the city and, at
last, we got a shape of it. The great mosque dominates the
scene standing in its lovely width of courtyard. The busy
little Orthodox Russian and RC churches are muddled
together. There was a lovely light on the Golden Gate.
The puckered coffee-coloured mountains to the Dead Sea
looked sinister, I thought. It is a cruel landscape and the
unmarked surface of the Dead Sea adds to the mystery.
Don't like it. Beyond this big country the upper plains
turned into a modernistic Kidderminster carpet, all
autumn colour and angled jazz stuff. (John Barker-High
Street Ken. and every villa on the Great West Road.) We
flew yesterday through the kindness of Air Commodore
Coleman. He bade us lunch with him. Mrs Coleman has
just come out from England, travelling six in a two-berth

cabin for three weeks. She is Australian, I think, with a most lovely profile. The tautness of skin over beautiful bones is mighty satisfactory. She is a very warm person and was so sweet to us, being thrilled with our life and the job and giving us handfuls of Kleenex for the journey! She came with us when the Air Com took us out to the airfield after lunch and stood by their huge car waving a big white handkerchief at us as we circled over and away. Blessed her for that. For no special reason a sudden low panic assailed me in that little plane as we left the earth. The kindness of the thought, the warmth that that gesture had, established a comforting contact. We are to spend quite a lot of time in the little aircraft this next week. I must say it is wonderfully simple. Half an hour and we were at Amman. It takes our bus four hours to do the journey. Mercifully we weren't in it yesterday for it broke down two hours away. The Sgt thumbed his way in and telephoned me with the bad news. No hope of getting it or our piano or our dresses in time for the show. However we gallantly said we'd manage in our crumpled cottons and on their Naafi piano and it was in fact a good show, up at the RAF camp. Pleasant little theatre, wide and not too deep. Just what I like. It's those tunnel halls that kill me. I wasn't feeling too hot. Got a cold in the first hot-and-cold, come-and-go stages, and I felt very unlike performing at all. However it was alright and they loved it. Several of the airmen came up after the show and thanked us. 'Best show I've seen since I been in the Middle East – that's three and a half years,' and 'It's different – not like an ENSA show at all' . . . The spokesman of the station band asked if he could borrow 'I'll be around' to copy it out. 'London Pride' went well again. I looked pretty awful in my old red-and-white striped cotton frock. I did what I could to Maud and wore a scarf à la Mary Q. of Scots. Long frocks do help on a stage. Not that it seems to have mattered much last night. They came to enjoy themselves and enjoy themselves they did. The boy King Feisal is staying with the Emir, and his entourage are in the hotel.[1] The English governess, very pretty in a pink-and-white way, talked to us.

Monday, October 9th, 1944   Rutbah. Up the Pipe Line

Yesterday was another Tipaza day. W/C Stillwell came and fetched us from the Philadelphia Hotel, and with Major Barto, Sq L 'Chalky' White we set off for the Roman ruins of Jerash. Two-hour drive. Lovely rolling country, big. Stillwell said it reminded him of Cumberland. Hairpin bends, white dusty road. The dried brown ghosts of flowers on every hill, in every ditch. They told us it was perfect with wild flowers in the spring – fields of lupins, every iris, and all the anemones. We saw a little pink bougainvillaea in the valleys; and morning glory again. Once a long and larger yellow 'stinking willy'. Birds, unafraid of us, rose quietly out of the dust as we approached. Little crested larks, stonechat, swallow, a pair of slow-motion hawk-like birds – kites? hovered over a cut in the hill. We passed a few Arabs, all friendly with instant smiles. Coming back, a couple of camels found themselves in our path and instead of sidestepping, tried to outpace us down the long road until an Arab on a donkey coming the other way headed them off. They swung along in untidy rhythms looking remarkably silly. One patch of land on a mountain has been wired off for experimental purposes by the Agricultural Commissioners, and, because goats can't get at the undergrowth, the whole place is green and lovely. Views in every direction all the way. Layer on layer of rounded reddish-brown mountain. Now and then a collection of little mud huts, miles away, grew into a sizeable village. We passed one river, quite a busy one too. Some Bedouins were camping near its banks. The Agr. Com. had

[1] Abdullah, Emir of Transjordan, became King in 1946 on Jordanian independence. The boy King Feisal of Iraq, born 1935, reigned 1939–58.

planted poplars around a little field. They were just
starting to turn lemon yellow, fluttering like tiny pen-
nants in a gentle wind. You don't get any warning about
Jerash. One minute you are just looking on the rolling
view and the next there is the triumphal arch, noble and
awe-inspiring, growing up into the sky – for you
approach from a lower level. The whole city lies on a
slight incline in a faint dip of the hills. It is easy to trace the
plan for the great forum is intact, so is the main street;
and almost all the main buildings are outlined. H. V.
Morton[1] says it deserves the fame of Pompeii. I think that
its remoteness enhances the magic of Jerash. There are
two theatres, the North and the South – the North seats
3000 and was used for intimate stuff, just right for me!
and the South holds 5000 and is, in fact, the lovelier and
more complete. Perfect acoustically. 'Chalky' White
climbed to the top and I stood on the stage below, and in
conversational tones I said the only poem I know almost
all through – 'I remember'[2] – and then in microphone-
sized voice I sang, unsuitably, 'Hand me down my
bonnet'. He could hear every syllable, he said, and
without effort. A classical education would be becoming
on these occasions. One should be able to quote a suitable
Greek song or a Latin verse. I can't ever think of any
suitable quotation when I want it. I remember Myra
[Hess] telling me that as a student she always used to
dream of the days when her mind would be so full of
beautiful music that she would stroll across Hampstead
Heath with Beethoven and Mozart singing in her ears. In

---

[1] H. V. Morton: best-known British travel-writer of the period.
[2] I remember, I remember,
  The house where I was born,
  The little window where the sun
  Came peeping in at morn;
  He never came a wink too soon,
  Nor brought too long a day;
  But now, I often wish the night
  Had borne my breath away!
      Thomas Hood, 1799–1845

actual practice when she would have liked this to happen all she could summon up was some topical barrel organ tune she'd collected without knowing she knew it.

We ate our lunch under a walnut tree in the garden belonging to the guide. It was pleasantly hot. Biggish sandwiches with egg, cheese, bully and rose pink salmon inside. Baby cucumbers, tomatoes. Biscuits and ginger beer. There was real beer for the others. A rangy white cat grew brave through greed for our scraps. We did all our sightseeing after lunch. Jerash must have been a very splendid city. It is on a big scale with an immense fountain of the nymphs halfway up the main street. The water used to drain away through cunningly carved filters in fish designs. Much of the carving is still there. Lizards ran off fallen Corinthian pillars. We climbed to the roof of Artemis's temple and saw the four noble pillars of the entrance on almost equal terms. One needs to spend days there to see it properly. But me poor old feet and the heat sort of beat me and I sank with gratitude on to a stone wall by the car and drank a glass of hot ginger beer. The drive home is a confusion of low lying sun in the eyes, overpowering sleep and dust. A lovely day.

Back at the Philadelphia we ordered tea with lemon and sat on the porch talking to Miss Symons who lives out here among the Arabs, giving eye treatments. She is a sandy, rather attractive woman of about forty, with deep-set blue eyes and a curious nose with a square tip. She lives alone in an Arab village outside Amman and loves it. She gave us her card. It has 'Miss A. M. Soltan-Symons' on it and 4 Basil Mansions, sw3 in one corner and her Arab village, Fheis, in the other. The A. stands for Adela and the M. for Milly. She was amusing and informative and we listened fascinated.

Flat on our beds for an hour. Then dinner with Major Spencer of the Arab Legion. We'd met him in Bagdad, not that I have the faintest recollection of it, but he says we did. He is neat and dapper with a healthy if ungrace-

ful moustache. His vowel sounds are so nearly swallowed that he is practically inarticulate. I do dislike
misshapen vowel sounds. Particularly the kind that are
an overlay for something that must be disguised.
Spencer's aren't that exactly. More what is erroneously
thought to be an Oxford accent. We were a party of
seven. The evening was without interest except for the
magic view from the balcony overlooking all Amman,
twinkling in the night.

Tuesday, October 10th, 1944   H4, up the Pipe Line

ENSA has indeed sent us to isolated units, I'm glad to say.[1]
We flew up from Amman, yesterday, over two hours of
uneventful desert, brindled in colour, patched with yellow seashore sand. W/C Stillwell fetched us from the
hotel and showed us around his camp before we flew. He
does the garden himself. Thick yew-like hedges of
rosemary, still in flower, which is odd – some scabious, a
sort of fragile dahlia-like daisy, zinnias and lots of chrysanthemums coming on. He has a witless stone-coloured
bull terrier called Brutus whom he loves. Clichés come
true in these sandy parts. Men are, in fact, nothing but
overgrown boys. At Rutbah we met a couple more –
Captain Dale Robinson of Recce and Lieut Dick Meek of
the RES. Our Wing Commander Harris looks like a small
boy with his curly hair and hairy legs in KD shorts but he
is that strange complete product of the RAF, curious
vowel sounds, detached view and all. To watch him
handle his aircraft is a joy. We'd liked it on Saturday
coming from Jerusalem to Amman. It was more spectacular on Monday from Amman to Rutbah. No sign of the
landing field there – we circled low to look and then rose
and went round again. He finally guessed the wind from

[1] Earlier, owing to the extreme heat, the GOC, Paiforce, had cancelled all
entertainments, leaving the men to feel neglected. 'Hearing of this,
Joyce Grenfell gallantly offered to fly out,' wrote Basil Dean in *The
Theatre at War*.

an idly flapping Iraqi flag on the toy fort, yellow built with castellations, and we made a gentle landing on the gritty desert. The two officers drove us all over to their bungalow mess, squatting in its little patch of zinnias and a fizzy green shrub they called burning bush. Iced beer for them and the W/C and Viola and I had long cold lemon squashes. Captain Robinson is a pink plump little boy with long narrow bright-blue eyes and very startling curling blond eyelashes. Mr Meek is large and bony with a schoolboy giggle that closes his eyes right up. They began by trying to make us feel the party spirit; which is always rather *triste* for we aren't quite the ENSAs they'd hoped for, we feel. However, as we all made friends and relaxed, they forgot to try and were very nice and ordinary and looked after us beautifully. The camp is stuck in the sand with a few mud huts for the residents and a tented compound for the leave convoys that pass through en route to Beyruth. There is a small pool with fire fighting purposes which they swim in. The mess has Arab rugs on the stone floor, some ill-copied oversized drawings of the *Daily Mirror* heroine Jane, and a shelf full of books sent by Welfare at Baghdad and changed at intervals. An Iraqi called – or rather re-christened – William, waited on us in the mess. He was small-boned and slim and wore his hair in a fringe, but rather different in that he had a crossway parting starting one side of his head, crossing the crown and ending over one eyebrow. He was anxious to please but faulty. They abuse him a good deal but he doesn't speak the language and smiles back quite serenely. I sank into a thick sleep, induced by the journey, the increased heat, my good lunch, and my less good cold. We each had a small room, mud walled and cream washed with a straw sort of roof. The bed was some yards of rabbit wire nailed to a wooden frame. Not ideal but quite sleepable on.

Our washbasins were ex-petrol tins. The cupboard in the room was made of tins, too; flattened out. A Devon sergeant, regular, name of Lippett, said what he and all the others in Paiforce feel about Aunt Nancy. I did some quiet work on trying to dispel the false impression but it is seated deep and I can't see she'll ever make the House again if she's foolish enough to stand next time. They are bitter about it.[1] This same man said we were the first girls who had ever bothered to *talk* to the men – of home and ordinary things. He was nice, even if it was beer-induced.

Viola and I went down to the leave convoy camp about 4.30 and saw a big one on its way back to Baghdad and Shaiba. They were already loaded in their lorries, about ten to each, with bedding spread out and kit arranged to minimise the jolts. They were to drive through the night. Several of 'em remembered us from last April. They all looked wonderful after their ten days in Syria. Beyruth is 'smashing', they told us. We waved them off and they called out 'Good old London', 'See you in Piccadilly', 'Ta-ta for now' – Tommy Handley's Mrs Mopp[2] has a following out here, it seems.

And now I write on a very good Iraq Petroleum Co. bed at H4, thirty-five miles along the line from Rutbah. A sudden sand storm has blown up. The window is as dark as a November fog and the young trees – persian lilac, macracarpa, and a sort of cypress are bending heavily in the wild wind. This is a high square room with three extra ventilating windows just under the roof. One of these has blown open and the air is full of the strange slightly sweet smell of desert dust. This page is covered in fine

[1] Nancy Astor's biographer, Christopher Sykes, records how the following month her husband Waldorf had the painful task of telling her that she must not stand at the general election which would follow immediately the war in Europe was over. She had more critics in her local constituency association than supporters, her parliamentary performance had deteriorated and she was mocked when she spoke in the House.

[2] Tommy Handley: comedian whose wartime radio series, ITMA ('It's that man again!') made him the most popular comedian in the history of radio. Its catch phrases such as Mrs Mopp's (the cleaner) 'Can I do you now, sir?' and 'Ta-ta for now, sir' were on everybody's lips.

white grit, invisible to the eye but making a tiny crack as my pen writes over it. We came up here this morning in yet another bus. The original one was exchanged for what was hoped to be an improved one. This broke down near Jericho while we were flying down to Amman. Its replacement is a heavy old thing painted an elephant grey with hard glossy seats that you stick to and which stick, in dark browny red patches, to you. It bounces up and down and smells of oil but is said to be trustworthy. We ran into a short rain burst on that godless road through nowhere. And now, several hours later, the place is made nightmarish in a completely surrounding hurtling cloud of dust. I wonder how they all survive the weathers here.

We were made welcome at the RAF camp by the sergeants' mess. Presently Fl/Lt Coutts with a powerful Scots accent made further welcomings. After our coffee Coutts took us over to meet the manager of H4, Mr Clough. H4 is one of the many pump stations on the line to Haifa from Kurkuk, IPC. Mr Clough is an ex-sailor from Manchester, fat and forty and very nice indeed. Mrs Clough, Maisie, has a seven-month-old baby, name of Susan, a pleasing creature with rosy-soled feet and dark stone-under-water coloured eyes. She is teething and does it on edges of chairs, stools, ashtrays or whatever lies in her path. Maisie is very decorative with a *jolie laide* sort of looks. Incredible, novelist's delight, hair of the genuine chestnut. I don't think I've ever seen this before. She's got a smooth braided bun and a centre parting and her features are rather up at the corners with an amusing nose. She is an oil child herself. Born in Mexico and lived most of her life in Iraq. She once did hairdressing and has recently been evacuated to S. Africa.

We lunched in the IPC mess. Curry for lunch and the remains of the royal turkey left over from the little King's visit en route for home last night. Viola and I made for our beds after that. We have homing pigeon instincts where beds are concerned these days. I read a little of Nevil

Shute's book *Pied Piper*[1] and then gave in to sleep. A hot bath to follow. And on top of that, in clean clothes and a fresh face, we walked across the compound to take tea with the Cloughs. A lovely set-piece tea with silver and flowered china and an iced cake and rolled oat short-breads. I ate much of everything. We listened to the news and heard that we are slowly oozing the Germans out of Holland. Viola has tuned the piano with a piece of lead tubing with a nail through it, cunningly built for her by a Texan sergeant we found in the mess. Our frocks have got very crushed in the new bus. It's not high enough for the long ones. Mrs Clough's white Russian refugee is washing our smalls for us. This business of keeping clean and tidy is an uphill battle. Ideally we ought to travel with a slave. If Noël has his Bert,[2] Viola and I ought to have my Rene.[3] She *is* an ATS. By golly if we ever do go again I'll try and work it. To have someone to cope with bags and clothes would be heaven. It's such a bore as well as a chore. The Russian, who is a wizened wonder of about fifty, has just delivered our clothes and refused our proffered reward with many smiles and 'Pliz, pliz no.' She also conveyed in sign language and some English that she was herself a singer for thirty years, some in Russia and some in Iran. 'Now, fineesh – over, sleep. Now work, sew-ing, work. All over!' She is very gay and wrinkled with dead straight mouse grey hair bobbed into a ruthless Dutch cut. There is gold in them there teeth.

This place is plonked down in the middle of complete barrenness. They are 127 miles from H3.

Wednesday, October 11th, 1944   At H4

I am now 127 miles from H3. It was a trying trip in heat with the bus leaping vertically at moments and lurching

---

[1] Nevil Shute: best-selling novelist; *Pied Piper* was published in 1942.
[2] Bert Lister: Noël Coward's dresser for all his shows.
[3] Rene Easden: a local girl back home who looked after Joyce and Reggie until she was called up and joined the ATS.

horizontally at others. Few things make me angrier than being involuntarily tossed about. It took nearly three hours. We didn't get to bed last night till after twelve as Mr Clough had invited the sergeants and Fl/Lt Coutts to stay on for drinks after the show. The show was stiff going for us. Poor Viola had terrible trouble with the piano. The entire works have slipped inside and there was an ever-present hum whatever she did about it. The twenty or more RAF boys sat in respectful silence and were stricken with paralysing shyness at our near presence. Or so their CO said. They didn't like to be seen laughing, which wasn't a help to me. When amused they did their utmost to disguise or stifle it. Viola made the lead once or twice, which was a mercy, and as the evening wore on and they got more used to us they did relax and even sang. But as a forthcoming audience they lacked a certain something. Poor things – they were sort of stunned by the whole evening. Many of them had never seen an ENSA show (they don't know their good fortune) and most of them hadn't seen what the Fl/Lt described as 'a white woman' for far too long. We had made friends with most of them in their tented mess in the camp lying outside the IPC compound, but even so a self-consciousness prevailed, and only the uttermost slogging got through it at all. In the end it was evident that we'd won a triumphant victory but it took a good deal of doing. After the first song we tried to cope with the piano and while Viola and the sergeant tinkered with string and a penknife, I endeavoured to keep the company amused. I never was a teller of stories and like an ass I embarked on a long rather complicated cricketing one of Dickie Murdoch's.[1] Not only did I forget which cricketer it was about but I entirely missed the point at the end! After the show, which lasted one and a half hours solid, we moved into the IPC mess and beer was circu-

---

[1] Richard Murdoch, actor known chiefly at the time for his part in the long-running radio series, *Band Waggon*; later with Kenneth Horne in *Much Binding in the Marsh*.

lated and nice Coutts tried to make us play a word game which we did rather badly. Then I showed them 'Poisoned Handkerchief' and 'You are Green'[1] and later we moved on to tricks – wiggling 6d off the nose, lifting a table while one's head was touching the wall, lifting a man on two fingers each, etc., etc. Bed was delicious. Praised be the name of the man who chose the beds for these IPC guest rooms. They are amply long and bounce just enough. The bathroom off it had a plug that pulled and constant hot.

We took lunch with the Army, just outside the IPC compound here. The CO is called Capt Redfern and he is twenty-one. Looks about seventeen, with a round baby face, a wide mouth full of excellent even teeth and slightly sticking out ears. He and the Czech doctor are the only officers. It is a staging post. We had a really delicious lunch cooked by an immense old Sudanese. Young Redfern talked with the greatest enthusiasm of his time in Italy. He was a Black Cat boy in the 51st Division under Gerald Templer.[2] An explosion has perforated his eardrums and he is now permanently graded B; that's why he is up here. He is terribly disappointed for he'd thought his B grade was only a temporary thing, but a final medical in Haifa a few weeks ago has decided things differently. He comes from Staffs. Was going to teach languages and had got through all but his last exam. He is now learning German and French from the Czech doctor, who is twenty years his senior, a kindly plain man with bright red hair. Little Redfern telling us about the thrill of being among the first English troops in a certain Italian village was enchanting. 'You see, I went there with twenty men and we met a little Iti chap and my sergeant said "Inglese" – you know, "English" to him, and he went off and told everybody, I suppose, and they came out and gave us flowers and vino. It was – well, it was

[1] Games played at Astor house parties at Cliveden.
[2] Gerald Templer: knighted 1949. Career soldier with distinguished wartime career who became Chief of the Imperial General Staff in 1955.

embarrassing really, but rather nice. You get a sort of feeling of being proud you're English. They put flowers all over the corporal and he said or signed to them that I was the officer – we were all in battledress and you couldn't see the pips or anything, and so they put the flowers all over me. It was really rather embarrassing. All the men had flowers in their caps. We couldn't stay long though because we had to get back at a certain time.' During lunch, if there was a pause in conversation, he would sing a little. His batman, name of Jones, was a source of delight to us. Long and thin with literally no chin and a very heavy cold. His waiting was timid but dextrous and his mild brown eye was very endearing. Looked as if he'd been designed by Disney for a semi-human leggy sort of animal with the characteristics of Dopey. There was something very charming about that mess. It is the usual mud hut whitewashed. There are all the maps meticulously kept up with little flags marking progress, *Punches*, *Picture Posts*, *Illustrated London News*es all stacked tidily on a table. Not a bad coloured picture of the King faces a not good coloured picture of Princess Elizabeth. Both are there because Redfern said 'a mess must have them'. The doc did the *passe partout*.[1] He also does the garden. His English is new since last November and it is good but sometimes hard to get. 'What,' I asked, 'are those vines growing up the wire in the window?' 'Beams,' he said. 'A kind off broad beam, perhaps?'

Sleep all afternoon for me. A solid plumbing job on the piano for Viola. She says it is, temporarily, a bit better. We then took tea with Mr and Mrs Vile. He is the manager here. His assistant is Mr Murdoch. There are three attractive, thin little Viles and one solid pigtailed Miss Murdoch aged eight. We had scones and gingerbread and tartlets, all excellent. Viola and Mr Vile got talking on music and they went into a corner with his

---

[1] *Passe partout*: a French expression meaning 'all-purpose', and applied to a black tape used in framing pictures at this period.

gramophone records. I made domestic chat with Mrs Murdoch who has a very fancy hair-do consisting, in the main, of two tiny snail-shell plaited buns and a pompadour. She is startled looking and is, today, feeling 'queer' from a peculiar steak and kidney she had yesterday. Mrs Vile is attractive in a fragile, 'woodsy' way! – they both are from Cardiff. Their bookshelves are full of solid worth as well as things like *Antony and Cleopatra* and some Penguins. The children read everything, she tells me. Rosemary aged seven is now enjoying Oliver Wendell Holmes. In between times their father is introducing them to *The Wind in the Willows*. The Vile garden is edged in blue gums and filled, still, with roses and petunias and all the zinnias. To come into this oasis with its compound of cream stone houses, roads and gardens, is like getting to a glass of water when you are very thirsty. It must be extraordinary living here knowing that outside the gate there is nothing but miles and miles and miles of desert. Iraq is merely the bottom of a birdcage. Only this happens to be Trans-Jordan. We crossed the border this morning. I'd forgotten.

Next day: One of our better shows last night. Given in the company's mess lounge. A fair-sized room with pale yellow walls, soft lighting and apricot linen curtains. The men came up from the camp next door in two trucks. Much less shy than the RAF ones the night before. We did nearly two hours for them. All the Oil Co. and their families came. Four children, still as mice, and three other wives besides *mesdames* Vile and Murdoch. One of the wives had a Rainbow Corner[1] look with rolling black eyes and a glamour long bob. She must find life in this little compound rather restricting. Down to young Redfern's mess afterwards for half an hour. Poor Jones couldn't make the concert because of his cold. But he pattered about us with the drinks. We had a nightcap of

[1] Rainbow Corner: a club for the Forces in London.

cocoa with a biscuit at the Viles and just before leaving heard Rachmaninoff's Elegie on their gramophone which was very soothing; and disturbing. The night was very warm, with crickets outside. We felt very strange hearing that particular music in these surroundings.

Saturday, October 14th, 1944   Haifa

We left H4 and on to Mafraq camp. Accommodation primitive but camp bed remarkably comfortable. Tea with a few nice officers in the hut mess. The new magazines had just come in from England. Pictures of the *Caesar and Cleopatra* film with Stewart Granger looking far too pretty, Vivien Leigh looking deformed in a very curious wig and Claude Rains obviously brilliant, but looking like Edith Olivier.[1] The major in charge is an actor from the Abbey Theatre, Dublin, called Patrick Considine. There was an Adonis of a young doctor, blonde and bronzed, two or three spidery lieuts and a kindly character called 'Sailor' Seaman. The show took place in a largish hall but good for sound. Viola spent a full hour plumbing the piano again. She's an angel about it and it takes all her spare time keeping the beastly old thing tolerable. Was strangely scared of the show that night; a little vague, which comes from being a bit tired. But it went with fine ease and they were on the spot and met me more than halfway. While Viola played solos a beetle progressed towards her and only by self-control of the highest order did she prevent herself from deserting her post. Marmite sandwiches and drinks afterwards with theatrical chatter. Capt. Lane, garrison adjutant, was a theatre-goer of experience with a marked bias for Frances Day.[2] He found her 'wizard'. The lighting in our hut

[1] Edith Olivier: writer, confidante of the artist Rex Whistler, a frequent visitor to Daye House, her Wiltshire home. *Caesar and Cleopatra* became notorious as Britain's most expensive film; Gabriel Pascal produced.
[2] Frances Day: American-born actress and singer; appeared in revue and cabaret.

came from two glow worm lamps that choked us. I put on a very bizarre make-up by it. One cheek was a cheerful scarlet while the other remained a mere rose. The 'Ladies' was the usual 100 yards off across sand but once inside it was pleasant to sit and star-gaze at the heavens, open above one, and I got into a sort of trance out there and forgot to come in.

On at 9 a.m. yesterday to Haifa via the Jordan valley and Nazareth. Coming into agricultural country again was lovely. The mountain road was no pleasure to me as I grip the seat in front at every hairpin turn and my sprightly imagination hurtles us over every cliff as we come to it. Jewish settlements in the valley rather impressive. The Jordan a wonderful thick green-blue-grey, swirling through the fields of bananas and corn. In Tiberius there was plenty of local colour and when we stopped to ask the road, young Jews with little cardboard attaché cases sprang at us and tried to sell hideous strands of coloured shells. 'Beads,' they said. 'Very cheec.'

The Sea of Galilee has a wonderful peace over it. Or so it had yesterday. It has the ghost of the New Testament about it. One can clearly visualise the happenings there.

Nazareth sits on a mountain and I've got a blurred picture of pencil cypresses and a church and a few Arabs selling lace and postcards but otherwise it hasn't dented my memory much. We stopped at the Naafi for lunch and talked to some men reading very old *Picture Post*s and listening to a hideously distorted radio. It seemed they never got a show there as they were so very few – only thirty or forty. So. Sergeant Simpson went in search of the Town Major to tell him we'd love to do a short show for them if he thought it a good idea. He did. So at 2, word having been signalled around, about forty men arrived and we did nearly an hour for them. Our frocks were pretty messy after travelling so we changed in the bus and looked a bit better. Fun doing a completely impromptu show like that. We lifted two nice little

white-uniformed WRNS with us who'd hitch-hiked out
to see Nazareth from Haifa and who had to be back on
coding duty at 6. At the Appinger Hotel, Haifa, where I
now write, we found two small clean rooms and after tea
and toast I got on to my bed and went for six; a deep,
necessary sleep. The evening show was a bit of a worry to
us. It was at a very hush-hush camp some miles out of
Haifa where the men were undergoing very rigorous
secret battle training and were confined to their camp and
hadn't had a show. They were fighting troops due for
further ops. The main snag was that the show was to be
done out of doors. There would be 400 present. They sent
a guide in a jeep to lead us to the secret stronghold and
we left the main road and did some cross-country stuff
over boulders and up ditches. They were all ready for us
when we arrived. A canvassed-in stage was up with good
lighting and a little dressing room at the back. Simmy got
the piano in place accompanied by cheers and advice
from the audience, and at last I had to climb the very high
step, with Simmy's assistance, and go on. I was afraid
they'd never hear me, but they did. It went beautifully. I
couldn't let go, though, for one instant. Every consonant
shot like a pistol; a slowing down of all tempo to let sound
travel. Everything went well – monologues, sillies and
sentiment. Viola played Warsaw in response to the usual
request and we ended on 'Nellie Dean' with all the pub
effects. I must honestly admit I was surprised and *very*
pleased about last night. It wasn't easy. Wish I could
have seen more but the lights were smack in my eyes and
I could only get about three rows. There were olive trees
all around and stars above and the faces I could see were
smiling and well and I do think the English soldier is
wonderful!

As usual we were swept off to the officers' mess. I do
wish we could get to the other ranks occasionally.
However they mightn't like it. The officers' mess was in a
large, rather ramshackle marquee, held up with string.
There were a very few chairs but those giant wooden

spools on which telegraph wires are wound, turned on their sides, made sort of nursery school height sitting accommodation. The biggest ones were used as tables.

As with Mr Pepys my final entry in each day of this book ends, with relief, in bed.

----◆----

Letter to Virginia Thesiger

Saturday, October 14th, 1944   ENSA HQ Paiforce

Letter from you today dated Oct. 4th, which is fine and speedy when you consider it's pursued me all over the Holy Land and beyond. Saw the Sea of Galilee yesterday and it is *lovely*. Far more like reality than any of the other relic-y places. It has such peace and such space and looks so good.

. . . Well, it's going well and is unbelievably hard work. I'm just about dead but tomorrow is an off day so I'm looking forward to that to breathe in. It's these long journeys and one-night stands that make it more of a chore than the last tour where we averaged at *least* three nights in the same bed. We were literally off the map most of the week. *Miles* off. Just grit and grit and more grit. Heavenly little units and such hospitality and kindness. As usual the social side is fairly heavy. We make chat with the boys and with their officers, and we are expected to go to a mess after the show for drinks, when of course all we long for is bed. But it's all part of the job so must be done . . .

Last night was, if I say so myself, a real triumph and I don't believe even Noël could have done it any better. 500 rather tough blokes on a stiff battle-training course confined to their camp because it is all so hush-hush. Out of *doors*, dear, and *no* mike. The olive trees looked lovely in the bright lights they'd erected around my canvas stage.

Above were the stars. They were wonderful – got all the jokes, were moved when I wanted 'em to be moved, gay with me and they sang and were silent all at the right times. Goodness, it was fine. The hardest work, I suppose, I've ever had to do because of acoustics. They were the friendly kind who answer back but do it pleasantly and not smart-alicky.

----◄●►----

Sunday, October 15th, 1944   Haifa

My ignorance about almost everything is very shocking. I didn't know of the existence of the Arab Legion, nor of the Trans-Jordan Frontier Force, both of which are commanded by British officers. And then I can't tell the difference between a Roman ruin and a Greek one.

Viola and I had to go out to a Bakery Unit in the flat valley bit a few miles out. Out-of-doors show. The elements and nature weren't a big help. I had the sun full in my eyes and every fly in the area gliding in and out of my ears, nose and mouth. The wind blew Viola's music away several times – otherwise it was a daisy. And the audience, about fifty I suppose, were cosy and eager and easy and we enjoyed it. The major in charge was called Josephs, a nice man who minds about the welfare of his men. In these small units we get a chance to really talk to the men and they rallied round and asked all the usual questions about home and food and the Americans. Tea with Bakery buns in a pretty little green walled mess hut. A neighbouring unit had been asked over to join in the fun and it was one of the happier parties. Afterwards a group photograph was taken with Viola and me. As usual I stand a full head taller than them all, even in my old low whites. We drove back via the view from Mount Carmel.

We went to the hospital, 42 Gen., at 6.30 and did a

good show in a small Nissen. Courtesy from the hosp.
staff noticeably lacking. No one met us, no one asked us
for a cup of tea, no one did anything. Not very welcoming. However the show was very good fun. But bad
manners left a nasty taste in our mouths.

Monday, October 16th, 1944   Beirut

I have always wanted to go to Syria[1] and now here I am.
The Normandy Hotel, on the sea front, with private bath,
at Beirut. We drove up here with Captain Chamberlain,
ENSA officer for the area. He came and fetched us at Haifa
and had lunch with Viola and Wynne Rushton and me at
the Appinger. W.R. was up from Jerusalem to cope with
housing the *No No Nanette*[2] company from Cairo later on
in the season. His puckered little pink face worrying with
every intake of breath. He was fairly calm talking plans
with me but then when Viola joined us and we got on to
general subjects he fair leapt up and flung his arms wide
and his voice cracked with excitement. The Jewish Navy
for instance: 'My dear, they look so *silly* – they do, they
do, they *do*.' The last 'do' was said from a standing
position, followed by collapse. Well, he's done the job by
me with every consideration and efficiency and I bless
him for it.

A heavenly drive along the coast road through Tyre
and Sidon. The Mediterranean on our left was mighty
blue. We passed many practical and present signs of our
occupation. Tyre, or what we saw of it, was a few little
box-like huts. Sidon had signs of an old fort? or harbour?
The bright green car we travelled in turned into a buzz

[1] Beirut was actually capital of the republic of Lebanon, which had only
achieved independence the previous year after two decades of being
administered by France under League of Nations mandate.
[2] *No No Nanette*: musical comedy, ran originally in London at the Palace
in 1925–6 for 665 performances; revived at the Hippodrome in 1935, and
at Drury Lane in 1973.

bomb and made the most alarming noises all the way
from Sidon to Beirut. It was dark when we got here so I
have no very clear impression of the town except that it
has atmosphere, French smells, looks like stage sets on
corners with sudden harsh lighting making dramatic
shadows and I'm rather excited to be here. Captain
Chamberlain took us to dine at the French officers' club
and we met Major James Lasbury of welfare, ex-actor
known as Jack Carlton. Such a meal! *Omelette fines herbes
à* perfection. A little steak with fried potatoes and to
finish off with – a huge, crumbling but basically sticky
meringue Chantilly that surpassed all dreams and memories of past glory. Theatre shop, and Lasbury holding
forth on the excitement of amateur talent and how he
believes in it. Some pleasant anecdotes including one
from Chamberlain about a girl who was going to have a
baby. The doctor asked her if she was married and she
said no, so he walked over to the window and looked up
at the sky. She asked him what he was doing and he said,
'The last time this sort of thing happened a star appeared
in the East.'

Later: Four thousand feet up at St Andrew's, a Church of
Scotland leave camp run by Dr and Mrs Shearer. He is
American and she is Scots. It is the most lovely situation
with mountainy views in all directions and a piney smell
and peace about and I feel better just for seeing it. Viola
and I and our new Sergeant Sharpe, whom I liked at
once, and a very Glasgow driver whom I can't understand a word of, drove up in a station wagon after lunch
today. It is a slow winding mountainy road with nasty
corners but always the view back to the sea growing fuller
and more lovely and the mountainy people looking less
and less harassed as we left urbanity behind us. There are
little chalky rather French houses all with red roofs and
we kept passing open-fronted fruit shops with piles of
glossy melons, more purple egg plants, baskets of tomatoes, strings of red peppers, fresh dates on their yellow

stalks, lemons and oranges and candelabra bunches of bananas, both green and yellow. This whole country is a joy to the eye. Its greenness and the blue sea and the red roofs and the morning glory and scarlet hibiscus and a particularly brilliant geranium that bursts out all over the place.

This morning Tim Lindsay Peto telephoned from nearby. He came over in a jeep and took me to swim at the officers' beach a few minutes out of the town. Viola insisted on practising. Went to the YM and met Sylvia's[1] husband – Rupert Bruce Lockhart. Also Mrs Dodge of the American University here. I telephoned boldly to Lady Spears[2] and she was wonderfully welcoming and knew me which was a special surprise and tomorrow night we dine with her.

I'd gone earlier in the morning to the Naafi sports store to try and buy a bathing suit. All they could offer me was a plum coloured number that wouldn't fit a ten-year-old midget. So I had to take a pair of man's pants, also plum, and wear a scarf skilfully tied around my bosom as a top. The Naafi assistant wrote out the chit as '1 man swim trunk'. The water was soft as silk and *fairly* warm. I made a few gentle excursions from the descending iron steps, came to rest on a rock for a breather and then swam back to the iron step and out. We sat and talked in the sun while we dried. Tim is now ADC to a general in the Fifth Army. It seems a long time since he and Peter [Tunnard] gave us that cosy evening in Sorrento. We've been *so* far since, I suppose that's why. He lunched with us and we had a particularly good lemon squash that *frothed*. Also an ice of exquisite beauty – praline. Then we packed a few

[1] Sylvia Bruce Lockhart ran a mobile concert-van around London searchlight and gun sites.
[2] Lady Spears: otherwise Mary Borden, novelist, and mother-in-law of Joyce and Reggie's publisher friend, Rupert Hart-Davis. She was co-founder and leader of the Hadfield-Spears Hospital Unit, saving many lives in France and the Middle East during the war. Her husband, Major-General Sir Edward Spears, was currently First Minister to Syria and the Lebanon.

things and came up here. There are about eighty boys
here at the moment.

When we arrived it was teatime on the sort of terrace.
Mrs Shearer and some volunteer friends were helping;
little Lebanese girls of about twelve or fourteen were
taking around cups and sugar and milk. The atmosphere
of complete ease, friendliness and successful homeliness
was quite extraordinary. We talked to some of the men.
All are impressed with the place. The type of men who
choose remoteness and peace in preference to the gay life
and lights of Beirut are obviously a listening audience. So
it was. We did nearly two hours that evening in the high
whitewashed hall which is the main sitting room of St
Andrew's House. They sang a good deal too and we did
lots of old Cockney numbers – 'Old Iron', 'Old Kent
Road', 'Henry VIII', and 'Lily of Laguna', etc. The piano,
once blanketed, was less harsh than we'd found it. Viola
gave 'em Chopin and Liszt and Moeran and finally, when
asked for, Warsaw. I love to watch them listening. I seem
always to be saying 'they were a particularly nice lot'; in
this case it is specially true. We had supper with them
and at my little table there were men from Scotland,
London, Birmingham and Leeds. Bromwich was a very
shy boy of twenty-two with a slight chip on his shoulder
about overseas service and things in general. He melted,
with food in him and some cheerful general conversation
all about him. He said he was wasting the best years of his
life. I told him I thought twenty-five onwards were the
best, and we had a six-handed discussion about it at our
table. The other ages ranged between twenty-five and
thirty and were with me. Bromwich asked for a second
excellent chocolate pudding and got it and said: 'Don't
take no notice of me. I'm bitter, see!' At which we all
laughed and he said he was glad he'd got *somethink* to
look forward to – being twenty-five. At the end of the
meal when he got up to go he gave a heavenly smile
which transformed his sulky young face into something
lots better, and said, 'Ta for your company and pleasant

conversation.' I was very flattered. Dr Shearer, who is a Rev, Presbyterian minister in Beirut, I think, took Sgt Sharpe and me down to a little promontory called Inspiration Point to watch the effect of the sunset on the mountains. The sun was setting behind us, over the invisible sea. The gathering clouds turned apricot, then lemon, and the mountains were all sorts of sweet-pea shades, so help me heaven. Standing out on that rocky jut of land with the ribbed vineyardy cultivation falling below us to the valley and little red-roofed houses pricking into light on the heights, with the clear sound of children calling borne two or three miles with no effort – all this was so lovely and so special and I longed for time, oh *time*, to really be there and live it properly. I'd heard about Syria from lots of people and its little pine tree surrounded villages and the wonder of the views and the freshness of the air. It's all true. I'd like to spend time here. I could even live here for ever within reach of Beirut. It's got a quality entirely lacking in Egypt or Palestine. Partly freedom from racial and political strife? And yet they have the French. I don't know what it is, but whatever it is it's enchanting and I feel happy here.

Tuesday, October 17th, 1944   Beirut

I write from the hairdressing salon at the Normandy. I am under the drier that is burning my ears but we are dining with Lady Spears and I must get dry in time. Ladies of the Levant with curious French accents come in to be *coiffée* – not washed or set but nicely combed for the evening. I've already seen two with glossy black hair tortured into elaborate upstanding pompadours with wide side wings and busy back roll curls come in to be re-dressed. They must be leading very arduous lives on their cork soles with their gold-set modern jewels and huge white bags and dark fingernails. One is gossiping to Lazare, the head man, and telling him how she had to spend the

whole day in 'bigoudi' in order to look *'belle pour ce soir'*.
She is highly excited about something. One good man-
sized kiss and her tower of black curls will be all over the
place. But maybe she's only out to lure and not indulge.
She is alarming in her calculation.

We woke up today to heavy rain and a wild thunder-
storm. It was also very cold up at St Andrew's. I'd slept
fairly well only; but dizzy by too much show last night
and couldn't sleep at first and then when I did I had a real
horror of a nightmare with faces coming in very close. I
woke with a cry but fortunately Viola only turned over
under her net and didn't wake. I slept better after that –
hated to get up this morning.

Wednesday, October 18th, 1944   Beirut

Yesterday and today we went to No. 43 General Hosp.,
scattered all over a steep hill behind Beirut. Col Jory and
Matron Davis. The latter is a funny little Yorkshire character with a mole on her nose and sandy hair. She is deaf
as a beetle, full of chat and giggle and I liked her. Col Jory
is a sort of Franchot Tone[1] type; quiet, with a twinkle in
his eye. New Zealand born but lived in England. We did
three ward shows yesterday. The first was on a biggish
scale and I had to yell. Or so I thought. I was wrong, for
they turned out to be good wards, acoustically, and it was
quite easy to hear. Lots of Londoners. And a pink-faced
Yorkshireman who asked for the 'Nightingale Sang in
Berkeley Square' for a 'special reason'. Anything to
oblige, so I did it. He said it had been 'smashing', so I was
rewarded. We lunched with matron and her assistant,
Miss Hepburn, and had huge bowls of sweet rice pudding, which I loved. The last show of the day was in an
eye ward and it was smallish, by mercy of heaven. Nicest

---

[1] Franchot Tone: handsome leading film actor, notably in *They Gave Him
A Gun, Four Graves to Cairo* and *Advise and Consent*.

one of the day and we hated to finish it. The patients sat on benches near the piano and we had some worthy choir work with 'em. Today's first show was in a large and long medical ward. About 100 present, some in bed, mostly not. They were waiting for us when we got there and we used the hospital piano which was nicer than ours. It was a glorious hour! They were with us, ahead of us, all round us; in perfect accord. They were noisy and gay in exactly the right places, pin silent when we wanted it, and it was one of the happiest shows I've ever done. Their willingness to sing was lovely. 'Rose of Tralee', with a surprising number of unexpected tenor parts, was a treat. They slowed it up to get full flavour of the juicy bits and when we did 'Nellie Dean', at the end, they fair roared. After this a very quiet intimate show in the officers' ward. Tame in contrast but nice too. Lady Spears came and Viola played some lovely romantic Rachmaninoff and I did all the monologues I don't usually do and we had a delicious fresh lemonade and egg sandwiches. Am a little alarmed to hear that advance publicity in Paiforce is in large letters and says all sorts of wonderful things about my 'goodness' in coming back there! Wonder who wrote it? It's all very well to Go Big once; it's mighty tricky to do it again. I do hope it will be all right. At least we've got a lot of new songs.

Thursday, October 19th, 1944   Damascus

The Orient Palace Hotel is LMS,[1] Manchester, the wrong end of the Edgware Road and a bit of modernistic Paris all in one. It is beyond words hideous. Take the elaborate electric light fittings in the hall and dining room for instance. Strange chrome discs belch into large white bubbles of opaque light. The whole thing is a total of

---

[1] London, Midland and Scottish Railway. Presumably Joyce means typical railway station and hotel architecture.

distorted wooden branches, *garni de* chrome and resulting in an alarming horror out of all proportion to the room it is decorating. The bareness and lack of grace in this hotel would be hard to beat. We drove over the mountains this morning and Viola and I made a discovery. We crossed a frontier and found, contrary to our certainty, we were *leaving* Lebanon and *entering* Syria! I would have bet quite a lot it was the other way round. Even the constant hint of the Lebanese flag in and about Beirut hadn't told us. I didn't like leaving Beirut at all. It looked so pleasing lying white and gracious with the sea to set it off as we looked back on it from about 5000 feet. The bus we now have is a lot easier on the spine than the Jerusalem one. It bounces, but in a slower and a less frequent rhythm. Sgt Sharpe is about six ft four tall, quiet, with a slight stammer, a small moustache, kind brown eyes, curling greyish brown hair and a gentle consideration for our well-being that is a comfort indeed. He has recently had a hellish three weeks with an ENSA company called 'The Barnstormers' who all hated each other and were very bad anyway so that his tour with them had been a time of misery. He says he finds us a nice change. Our driver is Lebanese with carefully combed ink-black curls and eyelashes of an exaggerated length. He drives with a flourish but considers us on the hairpin bends and does it all wearing a costume à la Derek Oldham in *The Desert Song*,[1] or whatever that epic was called. White, short-sleeved jacket, beige knickerbockers and bright brown riding boots.

Last night's show at an RE dump was a honey. In the sergeants' mess, very what Sharpe calls 'Al Fresco'. And so it was. I was specially touched to see on their notice board the little cutting and my picture from the *Eastern Times*, mounted on a pale blue sheet of paper with the word 'welcome' written across the bottom. We were in a

[1] Derek Oldham: hero of many a between-the-wars musical, played Pierre Birabeau in *The Desert Song* on tour. Setting: Foreign Legion.

tin hut, good for sound – apart from the insistent tom-tom beat of a generator outside. I asked if it was going to compete with me all through the show and a voice said: 'Won't be no light if it don't', so there it was. They are so used to it that it no longer sounds for them, but it took me some time to forget it. Captain Chamberlain and Sergeant Sharpe both came to the show and sat in the middle. It was not new to Sharpe but Chamberlain was fascinated and, like Bill Whittle all over again, came up to me at the end and said, 'I don't know how you do it' and 'You'll kill yourself at this rate.' But they don't understand. You get back as much as you put in at this game. Or jolly nearly anyway. There were sandwiches and tea and a fine party feeling; and then we sang some more. I don't know whether we are better this trip but the programme seems more rounded somehow. We never do it twice the same. This is a typical one:

'I'm going to see you today'
'Hand me Down'
'Nothing New to Tell You'.

Then as a break from music,
'Canteen',

followed by the three Silly Songs,
'Long Ago'
and 'All the Things You Are'
together.

Piano solo by V, probably two,
'Skylark',
'Surrey with the Fringe',
'I'll lend you my horse',
'Swinging on a Star'.

Then another break from music with
'American Mother',
'Someday',

after which a group of home songs for various localities:
'Loch Lomond',
'Blaydon Races',
'Ilkley Moor', 'Widdicombe Fair',
'Lassie from Lancashire',
'Rose of Tralee',
and they join us in them.

To round off the group I do
'London Pride'
and do 'Ernie' after it.

'Only a Working Man',
'Journey to a Star',
a film medley of 'Where and When',
'How about You',
'Lucky Star',
and the horrible 'Mairzy doats',
'Rose O'Day,'
'The Tattoo'd Lady',
'I'll be Around',
'Turn Back the Clock',
'Old Fashioned and Dearly Beloved',
some old Cockney ones – 'Lily of Laguna',
'All My Tomorrows',
'Nellie Dean'
with chorus, and 'Goodbye Gentlemen'.

As an encore I use 'Solitude'.

I've left out 'Infantry' and several other old film ones but
this is an average programme. We've got nearly as many
again tucked away for when necessary.

Saturday, October 21st, 1944   Baron Hotel, Aleppo

It took us all day yesterday to get here. We left Damascus
at 9.45 a.m. in the bus. Damascus lies in a green plain,

rich with trees and gardens. Soon we rose and crossed some foothills on a tortuous and bumpy road with mountains rising on either side of us, pinky sandy in colour with a strange hard, greyish crust at the top, looking like a crumbling wall built by a giant child. The roads out here *look* so good but ride so bad. The piano at the back got loose at one point and the front fell off. Then our dresses were jogged off their hangers and we had to reorganise everything. Beyond Homs the villages started to change from square houses to beehive-shaped ones. Some were whitewashed all over, some had an iced-cake effect by being whitewashed only at the top. The Bedouins started, just about here, to appear in yellow robes. All sorts of yellows, no two alike. It was quite enchanting. The earth was Titian red, darker than Devon, – almost a purply-auburn colour. An Arab shepherd wearing a long overdress, or robe or whatever it is, in dirty yellow wool, surrounded by black goats. Little boys of six or seven dressed in saffron, others in a washed-out olive. Yellow, canary, banana, egg, lemon, – all the yellows there are. At Hamar we stopped to have Turkish coffee and sat in a garden while the local lads stared at us through the railings. Rather dressy young men had shiny black braid on their yellow robes. A blond one, smoking a hookah, had a pale blue and white striped dress heavily embroidered in what looked like white Irish lace. Over this he wore a navy blue cape coat – sort of things old ladies in the Cromwell Road still totter to Boots in – with a lot of black braid on it. Hamar looks rich. Its great waterwheels turn slowly to fill the aqueduct which surely is the Roman one? It was a soft greyish day, like dusk when all the flowers suddenly glow as if they were lit from within. The colours in Hamar were exquisite. A huge man wearing a lilac shirt smocked like a baby's dress all across his huge chest. A boy in a pink and white striped robe. All those yellows. A vegetable vendor's window with little cucumbers and red peppers lacquered brilliantly beside beans and tomatoes in great mounds. En route we saw endless groups that cried out to be painted. In a Damascus doorway as we hurtled past in our gharry we saw a beautiful woman's hand, long and pale with lovely pale nails. As we got nearer she looked out at us and had a long mournful face, not beautiful but very drawable. Somewhere lately I saw a really lovely girl riding a donkey holding a big black umbrella over her baby as she rode up a mountain road in the heat of the sun. She looked down at it and was smiling as we passed her. It was an enchanting sight. Today in Aleppo I watched a boy arrange a large sheep across the back of his donkey before he rode home with it.

This hotel is all the Damascus one wasn't. It is clean, light, comfy, and has atmosphere. We dined early and I was in bed and asleep by ten. The owner is known as Coco or Koko Baron. He is an Armenian about thirty-seven, speaks perfect English and is extremely kind and considerate. Viola and I shared a room last night but today we are in separate rooms. She had a beastly night and was sick several times. I slept solidly through it! Poor thing, she was very wan and gentle this morning, so wisely decided not to go sightseeing with our host as arranged last night. I did, though. We skimmed it a bit, but even so I know that the suk is far gayer and more oriental than any we've seen before. Miles of it. We saw the shoe quarter – fascinating Kurdish boots in yellow leather frothing into a great blue silk tassel from a silver fastening. Red boots and slippers. Children's little royal blue boots with red soles. Alas, they are madly uncomfortable to wear for they have no shape at all. But they are extremely gay to see. There was a whole section devoted to robes and dresses and sheikh's capes. I longed for them all – the striped ones, the velvet ones, the gauze ones. And there were curious little waistcoats heavy with white embroidery on striped silk. In a silk loom shop we saw a boy in a tarbush weaving a broad pink corded silk. It will be turned into a sort of bolero jacket and it is for me! Mr Baron bought it for me. I made protesting noises but turned them into gratitude for it was a charming gesture on his part and I didn't want to seem snooty. How very difficult it is to receive gracefully. We drove to see the citadel, an incredible man-made mound topped with an impregnable fort. It is an Arab fort built on a Hittite site. It stands out for miles, they say. From here to an antique shop run by an Afghan with a British passport. He had nothing but junk really but the kindly Coco or Koko bought a couple of heavy silver slave bracelets for me and Viola and they are rather attractive in a barbaric way. He makes his gifts with a gentle grace that is irresistible. He is small, bald with a slight look of Mussolini. We lunched with him at his table. Mr Jabri, who is local king in Aleppo, came too. There was a bowl of rice, spiced with onion and raisins and truffles, topped with chicken wings and then, from a separate bowl, curry covered with steaming saffron. And now, too full to do anything else, I lie on my bed while the noises of Aleppo go on below my balcony.

Viola and I slept till after 4, and then dressed and wandered a bit. Europeans are rare birds here and we came in for much staring and comment. Finally we took a fiacre and lollopped slowly through the evening up to the citadel where we climbed, saw arrow slits, cannon balls, Roman baths, Arab baths, incredible cellars and wells. The citadel really is something rather special, merely by its size. The sun was setting while we were up on the top of it. Aleppo spread around us in soft greys and creams. Beyond that there were green orchards and then the bare red brown earth and in the far distance were mountains, deep bruise purply blue. The sky was light green with apricot streaks and grey wisp clouds. Arabs, donkeys, children, men in fezzes, women in black swathings all passed below us like animated toys. It was infinitely sad. But then that's a sad hour. I had no mail and there are reasons enough. The way I make for my bed as soon as I get anywhere near it is a horrible indication of the sort of Briton-gone-to-bits-in-the-East type I'd turn into in time if I stayed here. Tonight we do a show for the RAF quite nearby. I've only seen three English soldiers today in all Aleppo, so I daresay we have come to do isolated troops after all.

Sunday, October 22nd, 1944   Baron Hotel, Aleppo

My tum was gippy in the night and I slept almost not at all. In fact a beast of a night. It was pouring with rain when day finally dawned, I ran to and from my bathroom and felt low indeed. It's so humiliating, too. I sent Koko Baron a note at 8 explaining that I didn't think the Arab village outing was quite in my line and would he please explain to Mr Jabri how very disappointed I was. It's maddening.

Tuesday, October 24th, 1944   Baalbeck

Two small signal corps units last night at Homs and the night before. The first disguised in hive-huts. My background was a wall entirely covered in pin-up girls, mostly stark naked. Princess Elizabeth in pale blue looked rather overdressed among them. Cheese sandwiches and sweet tea to follow the performance and I was shown the works. Last night's group were housed in small tin huts. The one we used for the show was a round one with a tin roof. Someone had rigged up a light for the piano and a little tin-reflected spot for me. They were an attractive group, friendly and not too shy, and evidently got on well together.

Three Armenians from the nearby village came to the show – mother and two daughters of about sixteen and ten. They sat in a row on the front bench, dead still, with their hands folded in their laps, their wax white faces entirely without expression and their beetle black eyes on us both without blinking for the whole session. Afterwards in solemn procession and without smiles they

shook us by the hand and filed out in silence. I wonder
what they made of it all. I talked to an earnest Yorkshire-
men who had been on duty so hadn't come to the
concert. He was reading a *History of the Jews* by a Dean of
St Pauls called Milman[1] – a solid looking wedge of fine
print. He said he found it quite di-gestible and of interest. He wasn't interested in the history, really more in
the reasoning out. He liked to reason out. No, he never
read novels. Wireless now – anything on wireless, tech-
nical books and the like, those he read with interest.

Lunch yesterday with Colonel —. He is the life of the
party but he is also a useful sort of pirate for wartime. He
knows no fear, has no scruples, no queasiness and lots of
self-certainty and so much vitality that he must kill
whoever is with him for long. 'What were you doing in
the Sudan?' I asked him when he said he and his wife
lived there for ten years: 'Everybody', was the answer.
'General merchant.' And his witticism for siesta is 'study-
ing for the Staff college'. He told me that his marriage is
over; but his wife doesn't know it yet. He's found an
American girl he's known for twelve years and when she
is free of a maniac husband and he has broken from [his
wife] he will marry her. It seems mad to me for he is the
sort of wild man who can't conform to conventions –
marriage doesn't stand a chance on his terms. He's a
picturesque figure – if you like brigands. Weight about
sixteen stone, with a wild moustache and a smile that
shows good rather small teeth. He can drink anyone to a
standstill and remain lucid himself. Useful in his job as
security officer. Ruthlessness is always a little frightening
to me. But it has its place in wartime. Wonder what
happens to such pirates as he after the war? And to the
arch pirate of 'em all, Winston Churchill?[2]

[1] Henry Hart Milman: wrote his *History of the Jews* in 1830; became Dean
of St Paul's in 1849.
[2] The Prime Minister had just returned to London, via Cairo and
Naples, from the very successful Moscow conference with Stalin, and
Averell Harriman for the U.S.

Bedouin, or nomadic tribes of some sort, squatting in little groups all along road from Homs to Baalbeck, surrounded with their belongings, hens, babies, goats, rugs and cooking pots. No tents and the camels and donkeys roamed free. They must be in transit, one supposes. Much colder here. Clouds over the mountains made lovely effect. First sight of the six great pillars of the temple visible from quite a long way off. Exciting to see.

Thoughts in the bus. Worry over new sketch for Noël's revue next spring – if it comes off.[1] Can't get at it; no time; no ideas. Wish I could get it written – one, anyway. Toying with idea of Fern Brixton.[2] In tea shop? Music talk? Won't come yet. Idea for song? 'I close my eyes and there you are.' Arabs in buses travel very thickly – on roof, on ladder at the back. It looks pretty tough going.

Heard a fragment of news on the hotel radio this evening and they are still having constant alerts and buzz bombs in London – also in Belgium now. Wonder if Reggie is overseas yet? How Dick is? What Pa is doing, Gin and everyone? No mail, no mail. This life is all very well from an escapist point of view but one can't ever escape if you mind at all, and I do.

Our nice Sgt Sharpe has come in with some of his pals from the sgts club and I ought to go into the bar and be matey but I just can't cope tonight. This job takes a whole lot of one and this evening is a time-out period for me and I've got to keep it. Too sleepy to speak anyway. Viola has gone up to our room already. She went for a walk to see the moon on the ruins but I wasn't able to get beyond an armchair in the hall – a cup of tea with lemon in it. Tomorrow we will take it all in.

---

[1] *Sigh No More* opened at the Piccadilly on August 22nd, 1945; ran for 213 performances.
[2] Fern Brixton: a character Joyce created for a series of radio sketches for the BBC.

Wednesday, October 25th, 1944   Beirut

We did. H. V. Morton is right – there just isn't anything to
be said about it. The temples are so vast, so lovely, and
they must have been so ghastly in their hidden besti-
alities – even human sacrifices in the Phoenician temples,
under the Roman foundations. One's mind can't quite
take it all in – the enormous pillars, orange and gold in the
sun. There are only six of the forty-five original ones that
surrounded the temple to the Sun. An earthquake in 1875
or thereabouts shook down the others. One can now see
the lilac lebanons – and they are; rosy, mauve, lilac,
through these pillars. The sky today was deep blue. We
climbed, we stared up at ceilings carved with heads of
Diana, Mercury, Apollo, Mars and Venus; we sat in the
sun and looked with awe at the immense, great blocks of
stone all *rolled* there by slaves. It is hideous to think how
much agony went to make that place. Proportion, as
always in Roman designs, is quite perfect. I was curiously
moved by Baalbeck, not as it was, but as it is, with the
ghastliness erased by time and only the grace and devotion that went to fashion it left. We took all the morning
seeing it.

Viola and I have been wearing our 'glamorous' ENSA
uniforms for the journeys and they do save our clothes
but not our faces. Whenever I wear the uniform I get the
'hi-babe' looks, approach and conversation with the soldiers. I never meet with anything but extremely friendly
and easy manners when I'm in my ordinary clothes. Even
though we turn our ENSA tabs under they seem to recog-
nise the uniform and out here ENSA stands for the 'easy to
get' and I resent it deeply.

Thursday, October 26th, 1944   Hotel Hakim, Tripoli

Viola thinks we are staying in a brothel but the Town
Major who lunched with us told us quite seriously, 'Oh

no, *this* is the only one that isn't.' Our room is like the stage set for Tessa's death in the *Constant Nymph*.[1] Its barren horror cannot be exaggerated, and when I get on or off my satinwood bed it makes a resentful noise in bass tones. We have a saving grace – a balcony which gives on to the noisiest '*place*' in all Syria and that says a lot. There is a continual hooting of horns, cries of sellers of drinks, nuts, ice creams, fruits and bootlaces. Fat and idle Arabs are playing a form of backgammon below us in a small open-air café and the sound of their checkers being moved clicks up at us, two flights above them.

Last night an RE unit. Winged Pegasi, of gigantic size! In fact tops of all time, even surpassing that night at the Shaiba club; and the unit near Damascus last week, and all the other shows put together. That is from a *success* point of view. Subtle, no. But enjoying themselves and flexible to our wind, yes. Yes. They loved it all, sang their heads off and came back for more and more. We did about two hours for them, including a mass of requests like 'Dinah', 'Begin the Beguine', 'Stare Yes', and endless others. They clapped, they listened, they laughed and afterwards we were surrounded by eager faces, questioning us about all sorts of things. One said: 'Query: Does or does not Bing [Crosby] always use a mike?' I said I thought he usually did. 'Right,' he said. 'Query: Have you been out before?' Etc., etc. Viola had a cold and did not do a solo so when it was all over she hadn't played, and some of 'em asked her if she did Warsaw. She said she'd play it for those who'd like it if they'd come up to the other end of the hall with her. We were sandwiching the far end by this time. It made a heavenly picture to see her entirely surrounded by concentrating figures in KD, mostly with their sleeves rolled up, leaning all over the piano and listening and marvelling with enjoyment.

---

[1] *The Constant Nymph*, adapted for the stage by Basil Dean from Margaret Kennedy's novel; ran for 587 performances in London at the New (now Albery) Theatre. Tessa died at a pension in Brussels.

Friday, October 27th, 1944   Beirut again

We left here yesterday morning for Tripoli. Coast road. Enchanting fishing villages, blue sea, nets, sandy beaches, rocky shore, bananas, lazy people sitting in the shade of their white houses with the red roofs. The mountains rise comfortably from the coast and have gay little houses on them and green pines. Usually a monstrous convent or monastery on the peak. Then it was time for us to meet Sgt Sharpe and go out a few kilos to do a 4 o'clock show for some RES. Most of them had been on an all-night exercise and come straight into the largeish hut in which we gave the concert. About 150 of them I should think, hot and rather tired but wonderfully receptive.

At 8.30 this morning two simple majors from the RES, named Appleton and Leggett, took me in a jeep to see the Krak des Chevaliers. Viola just couldn't make it so I had to go off alone. We were followed by a second jeep containing a driver and spare, a primus and sandwiches. It's a good road till you get to within sixteen kilos, when it ceases to try and is hardly a track. Its surface is that of a miniature Giant's Causeway. Only a tenacious jeep could negotiate it, one would imagine; yet a convoy of eight three-tonners carrying holidaying Sikhs made it soon after we did. We'd passed them on the road and didn't for an instant suspect they were going our way and it was surprising, standing high on the great ramparts of Krak, to hear an increasing sound of strange voices and to find the immense courtyard suddenly filled with about a hundred beautiful dark Sikhs in HM's uniform of grey-blue shirts, KD shorts and their own exquisite turbans. They are, mostly, of great good looks. Rather effeminate, with large liquid eyes, and all those shining curling beards. They stood about, arm-in-arm, ran up the little spiral stairways inside the towers and emerging at the top with delighted amazement to see the panorama all around them. It is worth the journey to see Krak des

Chevaliers. It is like all the toy fairy-tale castles ever imagined, only more so, and ten times the size. I was attracted to it when I first read H. V. Morton, one lovely summer up at Nannau,[1] 1936. I found Krak thrilling for its position, commanding a view of fifty miles in all directions. The lake near Homs shone like a sliver of silver, there was a wide carpet of cultivation in the plain, spreading to the distant hills that were increased into mountains, and all along one view was that lovely Mediterranean, reduced to a mere strip from this distance. There are enormous halls, dungeons, a Gothic chapel, a row of what might be lavs, or might be places from which to drop that dear old boiling oil on the advancing enemy. The whole place could house a couple of thousand men and their animals, I should think. When you first see it from the Tripoli–Homs road ten miles away it looks like a toy; pale yellowy pink on a brown hill. As you get nearer it grows in majesty and when you finally shake your way up the final steep bend it stands above you as Windsor Castle stands over the town outside it. There was no guide, only a disinterested Arab in a small white skull cap and dirty Turkish trousers who said 'Good' to everything and took our piastres and sold us an aerial view of the castle. The thing that strikes me most about all the places we've seen out here – Baalbeck, Krak, the citadel at Aleppo, etc. – is the philosophical, long view taken by the men who first thought them up. There wasn't a chance for them to see the fulfilment of the early dream. It took 300 years to complete Baalbeck. Such unselfishness is beyond my understanding. I wouldn't want to start anything I couldn't see finished. Not a worthy sentiment but my own. When we climbed down from Krak the drivers of our pilot jeep had done a 'brew up' and tea was ready. Hot and sweet and in mugs. Tongue sandwiches, too, wrapped in damp khaki hand-

---

[1] Nannau in Dolgelly, North Wales, was a house regularly rented by Colonel Arthur Grenfell (Reggie's father) and Hilda, Reggie's stepmother, for their holidays. Joyce was a frequent visitor with Reggie.

kerchiefs. Very comforting. Then down that rocky incline
and so to Tripoli.

Sunday, October 29th, 1944   Oumayad Hotel, Damascus

We saw an hour of 'The Fol-de-rols' in the open-air
theatre. They are very good. Rex Newman's own pet
pigeon and well rehearsed, dressed and produced. We
loved it and roared at the comedian who is a really funny
little man not, for a change, the usual ENSA copy in-the-
style-of . . . The men loved it. I tried to imagine how it
must feel at the end of a five-day trip in a three-ton lorry
from Paiforce to sit in the moonlight by the sea and look at
an attractive show. That is what it must be for most of
them. We didn't want to leave but had our own RASC
Petrol Company show to do at 8.30.

A long morning packing, letters, and getting dressed
for lunch *chez* Sursocks. It was sweaty work; incredibly
hot. We took a taxi to Villa Alfred Sursock to lunch with
Donna Maria Sursock, a couple of elderly Sursock sisters-
in-law and her daughter Yvonne, a pretty little piece of
twenty-two. I'm a bit vague about them all but gather
they are the richest Lebanesers in the world; *the* first
family. Their villa is of an opulence I didn't believe. You
could translate it into rich Jewish St John's Wood or
Kathleen Norris's descriptions of Santa Barbara high
society. A vast white marble hall with marble screens
making a sort of inner hall. Carved like mad. Oriental
rugs, Persian, I suppose. A cheery but rich floral gerbe
with dark red hothouse horrors and spear-straight tuber
roses. A set of ten high-backed chairs all covered in
Damascus brocade, loaded with gold and silver thread
and now selling at £6 sterling the yard. Iron-work
abounded; also Italian art. An olde volume on a Bible
stand stood open at an engraving. It was cool, and, of its
sort, *good* if ugly. The sea was visible from the great
windows; a row of cypresses kept the utilitarian view of

the harbour from sensitive eyes. Very unreal, the whole thing. Three menservants in crocheted gloves doing a tricky sort of waiting on the table in which they removed the used plate and substituted a clean one all with the greatest difficulty and in one movement. Far too much food; special dishes for the two old ladies and slops for Yvonne who has just had her tonsils out. We spoke in French. Donna Maria's was with an Italian accent, the old sisters-in-laws in thick Arabesque ones, and Yvonne well. We spoke of the war, of food in England. And there was talk of the hard life one must lead in the war. Their look of suffering was well disguised. The whole set-up was a little horrifying in its richness.

There was an English nurse at lunch, been with Yvonne for twenty years. A nice simple nanny really, called 'Miss' and speaking French with a Mill Hill accent to add to the confusion. One of the old women accompanied me back to the hotel afterwards in a big Sursock car and all the way she and I carried on a wonderful conversation about Paris dressmakers in which I gave, I hope, the impression of being very particular, colossally rich and fussy about Molyneux and Lanvin and Schiaparelli, and to substantiate my liberal flow of information about it all I had the evidence of my little red jacket, given me by Nancy Tree[1] about four years ago and carrying a genuine Schiaparelli label! By not catching Viola's eye I was able to keep it up and we parted from the old wreck with her regarding me with a new respect, almost as an equal. Wonder what will happen to Yvonne? She is pretty and attractive and worth millions. One can't see her weathering English climes but we hear that it is the ambition of all Levantines to marry with an Englishman.

[1] Nancy Tree: Joyce's cousin; daughter of her mother's eldest sister.

Tuesday, October 31st, 1944   British Embassy, Baghdad

It is very nice indeed to be in Baghdad again. We flew up from Damascus yesterday and are staying at the Embassy with HE and Lady Cornwallis.[1] Last looks at lovely Beirut as we rose higher and higher over the mountain and she kept appearing, smaller and smaller, as we climbed and she came into view at intervals. Not even cool on the top that day. It was too hot at sea-level. Very sticky. Coming down on the other side Viola, who suddenly felt better after her thick cold, went to the piano and played it at the back of the bus for nearly an hour, sitting on a suitcase. Whenever we went into second gear she was almost inaudible, but now and again I heard bits of Bach and some nursery rhymes with Tunnard arrangements (lovely) and some Handel. Approaching Damascus among the mulberries it was lovely to have an accompaniment by Rachmaninoff.

I dined with Bryan Guinness[2] at the Orient Palace, following drinks with Col Frank Stirling and a Captain Porter. Bryan grows fat, a little vague and odd but I'm gently pleased to see him again. He wished to go dancing. Felt far from any such desire myself but I went and we dipped in a tango or two and had a couple of energetic waltzes all among the knee-high Levantines in their zoot suits (male) and cork soles (female). Many French officers in a variety of indecipherable uniforms. Damascus lovely under a big moon. Woken early next morning by the call to prayer from three minarets, lit with electric bulbs but looking entrancing. Early breakfast, goodbyes, and off in the Lodestar to Baghdad.

A royal welcome – a press photographer (Army), a Sgt for the bags, and Lt Raitz who is in Bill Whittle's place.

---

[1] Sir Kinahan Cornwallis: career diplomat who specialised in the Middle East, including spells in Sudan, Egypt and Iraq.
[2] Son of Lord Moyne, who was assassinated in Cairo five weeks later. Bryan Guinness, who became second Baron, doubled as a director of the family brewery and as an author.

We emerged from the plane carrying coats and cases and I had Aunt Pauline's fur boots. We were snapped at all angles and made much of. Ego soared at once. It was lovely to see Baghdad again under the plane. The Tigris is a noble stream and the town clings narrowly to its banks in a profusion of pale honey coloured buildings. Penny drove us to the Embassy and Lady Cornwallis made us feel so welcome at once. I've got a huge room giving on to the river, private bathroom and roses everywhere. A smiling slave whose English seems limited to a cordial 'Berry well' swept away all dirty clothes for dhobying and helped me unpack. Lunch on the terrace in the shade. It is still hot here. Ninety in the shade. Thank God we are to have three clear days off.

Morning ENSA office. Change money. See Sgt Holding. Call on Joan Wilson, still at YWCA. Meet Sheikh from silver suk who is going to make a cig. case for Viola from me for Xmas. Later Lt Raitz came to Embassy to show me map and our planned itinerary. It looks terrifying but I hope we can cope. All up in Iran this time. Sometimes two shows a day and 100 miles to travel.

November 1944

Reggie's and Gin's birthdays. Wonder where they are?

Yesterday at 4.30 Queen Ali,[1] her daughter the present Queen, and the Regent's two youngest sisters all came to tea at the Embassy. They are strictly in purdah and arrived veiled; the chancery, that opens on to the riverside terrace, was barred for the afternoon and HE kept out of his office. We curtsied all around. The older Queen, about sixty? was in a black silk dress and wore her veil unbecomingly thrown over her head, low on the brow and behind the ears, and sat on a sofa in enforced silence knowing no English – not even joining in when Arabic was spoken. Her little legs were slightly bowed in their sheer sunburn stockings. The Queen was in a bottle-green and white print with a scalloped crêpe de Chine collar of great dullness but her face is enchanting. No make-up. A pity, for she needs the accent of lipstick to balance the importance of her lovely dark eyes in a very pale face. She looked amusing. Understands English but won't speak it. Her eyes had the entirely unsophisticated look of a little girl's. I talked to one Princess about being in purdah – 'veiled' she called it. I said that perhaps things would change for them someday. 'Not before I am old,' she said, not with passion but sadly. I asked her what she

[1] Queen Ali: widow of Ali, formerly King of the Hejaz. Their son, Emir Abd al-Ilah, was Regent of Iraq until his nephew, Feisal, came of age.

did all day. 'Garden,' she said, and I said it was fun when it wasn't too hot and what did she grow? 'Oh, not *do* garden, sit in the garden,' she explained. 'If we had not wireless and the films our life would be very sad.' Indeed, yes. She and her young sister are about twenty-two and twenty, attractive with lovely figures and neat feet and hands. They are destined to marry one of their already inbred cousins, or not at all. One of their aunts ran away with an Italian waiter in Sicily and was not only cut off for ever by the family but a law was actually passed proving she no longer existed. Later the waiter tired of her – she had no 'dot'. No appeal from her was heard at all and heaven knows what has happened to her. So it takes a lot of thinking before it would be wise for one of them to cut a dash out of the royal circle. We talked in English. They had an English nurse and a governess. Later I sang three songs, including 'Yours' by request of a princess.

Piano situation looks black for Viola. She is in a strange fey mood and speaking in faint voice of ghostly tonelessness. Alec Waugh[1] for dinner. Nicer than Evelyn; kinder too, I'd say. The moon is full and we dined on the terrace by the Tigris by its clear light. HE sent for a coat afterwards but I found it just deliciously right. Wrote to Noël tonight because if he isn't going to do the revue early in the year I'm going to stay out longer. Nothing to go home for.

Friday, November 3rd, 1944   British Embassy, Baghdad

Show out at the hospital at 5. Several patients we'd met all over the Command last time. Viola's piano was beyond anything. No form of pedal so it went on ringing

---

[1] Alec Waugh: novelist; elder brother of Evelyn and currently serving with Paiforce. As a novelist, he made a sensational début, aged 19, with *The Loom of Youth*.

continually and was loud anyway. However, it was a success. Lady Cornwallis, Eliz. and Madeleine all in their black on account of the late Princess Beatrice,[1] came and sat at the back. After drinks in the officers' mess, Penny took us back to White Lodge to wait a bit before going on to do twenty minutes at the Semiramis where welfare, under Brig Blight, assisted by Captain Drain (fragrant names), were entertaining the locals who help them look after troops in this Command. They had been given drinks and a propaganda film before I did my bit so I kept it brief and the mini-piano we had this time was a slight step up over the other. The audience was a mixture of English residents and Iraqi ladies who help. There were some astounding middle-aged women in beadwork and beaten jewelry. But they laughed and were easy, for which I thank them. While I was waiting at White Lodge Penny turned on the radio and we heard a recording of Noël singing 'London Pride'. I think I do it much better than he does! I now work it up into a full-sized piece, speaking the middle bit and fair roaring the final line about 'every blitz her resistance toughening'. It goes a treat.

Incidental items. The Embassy cook calls Bubble and Squeak 'Babylon Quick'.

Saturday, November 4th, 1944   Habbaniya, RAF Camp

Last night was one of those nights that start by adding ten years to one's growth and then subtracting twenty. This is a huge, vast, enormous impersonal camp of un-equalled luxe in the middle of the desert. It cost many millions in about 1935 and was built on the sand near the Euphrates and its own lake Habbaniya to be a very important air base. I believe Aunt N. asked a lot of silly

[1] Princess Beatrice: Queen Victoria's youngest child; born 1857, died 1944.

and awkward questions about spending public money
on it. Anyway it was spent, lavishly, and the result is
very splendid and rather unreal. From the air its lay-out is
fascinating, like a child's model. Must have been great
fun for the man who planned it. It's got everything –
pools, polo, football, tennis, a huge movie house, clubs
galore, a first-class hospital under a pet of a plump
matron called Miss Polus, bungalow quarters for everyone with bathrooms to every room, trees, gardens, –
everything. And in 1935 it was just twelve square miles of
dust. The hand of man . . . We flew up yesterday from
Baghdad in a Proctor with an unshaven pilot called
Hennel. Canadian. The station commander met us and
took us for a tour of the camp and the civil cantonment
that's grown up here. Native bakery was rather fun and
very skilled. The baker took a lump of dough in one
hand, threw it on to a plate-sized but rounded mould and
then flung it into an oven where it adhered to the roof till
cooked and then it was removed by tongs. His rhythm
was perfect. The thing about the RAF is that it is first class
in its work but not in its personnel. A general and
dangerous statement but there is a lot of bounding done
in the RAF and I do dislike its slickness and all that gen,
prang, wizard, cue slang stuff.

. . . We did a quiet and gentle little show in the
occupational therapy room at the hospital. Not laid on
properly. So easy to have organised it in a ward as I'd
asked, but too much trouble. These uneventful off-the-
map places are far less on their toes than the ones near the
war; which is, I suppose, natural. But with all the time
they have and the few events to disturb it one would have
thought that someone might have had the imagination
and energy to organise the show where it would do most
good. But no. However, a pleasant hour went by. They
were very shy and silent but I know now when they are
happy even when they take pains to hide everything.
Afterwards a pretty little Aberdonian sister called Caird
took us around the wards and we found a very sweet

man who remembered us with affection from that good RAF show we did in Basra last April. 'We still talk about it,' he said. We glowed.

Viola from the bathroom where she had gone into a matutinal trance, called out to me in gloating tones: 'Isn't it wonderful – we have had five days of lavatories we could *sit* on.'

From the men's ward to the officers'. Extraordinary to see those lovely buildings and that equipment, bowls of zinnias and roses, and to know that a few hundred yards away is wilderness and nothing. Did a few songs at sisters' tea party with Viola at a mini-piano of bizarre appearance and tone. Then to flop in our room for an hour or two before the third show. Tussle with a flea, which I saw and pounced on three distinct times. Flea won. I bear many a scar. We were warned that the audience at Hab. is very blasé – we might have a full house of 1300 or only a few hundred. There was to be a mike and the piano was a grand. In deep gloom we prepared for the evening. I'd left all my stage make-up in Baghdad but there was a stump of eyebrow crayon in my hairpin box and by overdoing the rouge I looked odd but not too deathly in the piercing whiteness of those merciless spots – there were three. The mike was a good pick-up one, the audience liked what they got, my palms dried up and we had a wonderful hour. It was mighty frightening at first and Viola said afterwards that I sounded *so* well-bred and careful in my first fear but once launched I relaxed! After the show we were bidden to feed at the AHQ mess but they were showing Bette Davis in *Watch on the Rhine*[1] to finish the evening programme and we went up into the circle to see a bit of it first. Paul Lukas was charming but his great restraint went to lengths of immobility and dreariness while Miss D. was

---

[1] *Watch on the Rhine* by Lillian Hellman first produced in London at the Aldwych in 1942; the Warner Brothers film, with script by Dashiell Hammett, was released in 1943. It won Academy awards.

to be seen Acting in Capitals, which is a pity and not worthy of her. We left halfway through. Eggs and bacon with three nice middle-aged group captains, demanding no sparkle. Very restful. For a de luxe set-up our guest room lacked the finishing touches in that the knobs of light switches had gone so it hurt to turn 'em on. The bath plug had lost both its chain and the loop to which the chain would hook if there had been a chain, with the result that once the plug was in no power but will, sacrifice of fingernails, and finally a hairpin, could get it out to let the water run away. Petty complaints but ones that could be remedied, but Hab. is so big and so impersonal that it's never anyone's job as far as one could see. Easier to pass the buck.

Saturday, November 4th, 1944. Later Station Hotel, Mosul

Two Proctors were laid on to bring us here today. We played tonight in an ex-hangar, echoey for sound and this afternoon when we went to see it for Viola to try the piano, tenanted by a thousand choral sparrows. I trust sleep will be on them tonight. We are at the Station Hotel. Very clean, comfortable.

Next day: I wasn't a bit good last night. Not specially tired either. But the mere thought of having, physically, to do an hour or more suddenly assailed me in the first few minutes and it was then sheer hard work all the way. My own fault, I expect. Couldn't quite get through. They were a nice lot, too. Saw a man look at his watch and morale went down like a lead weight! How frail one is.

Taps in Iraq are unaccountable. In this hotel the hot is the cold and the cold is the hot. In Hab. both bath taps were marked cold but scalding water poured from one and none at all from the other.

Sunday, November 5th, 1944 Back at the Embassy,
Baghdad

Lovely flight this morning. Paul Hennel and I flew in the
little camouflaged Proctor and Viola, Baron and a sgt
were in the silver job. It was a cloudy day but cool, no
bumps. We cruised low at 300 feet and saw Arab village
life laid at our feet like a toy model. Chickens were scared
by our noise and flustered in courtyards, women looked
up from their labours. Children waved. An occasional
scarlet dress glowed among the mud huts and heaps of
yellow corn. Crossing a shallow bit of the river I saw a
sheikh fording it on a white horse, the trail he made in the
water arrowing many yards behind him. Hennel said,
'Lucky for him you're in here or I'd swoop down and
chase him.' I registered suitable horror. We saw wild
duck, flights of them, and clouds of sand partridge (?).
Low over Samaria today again. It isn't in the least 3000 BC;
a mere 600 AD!

Heavenly to be back here again. I quickly stepped out
of all my clothes and handed them to the smiling Jacob to
have them ready for our departure in the morning.
Which means I start off all clean.

Mail from Gin and Reggie. William Douglas-Home has
been cashiered and got twelve months' hard for dis-
obeying orders at Havre. What a ninny he is.[1] Gin hasn't
been well but is better.

Wednesday, November 8th, 1944 British Vice-Consulate,
Hammadan

To clarify our movements in the past three days I'm going
to tabulate them briefly. Just to see what we have done.

---

[1] William Douglas-Home: playwright, brother of Lord Home (Prime
Minister, 1963–4), objected to his superiors' decision to assault the port
of Le Havre without considering the fate of the French inhabitants. He
used the experience in his play *Now Barabbas*.

Monday.   9 a.m. Baghdad from Khanaquin.
           117 CGH 3 08 clock, show in ward.
           Khanaquin (NAAFI) 280 BCR's.
           Sleep OC Co's guest house.

Tuesday.   Leave Khanaquin 9 a.m. for Kermanshah.
           Call at CMP post at border.
           Call at CMP post foot of the Paitak, collect the
              6 men and all go up to CMP post top of
              Paitak.
           Show and lunch.
           On to Kermanshah in downpour.
           64 CGH 5 p.m. Ward show.
           9.15 BOR's social in Oil Coy's club room.
           Stay Mrs Sinclair, asst manager's wife.

Wednesday.   Leave Kermanshah 10 for Hammadan.
           Show and lunch on top Shah Pass, CMP post.
           Hammadan. Show 8 p.m.
           Stay Sq/Ldr D'Aeth, Vice-consulate.

I'm completely muddled in my mind about the past three days. All I know is that where I was hot I am now frozen. I lie on a camp bed in a bare room with two rugs and my coat over me and a sweater and bedsocks on under my dressing gown. The bathroom with its own self-contained log stove is the only warm place in the house. We are 6800 feet up. It was muggy and warm when we left Baghdad. Cooler, just at Khanaquin. Yesterday we ran into wild wind and rain up on the Paitak and it was suddenly winter. Aunt Pauline's fur boots which have been a burden for the past six weeks are suddenly my greatest joy.

General impressions of Persia: it is a far vaster country than I had imagined, but when it isn't being dramatically huge with valleys and fierce mountains it is of a delicacy that compares to its own lovely miniatures.

The colour of little poplar spinneys made me cry out. Sheer delight in every golden greenery-yallery leaf pennanting in the wind. They glowed for miles across the plain. Pale blue smoke curled up among dark Bedouin tents and a dying weed stained whole miles a brilliant orange. There was snow on the top of the higher mountains. My chief memory of today's sights was the little poplar groves – so light, so foursquare, so all I'd hoped to find in Persia.

Lt Col Warburton who is head policeman in these parts had sent me a letter with CMP posts listed in it so that we could call in on them all the way to Tehran. We picked up another escort in Khanaquin, Captain Connel and a CMP in a jeep who led us to the first post, at the border. We got out and said how d'y do's but it was only 9.30 a.m. and too early for a show; besides, this post is only ten miles from Khanaquin and gets in to shows. The next one was at the foot of the Paitak. A handful of men, mostly Londoners. Captain Connel told them to get into their jeep and ride up to the top of the pass where there was another, bigger post, and we'd unload our piano and give them a show. It began to rain when we got there but we jumped the first puddles and went into the hut they sleep and eat in. Neat as a pin, each little locker covered with snaps from home. A good radio, quite a readable selection of books. They weren't a bit shy – more Cockney! There were about fifteen altogether, including some signallers and a maintenance man or two. I did about forty mins. The rain hurtled against the tall windows, the gale blew the dead leaves over the door – used to thatch it for coolth – and we were far better off inside than out. Then mugs of hot, sweet tea and some sandwiches brought with us. Viola played Warsaw afterwards, and I had to do 'Yours', both requests. At Mosul on Saturday, an airman, due home by Christmas, told me he was going to marry a girl called Mabel in Kent and that they were going to have Warsaw[1] at the wedding. He was, he said,

[1] Richard Addinsell's 'Warsaw Concerto' (his best-known composition) from the 1940 film *Dangerous Moonlight*, directed by Brian Desmond Hurst, with Anton Walbrook and Sally Gray.

crackers about it. Seen the picture four times just for the tune. That's just one of a dozen incidents, all relating to the magic the piece has over the boys.

Cosy little show No. 64 CGH at 5. No time to change, we got straight out of the car, bit muddy and very stiff, had tea in the sisters' mess with the Col and a couple of Indian doctors and then had a heavenly hour in a ward. Only about fifteen patients, a few orderlies, sisters, etc. The matron turned out to be Miss Scrutton who was assist. to Miss Percy in Malta when we were there in March. She was in bed with a chill yesterday but we had a reunion in her tiny mud-built room. The sister who looked after us was the pretty little plump one we had liked at Khana-quin last April. Now married to an oil man and called Mrs Jones. It's extraordinary how the patterns of our last trip keep merging into this.

Mrs and Mr Sinclair, Jean and John, welcomed us in out of the rain about 6. I was about ready to drop and she was wonderfully quick on the uptake and within twenty minutes I was on my bed while Viola nobly did the social work over sherry and a cigarette. We dined with the Sinclairs about 8.30. Both from Paisley, so kind, so competent, so undeterred by the immense mountains outside their neat little suburban compound. Delicious dinner. Capt Moss, dizzy with desire to give everyone a good time, had laid on a dance at the oil company's club room with a wet canteen[1] going great guns and a pana-trope deafening us all with old dance tunes and into this mixture I was expected to do my stuff. The company sat around the edge of the room, the ghastly green-painted upright was at the far end, a sofa full of giggling Persian girls kept up a solid stream of conversation in full tones and the bar went on gaily. We did our best and invited people to come in closer, but it was a waste of effort really – so uncomfy, so wrongly lit, so like a cabaret act. However, not knowing that it could be better than it was

[1] One serving non-alcoholic drinks.

they appeared to enjoy it. Later there was more dancing and Viola and I were whirled off our feet. Endless Excuse Me dances in which one turned three times in the arms of a small corporal, changed to a sgt, a couple of CMPs and a little Scots oil man who danced like thistledown as do so many fat men. Each time he took me we were separated by a Geordie with two stripes and determination. The last time he said 'It do give me pleasure to do down a Jock', and off we spun in uncertain arcs.

Friday, November 10th, 1944   With Gen and Mrs Fraser, Tehran

Yesterday was eternal. Carpet factory with Town Major Woolley. Sweated labour. Little creatures of six and seven, cross-legged on boards hung below the looms, knotting away with little henna'd hands. Earnings average less than a shilling a day. The factory sounding like a bird cage. Mothers and children in rows, knotting away, never, apparently, looking at the pattern enlarged above them, slashing accurately with knives at the fluffy ends. Chattering and coughing and squealing. But doing the job. The women wear coloured cotton abbas and are only very moderately veiled. Flat faces, wide mouths, a little coarse but [Augustus] John and [Jacob] Epstein would enjoy them. The Persian manager, all gold teeth and careful English, told us magnanimously that if a woman cut her finger she was put iodine on at once. When Arthur Smith, the general, went round, he asked what welfare facilities the factory had – tea interval? insurances? canteen? The management were horrified at such pamperings. The carpets were mostly hideous. Only the traditional design lovely. All the colours good. Soft dark reds and greens with the half-crown design in them nicest. On, on, on, all morning. Huge country – plains – rounded hills streaked all colours. V. Sackville-West in *Passenger to Tehran* noticed it too. Coppery green patches, wine red streaks, yellow rocks, pink ones. A few camels when we'd dropped down, wearing dark brown for the winter. At Hammadan we were 6800 feet up. I felt a bit panty. But the air was lovely. Lunch Takistan. The mess very gay with a wide brick fireplace roaring with logs. Pink curtains, pretty pin-up girls and a little wooden bar. Old car seats for sofas. Delicious lunch all arranged with an eye to looks as well as tastes. Plates of raisins and almonds, sliced tomatoes topped with hard-boiled eggs, sardines, cheese, spam and Hotsweettea. We sang for half an hour and they were shy to start with and gazed rigidly at the floor. But by and by they risked a look and we ended very good friends. Warm handshakes and thanks for coming made us glad, as usual, we'd come. The Russians start at Takistan. Saw a girl in khaki looking very practical and quite without allure at the barrier. We hadn't gone more than five miles after lunch when the car faltered, hiccuped and gave up. 'Itsa ploogs,' said Wetheral in Yorkshire. There was a lot of unscrewing, blowing down things, screwing up and we tried again. No good. 'Itsa distributor,' said Wetheral. We crawled to the big US camp at Khasin. Their engineers were put on it. We were taken to the very highly decorated officers' mess by the Lieut. Slightly shaken by décor in the bar – life-size nudes in rich umber tones and pin-up girl lines. Subtlety was not the keynote. A naked bosom seen head on looks very like a target. The gals on the bar wall at Khasin are a suntanned lot in the very pink of condition. Chinese chequers, big log fire, tea and chocolate cake. Then the gloomy news that our car wasn't going to be reliable because something was definitely in three pieces and no spare parts in the camp. More Chinese chequers. A gangling lieut with a roaming cast in one brown eye came from Richmond; name of Southall. He guessed I must be kin to the Langhorne his uncle used to go with – the one who gets in all the papers for being in Parliament?[1] And

[1] Lady Astor.

kin to the one that married the painter who did the
Gibson girls?[1] I confessed I was. A command car was laid
on for us and at 7.15 in darkest night, Viola and I,
swathed in rugs and luggage and perched on the dignified rampart of a command car, set off for Tehran, three
hours' journey over the worst road in Persia. Staff-Sgt
Patterson, much concerned for our well being in front
with the driver from Michigan. Poor Wetheral had
started earlier in our staff car-station wagon travelling at
twenty m.p.h. with a CMP at his side ready with a tommy
gun. Captain Maurice followed us in his jeep alone. We
passed Wetheral; we lurched at fifty m.p.h. down what
seemed to be a completely straight road.

We drove up to Mrs Fraser's at 10 p.m. on the dot. She
and the General were silhouetted against the light of their
open door. Impression of big trees as we approached;
quiet. We were welcomed in and fed and warmed. The
house is simple with white walls and pale covers and
curtains. Books, old *Times*es, some Persian pictures on
the mantel-piece among photographs of two attractive
little grandsons. A yellow pottery vase filled with the
ghost of some large sort of parsley – now a pale gold.
Ovaltine, a hot bath in a strange tub filled from a tank
over a small stove, and bed. Mail from home! I slept very
well and woke to sun filtering into my little white room
through cream-coloured curtains, and the sound of
rooks. A Persian maid with far too many false teeth
smiled at me a little later and breakfast arrived. The
garden lies outside my room – very tall plane trees with
clean trunks, marigoldish flowers (candytuft?) and lawn.
A fountain. It is cool and clear and lovely. I'm dreadfully
tired, which is a bore. Captain Warren of ENSA came to
see me in bed this morning to go over the schedule. It

[1] Irene Langhorne (1873–1956): perhaps the most beautiful of the
Langhorne sisters, married the artist Charles Dana Gibson who im-
mortalised her in his celebrated 'Gibson Girl' illustrations. Nancy
Langhorne, later to marry Waldorf Astor, was the next sister, followed
by Nora Langhorne, Joyce's mother.

seems it's not practical as at present. Looks as if we may have to reorganise a bit and postpone departure for India for a week?

General and Mrs Fraser both darlings. She is practical and doesn't sit still for a minute. An apple face with bright eyes. Dressed today in a series of brown checks – jersey, jacket, skirt – all different, and on her feet some local sort of tennis shoes brightened up with woolwork flowers. She is mothering us like anything and I'm ironing out under it. He is soldierly with a sensitive mouth. We are to lunch with some Persians up the mountain.

Monday, November 13th, 1944   Isfahan

We left Tehran yesterday at 7 – little convoy of three. Only we weren't three till Qum, for the police car failed to start and had to catch us up later. Afterwards we were led by the police jeep with Captain Maurice at the wheel and his policeman, with gun and dog, beside him. Then the staff station wagon, painted desert yellow, with Driver Wetheral at t'wheel and Staff-Sgt Patterson beside him. Viola and I on the two comfy bucket seats and then the two suitcases, two canvas bags, our music cases, coats, and over all, the linen cover containing some of our dresses, laid flat on the top. The third car in our convoy is a three-ton lorry carrying a mini-piano. It is driven by a humorous Indian in goggles and a knitted cap and yesterday he was accompanied by a missionary called Miss Smart who wished to get back to her mission here in Isfahan. Yesterday was exceedingly long, dusty and faintly adventurous. Lunch with the few isolated boys at Qum, preceded by a show in their mess. Their isolation has knit them close and they were in good form. We'd been expected the night before (they were warned in time) so they'd laid on a party. Which means beer was plentiful and song resounded in their little green-walled mess. I was quietly grateful we'd missed it. I'm not much good, islanded in sobriety, while merriment goes on in a beery sea around me. They were a very good crowd. Qum provided a wonderful lunch – chicken, roast potatoes, peas, carrots; coffee; fruit salad. And all in giant helpings. There were four tables, and Viola, Miss Smart and I sat at different ones. I had an RC Cockney taxi-driver opposite me, a very young RAF meteorological boy whose father works in Shropshire on my left, and on my right a specially nice Geordie with a squint. There was a Yorkshireman with us with a poker face and a fine wit. I enjoyed it all.

Miss Smart rolled herself up in a rug and perched up beside the Indian, smiling behind the glasses, with her rust felt hat tied under the chin with a floral chiffon hankie. We had 175 miles to do. Exciting, untouched country. The hills streaked with colours – chemicals? Green, dark green, red, silver. No foliage, just Disney fantasia shapes sprayed with colour. Snow on the far-off mountains. All the way to Qum we were followed by the view of Demarand looking taller and whiter as we went. She is over 1800 feet and eternally snowed. Along the road somewhere our police jeep went wrong. There was advice and consultations and dear Driver Wetheral stood up on the wind while he coped. Earlier a coil or a lead or something had got loose in our Ford. He fixed both with dexterity and said in his thickest Yorks: 'Sorry to have kep' you wehtin', Miss.' It got dark. We'd eaten all Mrs Fraser's home-made sausage rolls and some marmite sandwiches. The jeep paused for an electrical readjustment and we were off on the last lap, twenty miles to go, over a ribbed road of great horror at about forty, when our back left wheel came off, rolled past us into the night, and we skidded, hideously, out of control, and came to rest in a ditch. No one was hurt. But we were all a little extra alive. The jeep hadn't noticed us at first but when they saw we weren't behind they came hurrying back. The first thing to be done was to find the rolling wheel. Wetheral got in the jeep and turned in wide circles with its searchlight trained over the flat desert. Camel thorn lit up like that casts misleading shadows and we kept thinking we'd seen the wheel. It was discovered 100 yards or more on the *right* side of the road. Must have crossed in front of us. All the contents of the car were transferred to the truck where Viola and I joined Miss Smart. Wetheral and the CMP were left with rations, a tommy gun and enough cigarettes, to guard the Ford. We shook on into Isfahan, our wild Indian driver trying to do just what the leading jeep did, which was silly for one three-tonner took up rather more space. We hit a hand-cart a wallop and I heard falling wood but on we went. He'd been told to follow the jeep so follow he did. No amount of cries from us three perched-up women in the back had the slightest effect. I wonder what will happen. The presence of a large yellow army lorry carrying a Union Jack on its paint isn't all that common in Isfahan. Perhaps the handcart owner will report it? We went on to the hotel – the Irantour – where a number of waiters and a man in knickerbockers helped us in. They'd had a signal and were expecting us. It is a surprising hotel – very clean, wonderful beds, space, blue tiles, good food. But it has very Eastern lavs and as my lav-life is of *great* importance to me, I'm affected here by having to do all from a stand or crouch position. There are two slightly raised little platforms for the feet, all else is a porcelain square with a small hole in it. However the plug pulls adequately and floods pour on and over and down. I am, or was last night, very Connie after having been Di[1] for a day in Tehran. I found it very hard work crouched over that damned hole. How do the locals like our form of seat, I wonder?

---

[1] 'Connie' for *constipated*; 'Di' for *diarrhoea*.

Friday, November 17th, 1944   Sisters' quarters, CGH,
Andameshk

There hasn't been a sec to write in here since Isfahan really. That was a magic day. We rang for our breakfast and a fire and two waiters came in and arranged an elaborate Heath Robinson affair by which oil dripped gently from a can through a funnel into a stove, a steady roar began and the room warmed up at once. At ten o'clock we went downstairs. Archdeacon Richards arrived to show us around. He's been in Isfahan for many years; Persia for eighteen altogether. Mrs R. and their daughter went home this summer. He joins them in Jan. We set off in bright morning sun, the yellow poplars everywhere fluttering in a breeze. We took a droshky. Viola and I sat facing the oncoming view and the Archd and a young RAF boy who was stationed there but hadn't seen the sights yet, perched on eighteen inches of seat with their backs to the two white horses. We drove straight to the Mardan which is the great square which forms the centre of the Eliz. part of Isfahan. It is wonderfully spacious. The buildings around it are, I think, of uniform two-storey height except for the Ali Kapu which was considered a skyscraper, being six storeys high. The Royal Mosque. Mainly impressive for its immense dome, the blue tiles flowered in yellow and white. Can't say I fancy tiling. *Salles de bains*. Nor yet do I go for mosques except as architectural wonders. The marble bases of twisted sugar candy columns in single spans of turquoise glaze were handsome but moved me not. On the other hand the Ali Kapu was one continual delight. I *think* it was the entrance pavilion to the palaces. Its main feature is a great verandah room on the first floor from which the Shah and his court watched the polo going on in the sun below. The original goal posts are still there. Stone ones; uncomfy to run into on a pony. The walls of the Ali Kapu are all painted. Every inch of every little room from the big main verandah to the many little bedrooms up above.

Moslems have defaced most of the heads but the pictures
are still clear and quite enchanting. There were pastoral
scenes of ladies, *à la Chinoise*, posturing with beads in
hand and draperies flowing, while gazelle, rabbits, birds
and flora riot on steep hills among pencil trees behind
them. Soft colours; mostly terracotta-ish red and faded
indigo blue. Dusty greens and yellows still show palely.
Sheer fantasies with flowers and buds, also the Chinese
influence, and ladies done in the Italian manner with
more beads and a careless accumulation of urns and
graceful musical instruments decorating the corners. The
drawing is quite lovely. I could have spent a whole day
there among those walls. Why some nippy New York
wallpaper king hasn't swiped the designs I can't think.
Alas our own Sandersons prefer to clog on with mud-
coloured lincrusta and autumn leaved dado patterns.
Some day I'd like a house with really lovely papers in it
and one room, probably the dining room, done with
designs from Isfahan. Wonder if I'll ever see it again? It's
the only thing I really long to see again. The other
mosques, the bazaar, the Madrassah – all good, but the
Ali Kapu struck my own special note. We climbed to the
roof and gasped with pleasure at what we saw. Isfahan
lay flat around us, roof after roof, eyebrowed with trees
in straight rows. Domes winked in the sun. All around,
beyond the city limits, lay mountains. The sort Ed Dulac[1]
used to paint. Fairy-tale ones with blue shadows and
peaks and the far-off ones capped with snow.

The Persian women are, legally, unveiled; but in practice they prefer to go covered. In the ME their abbas are
black but here they wear coloured cotton or silk ones, cut
on the cross so they fall gracefully like bells. All the pale
colours. From the roof of the Ali Kapu they look like
flowers – pale pink, rather a common green and an
equally nasty mauve. Sweet pea shades again. But in the

[1] Edmund Dulac's rich, often fantastic illustrations – usually in watercolour – best represented in editions of *Arabian Nights, Treasure Island*,
etc. French by birth, Dulac was naturalised British in 1912.

wide sandy square they look right and very romantic. Distantly, that is. There was a good deal of bargaining going on. Dress lengths, it looked like. Merchants in felt fedoras held out materials. Six pale belles crowded in on him. Measuring took place. The group got closer while money was exchanged, and then, transaction complete, dissolved. We saw it happen a dozen times. Droshkies with their double teams clip-clopped past. Donkeys, unbearably burdened, disappeared under archways into the bazaars. From our roof it had the magic of an animated toy, lit with bright sun, framed first by the inner square and then by the line of mountains beyond the houses. Puffs of pale blue smoke here and there, many stripes of yellow poplars ever marching in perfect line; a few umbrella pines (or do I dream them?). Far off, behind the flat roofs of the bazaar a dye works is dying lengths of material – strips of red, indigo and soft yellow. The sky a clear blue except at the edge where some affected little white clouds wreathe a few dark blue mountains just to complete the picture.

Lunch with six or seven boys – signals, met. and field security. They were all enjoying Isfahan. It's a three months' posting – they'd all like it to be longer. These small units, out of the way, make their own life and are absorbed into the community as individuals. There are about twenty English people in Isfahan – missions, consulate, petrol, bank, etc. The nice little Archd fetched us again at 3. Poor Captain Maurice, Staff-Sgt Patterson and Wetheral had all spent the morning on the car. Wetheral and Wallace, the CMP[1], spent the night with it in the desert, letting off the tommy gun once just to show their mettle. They heard something and thought it a wise policy. So Capt M. came with us on our afternoon sightseeing. Our same droshky, black horses this time, fetched us. We jogged off slowly to the outskirts of the town to see the house of one Prince Ismail Muzda whose

[1] The Corps of Military Police.

grandpa – or pa? – was a friend of Queen Victoria's. He was the Shah of the day. Alas, the Prince had been called away since inviting us, but his servant met us and gave us tea in coffee cups and we wandered among the most extraordinary mixture of loveliness and horror. The front door cut into the middle of a long passage hung with rugs of rare beauty, hung at angles!, swords, mothy deer heads, helmets, views of Nice and Monte Carlo in p.c. colours on wood sliced straight from the tree and left edged in bark, photographs of relations in uniform, out of uniform, on and off horses. There was a dazzling lady in a picture hat, about 1910, signed in French. There were tapestry chairs, some three-ply porch furniture with spindly legs and a look of railway restaurant to them. And, best of all, a set of deck chairs painted black and hung with tired yellow plush instead of canvas. But among all these, lovely bits of silk and a bridal mirror and a painting of charm if not worth. In the drawing room stood an upright piano, candlestick style. Viola opened it and played 'Baa Baa Black Sheep'. It was so wildly out of tune that the octaves almost harmonised. There was the same mad mixture in here. Group pictures with European ladies in large hats and small waists. Every corner had something. More really beautiful rugs, some hung, some laid. The dining room's majesty was a little marred by a small job of airing someone was doing on the horseshoe table. Rather sad wool-wear gents' drawers lay in wait for an iron, which sort of took the edge off things. There were plates hung on the wreath of silver? or was it dark grey? leaves designed and painted on the wall to surround each one. It was charming.

We climbed into the droshky and went to see the Armenian Cathedral. Very dark and full of richness. The walls thick with contemporary murals (sixteenth century) telling Bible stories to non-readers and showing Hell in no uncertain terms. The tenants were mostly female. Then the Madrassah – it's a school for Moslem priests, lately re-opened. V. Sackville-West was specially taken with it. She saw it in spring, full of irises and lilacs and distant birds but now, in autumn, the garden bare from disuse and only three or four rather sinister young men eyeing us over the Koran and out of their fancy little beards, its atmosphere was less serene. But as a building it lies harmoniously about its wide garden with its pool to reflect the trees and the dome of its brilliant mosque. By this time it was getting cool – in fact darned cold – but we felt we must see the big square once more in the fading light. The belles glowed even more without the sun. There were crowds of them everywhere. Seen near to they were less romantic than from our elevated views of the morning, but the general effect was charming. One last drive out to the Holiday Bridge, an elaborate structure built not for usual pontine purposes but also for pleasure. It has two levels and each arch has a little platform on which families come and spread their rugs and spend the day picnicking. While we were there the sun went down and the sky got a strange smoky blue – like painting on glass. A flock of white birds sprayed across it in flashes as they turned and the light side of their wings showed. And rooks, very East Anglian, cawed slowly and raggedly across the autumn trees about the river. The whole picture vaguely Chinese. Strange sky, with pink wisps in it, the birds; the soft red, orange, yellow and lime-green trees veiled in pale mist; the river, a little movement in yellow-grey and a long-legged white bird by itself in the reeds.

What a day of lovely sights. We sipped hot tea in the hideosity of the hotel lounge and suddenly realised how cold and stiff we were; but how heavenly it had been. The Arch-D's enthusiasm was just contagious enough and never went on too long. He's loving it all so much and communicating it, all ready and willing, and he was the perfect guide.

In the morning we dashed through the bazaar, cleaner than most, less smelly, and saw an ancient oil press worked by a blindfolded camel in a Hollywood-designed dungeon hung with quite unbelievable cobwebs of tweedy texture. Entire trees, four feet in diameter, had their part in the elaborate system which included bits of string and pulleys and pins. Then up into blinding sunlight to a roof where a row of craftsmen, all independent, sat cross-legged in tiny eight-feet-square studios making antique playing cards, bone bracelets with miniatures, and book backs, all for us mugs to buy in Baghdad and Tehran. Then down into the cotton printing factory where small boys and men stamp on the designs from blocks about ten inches long and eight across. Each colour is blocked separately. A gay grey and bright blue sprigged design was being completed by a dash of mulberry red. Then we saw little boys hammering bird designs on to silver dishes and cups, filled with pitch so as not to give as they work. When it's done they drop the whole in boiling water and the pitch melts out.

We did the show at the Anglo-Polish Club. In a moment of panic when they decided their mess was too small the soldiers asked the English sec. of the club if they could borrow their hall and he said yes and he'd ask some Poles. (Refugees from Russia. Mostly women and old men.) It was too late when we arrived to explain that we weren't a concert and that the Poles would hate us, so we had to go ahead. The British element sat in front and about 150 Polish – schoolgirls in dozens – filled the rest of the hall. Quite idiotic, but nothing to be done so we went ahead with me telling the kindly but quite humourless interpreter just what I was about to do! 'This is just rather a silly little song', I'd say, not liking to start to describe 'My Bonnie' or 'I'd Lend You'. He'd launch into a spiel that was I'm sure not in the least what I'd told him. It was a tough assignment but went a treat. The English were sweet and loved it and didn't mind the boring pauses while I said, 'Tell the Poles this is just a film song' – 'What film, pliz?' 'Oh, it's a film called *Going My Way*.' 'Going where?' – 'Er – going my way, but it doesn't matter.' 'Who is in dis film?' 'Bing Crosby.' 'That is nice – I will tell them.'[1] And then a spiel. It got rather funny. Finally I took to telling the Poles myself – at his dictation. This went down big. All I hope is that it cemented the entente. It took lots of me to do it. I know I never caught one granny who was, I think, stone deaf and lost in her own sorrowful thoughts anyway. She wore her few hairs in a Dutch doll bob and sucked her toothless gums in a distrait way that got me fascinated and I kept almost losing my words.

Off next day to Sultanabad. Picnic en route beyond Dilafan, where the men set up empty bottles and shot at them. Wetheral, whose name is Sid, scored a bull's eye with our rifle and Captain Maurice shattered his bottle with a tommy gun. They all took turns – Sergeant Patterson, CMP Wallace – but we declined. When he'd released three bullets rather off the target area nice Patterson said: 'That's the first shot I've fired since the war began, I'm afraid to say.'

A really grand evening in the mess, packed to suffocation with all the English servicemen in the station. We sang and played and they sang. An Irishman in a poignant tenor voice gave us 'Mother Machree', *lento lento* but with effect. I sang 'Yours' by request of Sid Wetheral. He is married to a girl in the ATS. 'She's a Roman Catholic, see, so we got married in her church, but I'm a Christian – English church, and I didn't turn. We couldn't have pomp or confetti or music. Only flowers. She were a bakeress before.' He showed us her picture. In ATS uniform, with glasses. She looks nice and has humour.

From Sultanabad to Malayer on Weds., 15th. About 11 we got there. Tea and biscuits with an Indian major and here we sadly parted from Maurice, whose area ends there, and were handed over to a welfare officer from Ahwaz, an egocentric of uncertain age who is definitely

---

[1] *Going My Way:* Bing Crosby as a singing priest won an Academy Award.

'touched'. Viola and I were horrified by him. He told us, in the first five minutes, of his irresistible attraction to and for children – little girls in particular. Anxious to return to more solid ground I said I hope he had a gun to protect us with – Captain Maurice had a tommy one. 'No,' he said, 'I fill my pockets with pennies and sweets to give to the little children.' 'Oh?' we said. He went on to say he'd been a schoolmaster but saw he was turning into a bully so gave it up because he loved little children so much. At Birjurud where we stopped for lunch and did a show in the men's mess he whipped out two photograph books full of photographs of little girls and some quite big ones, too. He is a most extraordinary character, very stubborn and pathetic in that he is so dotty and tries to win one by bribes of chocolate biscuits and tins of cigarettes. He gives me creeps and has made me extremely angry about twice but I am truly saddened by him for he is mad.

Our lunch and show at Birjurud were cosy and fun. They are, apparently, no one's pigeon – on the edge of Tehran's area and the Ahwaz one and get ignored by both.

. . . On to Doroud. Loveliest country of all, so far – valleys full of *little* cultivation, more and more poplar copses shining yellow in the afternoon sun. Little mud towns with fortress walls. Rice fields near water. Birds in swooping flocks. Always mountains of all colours; streaked in geological strata. Menacing and rocky and round and friendly.

Doroud at sunset. Roughing it again, mud hut and dust but a huge log fire and buckets of hot water and a very welcoming Scots major i/c the Signals. And a specially good show in the BOR's canteen. The 'Excerpts from the Opera' company were there and not working, so attended our show. Sandwiches and tea and talk with the men afterwards. Then 'Goodnight' to the sergeants' mess to please our sergeant and finally 'Goodnight' in the officers' mess, and so to bed. Our mad welfare captain, knowing he'd failed to impress or please, had left a tin of

cigarettes on my table with 'Best wishes – Uncle Dick' on
it. Oh dear. If only he'd stop trying to convey his bonhomie and the popular Santa Claus stuff.

Yesterday, November 16th, was, possibly the longest
in our history. It began at 6 with an Indian bearer in
knitwear cap bringing me very sweet tea and saying '*Goo*
morn Mem Sahib' in a high Welsh voice. We left at 7.30 in
a new station wagon. They found ours was full of faults
and the road to Andameshk was so dangerous anyway
that it was thought imperative to send us off in a safe car,
at least. So it was. Fine new tyres, heavily treaded; brakes
of great fierceness; a deep angry horn. We stopped at *nine*
signal posts, one every twenty miles. I longed to have
time to stay and sing at all of them but 7.45 a.m. is a bit
early and the first lot were eating their breakfast eggs
when we called. The next lot were hidden in mountain
mists. I sang a few songs and did 'Ernie' – at Sid's request!
He comes to every show, laughs at every joke and
analyses the audience afterwards. In my dream world I'd
have Sid Wetheral as my driver handyman. Wonder if
Mrs W. can cook as well as bakeress? At the third post we
met a boxer with a little silver trophy cup. At the fourth
we stopped longer for it was an HQ and had thirty men
including RES. We unloaded the piano in a downpour
and came with it into their canteen. The cooks, two
Welsh boys from Swansea, were whitewashing their
kitchen following a blackening fire at dawn, but they left
their job and joined us. They were best of all audiences.
Spontaneous, gay and really glad we'd come. So were
we. Cocoa all round and a thirty-five minute programme.
'You're the first ENSAS we've seen,' they said. We kept
quiet. They stood in the rain and waved us off. Two more
posts before lunch then at Malavi we stopped for eggs
and chips with five of the boys maintaining that bit of the
line. All day the captain urged us on, afraid of the dark
that would descend. I must say I share anyone's fear of
that road. It is 220 miles of endless snake, cliff-edged
way. Deep gorges, hairpins at impossible angles, blind

corners. They, in themselves, are enough but on top of
that there are the Aid-to-Russia convoy lorries, about
forty at a time, driven by opium-doped Persians who
don't give a damn and come at you like madmen. I had
almost no self-control though I didn't ever say 'Look out'.
Sid Wetheral drives beautifully, and grips the wheel in
strong, rather surprisingly fine-boned hands, sitting up
straight and bristling like a terrier. His only fault at the
wheel is one of excessive good manners. When he
addresses you he looks you in the eye. But I prefer the
less orthodox method on the road. I found it impossible
to relax, ever. We stopped at all the posts and drank lots
of tea. I almost floated by the end of the day. Something
could and must be done about getting shows of some sort
to those boys. There are five, or at most six, at each little
post. They live in good stone built huts and when I asked
them whether they preferred life in a big unit or their
separate existence cut off in the mountains they were
unanimous in preferring the quiet life. They fell into a
happy working unit in almost every instance. Major
Wilson told me late in the evening that the line boys hate
going back to a larger life. Seems to me that a two-handed
party like Viola and me could work that route quite
comfortably over three or four days.

Sunday, November 19th, 1944   Ahwaz

Viola and I fell out of the car at Andameshk Friday
evening in a somnambuling daze. It really had been a
day. It was arranged for us to stay at the hospital in
Andameshk, No. 36 CGH. We were housed in a large
room, part of an old Persian barracks. The furniture was
just adequate – an iron bed each in the middle of the room
and two chests of drawers. No chairs, no mirror, no mat
for the floor, no jam jar with zinnias in. Coming as it did
at a moment when we ached for a little Ritz life with hot
water at the turn of a tap and carpeting to sink into, it was

a little lowering. And not really necessary, for we've stayed in far more remote places and found imagination run riot with army blankets for rugs and at least *two* jam jars with zinnias. Here it was a case of nobody's special job so nobody cared. We ate supper in the sisters' mess soon after 7.30 and were in our cell soon after, looking for nails in the wall from which to hang our clothes. The plaster, pale blue, looked as if a maniac with a pistol had fired at it in a frenzy. Pockmarks all over. Mrs Pollock, a pretty little Scots nurse, showed us where to wash – a hundred yards away in the main block – so in my fur boots, dressing gown and overcoat carrying my sponge bag, towel, nightie and talcum powder I toiled over the cobbles and had a zinc tub bath. It was quite pleasant and bed was heaven. Lights out at 9.15. Viola's itch kept waking her, and me. But on the whole it was a good night. Hospital life begins with the first light. Indian bearers bore us our breakfast at 7.15. Letters and writing in this book all morning from my bed. I'm afraid we may have missed the Christmas mail. The last dates are over; but they may be extra cautious in order to clear the way. Hope so. I wrote to Reggie, Dick, Pa, Gin, Myra, Winifred, Victor, Joyce, Ann.[1]

Mad Captain —, whom I'd dodged by staying in bed, tracked me down in the afternoon even though I was, again, on my bed resting. He has lost all grip, poor thing. I now hear he is going to be moved but I don't think he knows yet. He's the sort of egocentric who thinks he can win by playing for sympathy. He entered with a long list of his woes in connection with the 'Excerpts from the Opera' company. I wish, too, he wouldn't keep showering Naafi goods on us as 'giftes'. Just as we are leaving he comes dashing through the rain with biscuits and sweets and cigarettes and thrusts them at us through the car window as if he hadn't done it and then buzzes back to

[1] Ann Holmes: Joyce's cousin, her mother Margaret being the sister of Joyce's father Paul and Miles Lampson's first wife Rachel.

his truck and we do hate it so. Even the Indian driver in our truck thinks he's dotty. He said to Sgt Patterson: 'Policeman nice (that was Maurice) – Captain funny,' and he tapped his head suggestively. I can't see what is to happen to a man like that. He's lived in India all his life; I don't suppose he's got a penny. He can, perhaps, go back to schoolmastering and bore the hides off little children. It's a sad thought. I wish he didn't give me such creeps. Last night we dropped in at the local signal corps BOR's mess and did a few songs and it was colossal. I don't know quite where I got the extra energy, for we'd come on from doing two other shows and in the car I'd just said to Viola, 'I've got nothing left. This'll have to be a short one, I'm afraid.' However there they all were sitting at tables playing cards and eating nuts, and they were so darned receptive and cheerful that I was completely recharged and we did about an hour. I enjoyed it. So did they. Cheers and yells and handshakes and speeches and just when everything was in a fine glow and we all felt good up gets the mad captain and makes one of those really embarrassing little talks about us. I thought Viola would hit him. I stood behind him hissing 'Do stop' – but on he went, attempting to be funny – 'Ladies are always such handfuls, as you know' – and the boys hated it as much as we did. However, we took the taste out of all our mouths by singing 'Auld Lang Syne' and Viola and I in a moment of extra elation gave them a duet of '*You* are jolly good fellows' which sounded slightly silly but came from our hearts. A Londoner with a broken nose and a voice like a foghorn came up to me and wanted to know if it was true I'd 'turned down a dinner invite to the Brigadier at Doroud so's to meet the boys?' Rather surprised, I said I had and he was delighted. 'The boys heard you had,' he said, 'and they're all tickled.' I asked him how on earth they'd heard about it anyway. 'We're signal corps,' he said. 'We hear everything.' At the time I was amused but I wish now I'd said something more intelligent because this attitude that officers snatch everything and that I'd

socked 'em one by denying them the privilege of our
presence is silly and no good. As it happened I explained
to the brig. after the Doroud show, that we made a policy
of staying on and talking to everyone because we found
they like asking us about things at home and he said he
was specially glad we did, and, of course, quite understood. When it's possible and the place isn't too big we
best like to have everyone in the same room afterwards
for food and drinks; the men and officers. It works very
well. Specially when the officers are good and mind
tuppence for the men. It's only the duds that want us to
have a party in the officers' mess and when they see how
dull we are – from that point of view anyway! – they
withdraw.

All the shows this week have been fun. The hospital
one at 36 was a treat. About sixty people there including
three Americans. I wonder just how much it has to do
with us when the show goes completely well? I think
room and lighting and sound are enormously important.
But after that? Often when I feel unlike it, as last night, it
goes best of all. There are no rules, I suppose.

The rains have certainly come. We left Andameshk in a
downpour and the eighty-mile run over good flat road –
not a single cliff or hairpin bend thank God – was made in
blinding rain. We move on down the Gulf by RAF tomorrow. Oh lor' and then India. Too quick, too quick. Sid, in
his moment of expansion, said he was enjoying every
minute of this tour – 'Better'n driving any officer,' he
said.

The Ritz we craved is ours. Room and bath, constant
hot from an electric boiler and a *bedside lamp*.

The co here is Col Boyd. He came to the hospital show
and looked a bit bored at the back and had a hacking
cough. Afterwards, in the matron's mess, he was very
civil and he asked me what sort of Grenfell I was. I told
him and discovered that Lionel Bulteel is his uncle so that
made us almost kin. When I said my own name was
Phipps a flash of recognition crossed his dark, rather

saturnine face. 'Not Nora?' – 'Yes,' I said. 'She's my
mother.' And he turns out to be Eddie Boyd, one of the
three brothers who beau'd my Ma at Plymouth in 1915
when I was five. I remembered him then as a leggy young
officer. There are photographs of them and their sister
Doris, all on the front outside The Terrace. Mummy has
them in her book.

There *might* be mail at Abadan today. I daren't think
about it.

Tuesday, November 21st, 1944   In the air, in the Ensign to
                                                    Bahrein

There was mail but none from Reggie, Pa, Dick, or Gin.

Abadan is a caged-in garden city – worse than Welwyn;
more of an outskirts to Birmingham or Preston. And
always the smell of oil. We drove over from Ahwaz in
heavy rain and the last bit was uncontrollably skiddy.
Desert dust turns into a particularly nasty mud when
wettened. The mad captain, martyrising, leapt out in the
rain with more offerings of biscuits but we waved back
two packets still unopened from the day before. When he
left us at Abadan he wished us well and told a whopper
about enjoying every minute of it. He knew we didn't
much like him and he knew I knew. Unhappy man.
Endless ego references to his own goodness to the men.
Welfare is his business. For the work's sake I'm glad he's
going. Apart from Penny and MacCollum, the welfare
officers we've met out here have been obvious throw-
outs – no good for any other job. Really poignant
farewells to the Sarge and Sid (who'd followed on to
Maqil in the car) on the steps of the hotel. I really hated to
break up what has been quite the happiest of all our little
units. Sid was at strict attention, his face rather too tired
and glistening with the muggy damp of Maqil. 'Goodbye, miss,' he said. 'It's been very enjoyable.' I agreed.

The sergeant looks tired too. I expect we are quite hard work. They looked after us a treat.

Wednesday, November 22nd, 1944   Capt Shillington's
                                                          house,
                                          The Naval Base, Bahrein

Very warm again, muggy too. BOAC sent us across the island to the naval base where we are staying while in Bahrein. Capt Shillington came out to meet us. Liked him at once. Large, kindly, with an Edith eye, one lower than the other[1], of bird brownness and a booming squall-beating nautical voice. His bungalow faces the Gulf and any little puffs of air that may come over the water and is full of windows. The humidity of Bahrein is as much as a hundred per cent in the summer.

Look at the first air editions of *The Times* I'd seen. It's a most lovely piece of work. India paper, about ten inches by seven, I should think; tiny print but very clear. Lunch in the officers' mess at the naval base. Captain Shillington's solicitude for our well being is complete. He has nobly given up his lovely big bedroom to us and made us feel so welcome and warm. I lay on the bed all afternoon reading old *Sketches* and *Tatlers* and marvelling at the race meeting pictures (Dublin of course) and the portraits of peeresses in Red Cross or St John uniforms. Their remoteness from the world we are seeing now is very noticeable.

The show was in a long and rather narrow hall with a deep and well-lit stage cleverly hung with yards of that sort of no-colour stockingette they use for cleaning engines and wiping oil. It comes in strips about a foot wide and they'd used hundreds of yards of it nailed to the wings and flies and back screens with very attractive effect. Captain Shillington's idea. He's a bit up in things

---

[1] Dame Edith Evans, the actress, had this peculiarity.

theatrical. Friend of Fanny Day's. We told him she is due to play Peter Pan this Christmas and his surprise measured equal with ours when we learned the odd news.[1] Last night's audience was a mixture of Navy, Air Force, American construction company, Anglo and American oil company personnel and some Indian sailors. Considering all things they jelled beautifully and it was fun. Swelteringly hot I got. In the night the storm crashed about the bungalow and Viola had to get up and push her bed out of the direct line of leaks. I didn't sleep much. It was very hot and sticky. Am a little perturbed about our outdoor show this evening. It is still wet with more storm to come, I think.

Thursday, November 23rd, 1944   In a Warwick flying to
                                                                                Sharjah

I had every reason for disquiet about last night's show (RAF). The rain stopped before lunch but the wind rose and was insistent. When we drove up in Sq L Alder's car to the outdoor theatre we found the audience huddling together, collars turned up. Overhead a young moon sailed in a starry sky and it all *looked* entrancing but the wind swept clean across us all from my right and the audience's left and for the first ten minutes I had battles with both my skirt and my hair. Maud just gave up and had a fine time standing up and being dragged across my forehead. Wisps got loose and blew into my mouth and tickled my nose. Viola couldn't think of using music. Sat on it instead. Funnily enough the wind wasn't too bad for sound. It came from the side and therefore bore my songs and words to the audience. But it didn't exactly make things easy and all subtlety and quiet effects were out. Pity, because they were a very good audience and it could

[1] Odd because Frances Day was best known as a cabaret and revue performer and the part of Peter Pan was usually played by a straight actress.

have been rather extra fun. I attempted to cut things a bit
– they looked so cold – but they wanted more and more so
we carried on to almost normal length. After the show
Viola and I went to the airmen's canteen and started all
over again in there, warmed with tea and a great many
people in a very small space. Mostly requests. Sq L Alder
collected us after about forty minutes and took us off to
the officers' mess for supper. Suddenly I realised I hadn't
eaten since 1 o'clock and it was now 10 p.m. Delicious
savoury omelette. Then Captain Shillington arrived and
took us across the island to a mess warming party. It was
rather a good little party. Dancing to a fairly tolerable
gramophone disguised as an Arab bridal chest. We were
about forty people, I suppose. We had plenty of Paul
Jones's and Excuse Me dances and all the girls wore long
frocks and some of the oil men had dinner jackets and it
was a success. Viola and I danced ceaselessly and then
caught kind Captain Shillington's solicitous eye and left
about 1.30. Bed was a pleasure.

Friday, November 24th, 1944   Sharjah

. . . That was rather a bumpy little flight. It was good to
get out in *Arabia*. We are staying in the BOAC fort – it's a
series of buildings around a square with the offices and
radio rooms on one side and the guest cabins on the
other. We've each got an attractive little cabin to
ourselves and as soon as we'd unpacked a bearer came to
collect washing, all of which he returned completed two
hours later. Allison, the BOAC boss, took us down to swim
about 4. We drove a mile or so across flat sand to a creek
where we were ferried over by a patriarch in a beard who
kept the small fry away, dozens in number, by bran-
dishing his oar, and, I imagine, cursing. A silver beach
divides the main water from the creek and the sea rolling
up in fine Atlantic manner. An audience soon assembled
and sat in a fascinated row, cross-legged in the sand, to

watch us leap in the waves and get our hair soaked. It was quite lovely. Warm as milk and very exhilarating too. It felt like holidays used to in France when I was young. The locals kept a discreet distance and I emerged from my gent's swim trunk and the silk handkerchief top into cami-knickers and a linen frock without incident. They are darker and skinnier here, and I quite see why Freya Stark[1] finds them so fascinating. An angular man in a fringed turban showed us a brown hand full of pearls but we declined to do business. This is the pearl part of the Gulf. I fell asleep after tea, stretched out very pleasantly on my good bed.

Saturday, November 25th, 1944   Sharjah

Outdoor show last night to a mixed audience of us and us. They seem to have enjoyed it for we did an hour and a half and they wanted more. 'Good King Wenceslas' has joined the programme. We divide the audience in two and make half the Monarch and half the Page. Watching them doing it last night under that half full moon I had a sudden vision of a world map and saw us all perched on that bare brown bit, Arabia, singing a Christmas carol, miles from Burton-on-Trent or Mobile, Alabama, and the familiar surroundings with which we usually associate that feast. A funny sort of compassion hit me and I wished things could be otherwise for them all. If only, I thought, any of us had learned anything from these transplantations and mix-ups it would be comforting. But I wonder, I wonder.

---

[1] Freya Stark, DBE: Travelled widely and adventurously in the Middle East; author of a number of books on her travels. Briefly married to Stewart Perowne after the war.

[Undated]   Karachi

About twelve o'clock yesterday morning Viola and I were
sitting on the roof of the fort at Sharjah, rather gloomily
wondering if we'd ever get to Karachi, when I was called
to the telephone and RAF Movement said that a York had
come in and was leaving at 1.15 sharp and would take us.
We were fully packed so there was no panic.

Sharjah was pleasant for us, knowing as we did that we
needn't stay indefinitely. As a permanent post I'd say it
had little to commend it but the RAF make the best of its
nothingness and I give them marks. I picked up an old
Tatler or *Sketch* – don't remember which – and in it I read a
notice by Elizabeth Bowen on Noël's *Middle East Diary*.
She quotes a bit about him saying how profoundly impressed he was with our men – he'd been doing hospitals
in Egypt, I think. He said, roughly, that their manners
and unselfed discipline and their ability to 'take it' filled
him with respect and wonder. And he finished by re-
marking that we'd got to see that they were well served
after the war. Oh, I do agree, with every fibre of my
being. What we saw in the hospitals in the Mediterranean last spring told me that. Seeing them all, perfectly
well, in dreary places doing, apparently, nothing much –
or anyway nothing spectacular – but doing it with great
good humour and a tidy bit of grouch, all of it has filled
me with deepest admiration. The more of England I see
in these forsaken places the more certain I am that the
English are the salt of the earth – or, remembering Jock, –
maybe I should say Britons!

On Sunday afternoon at Sharjah there was a cricket
match between the signals and officers and sergeants.
The latter were beaten. Viola and I watched for a while
under a little straw pavilion. The players were all naked
to the waist and a uniform suntan was worn by all. The
pitch was matting and the field sand. A beige picture,
accented by the sharp whiteness of pads and the screens.
We hadn't been watching very long when MacGillivray

and Jock Frew came by in the BOAC Ford to take us over to Dubai where Mack wished to buy a pearl.

The pearl outing was decidedly worth it. Very colourful. Mack led us on through little alleys and finally we climbed an outside staircase to a first-floor room where some pearl merchants sat cross-legged on flat mattresses in a very confined space. About eight pairs of shoes stood tidily outside the door. Their owners rose when we arrived, and room was made for us to join them. Two chairs were produced but Viola and I, anxious to do things in 'the manner of', squatted down. Silence and staring reigned. Mack then said he was looking for a pearl knotted in one corner and everyone leaned forward to look and a flow of Arabic began. A bare-headed Indian in a white cotton vest and swathed linen skirt talked to us in English. He was, it seemed, a very big merchant indeed. He told us he'd sold a string of enormous pearls to Cartier for Barbara Hutton.[1] Conversation was dripping rather painfully. Small cotton bags of pearls were handed to the merchant Mack had come to see and he poured them into a series of little bowls, all bored with different sized holes so that the pearls graded as he poured them through. They were a poor lot, I thought. Either too white or too yellow. No rosy ones at all, nor the bluish which I love if they are good. For something to do I opened my little blue jewelry box that I carry in my purse and showed them the star brooch and earrings Hilda [Grenfell] gave me, pearls set in gold. Very Victorian and I think attractive. More leaning forward and comment. The Indian asked, rather nervously, if we understood Arabic and we reassured him. I don't think he was afraid of what they were saying about my jewels but about ourselves. Against the opposite wall and only six feet away was a row of five rather grand men, tailing off into a skull-capped podge who never spoke but took it all in. The first

[1] Barbara Hutton: Woolworth heiress. Much married, including Cary Grant.

three were elderly. No. 1 had all the front teeth heavily plated in gold. He wore his full turban high on the back of his bald head. The tufts of rather half-hearted beard on his chin were henna'd. He wore a robe of very fine navy-blue cloth, braided in gold and he pared a pearl with a sharp blade all the time he stared – except when he held my brooch and muttered. Next to him was a delicate old man of incredibly fine-boned features, almost womanly. Small skull, graceful little hands with henna'd nails. His abba was gauze-thin wool and his turban snowy white. Viola said they appraised us inch by inch. I caught Jock's eye. He was sitting stiffly on a chair near the door. I shook my head and made some slow but polite conversation with the Indian. Later Jock told me he sat nice and near the door so's to catch any of them if they'd tried to bolt with my brooch! One of the sheikhs said he'd got a pearl to match Mack's, for our host had failed to produce one, and he made off to fetch it. We sat on and on. The little pale blue washed room felt smaller and smaller and outside the world turned pink as the sun went down. At last we decided we couldn't wait any longer and Mack arranged to leave his pearl with his friend who would match it and deliver the pair to Sharjah. We shook hands – two new figures had joined the party, very handsome with curled beards and khol'd eyes and daggers at the belt with curved scabbards. Sailing back along the creek was delicious. The sun behind us. All the sand-brown dhows – colour of pickled pine panelling in New England – glowed in the low light. Men and boys in their feast finery stood and stared. We got back to Sharjah just as it grew dark.

Sunday night at Sharjah there was a non-denominational service in a small rush hut. Viola and I went across the sand to it. About twenty-four of us there. Welsh padre of great earnestness and not a lot of inspiration. We sang four or five hymns but never got going, chorally, for the wattles, or whatever made the hut, sucked up sound and it was a dull rather than a joyful noise we made unto the Lord. An officer read the first lesson and a corporal the second. One felt the waves of homesickness lap all through that little hut. Religious fervour there was none but I rather fancy there was consolation in the familiarity of the words and the tunes and both Viola and I were uncomfortably moved by the whole thing. One clings to the familiar in a pagan sort of way. It is, I think, astounding that Christianity has endured so well in spite of man's lack of what it's all about – except in a vague general sense. Britons are naturally on the side of right; which of course has its roots in Christianity. But we do so awfully little about anything further. However there's a lot of practical Christianity about and that's the thing and even if it isn't called by the name that's what it is.

Thursday, November 30th, 1944 –   Somerset House
   Tommy's [Joyce's brother] birthday   (BOAC), Karachi

And now India! We breakfasted in bed yesterday morning. Then a mooch into Karachi where we bought ourselves nylon toothbrushes, Pears soap, (Australian made), and Pond's cold cream.

Captain Caldicott Bull is ENSA for the NW area. He looks a *little* like Alistair Sim.[1] Is an actor. Driving back in the station wagon from Karangi Creek last night where we did an RAF show – outdoors, about 500 men – exceptionally good audience – his sergeant (too thin) revealed his past to us. He was on the halls with a dressmaking act. It seems he created exclusive models then and there on three living models – a blonde, a brunette and a redhead. He married the redhead. They came on in brassières and

---

[1] Alistair Sim: Scottish actor with a lugubrious face, associated with the plays of James Bridie, but best remembered for his many films including *Belles of St Trinian's*, *Blue Murder at St Trinian's*, in which Joyce also appeared as Ruby Gates.

panties and he draped them. He did three numbers, all to music. First there was a black and white picture. One of the girls as an usherette held a tray with accessories, flowers, jewels, gloves, shoes and then the sergeant, in tails, draped. No. 2 was a wedding creation. No. 3 a patriotic number. The orchestra played soft music while he draped the first girl in a US flag and when he stepped back to reveal the completed costume the music burst into 'Stars and Stripes'.[1] Same procedure with a red flag and the Soviet National Anthem and then, on the central model he'd swish around with a Union Jack, whip out a trident, shield and helmet and Lo! Britannia and the finale. He boasted quite simply that he'd stolen the idea of the act from America. He'd seen it done at the World's Fair in Chicago. Dress designing is his forte. Up in Rawalpindi where he is stationed they have their slack periods between ENSA parties and he does 'exclusive designs' as 'Michael' in the dress shop of a lady friend. He likes to study his subject and always attends fittings. He's done a gown for a major-general's wife and is now about to go into the groove over a wedding. 'Solid silver larmy,' he says. 'The bride has a mahvlus figure.'

I begin to enjoy these outdoor shows. So long as it is good for sound I don't much mind where I play. Last night's was rather well arranged. They'd put up a platform against the wall of a long hut and fitted it with a row of dazzling footlights that completely blinded me but otherwise did their job nicely. The audience crowded around on forms, chairs, standing. It was a warm night. Astrakhan clouds about the full moon and a mild little breeze. Viola and I have been polishing up 'Begin the Beguine', and 'I'll be seeing you' and 'Sweet and Lovely', but we couldn't use them last night because the breeze carried off the music and anyway Viola had no light to see by. I wonder, I wonder how much it has to do with me whether an audience is responsive or not? I can't quite

[1] 'Stars and Stripes Forever', a march by John Philip Sousa.

decide where the balance lies. As so often happens, I wasn't feeling in very good form last night, no special reason, but as soon as we got there and saw them all sitting expectantly, that old circus horse within me leapt up and I was suddenly right on top. When this happens a new strength seems to enter into me. Afterwards I spin a bit and then am spent. Col Malherbe in Tehran said it was virtue gone out of one like Jesus in the New Testament! Giving out, unless one knows the source from which the power flows, is apt to be depleting. And even when one does, it needs peace and quiet for restoration. I am continually amazed and awed by the feeling one has when the thing – spirit? – whatever it is – flows from one, without effort in perfect ease.

Jesus said 'Heal the sick'. For a brief moment I think I one day might possibly want to make that my life.

INTERMISSION

'Organising ENSA in India during the war,' writes Jack Hawkins[1] in his autobiography, *Anything for a Quiet Life* (Elm Tree Books, 1973), 'was a comic and sometimes downright depressing business. I don't suppose that even the world's most unsuccessful theatrical agent has ever had to handle quite so many deadbeat acts as were sent to me. We called ourselves the arse-end charlies, for we were at the end of a very long line. So far as ENSA Headquarters in Drury Lane were concerned, we were not only at the bottom of their catalogue of priorities, we *were* the bottom.'

He tells of receiving telegrams from ENSA, telling him of the imminent arrival of an exciting musical act, who would turn out to be a solitary pianist deprived of the violinist, or a frantic dancer without her partner. The whole organisation, as far as India was concerned, he describes as a shambles. On one occasion he was landed with a group of actors which included an actor who was deaf in one ear, a stage manager with a wooden leg, and a shell-shocked leading man, an elderly character actress who had come straight from an amateur company in Devon, and two young actresses. This troupe was followed by a stream of entertainers, 'a deluge of fragmented acts; bottom of the bill comedians, contortionists, conjurors, the remains of dancing troupes, strident lady vocalists, and booming baritones'. The nearest any of

[1] Jack Hawkins: stage actor who became a film star after the war. His work includes: *The Cruel Sea*, *The League of Gentlemen*, *The Bridge on the River Kwai*, and *Lawrence of Arabia*.

them would get to the West End, he observes, was a show at the end of Skegness Pier. In the meantime the Army in India was complaining at the lack of entertainment, and he started receiving demands from Drury Lane why he was not providing 'blanket coverage' of India. Finally, fed up with ENSA's unreasonable complaints, he had a map drawn, superimposing India on a map of Europe, showing that the distance between Bombay and Calcutta was the same as London from Moscow, and not, as ENSA appeared to think, from London to Windsor. Thousands of miles were involved and they had no transport of their own. 'I had to spend hours begging lifts,' says Hawkins, 'and since the Japs were pressing our troops pretty hard, there was never much room to spare military transports for knock-about concert parties.' He describes one incident which served only to confirm his colonel's worst doubts about ENSA. Another concert party had arrived and Hawkins was informed by the ENSA people in Cairo that this was the tops. Taking them at their word, he booked the Town Hall in Bombay and heavily advertised the concert, in consequence of which, the hall was packed.

The show proved to be ghastly, 'an impresario's nightmare'. The singers' voices quavered and were off key; the dancers wobbled on their points, and the comedians' jokes were so bad that they failed even to raise a titter from the audience. At the climax of the show Hawkins's assistant turned to him and whispered, 'My God, I feel as though I've got ENSA stitched in sequins on my back!' It is no wonder that after this experience Jack Hawkins felt ready to volunteer for any suicide mission into the jungles of Burma!

During the nine months that followed, Hawkins expanded ENSA, moved its headquarters to Calcutta, took over the garrison theatre there, and mounted his own productions, presenting John Gielgud in *Hamlet* and Edith Evans in *The Late Christopher Bean*, as well as inviting the great pianist Solomon to play Chopin. When he

was demobbed in 1946 he heaved a huge sigh of relief.
'Trying to run ENSA in India and the Far East might not
have been as rugged and as dangerous as fighting
Japanese troops in the jungle, but there were times when
it stretched the limits of sanity.'

December 1944

Eric Dunstan (ex-BBC) is older than I'd expected with a
long neat head covered in silver white hair. I'd say he was
once red-headed. His blue eyes pop a trifle and he is fairly
sure of himself but he is considerate and imaginative and,
unless crossed, I feel he will be easy to get on with.
There's something of the bully in him which I don't fancy
and his temper is very touchy. But that may be the
climate and he is rather overworked. He's got more to
come, too, for B. Dean has sent him forty artistes in a
convoy due today and a further ninety in a month's time!
I'm glad we got here in time to get out of the way before
the avalanche descends.

We were met at the airport on Friday morning by an
ENSA sergeant with a truck for our bags and Eric's own car
and driver to take us straight to his bungalow at Malabar
Hill for late lunch. The bungalow belongs to Joan and Aly
Khan and it is attached to a slightly bigger one belonging
to the Aga. It is low and rambly and pink in colour and
has no carving and only marble in the very comfy bathrooms which is the right and proper place for marble. It
faces straight on to the sea. Just below Aly's bungalow is
a tennis court, walled in, and beyond it dark rocks and
the water. There are gardens in front of the Aga's end.
The whole place is quiet, comfy, slightly run down and
full of charm. As soon as we'd eaten, Eric drove us into
Bombay, about twenty minutes away, and saw us to our
room where roses welcomed us and all our luggage was

assembled. The roses had 'Welcome to India from ENSA' on a card with them.

I've got to revise my views and prejudices about ENSA. Eric has raised its standard high out here and is determined to keep it that way. He is very ruthless and if a show, although rehearsed and passed by Drury Lane, doesn't pass his standard, he re-orders it and sends home the artists who won't do or who don't know how to behave. In fact he has discipline and enforces it. Long may he continue. I can see that out here one needn't be ashamed of admitting to being under ENSA's flag. Makes a nice change! Basil Dean is due here soon and I fancy he is going to get quite a few surprises.

It is very hot here. Viola and I unpacked in spasms and in the middle of it a coolie came over from the office next door with a great wodge of mail for us. With incredible control I finished all my unpacking before opening any of mine and then I luxuriated. Three from Reggie, four from my Pa, five from Elliott, one Aunt Pauline, and a *very* old one from Mummy written in September and coming from Ennismore Gardens. Also various oddments. Eric sent his welfare officer over to cope with our washing and cleaning problems and a coolie went off with armfuls.

We were invited to attend the first night of the big services show *Men Only* on Monday night and then Eric took us over to the Yacht Club for a light lunch before the races. The Yacht Club was large and cool and spacious and very respectable. In the 'Ladies' a pretty Indian maid in a saree saw to our needs. It was all very Bath Club or Grosvenor House. Out to the races. Knowing nothing about the form or in fact anything, I gave myself entirely to looking. So much to see. The lawns were brilliantly green. Flowerbeds frothed with a funny little chrysanthemum. Tiny yellow button flowers. There were big yellow callas flanking the entrance pathway. It was lovely to look at – ladies in their sarees were a constant delight. Someone said they were only wearing their more ordinary ones that afternoon as it wasn't a big day but they looked ravishing to me. I love the white, sheer ones with silver and gold borders. And the rich delphinium purples, flame reds, sprigged yellows, incredible greens. European dresses were sadly dim. We sat in the Aly Khans' box. I had one small bet just for the hell of it, and lost. The Arab ponies were glorious. We saw them parade in the paddock, gleaming red gold flanks, satin greys – I'd never seen horses to such an advantage. I begin to see why people care! We did the whole afternoon in comfort, wandering gently under trees, staring and stirring in breezes, drinking lemonade, seeing one finish from the rails and the next from the box. I enjoyed it and let the colours and sun and strange feeling of peacetime soak in. By closing up the shutters of one's mind it is possible to forget buzz bombs and the people one knows in the fighting and the strain of life at home and the leaden skies they've got now and the cold and the long winter. If only they could all have a whiff of this, though, to get them through!

Tuesday, December 5th, 1944   Bombay

Insect life has entered into our Room 203. Going into the bathroom late last night – no, early this morning, 2.30 a.m., I was faced by a very horrid and enormous sort of cockroach with a body nearly two inches long (bright brown) and antennae two and a half inches above its beastly head, waving wildly in search of something all over the bath taps. I gave as controlled a cry as I could and Viola nobly took over. That beetle took a great deal of killing. Drowning was the first idea but it could swim and did so vigorously. Finally Viola held it under the water with a toothbrush handle and it succumbed. The idea was then to pop it in the lav and pull. We did this but it had become light as cork and sank not. However a sharp surprise pull this morning has vanished it. *But* – its mate, or its ghost, was in there this morning. With accuracy and courage I have trapped it under a glass vase and it is now staring out from its confined space in a pretty angry way. The bearer[1] says he will fix it later. Meanwhile two separate ant swarms have appeared. We rang for help and a Flit gun has put down the trouble for the moment but I've a shrewd idea those ants will have the upper hand in no time. I do *not* like insect life.

We dined with Kenneth Villiers, Michael Lord and Douglas Cameron and Bruce Belfrage.[2] The latter is in the Navy and out here to lecture on and propagate security by film and talk and all methods. We went to the Excelsior to witness the first night of the Navy's amateur show *Men Only*. It has had a fanfare of publicity and was patronised by the Governor and the various leading lights. Posters all over Bombay – money spent fairly freely on clothes and sets and months of rehearsal. We apprehended the whole thing and weren't far wrong really. It was full of good intentions, entirely without originality and far, far, far too long. There were chorus girls – male ratings with knobbly knees or, once or twice, rather alarmingly feminine graces. There was a robust baritone who sang from one side of his face and made very nice noises indeed. There was a top hat and tails number of embarrassing dullness and lack of talent. There were a couple of sketches by Bertie [Herbert Farjeon] – 'Cricket', and 'Winter in Torquay' – both done FFF[3] but failing to penetrate the Bombay audience which was easily the dumbest I have ever seen. There were Indian dancers in a battle number; rather fascinating and too long. There was a fakir who threw himself about on broken glass and ate a razor blade and an electric light bulb *and* fire. That was impressive but revolting and gave me hiccups. What else? A beach scene in the gay Nineties style, with the pier concert party act swiped whole from 'Sweeter and Lower' re-written to suit local conditions.

[1] Ghulam Mohd: the bearer provided by ENSA. 'We grew fond of him,' says Joyce in her autobiography.
[2] Bruce Belfrage: Famous BBC news announcer.
[3] Fortississimo.

The whole evening was derivative and precious and lacked middle. Nothing to get to grips with and the peak of horror from my point of view was a performance of Warsaw in total darkness with the exception of a back set representing the bombed capital with flashes of fire and gun effects to drown the piano at stated intervals. The pianist was glib at runs and he had the music there with him in the inky blackness but he played a version entirely his own and did things to the rhythm and the note values and like everything else it went on far, far, far too long. Needless to say it was a big success. But how Dick would have writhed. Viola and I did it for him.

Kenneth Villiers took us on to a flat owned by a very pretty Indian author, style Ivor Novello, and a sibilant friend whose name, appropriately, sounded like Rodent. There we found a collection of pansies that fair shook us. Soldiers, sailors and one airman. Waving hair, gestures of the 'my *dear*' sort and soft, gentle, wholly peculiar eyes and voices. Into this set-up arrived three black-haired popsies of extraordinary curve and chocolate-box looks. Just what they were doing there I cannot tell. We sat on a large bed in a big room, with a number of books and some fretwork Victorian furniture and time went sluggishly by. Bruce Belfrage and I exchanged news and views and raised our eyebrows; Viola was pinned in conversation by an elderly art critic called Garrard. Liveliness was not the keynote of the evening and at 1.30 we slipped away and Kenneth drove us home through the balmy moonlight.

Wednesday, December 6th, 1944   Bombay

I've just spent the evening laughing with Jack Hawkins and George Devine.[1] Jack told us about the week that the

[1] George Devine: Actor-director, and artistic director of the Royal Court Theatre at its peak; received the CBE in 1957.

Gielgud and Fay Compton production of *Hamlet* visited Denmark.[1] It was a propaganda tour to promote cordial feelings between the Danes and ourselves and Jack says that it resulted quite simply in the Danes *not* allying themselves to us, largely, he thinks, because of the mad English escapades they all indulged in. It was Practical Joke week and I must say that much as I disapprove of the Joke Practical, these, with distance to recommend them, did sound funny. For instance, the Motley girls'[2] four hours hard labour on all Glen Byam Shaw's buttons. First they cut them off and then they sewed them on; only two stitches per button so that starting with the bottom one on the flies of his pants they pinged off at each attempt to get them through the buttonhole. George Devine told us of the ghastly frolic perpetrated at Balliol College in his day on an unpopular student. They filled every pocket of every garment he had, and his sponge bag, and dressing-table drawers, with fish. There were fish – sprats, I suppose – in his breast pocket rising to soles in his jacket pockets and finally one of those shop-window cod, in its entirety, was gently laid in his bed. We talked theatre and theatre anecdotes till they turned the lights out on us. Of John Gielgud's *faux pas* – horrific these; of Michael Redgrave's tricks, now habit-formed and possibly permanent; of St Denis[3] being back in France; of everyone forgetting the actors in the Army after the war; (I said No, vehemently), of Peter Ustinov's[4] precosity; of the dearth

[1] Midsummer, 1939; Fay Compton played Ophelia; Jack Hawkins the Ghost and Claudius. Glen Byam Shaw was Horatio.

[2] Motley: a disguise for a triumverate of stage designers, Sophie Harris (married to George Devine), Margaret Harris and Elizabeth Montgomery.

[3] Michel St Denis: nephew of Jacques Copeau; head of the Old Vic Theatre School; and during the war, disguised as M. Duchesne, was the BBC's French expert and translator.

[4] Peter Ustinov: actor, writer, playwright, and raconteur. In 1940 appeared with Joyce in Farjeon review, *Diversion*, when only nineteen.

of playwrights; of Basil Dean who is due here quite soon
now.

Letter to Virginia Thesiger

Wednesday, December 6th, 1944   DNSE (ENSA) HQ,
Greens Hotel, BOMBAY

Such a wonderful mass of mail met us here five days ago.
We fell on it in contented silence and only the odd 'oh' or
'ah' came out of either of us for about an hour. There were
five glorious letters from you, and yesterday I had
another which arrived in *six days*! Wonderful. Darling,
you *are* old faithful, and if you could but guess how lovely
it is to get your fair hand on an envelope you'd not stop
writing for a single second . . .

We are in process of assembling our kit for up
country . . . Now don't blanch or anything, but I think
I'll stay out till March *if* Noël doesn't need me before.
There is such a really important job of work to be done
out here, and so huge is it that I feel, having got here at
last, I must complete it if I possibly can. I've cabled Noël
and await his answer.

. . . We are both very fine and giggle constantly. Our
English settlers here are exactly like the jokes and carica-
tures. It's hard to credit them. Coo, I'm late. Haven't read
the lesson yet. Oh, dear. Go on writing *constantly please*.
Happy Noodle Year.

Thursday, December 7th, 1944   In the train to Poona

Looking out of the window at the early morning haze
with curious little mountains passing by and unusual
cows grazing, I try to take in the fact that this is India and

not one of the familiar journeys from, say, London to Birmingham. Goodness knows Victoria Station, Bombay, was very like Euston, and except for the fans, the compartment could easily be an LNER[1] one. But at the last stop two little girls of about six and seven, wearing a very few rags and entirely unwashed, stood under the train window and went into a sister act. 'Oh Johnny, Oh Johnny, How You Can Love' they sang, and then lapsed into their own tongue, finishing up with broad grins which belied their tragic utterances: 'No mudder, no fader, no sister, no brudder.' And the 'Give me,' with little skinny arms outstretched. We made them do it again before dispensing largesse. They were full of rhythm and will obviously come to bad ends. There is a calm Hindu lady in here with us. She is reading an English thriller, wearing a black cotton saree edged with red.

The Colvilles[2] asked us both to lunch at Gov. House but Viola was afraid she mightn't be done in time so I went alone. This was my first taste of Gov. House life in India. I cannot believe the dignity of the UK would suffer all that much if things were a little less pompous. We were asked, on engraved cards with a gold crest at the top, to arrive at 1.20. We were then supplied with drinks and when a bearer in snow-white uniform with red turban and belt announced that HE approached, the guests, three in number, were arranged in a line to receive him. First came Sir Mohamed Azlzul Haqur, then me, then a colonel with a Scotch name I've forgotten. An ADC led HE into the room and called out, 'His Excellency the Governor of Bombay' then, without looking to left or right, passed slowly in front of the guests and said our names as he got level with us. After which Lady Colville pattered in. She is small and a wee bitty provincial. So is

[1] London and North Eastern Railway.
[2] Sir John and Lady Colville: he was Governor of Bombay, 1943–8. Acted as Viceroy and Governor General of India, 1945, 1946 and 1947. Created Baron Clydesmuir, 1947.

Sir John. They don't impress one physically. For this elaborate setting you need giants. There is a daughter with small, delicate features and a very pretty colouring. She was coolly gracious. Aged about twenty-one, I should think and totally devoid in humour, I should guess. It was with amusement that I heard her say she did 'little sketches' – 'Stanley Holloway[1] ones'. I must say my curiosity would like to see her at it; but see her from an invisible fly-on-the-wall position. They are a very short family and it is always harder to impress from low down. When we moved into the dining room – a large, pale blue-grey room with carved screens painted white; good, I thought – there were footmen behind each chair. As we got nearer they raised their hands in white cotton gloves in the salaam gesture and held them there till we found our seats. I sat next to Sir John and Michael Scott, an ADC. The latter has been badly wounded and lost an eye. I should think he is the only officer in the British Army who is allowed to wear a beard. He had many face scars and this is probably to hide some. I found Sir J. a little distrait, with civil service bonhomie. He was quite jovial but you felt his mind wasn't really on it. I exchanged a few banalities with Lady Colville and the daughter after lunch but polite as they were none of us got carried away at all.

Saturday, December 9th, 1944   Chez Gosnell,
                                  19 Queens Gardens, Poona

We got here at lunchtime on Thursday. The mini-piano was unloaded into our bedroom and we unpacked. One Lt Carr met us. He is under the welfare captain and in the afternoon took us to the two hospitals at which we will play here. Someone had told him we'd be here for only

---

[1] Stanley Holloway, CBE: comic actor and monologuist; famous as Alfred Doolittle in *My Fair Lady* in New York in 1956, and at Drury Lane in 1958.

four days but when I saw the size of the hospitals and the work to be done I doubled our time here and now we are doing three days at 126 and four at Number 3. This means very hard going but it's quite a lot cooler up here. I think we can do it as long as we don't try to do anything so tightly packed anywhere else. Did four shows yesterday. TB officers at midday, surgicals at 2, neuros at 3, and TB other ranks at 6.30. I'd forgotten how heartbreaking this job can be unless one disciplines oneself and keeps things quite clear in one's mind. The first impact here yesterday was a bit much. The last show of the day was in an enormous TB ward. Most of them were able to move up to one end and it wasn't bad for sound. They were a very tragic lot and I was haunted by their unseen homes and families. No sentimental stuff in there. We kept it all as speedy as possible but even so we were there for nearly an hour and a half. Two Anglo-Indians just arrived back here had seen us in the hospital in Jerusalem. They told me that the Indian boy in the draped white bed, who looked so beautiful, had died before they left.

This is an alarmingly enormous country. It's better to do what we do very completely rather than rush by scratching surfaces. Thus we've arranged to stay two weeks in Secunderabad which means we'll be there for Christmas. I gather we'll find a great deal of work there, and we are staying in a private hotel which should be all right and is really preferable to having duties towards hostesses one doesn't know. We have been warned to look in our shoes for snakes!

Sunday, December 10th, 1944   Poona

The organisation at 126 went to pot yesterday. We arrived to find no fatigue party to move the piano, no poster up in the wards we were playing and the ward itself unaware of the show. Thus forty-five minutes were wasted. I showed my teeth a little in what I hope was a dignified manner but it's such a bore and takes so much effort. The second and third shows were laid on properly so all ended happily. The second was TB [tuberculosis] again. Fewer of them and we got them all down one end of the ward and had a really heavenly intimate hour. I'd had to yell in the first one that afternoon – it was about 100 yards long, ninety beds. But the second was more concentrated and of course much easier. I'd had Noël's trouble in the first one just to add to the difficulties. Birds. Dozens of cheerful, piercingly vocal birds. The more I sang the more they sang too. It was an unequal struggle and the birds won. The TBS in the second ward roared with laughter and loved the monologues so I did more and more and we cut out all sentiment quite deliberately. Except a request for 'I'll be seeing you'. One can't – or I can't – bear to sing songs like 'Someday' or 'All my tomorrows' to people who have no future.

When we got back here about 6.30, beaten and longing only for peace, we found the first four of Mrs Gosnell's eight BORS [British Other Ranks] invited for supper, sitting in a circle on the lawn, so social sense took control and we sat and talked to them for an hour. Then an escape to the bath. We had a good evening with them. They were very neat and tidy in fresh KDS, some of them wearing the greeny khaki issued to Burma boys. I've forgotten most of their names but I know there was Jess Rodgers from Cheshire, McVean from Ayr, Hodgson from Huddersfield and Cleveland from Stoke-on-Trent. Two Cockneys – one from West Ham – an Englishman from the Argentine and a silent lance corporal from Gracie's home town, Rochdale in Lancs.[1] A delicious dinner. I sat between Ayr and Cheshire and conversation was easy. Being in a proper home was, we decided, pretty good. They had good things to say about hospitality in Poona. After supper Viola and I 'entertained'. They

---

[1] Gracie Fields: singer and comedienne who capitalised on her Lancashire background.

sat back in comfy chairs, Mrs Gosnell knitting between two of them on the sofa, the Col on a 'pouffe', wearing a blazer and grey flannels. We all sang carols. West Ham gave us 'My Devotion' in a profound if trembly baritone and the Col shamed me a bit by going into a sprightly comic version of the 'Old Folks At Home'. At one moment we were all on the floor playing something called 'Little Old Man', involving tapping when your own number was called. Then we did the matchbox relay race. I showed them how impossible it is to wiggle a four-anna piece off the end of the nose. We played a rather difficult game called 'Predicaments', then I did 'just one more monologue' and Viola and I made our excuses and came to bed. But not, alas, to a solid night. Tossage and uneasy dreams and my pillow is like a rock and the air cushion rolled and made me feel sick. Three more shows today. Ah me. But *not* Ah me, too, for it is the most exciting feeling to watch the very ill ones forgetting things for a minute – I think it really must be a good thing to do.

Monday, December 11th, 1944   Poona

Someone called Mrs . . . came to call on me. She is head girl of the wvs here in Poona and takes her duties with much seriousness. Whether curiosity or a Christian duty towards her neighbour propelled her this way I do not know. Anyhow there was spitting up of gravel as her bicycle took the corner and a completely joke figure in a topee, pink blouse and blue skirt, the total ringing the bell at about fourteen stone, came in and was grand. But you can't really be grand and look like a sugar pig at the same time. She made conversation and when she thought she'd done the social thing long enough out trotted the purpose of the call. Would I do a show for her officers' hostel? The answer was that as I'd come to India to play hospitals and as we are playing three shows a day I was afraid I must say No. A look of surprise; but she took it quite well and soon was arranging the right pedal of her bike in starting position, adjusting the topee and, swoop, off she'd gone.

We did a medical ward for the first show yesterday. Lots of Cockneys. We went to another neurological ward after tea, the third in three days. 126 is *the* centre for this.

We were bidden to drinks with the RAMC [Royal Army Medical Corps] officers. We did the show after supper in the infantile ward. Patients brought in from other wards and all the walking cases and a few friends; several medical orderlies and nurses. About a hundred or more. It was good fun. We'd got a proper piano with enough notes and they were prepared to listen, as opposed to having stuff poured over them. Very helpful. There was a boy called Colin from London, aged about twenty-three, who is entirely crippled with infantile. He lay making almost no shape in a bed just beside me and laughed and even sang with us. Somehow I just couldn't do 'London Pride' just because of him. He has no chance of seeing home again. Viola played 'Claire de Lune' like a dream.

Just got Noël's cable: 'DEAR JOYCE PERFECTLY ALL RIGHT IF YOU RETURN MARCH AS PLANNING DO OPERETTE BEFORE REVUE HAPPIEST POSSIBLE CHRISTMAS ALL LOVE NOËL COWARD.' So that is my answer.

Wednesday, December 13th, 1944   Poona

Yesterday was our fifteenth wedding anniversary. Lordy it doesn't seem that long. Cabled to Reggie for it last week but haven't had anything back so he may be overseas now. Viola and I started at No. 3 hospital on Monday. Can't quite decide why it is so much better than No. 126. The reasons are hidden but the proof is evident. The whole business of our visit beautifully laid on. Each ward expectant and prepared; poster up. The wards on either side of the one chosen warned and the bed patients carried over. Not only does the organisation make it lots easier for us but it also makes it far more fun for the men. The RSM at No. 3 is a first-class man. He precedes us everywhere at top speed on his bike and he appears to be really interested in getting it done properly. So far we haven't met the matron. Mrs Gosnell says she is rather spinstery and fierce. On Monday we did three medical wards, all of which are now rather confused in my mind except for a very sweet East Ham boy who has malaria and been in hospitals for four months. I'm going to write to his Ma and say I've seen him. He was very gentle and shy. Engaged to a Geordie girl from Newcastle. Yesterday we did a jaundice ward and two surgicals. The first were wonderfully gay considering, and I was *so* bad. Don't quite know why but I found I was working from the centre of a thick and impenetrable cloud of cotton wool consistency. Forgot words and was generally vague. With a huge effort I fought my way out and ended on my toes, but the first thirty minutes were a waking nightmare. The orthopaedics were, as orthopaedics always are, a perfect audience. I was awake by now and we had a fine time. The sister on that ward had made delicious drop scones for us and we had a cuppa with the boys when we'd finished. She had seen us at No. 29 at Shaiba last April; also at the Port Club there. We moved on through the evening sun to the facial maxillary[1] ward where we had an especially good time, too. They were chatty and responsive and we did a lot of requests. Their MO made a little thank you speech at the end and I gave him full marks for it, for he, like some of them there, has no roof to his mouth and his articulation is very poor, but they obviously like him a great deal and were with him from the start. No looking away in embarrassment or surreptitious giggles, which says a lot for him. Name of Brears. Among the audience were several West Africans. One enormous coal black one sat on a table in the middle

---

[1] Maxillary: of the upper jaw.

of the ward, quite motionless, with a snow white plaster across his nose. The effect was a little startling. After we'd finished more tea was produced and we sat about and talked to them of radio and theatre and bombs. It seems Vera Lynn[1] is waning and Anne Shelton[2] has taken her place. I asked in both surgical wards if they ever heard 'Here's wishing you all well again' and they all listen to it. No competitors, though, as far as I could see. Yesterday was a good day after a poor start.

Thursday, December 14th, 1944   Poona

Shopping in Poona with Mrs Gosnell. I feel a bit of a pig in not calling her Kay, but now I've let it go on too long without and it's too difficult to start. Col Gosnell's immediate Christian naming of us put us off and made me, anyway, get further away. But I like her very much. She's completely natural. Her heart is large, *and* practical, and she is gay. We had coffee in the local coffee house, went into five or six Kashmiri shops in search of fur jackets and then took a tonga to an underclothes woman who lived upstairs in a side-street among more awful housecoats and spangle-on-net dance dresses than it was possible to believe. She was an Anglo-Indian of vast proportions, speaking a sort of Muswell Hill with a lot of Mad*am*-ing. I bought quite a pretty pair of cami-knickers for Viola for Christmas. Then we tonga'd on to the Napier Hotel where Mrs Gosnell remembered dwelt a poor widow who sold underclothes on commission to help her eke out. So we had all her wares spread around a small dark room and she talked at us brightly with a little ripply

[1] Vera Lynn: was twenty-four when she volunteered in 1944 to sing for the troops in Burma, for what was known as 'The Forgotten Army'. It was her singing of 'The White Cliffs of Dover' which made her the Forces' Sweetheart, and she was awarded the Burma Star. Subsequently she was made a Dame of the British Empire.
[2] Anne Shelton: a popular vocalist; her success continued into the 1950s.

laugh while I fell for a really lovely set of white night-dress, petticoat and pants, all done in triple ninon with a small affair of palest green lilies of the valley appearing in appliqué in appropriate places. I shall keep the night-gown; Viola shall have the rest and I'll give the first cami-knickers to Mrs Gosnell as a parting present when we go tomorrow. We were very late for lunch. The Col was doing a self-control act, belied by his little blue eyes. I don't like the way his mouth smiles automatically while his eyes stay stones.

Washed my hair and wrote to Dick to tell him I wouldn't be home as soon as I'd said. Viola spent the morning swimming at the local club and the afternoon practising on a very horrid piano in Poona. In the evening we went to the forces club weekly dance and were whirled off our feet for a couple of hours and made to feel fascinating. Competition was faint, I'm bound to admit. We were asked to do 'just a little something' in the interval and were announced by a bounder called Somer-hayes as two well-known artists who had been flown out from home specially to entertain men in bed, which was a misinterpretation of facts guaranteed to put ideas in the head! Viola heard a man behind her say: 'Coo, so they've laid that on now –' But otherwise they behaved beautiful-ly and no one tittered.

Friday, December 15th, 1944   Poona

Viola and I walked into Poona about 11 and had coffee at the India Coffee House where we met Mr Carr, the welfare lieut. He says that Secunderabad are having billeting problems and have placed us seven miles apart. I've rung up Plunket-Greene[1] to see what can be done because I've no intention of such goings on. Far too

---

[1] Terence Plunket-Greene: became, after the war, a leading theatrical agent.

unpractical. I thought the hotel accommodation was all laid on ages ago. It's rather depressing. We've got fourteen days there.

Three more shows over at No. 3 in the afternoon and evening. First a surgical ward where they were very shy but appreciative in a not very demonstrative way. Then an outdoor show between two isolation wards far out of the hospital compound. Here we had five BORS in beds on one balcony and five officers in dressing gowns on the other. The sun was going down and, high above us, in the cloudless greeny blue sky, kites flew and glided many hundred feet up. It was a bit tricky singing from side to side across about fifty yards of space and I wasn't ever sure if the side I wasn't facing could hear me but we had a very cosy time considering the difficulties and did a lot of requests. 'White Christmas' crops up a good deal just now.

We did a show about 8 o'clock in the junior officers' surgical and all the others came in. Viola had the full-sized piano, for a blessing, and it was very good in that green vault for sound. Five or six leg cases were unable to come in from their balcony. I tried my best that they should hear but only the first three managed, so when it was all over I did a few extra monologues for the others outside. They were an ideal audience, both in and out. Several old fans from the Little days. General impression of No. 3 hospital is very good. I put a lot of it down to the excellent RSM, name of Horne. He laid on everything for us and it was beautifully done all through. We never saw the matron, which I think is a little dull of her, but I gather she's a bit sticky, so we haven't missed much. But three days in her hospital and she didn't bother out of curiosity to see what we were at strikes me as a little strange. When I'd done just over an hour Viola took over and played for a bit and they loved it. Bed was exceedingly good last night and I slept solidly for the first time for too long.

Sunday, December 17th, 1944   British Residency,
                                             Hyderabad

We are both staying with the Lothians[1] in this enormous
palladian-style mansion for three days. I'm not quite
clear how we happen to be here but I gather it's in the
nature of a royal command so here we are. Lady Lothian
is in bed with a cold. The daughter is a nice schoolgirlish
type in a cotton frock and no make-up and the father is
first and foremost a Scot. Whether his rather racy anecdotes at dinner last night were an attempt to speak what
he forlornly believes to be actresses' language I don't
quite know. He's a middle-sized man with large blue
eyes and a queer trick of clenching his teeth in an open
grin now and again. I think this is because he's had
trouble with his inner ear and it may be a method of
flexing his jaw muscles which might pop his ears. He's
slightly Athenaeum, a little majestic and rather tired.
Brigadier Russell, who is in command here, told me (off
the record) that Lady Lothian wants me to do a Red Cross
show for her in March and that is behind her hospitality. I
shan't be here in March. We lunched with the Russells
yesterday. It was quite a shock to go into a house with
real individual flavour to it. Joan Russell is what Mrs
Gosnell calls 'Artistic'. Which, in this case, means that
she had a deliciously fresh drawing room with white
curtains edged in blue. And her covers are gay blue and
white and red and white cotton in all-over patterns. A
slightly *Ladies Home Journal*-cum-Fortnum and Mason
Victorianism predominating and the general effect of
great gaiety and cleanliness. Mrs Russell does Diver-
sional Therapy at Hospital 127 where we start work
today. We spent the afternoon there meeting Miss Lang,
the matron, and Colonel Douglas the CO. They were all
very co-operative and with the RSM we've laid on a very
formidable programme for the next five days.

[1] Sir Arthur Cunningham Lothian: British Resident at Hyderabad
1942–6.

Viola and I played the crossword game and got very low as the sun fell and the size of the room increased. We felt very far away from home and definitely sad. Dinner with the Resident was a quiet affair apart from shouting owing to his poor ear. We ate well and there was home-made fudge to finish things off. The daughter was out. We came to bed at 10.15. I've sent Christmas cables to Reggie, my Pa, Aunt N., my Ma and Dick.

The drawing room here is good. The Resident told us Cecil Beaton was very pleased with it. Dates from 1803 and much of the furnishing comes from the Royal Pavilion at Brighton and was brought out here by the East India Company.

Monday, December 18th, 1944   Hyderabad

The Lothians were all out at their shoot when we came down yesterday morning. Viola got up first and explored the garden. I was lazier and didn't emerge till about 11.30 and then arranged myself in a long chair under a giant tree and read Eric Linklater's amusing autobiography called *The Man On My Back*. Viola soon appeared and we watched some idiotic black and white birds doing clown antics in another large tree, tumbling off branches, swooping down and stopping suddenly on a twig and generally being very entertaining. There were lots of very tiny little wrens roving without disturbances among the intricacies of an acacia sort of tree over me. Great delicacy of foliage burgeoning from a thick giant of a trunk. Flowers in India have a slightly nightmare quality. They are brilliant and big and have the consistency of rubber but they awe rather than delight the eye. I'm thinking of the calla lilies. And poinsettias. There is a whiskery sort of stock in the beds here. Smells delicious too; pink and white and when it dies, as the bowl full in my room has done, it turns into a weeping tragedy of falling petals and long streaming antennae. After lunch, which we ate alone under the rather scornful eye of an Indian butler, we walked in the garden. Viola had discovered a cemetery, circular and walled off, full of Regency monuments and telling a sad story of early deaths among the English who started out here. Stillborn babies, sons of ten months old, brave soldiers of forty-seven and some wives. We walked through coarse cropped grass, my eye ever out for snakes, and found a pleasant shaded plot with a model of this house in the middle of its grass where a sundial or fishpond would have been more in keeping. Sikhs were on guard at the foot of the wide front steps and they presented arms every time we got within sight, which was nice of them but which presented a new problem. Should one ignore the gesture, or smile, or say thank you, or what? I found myself murmuring 'Good afternoon' and I think Viola probably said 'Thank you most awfully'. But neither seems quite right. Of course a salute is the right thing but you can't in a cotton frock without a hat.

The car ordered to fetch us at quarter to four arrived to do so at quarter to two so it backed into the shade and got on with some chores like pumping up tyres and dusting till it was time to go. Cars in India are of the more fragile sort. We had a couple of honeys in Poona. A baby blue one with no glass in it at all and only one door that worked. The car we used yesterday has a bold bluebottle gloss to it but only half the correct number of windows and a horn that hurts clear through ear, spine and stomach. It is of a ferocious brutal tone that can't be ignored and we found ourselves tensed, awaiting its fearful blast. We set off yesterday afternoon at 3.45 to do a couple of shows at 127 hospital. About half a mile from our objective we had a puncture, and despair covered both the driver and his winder – a passenger who travels entirely for the purpose of winding, for the car has long since ceased to selfstart. It was, they indicated, the second puncture that day. They were very sad about it. We set out and walked, not too quickly because of getting too hot, but not too slowly so's not to be late.

Two medical wards, both very well laid on. We signed a great many autographs and in the second ward someone started a fashion by asking me to 'put something' in his airletter card and several others seemed to think this a good idea and that took ages. Hope the idea doesn't spread. I ask what the owner's name is, whom the letter is going to, whether they know he is in hospital, how he is, and from that evolves a three-line message saying I've seen Sid and he looks splendid and was singing with me on Dec. 17th when I was visiting the ward in which he is staying and I hope it won't be long before he is back in W. Ham or Hartlepool or Widnes or the Isle of Aran. I try hard to make each one different and try to imagine the homes the letters are going to. But it takes time. However, it seems, mysteriously, to give pleasure.

I wish Viola felt happier about her playing. She said, coming back in the car, that it had completely gone from her; she'd lost her ability *really* to play so that it made sense. This isn't true but she believes it is. I never knew anyone with less faith in herself. And it's sad really because she has *so* much; looks, a real sweetness and unselfedness, and her music is literate and articulate. I still feel she has a ghost somewhere that must be laid – a sort of sour something that gets in the way from time to time and takes control even when she doesn't want it to. She is a darling person and I love her. Can't bear these disappearances that come over her from time to time. She suddenly vanishes behind a blank wall and it's very hard going to get through to her at all when that happens. She had one at Isfahan and a sort of minor one in Poona. But on the whole I think they are less fierce and frequent than they were.

Tuesday, December 19th, 1944   Hyderabad

We are moving today. People called Slaughter are having us which is very good of them. I shan't be sorry to leave the Residency. It is haunted by a faintly unhappy atmosphere, hard to define. We met the Lothian family at lunch yesterday. It was the first time we'd seen them together and they were a bit depressing. She is still full of her cold and was distrait, disinterested and definitely dull. No warm spark kindles behind that respectable shell – pearls, a 'good' linen dress from Marshall and Snelgrove and a hairnet. Alison, the daughter, is a perfect prig and needs an emotional jolting to reshuffle her certainties about everything. He has warmth, now overlaid by a sort of bitter veneer; can't discover why. Not a very happy or cheerful trio. The subject of artists for her Red Cross show in the spring was skated over and left. It is odd that this great pile has absorbed the discomfiting atmosphere of its tenants. It could have been so different and probably has been. Somehow none of it is jelled. There is no feeling of amity or affection between staff and family or family and family.

We played two more wards at 127 yesterday afternoon and evening. A nice toothless Londoner told me if ever I was in Finchley to pop in on his mum who'd love to give me a cuppa tea anytime. I've got her address in my notebook.

Wednesday, December 20th, 1944   Chez Slaughter,
                                   The Gables, Secunderabad

Our spirits have risen. This is a large, low rambling family house in a wide compound. Mrs Slaughter is kind, gentle, and human. He is small and dynamic and a quite lot older than she is. There are three very attractive children. Jenny, ten, Tom nine, and Mary Ann, five. Solid blonde and forthright. We have a large pale pink room with pale green woodwork, our own porch and our own bathroom and it feels like heaven! We moved in the morning. The Lothians came to see us off and I feel a slight guilt in my criticism of them for they mean well. It's

just that they don't start burning in the right places. Not
their fault. Lady L.'s cold is receding and she emerges a
little less dim than I'd foreseen. Mrs Slaughter, he too,
says they are dears and do the job very well. So I'm quite
wrong and horrid. This room opens out on to a little
porch and beyond it is a square of grass and then the
tennis court. As I lay on my bed by the open double doors
a procession kept passing that drew my attention very
successfully from the book. Mrs Slaughter was lending
the house that night for a charity dance. Or, to be more
accurate, lending the garden. All afternoon bearers went
by bearing objects. A potted plant, a table on the head,
three chairs in a feat of balance, an ayah with tablecloths,
more plants; then four men in a funny little puttering run
carrying a bigger table. Mrs Slaughter, who is about
thirty-eight or forty, with tired good looks and very
gentle eyes, was supervising in an apron. Distantly I
heard Tom playing 'D'ye Ken John Peel' on his fiddle.
There was much Indian conversation among the bearers
preparing the party and quite near this room is a pen full
of turkeys that gobbled pleasantly. I set off about 4,
dressed for the first time, on the job that is, in Nancy's
black chiffon with the little satin bows and wearing my
new bright green silk scarf on the head. I was a little
alarmed by the whole thing – black gloves, bag and
shoes, but Viola says it was all right once I'd started
singing! When we got back to the Slaughters the first
guests were arriving for the party. There were lights in
the garden, a huge log fire burned on the gravelled
terrace above the beds surrounding a long shallow pond
– lit from within among the goldfish and lily pads – and
the RAF orchestra was establishing itself on the grey stone
dance floor that the Slaughters had laid down when they
first came here ten years ago. Viola and I changed and
rather unwillingly joined the party. I'd expected that as it
was a charity dance everyone would come in parties
already partnered but I was wrong, and there were a lot
of unpartnered soldiers, mostly from the big hospitals

here. Mrs S. introduced us to a group of six officers, most
of whom had wild and fierce moustaches but all were
dwarfed by the magnificent hirsutic triumph of Captain
Joe Dashwood whose handlebars were visible a good
inch on either side of his head even when seen from the
rear. They were any easy group: Capt D., Majors
Whitson, Townley and Powis and one, mercifully unidentified, two-pip lieut of ghastly bounce. Would I, he
asked in an overloaded accent, care to risk myself in a
dance with him. Upon my head be it, he warned. We did
some simple steps, me held very tightly in his practised
arms. 'I suppose you sing even more divinely than you
dance,' he sighed. 'I'm a lucky devil to have you like this.'
To which I could find no repartee at all. We got a bit
confused over a glide-throw-away-your-gal-and-then-
swoop-movement, and his shocked voice said, 'Can you
ever, ever forgive me. A thousand million apologies – but
of course it's your own fault for bothering to dance with
me.' I wonder where he picked up the act? Powis was the
nicest of the group. He talked well and with enthusiasm.
Told me of a Mass he'd seen celebrated by a lot of West
African Catholic Negroes a hundred yards behind their
guns, and how they ran forward to relieve the firing party
who, in their turn, ran back and took part in the Mass.
You could hear the faint tinkle of their little holy bell
between crashes of gunfire. An extraordinary sight to
see. And then he told me about a very still night in the
jungle when the men were all in their huts or tents and
the radio in the sergeants' hut came through very clearly
with an orchestration of 'Stille Nacht' and how the
sergeant beside it started to sing in a rich bass voice and
how the occupants of the huts all round joined in out of
the darkness, singing in parts, and filling the night with a
loveliness that had moved him a good deal. The party
went on till 11. Our group broke up a bit when Powis and
the arch-bounder had to get back to their hospital at ten.
Dashwood took me for a ponderous turn on the floor,
apologising for the iron tips to his desert boots and

bringing one of them down on my toe as he spoke.
Whitson, with a ginger moustache of inferior size,
danced like a crab but with 1925 rhythms, and Townley,
who was rapidly getting tighter but in a respectable way,
led me rigidly round the floor with great dignity and care.
We all laughed a good deal and the time passed quite
pleasantly. We sat down to hot soup with the exhausted
Slaughters at 11 and came gratefully to bed a little later.

Breakfast this morning was enhanced by a spray of
yellow daisies on Viola's tray and some pale lilac chrysanthemums on mine. The hand of Mrs Slaughter. And then
Jenny and Mary Ann, knocking cautiously, came in with
four very short-stemmed but delicious violets. Mary Ann
is five and has a pair of pigtails about two inches long of a
ferocious tightness and stiffness that stand out like wires.
She is solid and rather shy and came in clutching some
minute knitting on enormous needles.

Thursday, December 21st, 1944   Secunderabad

Mary Ann Slaughter has immense personality. She had a
cooking session yesterday morning and appeared very
flushed with a plate full of burnt brown crumbs. 'You
must put butter in the frying pan,' she explained, 'but I
forgot.' She thought I ought to see the hammock so, hand
in hand, we walked through the pleasant garden here
and she kept up a running commentary about flowers
and her ability to jump off a three-foot wall. This morning
she came to call on us at 8.30 carrying three large white
lilies. Her pale green cotton skirt stuck out in a short frill
under her sweater and the pigtails were tight and stiff.
We got on to the subject of bathing. She goes with the rest
of the family to Bombay[1] today and expects to get in the
sea sooner or later. Her bathing suits are 'yellow, all

[1] The Slaughters went to Bombay for Christmas, leaving Joyce and Viola
on their own. 'Few luxuries compare to staying with people,' wrote
Joyce, 'and having them go away!'

flowery and one with bows'. We asked her if she could swim, knowing it was one of her best accomplishments and had been mastered at the age of three and a half and we asked who had taught her. 'No one did,' she said. 'One day I said I will swim and I swam.' Sometimes, she told me, she felt like biting people and when she did she liked to bite *skin*. She seemed pleased with the thought. She sings perfectly in tune and with much gusto. Tom plays the fiddle with bold strokes and heavy breathing and we had a brief musicale after lunch yesterday with Viola at the piano and all of us contributing. She demanded 'Daisy' and whispered hoarsely that it was the one that began with 'Two Daisies'. Poor Jenny is the left out one. She's the eldest and isn't musical. Tom gets attention for being the boy and Mary Ann gets it for being Mary Ann. But Jenny is left out and this makes her a bit extra noisy and showy-off. My heart bleeds for her.

Friday, December 22nd, 1944   Secunderabad

We had our beds moved out on to the verandah and slept there for the first time last night. 'Slept' is going a bit far; we lay out there disturbed by distant pi-dogs, nature giving tongue in all manner of unusual sounds. 'Something' fought its way through bushes, footsteps came and went. I saw the stars change position over the tree tops. It was not a very restful night. Added to which we'd done a long and tightly packed show in the officers' ward at 127 that evening and I was still spinning. Which probably accounts for the whole thing. That show was our last at 127. We've been there for five days and have grown fond of its sprawling pale pink porticoed appearance. Like so many of the present hospitals out here, this was originally a barracks. Someone with taste designed it. Faintly Spanish flavour – pale pink plaster, with red tiled roofs, flower beds and a pleasing sense of space. The RSM, Jackson, with large, circular eyes, saw to all the

details very faithfully and everything was laid on well.
Our last BOR show took place in a jaundice ward and was
uphill work through deepest mudlike glooms in very
heavy boots. Poor things. They were locked away in sour
depths and it took all I had to get the very faintest
response to anything. I kept thinking of Dick when he
had it; but oddly enough he never got impenetrably low.
These boys lay yellow and inert and unsmiling most of
the time and then, right at the end, some of them seemed
to break through their cocoon of gloom and that helped.
But it was about the toughest going I've yet had and was
made even harder by the unimaginative arrangements of
the beds and the piano so that I was never quite facing
anyone and kept turning from side to side, hoping that
my voice was audible to someone at least. They had
punkahs in these large wards – heavy strips of canvas
about two yards long and one deep, hung on wires from
the ceiling. They do a very efficient job in mopping up all
sound which can't be said to help the singer.

Monday, December 25th, 1944   Secunderabad
– Christmas Day

Looking out of my mosquito net at the first light this
morning I saw what appeared to be a stocking hanging
with all the right bulges from the post on the corner. So it
was. Viola had found a pair of very small red and white
striped socks and filled them with soap, a pair of Indian
bracelets, some chocolate and a paper full of sparkling
silvery devices to be tied on the head or the dress. It is
only 9.30 now and already the room is a shambles.
Ghulam is celebrating Christmas for us too and brought
us garlands and a coconut each. The head peon has
presented us each with small mixed bouquets, a little
lopsided but infinitely touching. Viola arose with the
dawn and fixed me a bunch of orange and yellow candy-
tufts and plumbago. The cook went mad and sent the

trays in sprigged with bits of maidenhair fern, and we had bowls of yoghurt and a fancy macédoine of passion fruit and raspberry jam that was a bit startling for breakfast. I wrapped my gifts for Viola in puce, green, and yellow paper. We ate breakfast and undid each other's parcels amid falling rose petals from our garlands and much genuine surprise; for we'd kept our secrets well and she didn't know about the frock I'd found for her and I didn't know about the delicious white and blue saree she'd found for me. She wrote me a tune – simple enough for my feeble fingers – and I did a Christmas poem for her. She gave me Linklater's *The Great Ship* and I had a pair of red and gold slippers with the toes turned up for her. It's being a lovely Christmas. Viola has now got back into her bed, having arranged all the flowers in vases brought us by Ghulam, and hung the garlands from the posts of my bed where they wave gently in the morning breezes. They are composed of tiny white chrysanthemums or something very like that, strung on white cotton and spaced with pink roses and little tinsel affairs to give sparkle. Viola has hung all the name tags I made for her from the top of her net stand and arranged all her presents around her. I write from a welter of stockings, petals, bits of silver ribbon and my tune which I have yet to hear performed.

When I woke up at 8 I counted back the hours and found it was about half past midnight in England and I wondered if Aunt N. was in the little room behind her boudoir as she always used to be on Christmas Eve.[1] It won't be much of a day for her with both Jakie and Michael away; David too, perhaps? I count myself lucky to be away really. It's a sad moment somehow with the war getting longer instead of finishing as we hoped and the news being generally disquieting. I wonder if Reggie is at Oxford. And Ma and Tommy? And how my Pa is. Apart from these little anxieties – concern for the loved

[1] See *Darling Ma*, and Christmas at Cliveden.

ones is a continual presence, I find – apart from these, though, it's good to be miles off in isolation, with a job to do that involves a certain amount of self-immolation. Viola is a heavenly companion and we have reached that comfortable state of sympathy when silences are often more articulate than speech. Added to which she is almost as silly as Gin; and that's high praise. I do love an ability to be really silly.

Our two shows at 128 were lovely to do. It was Christmas Eve and the wards were decorated – or almost completed. We were told they were keeping the final details for the very day itself so that no one could swipe their ideas. There was a prize for the best ward. Very elaborate schemes they had – a complete tavern, a ship, and a garden. We were told that the patients were going to dress up too. One ward became an olde worlde village and had an oldest inhabitant and a village idiot. For weeks past the patients have been planning and making the decorations and it says a lot for the unit there that they have known when to shut an eye to strange goings on – such as the presence of two pet kids and a white kitten, all needed for the decoration plans, as well as pets. The last show of the day was in the penicillin ward. Many bed patients, mostly feeling pretty low, for I gather that penicillin isn't much fun; it hurts and the treatment includes injections every three hours. We had about 150 knee cases, all 'up' and they were in gala mood. Apart from rather a trying type who'd been drinking and had got to the stage of needing to express himself, all was fine. At frequent intervals he found it necessary to say 'Yeah M'am' and his neighbours, and I, wished he wouldn't. We stayed over two hours in this ward – lots of requests and communal numbers. I was asked for 'Just a Song at Twilight' which ordinarily I avoid because it's so sad but the asker was the illest man in the ward, a creature of bone in a cast, so we did it and they roared it in a comforting sort of way. Man called Lucas who has been in bed there for about seven months in a double cast, both legs, gave me a couple of little golliwogs he'd made out of red and green wool. He'd heard that day that he'd got to have one of his legs off. Once again we noticed their goodness to each other; a tenderness that is the more moving for its gentle fumbling clumsiness.

. . . I had a couple of rather bad come overs and nearly blacked out which was alarming, but I didn't quite and it passed. This business of weakness following the curse has got to stop. I've got now so I expect it and that's ridiculous.

Tuesday, December 26th, 1944   Secunderabad
– Boxing Day

On Christmas Day we had Palaw or Pilaw or Palov for lunch. Anyway it's a mound of rice and raisins topped with chicken and garnished with everything else in the house, some of it curried. We had two goes each and panted. The fruity mousse to follow filled in the only remaining gaps and after that sleep was the obvious cure, but instead, we sat in the drawing room and for some unknown reason fell to talking of when my Ma left my Pa and all the nightmare days there were when we sought her in Paris and the South of France. Some of it has hardened with time and I can see its funnier side but for the most part it's an experience that hasn't healed and my stomach goes cold when I remember the night when it all happened. Not a very gay subject for Christmas Day. It threw me into a mood indigo all right. Complex thoughts haunted me and from this distance I wished I had a few more answers. After a while Viola went off to do something with the candies we'd got from the Russells and I fell asleep on the sofa, sad as a sigh.

About 5 our taxi came to take us up to 127 where we'd planned to do a little secret visiting in the wards where there were the most bed patients.

Dinner at the Russells. The King on the air from home came through clearly and he spoke very well. I did a hurried flashback to all the places where I knew he'd be listened to – 37 Chesham Place,[1] Daddy's flat? Cliveden, and I wondered if Dick had him on. Wonder if Reggie was at 37? No mail, no mail. The evening was easy and pleasant. Food was un-Christmassy except for a flaming pudding. I had an argument, friendly, with Dan Russell about the bullying treatment of servants out here. He implored me not to write a book about my experiences in India! After dinner we played paper games which was a good way of making us jell for we were a mixed group.

Thursday, December 28th, 1944   Secunderabad

Boxing Day brought us a small batch of very old mail. Can't think where it's been all this time. Reggie writes that Harry has got to lose the other foot too. It's damnable; really bloody. He is at Roehampton. Strange pattern that has made – back to Roehampton again after twenty odd years. I've seen pictures of Reggie and Harry and Vera[2] there as small children with their Shetland pony under a giant cedar tree. That was in the Col's palmy days. Hilda was there – deliciously slim in a flowing white dress and the Col, in a high collar. Lord, what a lot has happened in between. And now Harry, hurt in Burma, is back at his own home as a patient. Nothing from Pa or Gin. No other mail at all. I wrote a few letters in the morning while Viola played. Lunch in the garden. Really, the loveliness of these days. Only trouble about so much space is that it gives one time to think. A bad practice at the moment, I find. It's a bloody world. The war gets longer and longer. Dropping V 2s in the North now. Churchill and Eden went to Athens on Christmas Day to try and clarify that little muddle.[3]

---

[1] The home of Reggie's parents.

[2] Harry and Vera Grenfell: Reggie's younger brother and elder sister.

[3] The Greek rebellion: a conference, attended by Churchill and Eden, Archbishop Damaskinos, Field-Marshal Alexander and Harold Macmillan began on December 26th, 1944 aboard the *Ajax*.

We started working at 134 on Tuesday. Tea with Col Hyatt and Miss Colman Turner first. Everything very well organised here. We did a couple of good shows in surgical wards. Playing at 5 and then again at 7 is about the best timing we've done so far. Neither show has to be hurried and we did an hour and a half in the second one to the most heavenly audience ever. Two bed patients near the front were in flattering ecstasies. They shook with laughter, their eyes grew round in sentiment; they clapped and clapped. Viola has got a horrid crack at the top of her finger and playing the mini doesn't help at all. Later, dinner back at the bungalow and then we played some duets for fiddle and piano. I knew Viola had done the fiddle at the Academy but I hadn't realised that it was more than that and there'd been a struggle to decide which instrument to do. There was only Tom Slaughter's little plywood fiddle but she made it sing and even my poor accompanying took colour from it and we had a fine time going through a book of Gems for Piano and Violin – First Position. Everything in it from hit tunes from the operas down to arrangements of 'Swanee River' and 'The Blue Danube'. Then walked in the garden. The moon was high and the shadows clear-cut and beautiful. Hindus, not far enough away, were beating at drums in some sort of celebration.

General approval of the job we're doing here reached my ears in whispers last night. One rather drunken major told me the boys in his hospital were frankly suspicious of us and had an antagonistic attitude to these stars who come out slumming from England. But that after they'd heard us . . . etc., etc. Nice for the ego. Being able to do the job slowly does make a lot of difference to them and to us.

Two mornings ago at 9 a.m. the butler knocked on our door and handed Viola a card. Mr M. Pradhan, it said, was a lawyer from Bombay and on the back was a message saying he would like an interview with Miss Grenvile. Viola went and saw him and found a youngish-old – thirty-three – Indian in glasses who wished to join ENSA. He was persistent and intense and she urged him not to give up his lawyering on the flimsy hope that ENSA needed him, which was his intention. Finally, to get rid of him, she said that if he'd write a letter stating his qualifications and asking what he required we would hand it to someone in ENSA. He was then bidden to tea next day and of course came, arriving early and moist from the long bike ride from Hyderabad. He had a soft smooth ageless face and greying straight hair. He spoke fluent but quaint English: 'In Bumbi (Bombay) they are putting up *The Doll's House*, I have studied the Scandanavian drama but it is not appealing to the masses.' We sat down to tea, which he drank with his left hand, slowly. He was oddly lifeless and far off but he said that the theatre was his 'craze'. He had produced some sketches of Noël Coward's; but they were for intellectuals. He wondered if Sheridan's *School for Scandal* – he called it Skendel – would appeal to the masses? It is comedy they wish? We asked him what his experience had been in the theatre. 'I am watching it for three years,' he said. 'Also in Bumbi, I was putting up Ibsenesque plays. A friend of mine has made translation of *The Doll's House* and *The Honeymoon Couple* and put them together in Hindu, changing the watching of the fire from one play to something else with significance. It is all symbolical.' We passed him another egg and tomato sandwich which he bit into very gently and chewed as if it tasted of nothing at all. Now and then he would raise his right hand and thoughtfully scratch his head with an unbent finger; the whole thing without interest. We asked about professional theatre in India and he said there was none. Some people in Bumbi had tried it but it has been a flup; they lost financially. In Hyderabad he had wished to put up 'Candida' but it was too hard to cast. There were four or five Mohammedan ladies there who were interested but none of them was fit to come on the stage. Somewhat tentatively we asked him what he wished to contribute to ENSA and he said he could produce plays and farcical sketches together with Scandinavian drama. He had studied (by watching?) the Ibsenesque technique. We told him as kindly as we could that ENSA wasn't entirely concerned with the higher sort of theatre but he wasn't discouraged and suggested he came to Bangalore with us on Sunday to see Plunket-Greene about his chances. This we hurriedly told him was no good. We'd show his letter and credentials to P.-G. and then, if we weren't wrong, he'd suggest our taking them all on to Calcutta to show Jack Hawkins; which we'd do. Of course it would be kinder to be cruel now and say the whole thing is quite useless, but we just couldn't, even though he was a bore and without charms of any sort in the world. His letter to Plunket-Greene makes plain the whole picture.

Sir, I understand you are the officer in charge of the ENSA for this area. I shall be much grateful if you would consider my case for an appointment in the organisation. I did my BA and LLB from the Univ. of Bombay in the years 1933 and 1935 respectively. Since 1932 I have associated myself with the stage-craft and I have been acting in the Plays and directing them; also to a certain extent I have tried to study 'Modern Drama'; in proof of this I am enclosing a certificate from the President of the Assocs. for which I have been working all these years. The Plays put up by the Assocs. for which I have worked are of the type of Farcical Comedies, Sketches and Problematic Plays. I presume that my services would be of some use to you in running the shows for ENSA. I am enclosing 2 certificates from the College authorities where I completed my Academic Career; and one from the Rector of the Hostels where I was Resident-Student. My birthdate is 6th Aug. 1911. If any reference is required to be made the same may be made to 1. Justice Naik etc., etc. 2. Rajah Bahadur etc., etc.

In the circumstances I shall be much grateful if you would, without going through much red-tape, kindly consider my case favourably for the Appointment to ENSA.

Yours faithfully,

M. R. Pradhan.

It should warm Basil Dean's pinsized heart to know there are people who regard the organisation with such esteem and respect.

There is what Mr Pradhan calls a 'certificate for him' written by the President of the Hyderabad Music Circle and Kala Mandal. This throws further light on the set-up:

Since 1932 we have been staging 'Modern Drama' and Mr M. R. Pradhan has been a precious asset to us as he has been personally acting in the plays and directing them. Mr Pradhan has played the leading roles in most of our dramas and I may mention *Baby*, *Lapandas*, and *Hach Mulacha Bap* – the most important plays in which he played the roles exquisitely. I may also mention that Mr Pradhan has studied the technique of the 'Modern Drama' and is well acquainted with the Modern Technique known as Ibsen's technique or Scandinavian Technique. The plays staged by us are after the technique of the American Burlesque, Ibsen's Plays and Bjornstjerne Bjornson's Plays. In view of this experience acquired by Mr Pradhan I am sure that his study of stagecraft and his superb acting would be widely commended. Incidentally it was Mr Pradhan who directed the tunes in the lyrics of the play 'Lapandoo'.

We had to go off to the hospital at 4.30 so Mr P. held out a limp hand with grey nails and mounted his bike for

Hyderabad. It is all very sad and there's just nothing we can do about it. He hinted hopefully that he thought the ENSA might take him back to England with it after the war and we tried to clear that one up but he is living in a realm of dreams in which all things are possible.

Saturday, December 30th, 1944   Secunderabad

The birds in this garden make Surrey sounds and please the eye with their colours and flights. We have found a small bright green woodpecker (it turned out to be a copperpot) who is hollowing a dead branch on a wide pressed-fern-looking tree near the back gate. We stood under it for ages while butterflies lolloped through the finely drawn branches and the woodpecker pecked at his branch. Higher up still, his wife, less giddy to look at in her duller colours, watched out for him. He's been there three days running but we've only seen her once. And there are slim graceful birds who flash like Bible-edge gold, as Viola said; and some excitable bulbuls who feel good and say so at the top of their voices. Tree rats who are really sort of squirrels move at great paces and take flying leaps and squeak at each other and there are lizards and two very horrid cats with hideous voices. One reason we have had so many poor nights here has been the presence of rather too many enormous clumsy birds in the tall trees outside our room. They land among the leaves with a great crash of sound and then take off again in another. In a fit of whimsy I called them the albatrosses and they have now become Mr and Mrs Albert Ross and all their horrible little Rosses and we hate them. On these white nights with the moon staring coldly over the whole garden, making snow scenes and thoroughly upsetting us all, they lurch out of their trees and flap noisily over our little spread of lawn, throwing alarmingly large shadows and causing me to shudder. Nature, O Lord, is mighty complex and not always understandable.

January 1945

I write in the train to Bangalore. We left Secunderabad early this morning, having been allowed to board the train about 11.30 while it stood in a siding. Ghulam had made up our beds and laid a towel on the table – bananas, biscuits and water bottles were all arranged for our comfort. Indian trains do a disconcerting leap movement and, when we hurtle, as we do now and then, my pen is thrown all over the page and I get angrier and angrier about it. And about the heat and dust and the length of this journey and dullness of scenery to see through the eye-dazzling mesh of the fly screens. We are travelling as comfortably as it is possible to travel in wartime India but it lacks a certain something. However at least we can lie full length and at least, so far, we are in this compartment alone so I feel I should not complain.

Yesterday we had our first bit of real India. At 10.30 we drove over to Hyderabad to pick up the Bilgramis, Naqui and Mariam, and they then took us to see the palace and jewels of Nawab Salur Jung. I don't know where to start in that enormous messy conglomeration. He is by way of being a collector and we saw room after room full to the ceiling of pictures, furniture, objects, swords, daggers, more pictures, a collection of walking sticks about 400, etc., etc. The pictures were for the most part large and Italianate and almost all had a nude woman in it. They were of the every-picture-tells-a-story school and we had mythological subjects, life size, rioting all over sagging canvases left to lean against the wall in thick dust. There was a Leighton and a Landseer (rather a touching sheep dog guarding a pink bag!) and a very large story picture, called 'The Stigmata', of a comely nun in complete undress being branded by some bearded old men while younger, clean-shaven ones looked on in interest. We saw more junk assembled in one place than I hope ever to see again. And the filth of it all! Thick dust everywhere and rather hideous but quite good French furniture bursting out of its silk covers and just left to go on bursting further. We saw a room entirely hung in needlework pictures; astonishing work but of no aesthetic merit; and another full of miniature mosaic pictures. More dust, more pistols, more daggers and a pile of gun cases, mostly new. We rambled on through more rooms and downstairs into a reception hall hung with copied portraits of all the British Residents there had been in Hyderabad since Victoria's day. These gentlemen, faithfully copied by the secretary's secretary who showed us round and had long-range halitosis of the most powerful sort, were skied fifteen feet up, right against the ceiling where no light could reveal them and all dust could blur their features. It was rather an attractive pink room with Queen Anne-ish plaster-work painted white. There were chandeliers everywhere – some hung, some stood and all were covered in dust. There were Indian ones and English ones and some beauties from Vienna and in the larger banqueting hall next to the portrait gallery there were six or seven more, all hanging and in alternate colours of green glass and white glass. In this room there were sofas and chairs in Holland covers and a Victorian carpet worn thin with bare toes wriggling, one supposes, and covered, in patches, by a cotton drugget. More junk in here, screens, objects, more skied portraits of Victoria and her Albert at various stages of their lives. There was a ping-pong table set up in here among the shrouded furniture and beside it a large low divan bed. 'Where the Nawab sleep,' said the secretary. 'He has many room but he sleep here', and he turned back the faded paisley cotton covers and brought out a small hard narrow pillow which he told us the Nawab had had all his life and without which he couldn't sleep. It had a new cover on every day, the sec. said with pride. By the noble bed was a pile of books. One was called *Love at the Courts of Russia*, or some such title, and the others all dealt with amorous subjects. Out in the courtyard the sun beat down on steps roughened by pigeon droppings, and an old bearded gardener in a plaid rag scratched away at some defeated greenery. Inside there was a bright new sun-ray lamp. We saw the inner room where the sec. obviously thought the Nawab should sleep and it had walls entirely hung with reproductions of colour prints of romantic pictures mixed in with some rather lovely Indian historical minia-tures celebrating battles. By this time we were getting tired of looking but still hadn't seen the jewels we had particularly come to see. Back to the first courtyard, pool in the middle, potted plants and shrubs and ferns and, along one shaded verandah, rows of canaries all singing in cages. The Nawab came forward to greet us. He is fifty-seven with joke ears that look as if they'd been taken off and ironed out and then stuck back like handles on a sugar bowl. His hair is duck's-tailed and grey and stood up rather endearingly under his high fez which he wore at an angle. A pretty nasty old man, I suspect; but quite gay to meet. Hideous with a bulbous no-boned nose and a flabby Charles Laughton mouth. And dull eyes. He wore one of those long dark blue coats buttoning up to the neck and over his unfortunately low-hung and pot-bellied tum. His hands were also quite boneless and the nails were bitten down into tiny little pale strips. We were arranged in chairs around a low baize-topped card table. Two wooden cases, made like little toy chests of drawers, were elaborately unlocked and the drawers put on the table one by one. The sec.'s sec. had now gone and the sec. took over. He was fat and flabby and had a roving eye. Mrs Bilgrami sat next to the Nawab and came in for a certain amount of cheerful nudging and patting. The Nawab removed the shammy leather square on the first drawer and our eyes widened. Strands of pearls, knotted with emeralds; pendants of enormous size and elaboration to hang from turbans; ankle bracelets, rings, earrings, necklaces, belt buckles. All the first cases filled with old family stuff of beauty. Each piece set in heavy silver or gold and backed with exquisite enamel work. Bracelets always came in pairs. There were elephant-headed ones set in precious stones and weighing a lot. The whole thing designed in flowers. And there were lion-headed ones too. Many of the diamonds were as large as my thumbnail, and all these old pieces were cut smooth so there was no brilliance in them. The rubies were often pale and probably not very good but the settings were so lovely and so rich that we were delighted by all we saw. And the pearls. Dozens of ropes. One quite short strand was finished at the end by a pair of perfectly matched blue-tinged pearls – they were completely round and of identical weights and had been bought separately by the old man who was very pleased at his own cleverness. Indian jewels for the most part have no clasps. They are strung on silver or gold threads ending with strands long enough to be tied. We held heavy chest ornaments against our bosoms and Mrs Bilgrami put on earrings while I tried on rings and Viola played with bracelets. The Nawab was all eyes as if he expected us to swipe something and I must say I would very much have liked to do so for they were really lovely and very decorative. After an hour or so coffee and iced cake came round and only just in time. We were all visibly wilting and our eyes were dancing with the sights we'd seen. By this time we'd seen most of the stuff in the wooden cases but now a tin trunk was produced and we saw further pearls and gold thread belts with astonishing buckles of rubies and diamonds; more emeralds and more lovely enamel work. When we'd finished with this the Nawab's own little private box was produced: 'The things I keep with me,' he said. There was a gold cigarette case from Cartier set round with square cut sapphires; there were buttons of diamonds and rubies, studs, lighters of incredible vulgarity – modernistic style in rubies on gold – and endless more cigarette cases and tie pins and watch fobs. By now we were reeling and made signs to each other to go, but as we did so a procession suddenly appeared. There were ten bearers, of great filth and poverty, and on each of their heads was a black tin box and in each box more and more and more jewellery. We saw one full of cigarette cases – unbelievable mixture of hideous taste and good workmanship. Some had whole horses on them in diamonds; one had a large horseshoe all over the back in square-cut diamonds of great size. There was a wooden one among the precious collection. I was glad to see it. We made more movements to go but the Nawab wasn't ready. It had taken him some time to get started and he was apparently reluctant to do it at all – only two boxes worth seeing, he'd said – but, once he was at it, there was no stopping him. We had to see his earring collection; rather mysterious these, for he is unmarried. He made no comment, just opened case after case. They were a little shoddy, I thought, but at least I expected he'd give some to Mrs Bilgrami for he was so very insistent that she should see them all. But no.

At last we got away, glutted with richness and dizzy with looking. Rather frightening to see one ugly old man surrounded by those piles and piles of junk and all that jewellery, living in semi-squalor with dozens of inherited servants slopping around in dirty white uniforms and faded turbans. The Nawab's trousers, I observed, were worn at the cuff but his mother of pearl buttons had his initials on them. Those were the only ornament he wore, apart from a twisted snake ring in two golds.

When we'd been in the ping-pong table room I looked around for a piano. He is reputed to own half a dozen or more and we hadn't seen one yet. However in a sort of sky-lit cupboard room off the big one we found one under a cover, nose in to the wall as if in sad shame. It was a Bechstein and a beauty. Viola opened it and saw the strings were red with rust and all the usual dust everywhere. The sec. assured her it was tuned every week and didn't register at all when Viola suggested it might be used and cleaned every now and then as well.

We drove away, glad to be rid of the bulk of stuff we'd seen. Collecting on that scale amounts to madness. The Nawab is said to be building a palace to house it all some day. But it never gets any further and the present falling-down palace is nothing but a store house full of rotting furniture and useless objects. Very depressing. He is a feudal lord and within his walls and under his command lives a complete little world. He has his own bedraggled army, police force and ministers. Some of these were lurking in a courtyard room when we arrived. Gaunt men in co-respondent shoes wearing long coats and fezzes. 'Courtiers,' whispered Naqui Bilgrami as we passed them.

Tuesday, January 2nd, 1945   Central Hotel, Bangalore

And now here we are in Bangalore. Captain Terence Plunket-Greene met us. He is an actor; handsome in a smooth Henry Tiarks[1] way. Not much humour, but friendly and worried for our well-being. Young. Was wearing Burma green battledress and a swashbuckling felt hat. We have a room with a screened-off sitting room attached and a bath off it. We are washed and tidy and now await lunch. Calcutta is five days by train from here so it looks as if we must send Ghulam on ahead in a day or two's time, for we fly up on Tuesday next. Mail here. Two from Reggie, two from Gin, and a cable from my Pa for Christmas. Still no word from Dick for far too long. Hope he is OK. Harry is back, in excellent form. Gin has written

---

[1] Henry Tiarks: businessman and banker; friend of Joyce's family.

a good wartime parody to 'I'll See You Again' and writes of the bomb on what I interpret to be Penberthy's in Oxford St.[1]

Thursday, January 4th, 1945   Bangalore

Visit Miss Bremner, matron, and Col Scott at the BMH [British Military Hospital] here for tea on Tuesday. And what a tea. Hot buttered scones, choc sponge cake with icing; plain sponge with lemon filling and Christmas cake with almond paste *and* white icing. I ate all. Miss B. is a pet. Plump and nannyish. Her little sitting room is full of matronly calendars and flora and objects and she is passionately loyal with a fierce drawing of Winston Churchill on a table and a photograph of Wavell on her desk. We laid our plans and inspected a ward or two to decide just where to put the piano. That evening Viola and I dined with Plunket-Greene at the club here. We let him down, in our innocence, by going in day clothes, for we were going on to the movies. It seems the club demands long frocks. Well, it didn't get 'em and to be honest Viola and I decided we were a good deal more suitably and more chic-ly dressed than the rather tawdry little numbers the local ladies were wearing. The movie was *Song of Bernadette*[1] and I'm afraid we couldn't quite take it. True, Miss Jennifer Jones had extraordinary distance and a high-cheeked charm and was faithfully served by the camera and the lighting. But the piece got us down and when, as a nun, she started the dying sequence in a dreadfully public convent surrounded by Princes of the Church in lace aprons, not to mention various nuns who glid by, headed by Gladys Cooper, we got bad giggles brought on by a shaft of light that smote

[1] Penberthy's: well-known glove shop.
[2] *The Song of Bernadette*: sentimental 1943 American film. A huge success. From the novel by Franz Werfel, based upon the real life story of St Bernadette of Lourdes.

me. She was shown wearing a sort of goffered cap and suddenly I realised she looked just like a cup cake and said so to Viola who found the notion as funny as I did, and we lost all control from then on to the final holy fade out with unseen choirs of female voices singing in thirds, way up in the treble clef.

Two good shows out at the hospital. Both audiences were on their toes. No lifting or yanking at all. The last one was in a small [ear, nose and throat] ward and we had a really cosy time with solos from an Irishman with a childish high tenor of great sweetness and 'I'll Walk Beside You' from Sgt Redpath of ENSA who'd come with us. This was much appreciated. His falsetto high note at the end got them properly. We stayed on and on in there and now we've had a late dinner, got into our trousers and Viola is lying on a sofa reading *The Craft of Comedy* which is a correspondence between Stephen Haggard[1] and Athene Seyler.[2] All that Athene has to say is of point and interest; but I doubt if S.H. ever had an inkling of what was funny and what was not. He reads as a solemn fellow delving deep in an earnest attempt to find humour. I read it yesterday.

Sunday, January 7th, 1945   Bangalore

Morning wandering along South Parade, window shopping and getting a thriller for the next day's journey. Three shows in the afternoon and the first easily the worst I've ever had to do. Officers they were; surgical

---

[1] Stephen Haggard: actor who did his best work in the second half of the 1930s. Died in February 1943 aged thirty-one. *The Craft of Comedy*, written in collaboration with Athene Seyler, became a minor classic.
[2] Athene Seyler: character actress, born 1889. Made her first appearance in 1909; thereafter specialised in comedy; was in several Restoration plays, in Wilde, Chekhov, and as the Nurse in *Romeo and Juliet*. Married to actor Nicholas ('Beau') Hannen, and both were close friends of Joyce and Reggie.

officers. The bed cases weren't feeling very good but
were on their toes and appeared to enjoy themselves but
there were about ten or twelve up patients sitting on beds
gazing into space and looking as dumb as they in fact
were, who made me despair. Shock tactics were no good;
sentiment failed; some of them tried *not* to smile and for
the most part were quite successful. Viola and I exchanged looks and as I got angrier, which was silly, I also
got an internal *fourire* which was dangerous and I had to
take a real pull. It was 5 p.m.; not too hot, they weren't
too ill; I was on my toes – but, try as I did, they remained
morons to the finish – with exceptions. One of these was
the mouse-like wife of a gaunt grey man propped up on
pillows. She loved all the things we did and was brave
about laughing out loud. And there was a colonel in a
brocade dressing gown, and a baby lieutenant, in a
foulard one, both of whom had a fine time. But taken all
around they were a group of dunderheads and we
finished with a sigh of relief. I always wonder on these
(rare!) occasions how much of it is my fault? It's no good
being angry when the audience won't play. That is
obvious. But, presuming they would *like* to enjoy themselves, how is one to help them? It's one's job; but on this
occasion a very uphill one. There were shy titters here
and there, and applause was adequate, but it is quite
despairing to say, sing and do things that just don't
penetrate at all. You can see them actively NOT hearing;
not clicking. It is particularly true of people who've been
out here a long time. They are incapable, some of them,
of absorbing an idea. It's as bad as that. After this show
we crept wearily along to the isolation ward where we'd
asked to do an outdoor show for them on their balcony.
This, mercifully, went over BIG. So the ego was in some
measure restored. And later, after supper, it was swelled
considerably by a really wildly gay performance in the
other officers' ward where we went on for over two hours
and were appreciated no end! It was indeed enjoyable; no
exaggerating, no lugging up hills through mud – they

were with and ahead of me, and I had a lovely time with all the monologues. Viola was angelic and played on and on, on such a beast of a piano that it makes me sick to even think of it. One of those gutless, toneless, Woolworth affairs with notes that stick and hum and some that do not sound at all.

Packing all morning and at lunchtime Plunket-Greene arrived to say he'd made a muddle about dates and we weren't on the 3 o'clock train and in fact couldn't get off to Madras the next day. I could cheerfully have slapped his pretty face. He kept saying it was entirely his fault which didn't mend matters. Then I remembered one gallant Maj. General Rankin's[1] rash invitation to call on his help if ever in need, so accordingly I telephoned to him with the result that at 8.50 we were on the Madras Mail sharing a four-berth compartment with Mrs Taneje and her two children. The elder 'child' was a gangling youth of fifteen with a heavy black moustache and spectacles. We got into Madras at 6.30. The Tanejes had another train to catch so Viola and I remained in our bunks to leave the way clear for her and the children and the bearer to pack up and get away. Then Ghulam came in and took over and we finally assembled ourselves and were escorted by a missionary, now welfare, called Captain Greet. We are at the Connemara Hotel, large, modern with excellent beds and no service but, until he precedes us to Calcutta, we have Ghulam.

Wednesday, January 10th, 1945   Madras

Madras is very hot and depressing. Been having an unaccountable low in which the map grows larger and larger and distances wider and wider and all in all things look strangely grey. But it is undoubtably stomachic and will pass. Is passing.

[1] Deputy Director of Medical Services, Southern Army, India, 1943–5.

Mrs Robertson, the Col of the BMH's wife, suddenly invented a cocktail party to meet me which was kindly meant but a chore. Oh, the endurance done in the name of kindness. I stood for an hour in the writing room at the Connemara Hotel talking to people I didn't know or care about. It was well done in that the guests were circulated and I had about three mins by the clock with them one by one. I don't quite know how the whole thing started but if, as I find it hard to believe, it gave the Robertsons any pleasure then I'm glad we had it. But it struck me as a waste of time, energy and money.

Thursday, January 11th, 1945   Madras

Met His Excellency Sir Arthur Hope who joined us for a drink. A jovial type with the human if unworthy weaknesses of gossiping and the convivial cup. We had an enjoyable half hour in which he was pleasantly indiscreet about the India Office at home and its inefficiencies. I must say his account of a private code telegram rushed to him from Amery[1] to ask him to locate a certain Sir Something in the Civil Service here in order to give him an important assignment was a little hair-raising. 'Do you know whereabouts or last known address of Sir Something', it said; or words to that effect. And it turns out that Sir Something is in fact Sir Arthur's No. 1 and has a two-year completion to fulfil; yet his employers in London seem completely unaware of the fact. Not very inspiring of confidence.

Out to Avadi hospital, No. 18, at 4. Lovely drive through little villages and rice fields of exciting new greenness; past an alarming Hindu temple with a row of five giant idols sitting with their backs to us on a high plaster wall in the sun. More bullocks sitting in more ponds up to their nostrils. Endless naked children.

[1] Leopold Amery: Secretary of State for India and Burma, 1940–5.

Gaggles of geese, motley brown and speckled ones, being driven by children in graceful rags. Water everywhere reflecting the blue of the sky and intensifying it. Palm trees of a weedy kind. One pond entirely covered with an orchidaceous pale lilac flower, lovely in the low sunlight. More Devon red earth; more brass pots on the heads of more willowy women.

At the hospital Colonel Helman said that owing to a very important football match he'd decided to ask us to do the officers' wards first. It went a treat in spite of yet another horror piano for Viola. The nightmare of these pianos must be beyond endurance for her. She does complain but not too badly and it must be one long hell never being able to make a sound that satisfies one's ear. It's bad enough to sing to but to make it must be agony. And that is no exaggeration. It is a physical agony to Viola who gets up from the chair at the end with a look of sick misery on her face, disguised to the unknowing but patent to me.

The second show was in a small room, miles better for sound. It was fun to reduce things to an understatement again. From broadening in the big wards I'm sometimes a bit scared whether the elastic will ever quite spring back to a subtle tightness. I'm a bit perturbed at the thought of Noël's show to come. Can't seem a bit creative out here. I did start on a couple of ideas while we were in the Gulf, I think it was, but they are ashy. Time hasn't jelled them, more's the pity. I wake up in the night now and then and panic about it.

Friday, January 12th, 1945   Madras

I wrote to Noël and to Celia yesterday because *This Happy Breed*[1] had made such a new impression seen again out

---

[1] Noël Coward's 1943 play, in which he appeared, with Judy Campbell and Joyce Carey, and also directed, was filmed in 1944 with Celia Johnson.

here. Yesterday in one of the wards out at 18 a young man came up and asked me if I knew Noël because he said he admired him so much; always had. And how he'd thumbed his way over twenty-five miles of jungle country in Burma to hear him last summer. 'It was worth it,' he said with feeling.

On to coffee with Lady Leach out at Adyar. Lady Leach,[1] who is wholly German from Bavaria, is a dear. She looks like an enlarged Pekingese, but her little blue eyes are sunsets rather than midday lights and they all but disappear when she smiles, which is often. She is the wife of the Chief Justice in Madras and they have a hundred year old house on the river. It has charm. We sat in a cool room with many windows shaded by those local venetian blinds that roll down outside on the verandah. There was an underwater light that blessed the eye after the glare. The Leaches were for some years in Burma and have picked up bits and pieces as they went. I don't like oriental statuary, furniture or daggers, but there was something pretty exciting about the enormous gong hung on an elephant's tusk that stood in the front verandah. It was black with age and rang a note so deep and so vibrant that it made one's ears beat. The strange pulsation rang on, wave by wave, long after the gong had been touched.

Tea in the officers' mess for me while Viola did some plumbing of the piano. Then two really lovely shows. They'd got all the patients down one end which made it much simpler and by turning off a fan or two sound was not too bad at all. Was on my toes. So was Viola. She played that bloody old Joanna like one inspired. The second show nearly got me for about two minutes. Had a sudden feeling of complete exhaustion; not a dread of the programme or a sense of eternal work but a drag that made me feel for a second that I just couldn't make it.

[1] Lady Leach (née Sophia Kiel): wife of Rt. Hon. Sir Lionel Leach, Chief Justice, High Court, Madras, 1937–47.

Horrid. But I took a grip and refocused and all was a treat. We called in on the sergeants' mess, to inspect their piano just in case it was better than ours; but no. Drinks all round and Viola played Warsaw, then the colonel's driver, Avenal, ex-Rolls Royce chauffeur, swooshed us back to Madras in a terrifying exhibition. There were moments when his prowess at the wheel had me doubting but we got back all right while he kept accusing us of being nervous and laughing in a Satanic manner.

Sunday, January 14th, 1945   In the plane to Calcutta

Yesterday was Culture Day. It began by a visit to the Church of St Mary, in the fort. Dated lateish seventeenth century. Enchanting, simple. White walls with restrained memorials, draped urns and literary outpourings on the nobility and high character of the deceased. The ceiling was painted a dark blue-black and was ornamented by white rosettes in plaster-work. The effect very charming. Our guide was Sgt Halliday, who knew all the answers. An extraordinary man, filled with knowledge and ready to fountain it to us in a torrent of well chosen words. We enjoyed him. He was clearly surprised to find that we had curiosity and all but gasped when we talked about the wild flowers here and Viola suggested that a miniature mauve thing I picked might be a sort of calceolaria or some such. We plied him with questions about trees, birds and Brahmins, and he came back at once with succinct answers. We sat on a part of the fort wall and talked of poetry and *Romeo and Juliet* and Life and Literature and it was as if the cork had burst out of a very tightly sealed bottle to see his eagerness and hear his enthusiastic replies. 'You can't think how much I'm enjoying this,' he said rather pathetically. His mental agility was stimulating and we felt quite bright ourselves. Rather diffidently he asked us to dine with him at a Chinese restaurant that night and we accepted. Sidney

Wilson came to lunch, looking ashy with exhaustion. He had spent the night before meeting and settling in the 'Red, White and Blue' concert party, all of whom were at loggerheads; the show was bad, the comedian drank; a girl had been found with two BORS sleeping in drunken stupors on the floor of her room (safety in numbers surely?) and Miss Una Cheverton, the violinist of the party, had a fever. Then in the morning he had been meeting and settling in the 'Good Music Co.', five sensitive Italians who have come in for a lot of rough treatment and whom he wished to cosset a bit.

More culture at 7 when the 'Good Music Co.' played for us. It was *very* good of them for they'd travelled all night and must have been tired but when they heard from Sidney that we'd like to hear them they said they'd certainly do it. We went into the private dining room of the Connemara, used for banquets and Masonic meetings, and bare of hangings or furniture except for a few chairs and a small table, and far too resonant for music. The baby grand had some strange notes and a broken pedal and was down. However, Spironello, the leader, rose above the whole thing and played the solo arrangement of the Mendelssohn for us. This was a competent, and now and then exciting, performance; but it was the quartet that really got me. First an arrangement of the Air on a G String. A little lush but Bach's lovely bones stood it. And then Beethoven – Opus 18 No. 4. They played it beautifully. I remembered hearing the Grillers[1] doing it at the National Gallery and watching Myra loving it with a score in one hand and a cigarette in the other, hidden from the public behind that huge curtain. It was good to hear real music again. Viola, in a moment of self-expression, got on to the floor and lay on her back under a table, all the more to enjoy it. I found myself forgetting to breathe in my pleasure. It was a lovely time. They finished, now thoroughly wound up and well away, with

[1] Griller String Quartet: founded by Sidney Griller, CBE, in 1928.

the last movement of a Brahms I didn't know. C minor.
The air was full of feelings and sounds. There we were in
an empty banqueting room, green with tropical tree
designs in the modern manner, hearing Bach, Beethoven
and Brahms played to us by Italian ex-POWs in ENSA
uniform! *Bien bizarre.*

Sgt Halliday and Martin Greet, the welfare officer,
came and fetched us at 8.30. We were bursting with
music and very hungry. The Chinese restaurant we went
to was very full but in one of the many small rooms we
found an empty table. We had a sort of omelette and an
accompanying dish of prawns, vegetables, raw celery,
bamboo shoots, all covered with a delicious sauce. And
we had noodles. Fresh lime-ade. New bread and butter.
While we ate we talked; or rather Halliday talked. For one
so chatty as myself it was a change to sit back! He talked
of psychoanalysis and revealed that he was a Buddhist.
Much that he said was of the *News of the World* sort of
interest; particularly his illustrative anecdotes. He really
did know something about the subject but as a man
obsessed. He was entirely preoccupied with sex and, like
the man in *Cold Comfort Farm*,[1] saw it in everything. But
he was intelligent and lucid about all he had to say; it was
simply that his balances were out of gear.

I've been reading Beverley Nichols's new book, *Verdict
on India*. It is full of gardenish path mannerisms[2] and a
little too facilely readable but it is also packed tight with
information I wanted and since reading it I've got a few
facts about India straightened out. Muslims and Hindus,
for instance; Pakistan; Gandhi's position. The truth about
British administration – far from being overpowering it
has often been too lenient – if B.N. and the quotations he
uses are to be believed. I'd say it was a fair picture. It is
certainly a very alarming one. Particularly the Hindu
aspect which strikes terror in the soul by its ephemeral

[1] *Cold Comfort Farm* by Stella Gibbons, best-selling parody published
1932; awarded Femina Vie Heureuse prize.
[2] A reference to Nichols' book, *Down the Garden Path* (1932).

jiggery-pokery and vice-like grip on simple superstitious minds. We talked a bit about India but didn't delve deeply. And then we got on to the Absolute; and I waded in with both feet when Halliday submitted that there was no such thing – no purpose, no governing principle, in fact nothing except reflexes. I couldn't have that and we had St Paul and Jesus and the Christian outline all before us over our iced coffees.

'"Christ exists", you say,' said Halliday, 'and so he does in your brain – in the cells at the top of your head. But you have no proof, no realistic proof that he rose again', etc. I did my best, backed verbally by Viola and with assenting grunts by Greet. It was quite fun and, as I knew I was right I wasn't in the least worried. It is only when one has doubts in an argument that one minds.

(I'm writing this in the plane to Calcutta. The very kindly Brigadier opposite – it's a DC 3, tin seats again – who fixed me up with a rug and gave us lunch at the last drop down, has just handed me a piece of paper with this on it:

> Old Father Hubbard went to the cupboard
> To fetch himself a hankie
> But when he got there, He found his wife bare
> And so was the goddam Yankee.)

We stayed talking for a long time. Before we got on to the Absolute and were still psychoanalysing, Halliday asked me if I had affection for any objects – all such indications having a profound significance. I told him about my little pillow that I take everywhere with me and he at once said, 'Of course you know what that is, don't you?' I said I didn't, quite. 'Maternal complex. My dear, if you had a baby you'd be able to forget your pillow completely in two months!'

It was an amusing evening. Sgt Halliday, who writes under an anagram of his own name as Lloyd Hai, looks rather like a late eighteenth-century pugilist in a print.

His nose isn't broken nor is he bestial to see, but there is a stockiness and thick-necked look to him that reminds me of that sort of picture. His eyes are very blue; his mouth rather thin lipped and mobile. He must be about forty-eight or fifty, I think. Very energetic, rather nervous, kindly, intelligent and utterly earthbound. Little Greet, with his broken arm in a cast and his greying fair hair a little tousled, has a faintly Leslie Howard[1] quality about him. Gentle and sensitive and very shy. He told me he was married to an Anglo-Indian and had four children and it emerged that their life's work was running schools for the illegitimate children of tea planters in Ceylon and India. It seems to be a full-time job too. I gather the tea planter is not a very highly intellectual type, usually someone who couldn't quite make it at home. They take a local girl as a housekeeper and mistress and when she has, as she almost inevitably has, a baby, he pays her off and, having salved his conscience, forgets about the baby, goes home and marries someone else. That story, they said, was very common.

Monday, January 15th, 1945   Government House,
                                      Calcutta

Sidney saw us off yesterday morning. DC 3s are not the most de luxe form of transport. The plug had come out of the air hole behind my seat and all manner of substitutes completely failed to alleviate a powerful draught of icy wind that played a constant tune along my spine. Even with Aunt Pauline's air cushion and a rug and a curious green pillow, lent by an enormous major with an amusing face, it was an uncomfortable six hours. Viola slept quite a lot in the plane but I couldn't settle and spent time reading a dreary thriller and writing in here with one eye on my watch in hope that we'd get in soon. Calcutta from

[1] Leslie Howard: distinguished actor both in theatre and films. Of the latter best known for *Pygmalion*, *The Scarlet Pimpernel*, *Gone With the Wind*, and *49th Parallel*. Killed in air crash in 1943.

the air is a sprawling collection of buildings, waters, trees, roads, and none of it, at first glance, has any relation to anything. The airport of Dumdum seemed to be in process of rebuilding. There were dozens of men and women and babies all over the front of the admin building, ostensibly laying a brick terrace, I think. In fact two or three of them were actually putting a brick or two in place but for the most part a nice lot of sitting about went on. It can't be all that easy to work with babies sleeping or playing underfoot and blank-faced wives either squatting or getting in the way. Wonder how the wage system is worked out. Per family? Per pair of hands? Per piece work? We killed time in an American Red Cross canteen. Good coffee and biscuits and a saccharine church service relayed through a distorting radio. Hymns in slow tempo sung in thirds by sentimentalists. That sort of harmonising is fun on a picnic – fun to do – but as a praise to the Lord it lacks gusto. Finally Major Bontemps arrived to fetch us. Nice, Scots; tired; overworked. Drive into Calcutta through pink-stained smoky evening. Impression of elaboration in décor on balconies – iron-work or was it plaster? Soft colours. Curious boxlike carriages. Brilliant gipsy-looking women. A wedding procession – or was it a funeral? We lifted two RAF boys, wireless, en route to hear the Calcutta Symphony Orchestra play the Maestersingers under a French conductor. One of the boys came from Boston, Lincs., and he and Viola had a home chat. We stopped in a crowded street to put them down and drove to the ENSA office in search of mail. Some for us. Most of it old. Reggie in *November*. Dick, December 10th, written with gastric flu at very low ebb. Everything on top of him. Nice letters from General Arthur Smith and Penny in Paiforce saying thank you and another from General Gardiner in Poona saying the same thing. Very warming.

Government House is camouflaged. Once a dazzling white, it now stands a great strawberry jam colour, mixture of Devon earth and wallflowers, with palish green shutters. General effect attractive – it is a noble pile. Learn it is a copy of Kedleston[1] at home.

Tuesday, January 16th, 1945   Calcutta

Grand piano here for Viola. Lunch yesterday Major Bontemps at 'Firpos'. Talked of Drury Lane's inanity and the small sense they show in the sort of stuff sent out – specially a company who arrived last year and at the run-through were found to be outfitted throughout in green and yellow jester's costumes complete with turned-up-toed slippers and bells everywhere! They got to India in the heat; their tights were wool and after the first performance they had to be cut out of them as they entirely failed to draw off! Bontemps found their pianist a little inadequate and casually asked him one day how long he'd been at it. 'Not long,' said the pianist. 'But there's a great shortage.'

General impressions of Calcutta dirty, dusty, full of Americans; spacious with some good official buildings dating back to the eighteenth century. It's very spread out. Bontemps says women are not allowed to ride in horse-drawn vehicles here. Big anti-vd drive has, mysteriously, something to do with it! Viola and I shopped for a bit in a Government House car.

This afternoon was a triumph of disorganisation, started by misunderstood messages. Viola, in response to sos from Jack Hawkins, who is ill today, was waiting for transport to take her to play to some convalescent patients at the golf club. Two army trucks rolled up full of men, and out of one got a small woman about sixty-five in a wvs uniform who asked if Viola was Miss Tunnard and where was her friend? It seemed they were expecting

---

[1] Kedleston: eighteenth-century house in Derbyshire, seat of the Marquess Curzon, Viceroy of India 1898–1905.

both of us so Viola telephoned up to me and I roused
myself from the armchair in which I was settled with a lot
of old *Times*es and a newish *Sketch* from home, powdered
my nose, and went down, trying hard to focus on the
public service angle, and feeling sore at being denied the
afternoon I'd planned. 'Get in, get in,' said the wvs
gnome. 'Divide yourselves – one in each truck.' They
were, as trucks always are, hell. We were thrown
together and shaken and it was very dirty. We drove for
half an hour along tram lines and over what felt like
cobblestones. Then the golf club. A good grand piano for
Viola. Echoes and a running buffet with lots of clanking
china going on the far end of the room for me. Also three
members of my audience of about thirty got psycho-
pathic sort of giggles and made me feel wonderfully
unfunny which didn't help really. The others got a little
annoyed with them and so did I. It got almost to the
exhibitionist stage in which they were doing it to show
off. And then as suddenly as it had begun it stopped and
they listened.

General Cantlie came to tea to help us plan our tour
from here. Hope we can keep Ghulam but it may be
difficult.

Friday/Saturday, January   At Mrs Denham White's,
19th/20th, 1945   4 Asoka Road, Alipore, Calcutta

We moved here yesterday after four enjoyable days at
Government House. We love Mrs Denham White. She is
hard to put on paper. McEvoy[1] would have made an
enchanting watercolour of her; Delius could have put her
to music; Yeats in poetry. She is also faintly comic,
entirely kind, good as gold, vague but with lucid patches

---

[1] Ambrose McEvoy (1878–1927): English painter influenced by Gains-
borough, encouraged by Whistler.

of practicality and everyone loves her. She has rather wispy grey and brown hair, very soft. Her eyes are the blue of French soldiers' overcoats, enormous and deeply set. She looks frail as lace but never stops bicycling and being kind and going to concerts and caring for Bill Denham White, so she must have steel somewhere in her delicate make-up. He is commonsense personified. Spare, with a long nose and rather thin mouth that widens into an enormous smile when he is amused. He obviously adores her; disapproves of her artistic side. Doesn't like music or poetry; pictures, yes. Is a very successful doctor. They've lived here in Calcutta for twenty years. The house is full of rather lovely Chinese bits and pieces. Too many of them and the general effect is gloomy but she has an eye for lovely things and loves what she has collected. The house is full, too, of books. They are everywhere – all the ones one has wanted to read and never had time to. I had a wonderful morning in the garden – square lawn with an undulating border – catching up on my old *Tatler*s. Pictures of Jakie's wedding. Both very solemn. She is very attractive and glamorous. Reggie writes that they are ecstatically happy. Long may it last.[1]

But RAF audiences are good. They expect you to prove yourself before they commit themselves in any way. None of your expectant enthusiasm until after they've taken a view. And they are right. It's more flattering to go well with the RAF for they are discriminating. We did a show for them yesterday at the Loretta Convent which has just been opened by them this month. It went very well. Lovely for sound which is more than can be said for the ward at Davidian School where we did one the evening before. The Army ought not to be the poor relation of the services but it is. The Davidian School is an offshoot of the big BGH (21) in Calcutta. It is

---

[1] John Jacob Astor ('Jakie'): fourth son of Lord Astor; married Ana Inez Carcano. The marriage was dissolved in 1972.

old-fashioned, dark, dank, and very, very noisy, for the trams pass its portals in a never-ending stream. In the contest between my voice and the trams' clang and scream I lost, with lamentable ease. The ward was ill-lit and gloomy and when it was time to turn on the lights only three naked bulbs came on. Of the forty or fifty beds in there I don't suppose that more than six of them were adequately lit for reading or the leather work they are so mad on. (That full-blown frigate sails across the cover of many a writing case and a modernistic antelope leaps on pochette and handbags. We've met both constantly in hospitals everywhere.)

The HQ is in a house that was once part of the Government House summer property – probably a sec.'s, I should think. We ate in a large white room at two round tables. Dark red roses in the middle; a general impression of light and gaiety. Drinks first with General Oliver Leese in his own little sitting room. More roses. We approached it through his bedroom and the sight of a battered panama hat on a chest of drawers adorned with an I Zingari ribbon was very endearing. He is a charming man, entirely English of the best sort.[1] Very tall with a slight, almost non-existent, stoop. Gentle eyes; kind. Like all people burdened with responsibility he has a certain distraitness, but misses nothing at the same time. My romantic leanings found much in the whole set up. Very struck by the atmosphere of common intentions; single-minded. One felt they all enjoyed each other. Didn't know about the Brigade of Guards practice of calling its officers by their first names – General Oliver, for instance. After dinner we did our stuff. The general had invited all his drivers and batmen and orderlies to come in. They were our favourite part of the audience. The general listened with half an ear but had his mind on

---

[1] Lt. General Sir Oliver Leese: C. in C. Allied Land Forces South East Asia, 1944–5, having previously commanded the 8th Army in Italy. A passionate cricketer, not only playing for I Zingari, the oldest of the wandering clubs, but becoming President of MCC in 1965.

other things for the most part. However he enjoyed 'Ernie' and asked for 'Lily Marlene'. The other generals and brigadiers were fairly solid; Jimmy Boyle, who'd thought up the whole thing, was suffering as responsible people must. The penny dropped more swiftly in the back ranks and I found myself broadening to them – gallery playing. But they were so very nice and friendly. Says much for the general that they behaved completely naturally in his presence.

Mail has been pouring in this last few days.

Got desperate yesterday about not getting to grips with ENSA over our plans. Wretched Jack Bontemps whom I like so much has had twenty more artists thrust at him from Bombay and nowhere to put them and no one to help him, so all in all the office was in a state of chassis when I got there at 12 by appointment. No one in. I left a terse little note saying I did understand the difficulties but please could we be dealt with as we were wasting time and it was being so difficult to ever arrange anything. We played the Loretta Convent Hospital at 5. Or rather at 5.30 for when we got there the piano hadn't arrived. Mercifully Jack Bontemps was with us and got things organised with wonderful speed but it meant a half hour delay and I chattered on and on about home and endeavoured to amuse till it got there. They were a lovely audience and we had a fine time with them. Noticed a marked prejudice to the RAF – because their term of service is much shorter than the Army's. A wired-off window at the side of the wall had three eager faces in it all through the show. They turned out to be prisoners. I went in to see them afterwards. One was awaiting his release, the second had a year to serve, and the third hadn't had his court-martial yet, but expects to get two years. 'What have you done?' I asked bluntly. 'AWOL,' [Absent without leave] he said; Lancashire he was. 'I come up on leave from the front and met up with a woman and I didn't want to go back, see.' I asked him how long he'd stayed. 'Oh, three or four month,' he said.

'Then the CMPs [Corps of Military Police] picked me up. That woman's got me in a lot of trouble. My girl at home says she'll wait for me.' I said she must be nice. 'She's not bad,' he said grudgingly. He was ashamed of himself and his slightly bravado act wasn't very convincing. 'Well, I've got two years to think it all over.' He hadn't shaved for two or three days and I don't think his IQ was very high, but he wasn't entirely bad.

One man in the main ward told me, with the air of one making a tremendous discovery, that I had got a very good pianist indeed. His tone indicated that I didn't realise it!

Mrs Denham White went out to dine with some Chinese. Col D.W. came in very late after we'd finished and were sitting by the electric fire in the green drawing room. He'd been expecting to dine there too but hadn't gone because he said he couldn't stand the woman who'd asked him. 'She hates me too,' he said. Told us some sensational stories about unexplained deaths in high up Indian families. 'Wiping out' seems quite usual here.

Thursday, January 25th, 1945   Calcutta

The noise was considerable for our outdoor show at Barrackpore on Tuesday. It was like singing from a dock to a liner rising clifflike over one; for the patients were ranged on two balconies, one about twenty foot up and the second ten foot higher. Matron had laid on some ward screens of official green rep set up on the asphalt sweep, in front of a flight of about thirty steps, to form a little background for us. The piano and a small table with my glass of water on it were awaiting us as we stepped out of the CMP's station wagon – mysteriously provided as transport and very comfortably driven by a taciturn Yorkshireman who had the traditional heart of gold under a gloomy exterior. We started off at once. My voice

seemed to get to the top tier boys more easily than the
lower range; I don't think it made easy hearing for any of
them, even though I did my darnedest and got a crick in
my neck from looking up. And just to make it harder
every crow in the area decided to gather round and join
in. So did green parrots. Low-flying aircraft came roaring
in just over the treetops; oxcarts rumbled by nice and
slowly; motor bikes spurted by nice and quickly; an
Indian in immense black boots scrabbled along the
asphalt and another, out of sight behind our screens,
watered some flowers from a trickling hose that made
very suggestive sounds and scared Viola to bits.

In spite of all these little troubles the show went a treat
and they were leaning over the balcony rail clapping and
calling for more, so we kept on for an hour and fifteen
minutes. Can't say I like singing at that angle; kept losing
my balance. Wore my black suit and the magnolia shirt.
On Monday evening we got in about 9 and dined with
Col Denham White who has opened up to us in the past
few days. He is slow to warm to one but when he does it
is doubly endearing. Mrs D.W. was out but he hates
going out and won't. They are an attractive pair and
complement each other. We hated to leave there this
morning. The hour wasn't particularly comfy: 4 a.m.
John, the little butler with the bifocal glasses and permanent duster over his shoulder, called us with tea, orange
juice and bread and butter, which helped a great deal. Mr
Ayling and the ENSA station wagon came to fetch us and
then followed a series of long and exhausting waits. I've
got a roaring cold and feel like a boiled owl or a very
heavy fuzzy moth. Finally we were airborne at 6.45 in a
Dakota full of sacked freight and four cross nursing
sisters returning from a month's leave, poor things.

Mr Ayling turns, like the wheels of the gods, very
slowly. When you telephone the office and he lifts the
receiver and says hello, and you say 'this is so-and-so
speaking, is that Mr Ayling?' there then follows a long
silence. Jack Hawkins got so mad once he said, 'Now let's

get this thing straightened out – are you Ayling – yes or no' and the startled little man admitted he was. I don't know what can be clogging the works unless it's adenoids. He is married to a piano teacher and has a seven-year-old daughter called Pam. He is mad on psychiatry and almost completed his medical training before the war. He is also a good card manipulator but he is a very, *very* slow administrator in an ENSA office. And it's almost impossible to get a direct answer from him, so that now Jack Bontemps has taken to Jack Hawkins's practice of asking a question and demanding *only* 'Yes or No' to it.

With Captain David Clowes to see the Khalighat Temple in D.'s jeep. We went through a bazaar of spectacular filth; the roads wet with a recent if half-hearted attempt to wash them down. As soon as we got near the temple a sprightly high priest in a brown shawl spied the jeep and recognised David, who'd been there recently with Jimmy Boyle and offered to guide us around. Having read Beverley Nichols's *Verdict on India* I now have a *faint* idea about Hinduism. One can't get a clear one. It's 'boxing wiv ve ephemeral' all right. The outward and visible signs, as seen in Khalighat yesterday, were hideous and without grace. There was a shoddy figure of Ganesh, badly painted pillar-box red and hung with fading garlands of little yellow flowers. And a goddess of knowledge, I think, with her tongue out, was hidden behind closed doors for a couple of hours, 'from the beggars' was the inadequate reason given by the high priest. We saw a picture of her. The courtyard was flanked by little shop-like pretty temples and overrun by children in all stages of poverty with sores; with flies, with nits and with deformity – idiocy, too.

The only thing to please one at all were the heaps of flowers being sold to be given as offerings to the gods and goddesses. We saw the little head blocks where the goats are slain each morning and a few pathetic goat heads were still lying at the feet of a beggar who was trying to sell them. Flies everywhere. Mercifully a cool evening and my cold kept smells off for me. But it was a horrific place. The apathy of the slightly better-caste Hindus squatting in their clean cotton sarees depressed us. I think it is the general paralysis of apathy that is the worst part of India. They just don't give a damn. Don't know *how* to give a damn, which is even worse. They are very animal of the bovine sort, large eyed, slow moving and apparently nerveless. I hated Khalighat. The beggars cross-legged in the dirt, covered in flies, the squalid gods, the dying flowers and above all the lack of any purpose. There wasn't even any religious fervour. No, that's not quite true because, on our way out, we heard a drum being beaten, and one of those powerful Hindu voices being raised in a powerful wail, and turning a corner we came on a group of prayers (people praying, i.e. pray-ers), official I think, surrounded by an apathetic crowd. In the middle of the sitting prayers was a fat figure with long greasy curls wearing a salmon pink cotton Gandhi cap and skirt with an off-coffee coloured shawl. Very like Elsa Maxwell[1] in style but in fact a Holy Man, so the high priest said. He got up clumsily and fumbled with the knot of his skirt which led David to suppose he was going to undress, but instead he tightened it and made salaaming bows to the four quarters without speech or expression. While he did this the drummer opened up and let forth an animal cry of such jungleness that we moved away instinctively. All his teeth and his uvula were revealed and the veins in his neck stood out at the effort. From the temple we progressed slowly through the evening crowds to see the burning ghats. David had already told us how the nearest relation had to witness the final destruction by fire, but before this the navel had to be removed from the body and when everything else was reduced to ash this must be taken down to the river and thrown in. The burning went on in a small back yard,

[1] Elsa Maxwell (1883–1963): Leslie Halliwell described her as 'Dumpy, talkative American columnist and party-giver'. Film appearances included *Stage Door Canteen* in 1943.

about thirty-five feet square, possibly a bit larger. There were five or six fires going when we got there, but all except one were in final stages, embers and ash. One was going well and two male relatives were poking and stoking with apparently no emotion of any sort. The guide said he could see bits of body within the mound of logs but I preferred not to look too closely. Suddenly, though, I saw a corpse on a bed waiting for burial. He had been a very skinny old man. His son sat in dull stupor on the foot of the bed, just waiting. Viola and I decided that was probably the first dead body we'd ever seen, other than the old familiar ones we'd met so often in the pages of *Life* magazine. And on the way out we saw another, tied up in a bit of calico with his feet, crossed, sticking out at the end. He was, the guide said, a starvation case, destitute. No kin had come to burn him so I suppose the authorities see to his dispersal. All the time we were in the yard a stark naked man, apart from a very small loincloth indeed, pranced among the fires. He was a mad holy man. On his head he had wound a scarlet turban at a rakish angle with the knot tied over one ear which gave him a look of great dash, and he'd covered his body with white ash so that the general effect was a bluish grey. His step was light and he looked wildly happy. At one moment we heard cries and he advanced through the arch with steps leading down to the river, carrying a burning log in his bare hands. It fell to pieces and he danced round it, rolling his eyes. We saw two other holy men. One sat cross-legged on a mat outside his four-foot hovel made of branches and old sacking. He was a little wizened man, not old, with a wrinkled body and a smooth monkey face. Near him squatted another with long curling hair and a smooth cocoa-brown body. He was effeminately good looking and about as holy as a boot. The river was a let-down, being very like the Regent's Canal in London in its worst reaches. There were Untouchables paddling in it, bending down to gather up handfuls of mud from the bed to look for gold rings that the rich fling into the water as offerings to the gods.

As an outing the whole thing was intensely interesting but abysmally depressing. I see no hope for India, ever, ever. Not while Hinduism goes on. And I see no hope for its cessation.

We returned to Asoka Road to pack for our 4 a.m. departure.

Captain Glynn met us at the airstrip at Comilla and we drove to ENSA House! This is an attractive whitewashed block with a little lawned garden, one of the few brick houses in Comilla. Most of the others are basha huts. Captain Glynn has made it gay with cotton curtains and covers from the bazaar. Flowers everywhere, mostly sweet peas. Ghulam here to meet us. It had taken him two nights and a day to get here by train and river. We'd come in one hour and fifteen minutes. We eat at the officers' club just across the road. It's very rural here, and quiet.

Monday, January 29th, 1945   Comilla

Dinner pleasant. General Symes[1] very nice and chatty. Viola sat next to Brigadier Winters, the medical brig. Full of vitality and enthusiasm. I must say we've seen a lot of both those qualities out here. It is the more remarkable because of the climate. It was cold-Sunday-night-self-serve-supper. We talked of Hinduism; agriculture; bluebells in Somerset; the happy experience the general had had in Belgium last autumn, seeing our troops genuinely welcomed and trusted. Deservedly so, he said, for they were – are – such a grand crowd. He said the cases of misbehaviour were so few as not to count. Couldn't quite say the same of the US troops. In fact the

[1] Major-General G. W. Symes: Commander South-East Asia Command 1944–45.

Belgian girls used to ask for British protection from them!
The general's driver, a Gloucestershire man, was waiting
for him outside a shop in Brussels one day and when he
came out he told the general he'd had four separate
invitations for supper. 'He never ate in the barracks after
that.'

Did a show in the surgical ward out at 92 at 5 o'clock.
Several cast cases; long termers. A Scot with prematurely
white hair, who held my hand afterwards, said pretty
things in a soft Highland voice and called me 'Madam'.
Also a sandy Cockney of astounding bounce, both legs in
casts. Full of conversation. When the show was over and
we'd been talking to them for about half an hour someone asked Viola to play, so she unpadlocked the Mini and
gave them some music. When she got to Warsaw the
Cockney, who had carried on a ceaseless stream of talk,
swept his eyes down to the far end of the ward where
Viola was playing and interrupted himself to say:
'Smashing pi-yannist you got. That Warsaw Concerto's
smashing too –' and on he went, a flow of words about
comics he'd laughed at, shows he'd remembered.
'Trinder's good for a laugh but Maxie Bacon's a funny
feller.[1] I ain't seen Sid Field yet but by all accounts he's
pretty smashing. My brother-in-law wrote me about him.
Phyllis Dixey's making a name all right – pays for it
though, I daresay.'[2] He said Vera Lynn was smashing
and no one couldn't tell him no different. There was a
quiet man in glasses with a pile of books by his bedside
who knew all about Dick's film music and wanted to

[1] Max Bacon: comedian and drummer; played in Ambrose's Band; had
his own solo act in variety and on radio. In later life became a straight
character actor.
[2] Phyllis Dixey: known as a 'Peek-a-Boo' fan dancer; appeared with
Ernie Lotings and Jack Tracy, whom she married, in a variety act, 'The
Sap and the Swell Dame'. During the Second World War the *Phyllis
Dixey Non-Stop Revue* played to full houses at the Whitehall Theatre. On
taking over the lease of the Whitehall she put on the farce *Worms' Eye
View* which ran for 2,245 performances.

know about Dick as a person. Noël cropped up again. One thought he was 'very clever' but too conceited. Another said he'd done enough with *Bittersweet* alone to justify his fame. All agreed he was clever – most of them thought he had done well out here. I was amused to find one of them saying that of course Noël Coward was of the privileged classes; 'public school and all that'.

Wednesday, January 31st, 1945   Comilla

Three very busy days have gone by and no time or strength to write. Monday. Wrote some letters – cold gone. Two shows. First at the head and eye extension of No. 92 IGH which is housed in the old courts of justice in Comilla and presided over by a brilliant young man called Major Johnson. Both he and the senior sister who run it are very enthusiastic about the job they are doing and the whole place is keyed to their mood. We gave the show at 5 o'clock on a balcony where they brought all the bed patients who were fit enough to come and there were about fifty up-patients too. It was a good place for sound and we had a very good time. They sang like mad. Several eye cases so I remembered *not* to say what I usually say when I introduce 'Long Ago and Far Away'. It happened, like all those things do, quite unpremeditatedly, ages ago. I said that if they felt like closing their eyes while I sang it, they could imagine I was Rita Hayworth, and it was smashing work. Such a roar of pleasure greeted this gentle little sally that I've said it ever since and it never fails! Gag lines – ! It's a pit into which one is bound to fall, I suppose. Doing so many shows one gets set even when making all sorts of resolutions not to.

Major Johnson took us through the head wards afterwards to see the patients who were too ill to come to the show. Some were still in the shocked state where they apparently didn't register. One boy made baby noises which were rather awful. Another just smiled. He said they'd probably all get completely well. In the furthest ward of all quite by himself lay a very young Jap POW. His bodyguard treat him as a complete pet and feed him and play with him while he lies there grinning with his head bound up. Lately he's started writing and they are trying to get his scribbles translated but there are no Jap linguists here so it isn't very easy.

We drove out to the RAF mobile hospital after this. For some reason I'd assumed it was just around the corner and we allowed ourselves ten minutes to get there, but it turned out to be full seven miles over roads that defy description and every few hundred yards there were diversion signs leading all over the place, round fields, through farms and over banks. It seems they are mending the real road and in order to keep it clear they have evolved these diversions. We arrived very late and shaken, in all senses of the word. Miss Black, the little senior sister who runs the place and looks just like Bette Davis, met us and introduced us to a circle of grand RAF doctors, down here for the big medical conference being held out at No. 14 all this week. They came to the ward where we did the show . . . The return over that problem road was lovely to look at, for the moon was full and her creamy light turned the wide fields into seas of snow and fell on the stagnant square pools and made them mysterious, edged with silver trees and haystacks.

On Tuesday we set off with a suitcase to spend two days out at No. 14, which is situated on a little ridged bit of country over even worse roads. Ghulam was already there with the beds and the piano. We hung out our dresses in our tent and walked up a little sandy hill above our tent to have lunch in the sisters' mess. As a novelty I don't mind tent life; not in January with fine weather and not too much heat. But my mind recoils at the thought of that camp, *all* tents, in the rains. Deep ditches are dug all round which make night progress a little involved unless one has a torch. It is dusty country and that dust turns into skidding mud when it gets wet and it must be sheer hell to live in and work in. The sisters regarded us with suspicion and no blame to them. However, when we left the atmosphere was very friendly.

After lunch Viola and I lay on our beds in our little tent and rested for half an hour. We had four shows to do that afternoon and evening and it was a formidable thought indeed. The light in a tent on a sunny day is diffused, golden, and very comforting. Ours was a worn old thing with stains on the sides. Birds seemed to be running races on the roof and it was all very near to nature and nice. The only thing that wasn't very nice was the inability to find anyone to empty our lavatory. It wasn't very large and it came into service at lunchtime on Tuesday and no one but contributors went near it till nearly twenty-four hours later, when things were getting very serious. However, matron called on us after breakfast next day and we confided our trouble to her and within a few minutes a skinny Indian in shorts had dealt with things. Viola and I and Ghulam had on six separate occasions failed to gain any interest or sympathy even though we'd approached orderlies and a sister.

February 1945

Flew up yesterday. Thirty minutes' hop. American crew in a DC 3 with the door open which I didn't particularly like. We are staying with a character called Miss Hodson whose brother Eric is in the police out here and is now loaned from the Bengal Government to the Army as a full Colonel to raise a Pioneer force – or something as involved. She is fifty-ish, stout-ish with a rugged face of great kindness, rather wild, fine hair that is waved a bit in front and gets out of hand at the back; large good teeth and all the trappings of a decent sort. Which indeed she is. Her voice is a little loud; her heart enormous and her energy very British and undiminished even after seventeen years in India. She is doggy, sporting, team spirit and backbone of the Empire – all things one dismisses with a smile but in her case you are a little moved and you know she is the salt of the earth. The bungalow is a basha one with plaster walls and verandahs all around it. It is quite new and they are still without ceilings. Col Hodson, who is away on tour, built it to catch any winds there may be, with the result that now, in the cool weather, it is crossed with draughts from every angle. The drawing room has two distinctions. One is the wall décor, nursery style, of a series of gnome-like creatures from fairy tales in fretwork from Bavaria, highly coloured and pinned in an ascending line to the white plaster. They are a surprise, seen among etchings of cathedrals and a print with the heads of Beethoven, Brahms and an unidentified composer that hangs near the piano. The other distinction lies in the ashtrays. These are held in the outstretched hands of wooden Negroes, a yard high, standing at attention in breeches and tail coat, the paint getting a little dim on their blue shoulders and red legs.

Viola and I have a large room and bath, with another of those all-enveloping mosquito nets that look so like a fantasy drawn by Emett.[1] We got here in time for an excellent tea. We bathed, put on trousers and had an excellent dinner with Miss Hodson, who sits with her feet in a cretonne bag with elastic in the top to cling to her knees in order to prevent mosquitoes getting at her shapely legs. After which Viola found some Handel songs on the piano and played a few of them on a brute of a barking upright and so to bed at 9.30 to read. I found *Tonight at 8.30* and read *Hands Across the Sea* and *Still Life*,[2] both of which are in Noël's very best manner. The second is the basis of the new movie he's making with Celia.

Our two days out at No. 14 were pretty strenuous but fun. First afternoon we did the medical section and two penicillin wards. Tents, as I've known since N. Africa, are no good for singing in. However the first show was very cheerful and fast moving and the tent packed to suffocation and the sides rolled up so that patients could sit on the scrubby grass outside and hear from there. Then the penicillins. These were much quieter. All bed patients.

It was about 6.30 when we finished and we'd been at it solidly since 3, so the bed was very delicious for a bit before dining with the sisters and then doing a show in the officers' ward at 8.30. This was a crammed affair and

[1] Rowland Emett: artist, especially remembered for his fantasy railway trains, and ingenious comic inventions, including those in the film *Chitty Chitty Bang Bang*.
[2] *Tonight at 8.30*, Noël Coward's nine one-act plays which came on at the Phoenix in 1936 and ran for 157 performances. *Still Life* was renamed *Brief Encounter* as a film, frequently re-shown, with Trevor Howard and Celia Johnson.

took place in the officers' surgical where there were several cradle cases and almost all the beds were full of immovable patients. There were up-ones on mattresses on the floor, visiting brigadiers and American medicals perched on beds, and several chairs were arranged at the far end of the tent in darkness. We were lit by a few hurricane lamps.

Next day I did a bit of ward visiting in the morning, and then we had three more shows after lunch. The gang who dealt with our piano for the two days returned it to the ENSA hotel that evening and we signed ten-rupee notes and shook hands. The corporal in charge was a Welshman of the semi-educated sort, smooth of vocabulary and polished of manner. 'If I may be permitted to say so,' he said to me, 'I have attended all eight of your performances' (there were seven) 'and in no instance did the programme pall.' Another Welshman, from Carmarthen, in the dysentery ward, told me he'd cried when we'd all sung 'All Through the Night'. He has been very ill and looks like a shadow but is getting better now. Since he came away, matron told me, he has lost his mother, father and all his family. He hasn't got a relation left in the world.

Sunday, February 4th, 1945   Dacca

Much colder up here at Dacca. In fact I can't seem to get warm *inside* even with bottles and rugs. It is warm in the sun but there's an east wind, just like home! On Friday morning Captain Glynn took us over to see a couple of matrons to plan our work here. We started at No. 17 that afternoon. Basha huts and heavenly audiences. The first were surgicals. Lots of bed patients inside and the verandahs crowded too. While we were singing the sun set broadside on to the ward, lighting it up, throwing the standing patients in the fringe into silhouettes, flooding the floor. It was a little like the naval hospitals in Bombay, only lovelier. The whole place glowed. The light was reflected from the ground up on to everyone's faces and they were all laughing and looked gilded. There was an older man, from Durham, just behind Viola, who had started off in deepest gloom. He got the giggles and laughed till it hurt his stitches. Yesterday the colonel told me he was better for the first time; and said it was our show that did it. Those are the rewards that pay us.

The second show that night was in medical ward. Jaundices; but they were pretty gay in spite of it. Back at Miss Hodson's we took off our frocks and put on jerseys and trousers for dinner. Early to bed.

We grow in dread of the unseen Eric Hodson. Life in this bungalow revolves round him. He is a bull of a man with a roaring voice according to Colonel Garner. He is quoted at us a good deal and we see that he is god to Miss H. Miss Hodson is locally known to everyone as Aunt Margaret. I've now discovered what it is she reminds me of, and it's that Disney squirrel or chipmunk with the two long front teeth. Maybe it's a beaver? Anyway it's drawn by Disney. She has just come in from church where a bug got up her knickers and has bitten her to bits. She tells me she is *very* fond of dancing.

Colonel Ted Garner took us out to see the sunset at a mosque three or four miles out of Dacca. It's a fifteenth-century mosque perched on a little green cliff overhanging an endless plain of paddy fields. In the rains it will turn into a vast lake. Now it is patched with brilliant green and the huge sky vaulted overhead in a shifting expanse of greys and corals in the evening light. Flocks of silent long-legged birds like small cranes – paddy birds – arrowed across the sky; no sound from their steady wings. Geese too, and an occasional small darting bird with a little cry. It was very still and highly romantic. Clearly the colonel was haunted by ghosts of former expeditions. 'Picnic,' he said, 'by moonlight.' A Muslim priest appeared with some little cows. A handsome old man with a grey beard and a small turban. We took our shoes off and went into the empty mosque. There is something rather good about little mosques. It may be in contrast to *anything* Hindu. We drove back along a road arched in mango trees. Children were still flying kites in the gloaming, their dancing toy a dull thing among the first stars.

Dinner and dancing at the gymkhana club. Col Carver, Col Garner, Viola and me.

'Aunt Margaret' is a Theosophist. So are they all. I'm not very clear what a Theosophist is but it makes Aunt M. into a vegetarian and keeps her busy doing kindnesses. Wonder if Eric is? He sings. Bass.

Tuesday, February 6th, 1945   Dacca

More and more emerges of the Hodson tapestry. It is weaving into a wide pattern, featuring Mother who was musical – 'the Martins are all musical' – Geoffrey the elder brother who is a Theosophist and has X-ray eyes; Phyllis Larkin[1] who has nightmares and no sort of proper inside at all, and 'whom we never leave alone for long'. A cryptic sentence, playing havoc with the imagination. And then of course, Eric. He grows bigger and bigger and more and more odd as we build him up from scraps. He, too, is musical but, in a sudden spurt of disloyal disclosure, Miss H. said she wasn't really in love with his voice. It can, she told us, fill St Patrick's in Calcutta, *easily*. She, alas, isn't musical but she loves it and always sings her troubles away. Her mother did the same. When she was unhappy she'd go to the piano and play till she was right again and so does Miss H. Only she can't play so she sings. Unfortunately Phyllis and Larry Larkin can't bear anyone to sing and whistle about the house so she has to remember that, but Eric understands and she always

---

[1] Phyllis Larkin: sister of Eric and Margaret Hodson, wife of Alfred Larkin, Commissioner Dacca Division, Bengal.

does it here. She can't, she told us, keep quite on the key, but she enjoys it. She has grown more and more lovable as she sits back in her chair with her legs in the mosquito bag, going into the past for us. And she becomes rather a tragic figure, though she'd be the last to admit it. We find that Mrs Larkin, and we guess that Eric is the same, use her for all she's worth and then conveniently forget her. We lunched with Mrs Larkin on Sunday. She was jolly, affable and pleasantly downright. Both of them still speak with a Lincolnshire accent. Both she and Eric grow into evil fairies sucking poor Margaret's blood; but as she seems quite happy to have it that way it is foolish of me to feel concern for her. But I do. So does Viola. Aunt Margaret revealed in last night's outpouring that once she had played the mandolin. She did it at school and they had a ladies' mandolin band and played in it wearing rosettes, about thirty of them, with their instruments hung with coloured ribbons. A tragedy befell hers though. She kept it on the floor behind the settee in the bow window and one day Phyllis came in through the window and stepped on it. However, later, on her way out to India many years afterwards, the ship stopped in Naples and she bought another. But no one told her about the things the weather out here did to stringed instruments and during the monsoon she left it strung up tightly and it broke its back. So that was the end of her mandolin playing. We asked what she played and she said there was a tune called 'Black Bess' which she started to hum in imitation of a mandolin and got the giggles over it and we all laughed till it hurt. Listening to her has a hypnotic effect on me; I sit entranced, living her days with her mother and the Ladies' Choral in Bedford, hearing about the time Eric was shot by a medical student in Dacca in 1930 and the awfulness that attended that. Of her friend Tibs in Northumberland who doesn't understand her children and whose husband ran away with the theatre sister who looked after his wife when she had her operation. Tibs won't divorce him so they live together as

Mr and Mrs right under her nose and have a family of their own. In the end Miss H. is going to spend her old age in a cottage next door to Tibs. She is devoted to her in spite of her faults and her hardness and they get on very well together. Eric talks of living in the S. of France but Miss H. says he wouldn't like it. He loves Germany for the opera and the good roads. *Not* enough good reasons. We asked if Eric had ever wanted to get married and she told us he'd been engaged to a girl called Marjorie, who was very bewildered by him but it didn't come off and Miss H.[1] said she was glad because he would have made Marjorie miserable. He isn't the marrying type. Just a boy inside; very lovable – but not to be married to. It was difficult, she said, because she couldn't say to Marjorie that Eric would be awful to be married to but he would. Eric *is* a Theosophist, too. Geoffrey writes books about it and one has a foreword by Mrs Annie Besant. I dipped yesterday and saw it full of fairies and earth spirits so I closed it up and preferred to stay rational.

We've been working at No. 17 the past two days. On Sunday morning I wrote letters and sat in the garden. Two shows that afternoon at 5 and 7. The surgicals first, noticeable for their high spirits and gaiety. Patients stay in surgicals longer than medicals very often and they seem to grow fond of each other and make a tangible atmosphere, a sort of unity. It was very marked that evening. We stayed on and on and afterwards a sgt major called 'Pop' did his stunt for me. This was a cleft-palate act which endeared me to him forever. Wish Celia could have seen him.[2] He gave me a leather wallet.

Yesterday, Monday, Viola and I took the dog for a walk. It is a terrier called Tigger. 'Ever since the Pooh

[1] In her autobiography, *Joyce Grenfell Requests the Pleasure*, Joyce confesses that the memory of Miss H., whom she calls 'Aunt Marjorie', and another older unmarried woman gave her the idea of writing 'Three Brothers' with Addinsell.

[2] In *Darling Ma* Joyce explains how she and Celia would pretend to have cleft palates and collapse in girlish giggles.

books,' Miss Hodson said, 'Eric has had a Tigger.' Nail in my shoe made progress less easy. Deep sleep in the afternoon before the show – only one. The luxury of *one* is so terrific that we can hardly believe our good fortune when it turns up. Pretty rare. They were medicals again – ENT and skins, but very gay. I stood at the far end when Viola played and the sun was doing its spectacular setting act right across the ward. The men were all with their backs to me and their ears were rosy in the low light. Nice sight. About four men to every bed. Still as mice, listening. General verdict that Viola's playing was 'smashing'.

Col Carver has just rung up to say that Lady Louis Mountbatten[1] and the Larkins are coming to our show in the officers' ward tonight. Also General Cantile. Lady L.M. according to the colonel considers me to be one of her favourite artistes!

Wednesday, February 7th, 1945   Dacca

Today has been filled with activity, starting with the Indian police arriving to investigate the burglary which has robbed Viola of our float – 400 rupees, her fountain pen, the silver cigarette case I gave her in Baghdad and her sunglasses. Also her pay card and Ghulam's too. They took a statement from Aunt Margaret and then asked her to write it all down and sign it. They demanded to see the bag from which the stuff was stolen and said they must keep it to produce in court and of course we said 'Don't be so silly' and kept it. It was maddeningly slow and we got nowhere. I wanted to hit the fool of a sergeant who was in charge but Aunt Margaret's carefully controlled temper set all a good example and I didn't say or do anything to show my fury, thank heaven. Then

[1] Edwina Mountbatten: later Countess Mountbatten of Burma, wife of Lord Louis, Supreme Allied Commander, South-East Asia 1943–6; Viceroy of India, March–August 1947, when he received his earldom.

to the All India Radio studio to record fifteen minutes for a programme that they run for Europeans each Saturday for half an hour! The studio was well equipped and tastefully furnished with outsize lamps shaded soberly in orange with tassels. The piano, ha ha, had no pedal and was out of tune. Viola produced her tuning key and dived deep into the inside, but there was nothing to be done about the pedal. Meanwhile I was photographed by a small-sized Indian in a crumpled white skirt with buff muffler and tweed jacket. The tripod was unmanageable and he could NOT get it right. It lurched drunkenly and the camera faced me at an angle, so he tried again and finally after readjusting it six times he just gave up and snapped me with a long click in semi-darkness. It is for the Indian *Listener* and should prove interesting. We ran through the programme and timed it. I held the stop watch and a pale turnip of an English girl wrote down what I told her, *very* slowly, with her left hand. She was an ex-sister from No. 62, now married to an airman and just what she is doing in the All India Radio station is beyond me. Any English voice for announcing, I suppose. She reads with mouselike intensity in a careful council school accent and with all the facility of moving through deep mud. 'This is All-IN-DI-A Ra-di-o pree-sent-ing Joyce Grenville with VIOLAR TANNER at the piano' – couldn't even read the printed word.

Letter to Virginia Thesiger

Friday, February 9th, 1945   c/o ENSA, HQ Greens Hotel,
                                      BOMBAY, India

Tomorrow I'm thirty-five and it's far too old. Very depressed about it, and I *know* one oughtn't to record ages and all that, but as I look at my pore old face and take a frank look at my wrinkles it all seems sad. However, I'm really in good form after two weeks off map, doing hard work but with little travelling and fresh new potatoes, peas and lettuces and lots of sleep and Ros Lehmann's *The Ballad and the Source* – so-so but she's always worth reading – and a garden full of sweet peas and dianthus and African daisies . . .

———◄●►———

Friday, February 9th, 1945   Back in Calcutta with the
Denham Whites

Flew down here yesterday from Dacca. But I must finish off Wednesday – after the broadcast, which wore us both out and earned me fifty rupees and Viola twenty-five!, we had lunch and took our usual sleep. When I woke up I saw Aunt Margaret pass the window with a large khaki figure and it was the fabulous Eric returned from the North! I was wrong about him. He is no cruel bully at all – he is a large overgrown boy scout with enormous hands and knees, bare, and something very touching about him. His fondness for music *is* real. Somehow we'd suspected it. Eric really loves music and knows a little about it. Two ornate chests in the drawing room are full of oratorio, operatic scores, Gershwin, Kern, 'The Gondoliers', Tantivy Towers, Purcell, Schubert and even Humperdinck. Fine mixed bag. We had two sessions with him, Viola playing for us both, to sing – Manon, 'Si mes vers', Messiah, 'Brother James' Air'. In between times he went to the piano and played for himself. His huge hands hovering gently over the notes, sudden crescendos with the left hand half a beat behind the right. He sang 'To Music' and 'Lovely Celia'. No voice left and he's only fifty, but it must have been charming once. It seemed very light and gentle but he wasn't of course trying to fill St Patrick's. It was sad to see Aunt Margaret

close up in his presence. She was allowing him his
rightful glory and one could see her pride in him shining
off her in a bright glow. But the attitude that Man, willy
nilly, must be right and know all the answers is a silly one
and I wanted her to contradict him or show her spirit but
she didn't and never will. He leans on her but doesn't
consider her. On the whole we found them a tragic-comic
pair. He reminds me of something Humbert Wolfe[1] says
of Cyrano in his translation. Can't get it quite clear but it's
about a man fumbling like a moth into the light it loves.
Neither of the Hodsons are articulate; he finds some
reality in music and I suppose her love and pride in her
family is her form of self-expression but it's not quite
enough somehow.

Edwina Mountbatten was among us for two days and I
took my hat off to her. She looks chic and attractive and
never stops working. Hospitals all day, Indian and British, meals in messes with sisters, and one night she came
to No. 17 officers' ward to watch us do our stuff and the
next night saw her at the BORS' dance where we all took
the floor solidly for three hours, including Aunt Marg.

The Hodsons' garden is the source of supply to all
Dacca, it appears. People kept coming and saying that
Lady Louis was lunching, dining or visiting and *could*
they have a lettuce and some sweet peas. Both Viola and I
did our share of sweet pea cutting. There were three
rows, about a hundred yards long. Every colour, some
stripy pinks, salmons and mauves. And smelling right
too. Eating peas were coming on and we had cabbage
from the garden daily.

Before going to the BORS' dance on Wednesday night
we did a show at 62 India General Hospital in the old
Government House on the race course. One of our very
best, fairly small ward with good sound and lots of nice
people. We were in form and did two new-old numbers,

[1] Humbert Wolfe (1886–1940): eminent Civil Servant, poet, and translator of *Cyrano de Bergerac*.

'He's my Guy' and 'Embraceable You', which gave us a fillip, for we do get tired of doing the same old ones twice daily. Requests continue along the same lines, though 'Deep Purple' was a bit different. This was asked for at 17. I apologised for not knowing it enough to sing it and the man who asked for it said he wanted me to do it in memory of his mother-in-law's varicose veins!

The dance was wonderful exercise. Quite early on a small Cockney (my fatal attraction for the middle sized) asked me to dance and he was my persistent beau all evening. He danced beautifully in a *palais de danse* way, many steps, lots of rhythm and a stolid balance that kept us both upright even in the speedier variations he would lead me in. He'd seen me in 17 where he'd been a patient. 'Goin' to sing tonight?' he asked, and I said I wasn't sure; and he said, 'Go on, you wouldn't want your mother to think she'd given birth to a jibber, would you?' Later on, we did three or four songs. It went well, but was entirely redundant and I'm against such things in the middle of perfectly good parties that don't need it. There's no two ways about it; the BORS dance far, far better than their officers. Haven't taken so much exercise for months. I don't like that very *lento lento* waltz that they seem to love. It involves so much poise and gives me little pleasure even when dealt with as well as it was with my Shepherd's Bush chum. When the party was over he put his beret on (Tank Corps) and looked wildly rakish with it adhering to the very back of his head. And saluted me.

When we got back to the bungalow we discovered the burglary. I still think it must have been an inside job for Tigger didn't bark and the guard wasn't roused and the thief went straight to the chest of drawers, found Viola's bag and took out a wodge of papers, her pen and cig case and left the rest of the room untouched. It was, of course, idiotic of her to have left things in the drawer after all the warnings we've had. But there it is. I don't suppose there is the faintest chance of the things turning up. Today I ordered a new cigarette case in the new market and it will be more or less the same except that it won't have that artless little wreath of flowers on it and I'm having the fourteen countries we've played in written on the inside.

Uneventful flight down from Dacca. We landed at Barrackpore and Ayling was at Dumdum so that created a delay. However he arrived in time and we learned the local news driving in through the dusk, smoky and smelly, back to Calcutta and the kindly Denham Whites. Formby and Beryl[1] are here and were doing a show for the local troops in the football field last night. Marie Burke's[2] company are off at last. The *Love in a Mist*[3] lot missed their train. Ayling has another cold and is slowed up to a very gentle ambling gait. Turgid!

Lots of mail, four from Reggie, two from Dick, one Gin, one Pa, one Stephen, one Joyce C., one Harry, one Harold Lindo, etc., etc.[4] Dick says Noël's revue postponed till Autumn. Oh *dear*. Rather low about that I must say.

This morning to office. Usual chaos but Rex Newman beaming, on a visit from Cairo. Said a lot of very extra-specially nice things to us. Told us Formby did a good job last night. 10,000 troops, lights failed once, mike twice and he didn't turn a hair. Rex said, as does everyone else I've ever met, that he was mystified to know how or why Formby holds 'em but agreed he did, magnificently. Didn't see Jack Bontemps so we left with much unsettled. Viola went to the financial section to talk about loss of float.

[1] George Formby: comic and singer with high-speed banjulele accompaniment; travelled everywhere with his wife Beryl, 'the unconquerable Beryl' as Basil Dean described her.
[2] Marie Burke: actress and singer. Best remembered for her Julie in *Show Boat* (Drury Lane 1928) and the Countess in *Waltzes from Vienna* in London and New York.
[3] *Love in a Mist*: comedy by Kenneth Horne.
[4] Harold Lindo: architect with whom Joyce collaborated early in the war doing troop concerts in the Home Counties.

Mrs Denham White said to me at tea, 'You know, Bill adores his work. He'll get up in the night to go and see decaying nuns without a murmur.' Her conversation is like a many-branched tree – a delicate thing suddenly sprouting new boughs. 'She – the mother was a brilliant creature; well, *very* clever – she had a companion who *had been* head of a convent, my dear, and *left* – got out of the whole thing, which is *rather* odd – and her daughter – such a good simple sort of woman, very straightforward with bones like Greta Garbo – well, the daughter couldn't bear any sort of fuss, not that it matters, and the Frenchman who dined here last week – such a clever man called Louis – face like a small monkey – he was very pessimistic about *everything*. I do *feel* people oughtn't to be like that, don't you, my dear? He said Ruth looks *awful* – he saw her in England and of course we feel Tom shouldn't have come out but it was a thrilling job for him and he *is* an ambitious sort of man. The boy designed a ballet most successfully and that of course leaves poor Ruth alone in England which is sad if you see what I mean.' I sit with my tea getting cold, in a trance. Mrs D.W.'s eyes are like star sapphires today and she is wearing grey. I feel as if I'd had a session under the water. Intoxicating, bewildering, refreshing.

Sunday, February 11th, 1945   Little Chevremont,
                                       Darjeeling

This is the Denham Whites' house, perched high up in the foothills to the Himalayas. It is very cold here. We are in trousers, cuddling the fire, while the BBC Northern Orchestra gives us Sunday morning light music all those miles away. It's 6.30 here. Sun is lost in heavy clouds. We've shut them out now. Hoped for a sunset but it didn't happen. The day started early at Siliguri station where we were woken out of a pretty good sleep in a coupé. We got on at 7 last night with sandwiches for

supper and our beds made up by Ghulam. Lt Perth, a
Viennese doctor from Lebong, met us. Breakfast at the
REME [Royal Electrical and Mechanical Engineers] camp
with two lieuts called Price and Alexander. Promised to
do show for their twenty BORS on our way down on
Friday. Then a long drive up here in an opalescent blue
taxi with Mrs D.W.'s bearer in front and Lt Perth behind
with us. Ghulam followed in a truck with the piano and
bed rolls. First we had four miles through forest said to be
jungle-y; tigers. Not a sign, alas. Then coffee and toast
and marm. at 4,000 feet. Women, small with flat faces
and pink cheeks. Nose rings. Shawls worn swathed like
cummerbunds, only over bosoms as well as over
stomachs. Tibetans? And finally Darjeeling. Too many
red tin roofs and Victorian villas. We left the car on the
main road and were told to walk up to the bungalow. On
and on we climbed, followed by Ganesh, the D.W.
bearer, who got muddled and set us off on the wrong
road. On and on. Then a mile up, and low down in our
minds, we decided it couldn't be right and started back. I
got ahead, calling to Ganesh. No sign – nor of the three
women porters who were laden with our bags on their
heads. And down in the main road the car was gone! And
then Viola and Perth (such an unlikely name for a Viennese but nevertheless his genuine one) didn't come. Ten
minutes. I suddenly had one of those ridiculous fantasies
– a dream panic – that they had all been in my imagination and never had really existed. The little lane was
Mary Rose's island.[1] I ran up it calling and calling to Viola
and about 500 yards up I stood still to breathe and she
answered me, higher up. They didn't know which turning I'd taken and had waited for me. The car turned up,
parked around the corner. A coolie aged seven led us the
right way and we climbed up to this house, sitting on its
own little nob of the mountain, bathed in sun. Bow

---

[1] In J. M. Barrie's play the child Mary Rose disappears while on a
Hebridean island.

windows to the views. Inside a scene of mad activity and we found they weren't expecting us. Mrs D.W.'s letter had come but, apart from the monthly cheque in it, no one had bothered with it much until this morning when the head bearer had taken it off to get it read to him, and he was out on that job, now, when we arrived. The drawing room was demobilised, chairs in the middle, rugs up, and dust. The place was cold as a dead stove. We turned our backs on the apparently impossible, a little depressed, and walked down to the car again. No one is allowed to drive cars in the lanes. They are narrow and steep and there are no places for turning in. By the time we got to Pliva's it was nearly two, but they produced an excellent lunch which we ate in a window full of sun, facing down over the square and bazaar and across to the mountains wreathed in clouds. There were four drunken Americans finishing off a meal of sorts and Viola and I showed our views on their condition which started us all off on a frank discussion of Life – and all its aspects. Perth was intelligent and realistic, as one would expect. He was also surprised (agreeably, he said) at our directness. He didn't believe any Englishwoman ever talked freely; and we certainly did. I liked him. He was gay and easy to talk to; quite funny and both sophisticated and fairly simple. It emerged that he was Schuschnigg's[1] secretary before the putsch. One and a half years in a concentration camp. Then escape to America for three weeks; then China, now India. He is really a gynaecologist, a branch in which he gets rather little practice at the moment, the British Army being what it is. Having had a skin condition he has been posted up here to clear it up. The Lebong hospital is mostly skins. The cool clear air is a help after the awfulness of the rest of Bengal. Being a two-pip lieut after his experiences and the positions he's held, must be trying, but he didn't indicate that it was. We sat long over our lunch and then walked very slowly up the mountain

[1] Kurt von Schuschnigg: Chancellor of Austria 1934–8.

again, panting. He picked a pale mauve primula for each of us. They grow wild. Rhododendrons are just out. Saw two. One scarlet with tight clustered heads; the other that voluptuous pale pink one they have at Ford.[1] Wild here! It's lovely being so high. It's very quiet. The views stretch everywhere and the air almost hurts when you breathe it very deeply. When we got back after lunch Ghulam had arrived, the fires were lit and the rooms all in order. Perth kissed our hands and said we'd given him a lovely day and we said we'd enjoyed it too.

Later: Now, unpacked and washed, wearing our trousers and two sweaters each, we are by a roaring fire. Supper was an omelette and fried potatoes and coffee. Now books.

Trivia. Saw two beggars at Kurseng. The first was about six years old with rather peculiar feet and on his chest was embroidered the appeal 'Please Help this Poor Lame'. The other was considerably older; he came striding down the road as we climbed up it in the car, and he, too, wore an embroidered front, a little less West End than the boy's, for it said

PLESEH
ELP THIS
POOR DUMB

Wednesday, February 14th, 1945   Darjeeling

This is a most heavenly spot. No aeroplanes, ever. Ghulam comes in at 8 wearing his eternal fur hat, a white muffler Viola gave him and his new blue tweed jacket, and he builds a fire for us. Our room is lit by two skylights set at angles high in the roof. No windows; which is good in this cold but prevents us seeing the incredible views. The light from the skylights is attractive and at 8 o'clock it

---

[1] Ford Manor, near Lingfield, Surrey, the home of Aunt Pauline – sister to Waldorf Astor, married to Bertie Spender Clay.

is just warming to yellow as the sun gets up over one of the ranges. A tree near the house shows its top branches through the glass and the sky gets bluer and bluer as the day grows. Breakfast in bed with glasses brimming with orange juice. One feels a little queer up here. Can't hurry. On Monday morning we went down a thousand feet to Lebong to see Col Wiggington of the CMH [Combined Military Hospital] there to lay our plans for the week. He is OC the hospital and both convalescent depots so we got the whole programme sorted out in his office. Miss Ferguson, from Australia, is the matron and she was friendly too. Wiggington is a live wire, about thirty, hair cut *'en brosse'* and the sort of person who Gets Things Done. So Miss F. told us. She likes working with him.

These climbs from the car are hard going. Takes ten minutes to get up from the main road to this house and cars aren't allowed so one *must* walk. We came back for lunch, on a little table in front of the fire. Excellent fish. Then we changed our blouses but couldn't get into dresses in this weather so went to work in our suits looking at least clean and tidy! A very cosy show in a small ward to about twenty patients. We all gathered about the log fire and they soon forgot the shyness they started with and we had a fine time – one and a half hours of it. The atmosphere, while beautifully friendly, got pretty thick with fire and cigarette smokes, and I found I was full of it and my voice became very rough when we finished. Tea with Miss Ferguson, late, about 6, and then, worn right out for no special reason unless altitude, we came back here and climbed the hill in the gloaming while the first star shone out of a stormy sky on us, and wind off the icier slopes lashed our legs. Distant Tibetan bells rang out and there were little fires glowing across the valley. Supper in trousers by our fire, me with *Ego 6* [volume six of James Agate's autobiography] and Viola finishing *Invitation to the Waltz* [by Rosamond Lehmann]. Agate is amusing, is literate, is clever; but he is also empty as a dry box and devoid of all loveliness. He leaves ashes for beauty; which is sad, for he'd like to leave beauty. Conceit in Shaw has its own rather gay quality, but in Agate it makes the hairs on the back of the head to rise. One just wishes he wouldn't. Bed, under six blankets, rolled in brownie with bedsocks and a bottle. Just right.

Yesterday morning, and today, I got up at 7.30 and put a coat on over my dressing gown and went out to see Kanchinjunga before the day clouds rose up and hid the range as they seem to do at this time of the year. Very high mountains, snowy topped, with the first sun on them and the heavens a pale new blue above them. Very good. They look higher than any mountains I've ever seen and most probably are. Exciting and remote and not to be dwelt on for too long. It was good to get back to bed again and watch Ghulam build his fire for us. Viola went down to explore the bazaar in the morning, but I took a notion to laze. Couldn't face that climb back, knowing we had two shows to do in the afternoon. So I played the radio and pressed a blouse and did my nails and nursed the drawing fire which had gone into a black heap. Then 'fish for luncheon'.[1] Then, oh so unwillingly, changing from trousers to black suit and frilly blouse and off to Lebong. Found 4 or 5 skin patients we'd known at Barrackpore. It's very flattering the way they eagerly come to the show again. These were walking cases from a distant ward and didn't have to come at all but said they didn't want to miss it. Same old jokes, same old songs. It's nice to know they like them a second time.

Ghulam said there was hot water for a bath when we got in, so we arranged the tin tub in front of the fire and went back to nursery days – Viola, with her head tied up in a red and white scarf with ends like rabbits' ears, sat and soaked in silence by the glow. Lying down isn't easy in tubs, bits get left out and go cold. But I managed to curl

---

[1] 'Fish for luncheon': Farjeon monologue, originally performed by Edith Evans in *Diversion*.

most of me under the water which was red hot and wonderful. Discovered, rather too late, that the tub leaked and the rug was sodden by the time we emptied the rest of the water away. The telephone is out of order 'because of the storm'. What storm? Wind has blown a good deal but not unduly. It has thrown the radio aerial on to the tin roof and something peculiar happens each time they touch and it sounds like big guns through the programmes. We abandoned the radio and turned the switch to gram. and had Beethoven. Symphony No. 4, Toscanini. Sat up much too late but it was so delicious by the fire and the magic of the music on this mountain was pretty good.

Today started with the whole range of mountains clear of cloud. Darjeeling, below here, lay indigo in early mist, very dark. I stood in the garden with sun on my back and my toes a bit nipped and took in the panorama. Later Viola and I walked down to the bazaar in search for *giftes* for the loved ones. So difficult. Don't want any carved boxes or curved daggers; nor art silk pyjamas in deep purple; nor yet a housecoat covered in rather wobbly woolwork. Got a cashmere shawl which I *may* give to Hilda. And a pair of apple green felt shoes with rope soles that are quite definitely for me. Otherwise we found nothing but saw some nice sights. A group of seven or eight dead-end kids in blackened rags, for they work in the coal dump near the station, sitting on a doorstep playing cards with an almost undecipherable pack of limp grey cards. Lovely design there – stone wall, stone step; warm stone colour. The children with flat little Mongolian faces, grey-beige with little slit eyes catching the light like chips of jet. Their rusty black clothes. Wish I could have drawn it. Better still someone to have done it in colour wash. We saw a tot of about two in candy pink wool bonnet, red jacket, purply pink petticoat, clutching an orange. And two elderly Englishwomen in men's tweed fishing caps and sandals. They were unperturbed, tub shaped and turning rapidly into natives.

Later: We have invited Lt Perth to sup with us this evening. It is all a deep laid plot because kind people have asked us to dine and we've refused all their hospitality, pleading the need to rest while we're up here. The real reason being that this house and its fireside win hands down over any proffered company. However, Lt Perth is a kindred spirit we feel, and so we've asked him very secretly to come and sup with us, assuming that he'll *love* to climb for ten minutes in a bitter wind to enjoy our company! The preparations have gone on since yesterday. We ordered a special dinner – we've been having eggs, but tonight it's soup, bird and coffee cream. We've bought joss sticks and the place is heavily incensed. We've fixed flowers, African daisies and a big bowl of glossy green leaves with unidentified clusters of tight white buds in it. We've got cigarettes, fixed nuts and sweets and built up the fire. We've giggled at ourselves over it – all these goings on. We've cleaned our faces and put on clean blouses and we feel very festive. All we hope is that these preparations won't scare the poor man.

We did a show in the officers' ward at Lebong at 4.30. Tea first, very elaborate and good with Col Wiggington and the matron and one or two other members of the staff. We played on an enclosed verandah but even with the windows tightly shut it wasn't very warm and I felt sorry for the audience but they were very good and the penny dropped with fine speed. Coming up our steep hill tonight we saw the new moon, the evening star and the top peaks of the Kanchinjunga range glowing pink above a thick whirl of grey clouds, all at once. Panting, we stood awestruck.

Saturday, February 17th 1945   Back in Calcutta
          (Denham Whites, 4 Asoka Rd, Alipore)

Mrs D.W. at tea today: 'I'm not *really* very attached to my brother. He is much older than the rest of us, and *rather* difficult. My father said he must do something and he said he was going to be an artist and he went to the Slade – he wasn't too bad – but then suddenly he came down to my aunt's and built a huge bonfire, my dear, of all his paints and pictures and brushes and everything right on the lawn. It was rather hard on my aunt because she was so fond of her grass.' And at lunch, about a missionary who is staying here too but whom we haven't yet met: 'She's an angel but she never stops talking – but she *is* an angel. All those blind people and everything. She *is* an angel, but an annoying angel.'

We got back this morning, un-met by ENSA; so that took up a lot of time getting things organised. Finally a sergeant turned up with a lot of mail and we left him to cope with the piano which was a bit complicated because the coach it was in was so far at back of the train that it didn't even get to the platform and no one would or could unload it. Chief item in mail was cable from Noël: 'DEAR JOYCE DEFINITELY PLANNING REVUE TO OPEN MAY OR JUNE WOULD LIKE YOU HOME AS SOON AS POSSIBLE CABLE ME EARLIEST TIME YOU CAN BE HERE ALL LOVE.' I've wired back saying I'm due to fly home on March 12 but have stupidly forgotten to ask if he wants me to return earlier. Nor have I put my address and as his cable dated Feb. 6th didn't reach me till now he can't reply. Must rectify tomorrow. Reaction confused. Had just rearranged my feelings about postponement as announced by Dick so that the breathing period had become rather pleasant. Now it is all a little close and frightening. It's the inspiration that alarms me; or rather the lack of it.

Darjeeling was a very delicious interlude. Was just getting used to the cold when we moved away. Our evening with Monty Perth (it really *is* an unlikely name for a Viennese) was cosy and successful. When he arrived he confessed that the prospects of us both was alarming a bit but that soon passed off and we talked endlessly over a delicious dinner and he and Viola enjoyed the whisky he'd brought as a contribution to the party. Viola took one of her notions halfway through the evening and did a vanishing act in order that I might have a tête-a-tête with the doctor. He was full of compliments and the ego swelled disgustingly. Asked a lot of pertinent personal questions and knew, all too soon, far too much, even without me telling him. Viola had gone, ostensibly, to the lav, but later to stargaze, and she came in later breathing frost and we had some Beethoven on the gramophone. Perth enlarged on his own history a little. Sister a professional pianist, married to a Jew. He hasn't heard of her for several years and imagines she is dead. He isn't married but lived with someone for a long time. She is now in England, a painter; of an RC family, so she can't divorce. He is a gay and attractive person and his English is very good but with an accent that we find fun. He and Viola were talking of something by, I think, Mahler. 'How does it go?' asked Perth. 'Weazle it for me.' We all sat up far too late and by the time we'd taken him halfway down the hill in the starlight and panted our way up and Viola had played another whole Beethoven concerto on the gram. it was 2 before we put out our light.

We left Darjeeling yesterday morning. Our usual little ritual of groping our way out of deep sleep in order to look on the mountain-range in all its pristine morning loveliness before the day clouds had crept up on it. Wonderful yesterday. Silver against blue grey; the entire range clear of the clouds below. I never was able to assess the height of the range when searching for it later in the day. I never looked high enough. Now and then the topmost peaks did pierce through and above the clouds. Packing after breakfast, and then we got Ghulam to summon the household that we might present largesse in a lump sum to Kuntza the head one. In our five days at Little Chevremont we'd seen two bearers, one sweeper and Kuntza. Yesterday the room was jammed with humanity and the two gardeners among them presented us each with a green orchid tastefully smothered in maidenhair and lashed to a little bamboo split by threads of red cotton. We hoped our thirty rupees would divide up into something slightly worth having; but we rather doubted it. We left Ghulam and Mrs D.W.'s Ganesh to cope with the horrors of getting our bedrolls, two suit-cases, two canvas bags, two music cases and some loose coats to the station a mile below the house without transport. Coolies did the carrying and Ghulam and Ganesh, with our baggage, crept down to the plains forty-five miles away in that joke train, like an Emett, in the space of six and a half hours.

Since getting here just before lunch we have idled pleasantly after quiet lunch with Mrs D.W. and then an orgy with *Tatler* and *Sketch*es arrived since our first visit here. Several pictures of Aunt N. celebrating her twenty-fifth anniversary in the House. Larry Olivier's *Henry V*[1] looks lovely and Pa writes that it is. Mail today was very good. From Reggie, Gin, To, Victor, Dick, Celia, Ruth Draper, Elliott [Coleman], and birthday cables from Reggie and Pa.

Monday, February 19th, 1945   In the train to Muri, and on to Ranchi

It is hot; we have stood on the platform among dirty travelling Indians, poor devils, and waited while Jack Bontemps, little Ayling and a large sweating Sgt got our accommodation changed from sharing a four-berth compartment with two Indian officers (male) for two Red Cross workers (female). I think God may have had a hand in the whole business, for one of the girls is copy of the most heavenly sort. She is Cockney, blonde, pointed of feature, dumb and full of bright conversation. Her companion, who is very pretty with soft wild hair and a very

---

[1] The film of Shakespeare's play, directed by Laurence Olivier, in which he also played King Henry.

careful modulated voice, has an automatic smile that flashes on and off like an electric sign. She is apologising in silence for the crudity of Judy the dumb belle, and is clearly short of patience with her and only a maddening self-control of the Prefect sort is enabling her to get on at all. The air is now fragrant with eau de Cologne, orange and a dusting powder that came out of an enormous tin container. Judy has interrupted Joan five separate times in her reading to say she does like a nice light book for journeys; isn't it warm; do we mind her undressing in public but the closet is a bit – well; her hair is a mess; and she does like something light to read in the train. I'm on thorns waiting for her next interruption. Here it is: 'Can I tempt you to a Thing?' (Peppermints) 'I never could fancy marzipan.' Irrelevant it would seem.

Today was mostly wasted at the ENSA office. It has now moved to 19 Chowringhee where it is housed more comfortably but, pro tem, even more chaotically. Saw George Formby and Beryl for a moment but didn't speak. Liked the look of George but Beryl was being firm which is never becoming. Large photograph has appeared in today's SEAC [*South East Asia Chronicle*] with inaccurate captions about me as Cabaret and West End Singer and no mention of the hospitals or of Viola. *Dear* publicity.

Thursday, February 22nd, 1945   Ranchi, staying
                                         Major Gen Briggs and wife

We got here on Tuesday morning after getting off the train at Muri about 5.30 a.m. and standing about a good deal while the ENSA sgt woke out of his sleep in his truck and got things under control.

Spent all yesterday morning on monologues – 'Interview' and 'Drama Circle' – so so.[1] Ideas good, lines quite

[1] In preparation for Noël Coward's new revue.

funny but I don't know. My old stuff is really rather good, I think, and it's very difficult doing anything that will measure up. I worked very hard all morning and Viola came in before lunch to hear my results and was clearly as disappointed as I was. We did three shows out at 139 yesterday.

Monday, February 26th, 1945   In the train from Khargpur to Calcutta

We left Ranchi on Saturday morning. The General, who is very attractive, laid on a picnic for us and he and Mrs Briggs drove us the first sixty miles through lovely rolling wooded country to a PWD [Public Works Department] inspection bungalow in a little village called Tibo where we ate lunch on the verandah while the two military drivers and Ghulam sat behind the truck and ate theirs. At least Ghulam didn't eat. His feeding arrangements are very mysterious and rare. He gets paler and paler as the day goes on and refuses all proffered bananas or cakes which must surely be quite legal even for fanatical Muslims. It happens on all our journeys. He takes a cup of tea in the morning but nothing else and while he is always irreproachable and affable with us, his temper grows shorter and shorter with what he regards as his inferiors. The little Indian soldier detailed to follow us in a truck with the piano failed to put any oil in his engine until the thing made awful noises and stopped. We missed it and went back to look for him. Ghulam's disdain and withering utterances were very alarming. 'This ignorant Indian,' he said with hideous scorn, 'he knows nothing.' I wish I'd written down some of Ghulam's conversation, for it is fraught with interest and surprise. We showed him the large and rather stagey picture of me that SEAC produced last week and he said it was not like me for 'memsahib came smiling' and this was solemn. 'Not much came smiling,' he said. His washing lists make good reading. They are headed with the word 'LANDRY' and the place where we are staying. There follows a list of fascinating articles like this: '1 tole, 1 pilow cover, 1 body, 1 scirt, 1 blose, 2 nicer, 3 petti coats, 1 night gone, 2 handkerchieves, 1 pair glove.' He tells us tales of his home life of which he is very proud. His mother and sister are tall-tall, which is good. The doubling of words is used instead of 'very', but 'much-much' comes in a good deal. He is ruthless and, under his control that is always exercised for those he likes and admires, lies a real wildness. I would never be in the least surprised to learn of violence. Indeed his face gets really frightening when he is moved to anger, which is frequently. Coolies and inferiors are all no good with him. In fact he is really rather a horrid character but even so we like him very much and his thoughtfulness and efficiency where we are concerned is perfect. If we were going to be here longer I'd feel morally bound to tick him off a bit for being so fierce but, as it is, he is spared what Viola calls one of my little talks!

The general sent us on in his car to do the other 140 miles to Khargpur. This was an underestimate for we'd reckoned about fifty miles short. However we got there about 7, just at dusk, and we felt we had at last seen something of the real India. The wooded hills were lovely. It's impossible to know just what season this is. Trees were burgeoning into new leaf – sticky red acacia-shaped things. There were autumn colours going on huge spreading trees whose dying leaves were scarlet in the sun. The plains were very bare and brown. Paddy fields like unshaven chins. There are aboriginals in Behar. Ugly negroid people, very dark and not very big. We saw their women working on the roads, stocky girls with lovely breasts and rather lovely arms; faces, mostly, dull and animal. We came upon a road-mending squad. About twenty girls of all ages were pulling an enormous roller. Older women carried reed baskets full of stones on their heads. Dirty white sarees. Silver nose rings, ankle bracelets.

It was arranged for us to stay with Brigadier Barlow of 351 Sub Area. He leads a bachelor life on the top floor of a surprising block of flats rising suddenly out of the ground in the residential area entirely populated by the Railway. He is a large man, underhung like a bulldog, with a low laugh that shakes his whole frame and a roaring voice. 'Boy,' he bellows, and one expects the startled bearer to say 'Yes, papa'. He is a dear. Gruff. Rough, Blimpish, prejudiced and bombastic. That is the façade. Underneath this rugged front is a heart of velvet tenderness, a growing tendency to withdraw from the world. We'd feared he might have expected us to be gay, it being Saturday night and we sank at the thought of club life after our eight hours' drive. But no. His idea of a good time is a book by himself. What sort of book? we asked. 'Anything that isn't trash,' he said. Above all, he missed music in India. 'What sort of music?' we asked. 'Anything that isn't trash.' An endearing character. After dinner when we'd all relaxed we said we betted he'd been furious when they asked him to put up two unknown women, and ENSAS at that. He said he was. His flat has three bedrooms all opening on to a balcony and until our visit the windows and doors had been uncurtained, but in our honour a green and white seersucker hanging had gone up over Viola's door and window, and a red and white one over mine. 'Hope you've got everything,' he said, anxiously ushering us into our rooms. There was a bed, a chair, a dressing table and a mirror. We hung our clothes from door knobs and window ledges.

We worked at No. 9 IGH [Indian General Hospital] on Thursday afternoon. Like all the hospitals there, it is new and only just in process of being opened up. Only fifty odd patients but with the orderlies and staff we were about 100 in a sunny ward hung with gay yellow curtains. I've got my introductory remarks set pretty deeply now. There are certain things that I've tried and proved and so they've stuck. Telling them that Viola is from Norfolk and Lincolnshire and that part of the world and wondering if there are any other Swedebashers there? That I'm from London, etc. When I do 'The Surrey with the Fringe on Top,' [from *Oklahoma!*] I tell them a bit about it first. How that a Surrey is a kind of carriage – 'You know,' I say, 'a thing with horses', and I go 'clk-clk', which is the BORS' audible sound of approval where females are concerned. And when the chorus of clicks that this arouses has calmed down I say, 'And as we all know that is the sound you make when you're out with a horse.' We did a 7 o'clock show at the Ranchi CMH that evening and had a very good time in a crowded ward. Like the officers' ward at 139 the night before, I felt conscience-stricken at making some of them laugh for it appeared to cause a certain amount of pain. There were facial mac. cases in 139 who held their faces as if in torture but when I asked them if they'd rather I didn't or would they like to go out, urged me to carry on and said it did them good. There were mostly newly done tonsils in the CMH who went on bleeding cheerfully, which seemed a pity.

Monty Perth appeared on Friday. He'd come down from Darjeeling on a Political Intelligence course; and to see us! The Briggs kindly invited him to lunch and we dined with him at the local club in the evening. He nobly gave us his precious white cashmere shawl to cut in two! This was a very generous gesture indeed. It is a beauty.

Sleep all afternoon following a curry for lunch that set me on raging fire within and no amount of water could quench its fierceness. Then out to Mednapur hosp. again, five or six miles over rough road in a car that had no windows to speak of and the rising red dust blew in and over us, entering eyes, ears, nose and mouth and was horrid. We played in a ward that was once the entrance hall to the Gopal Palace. There were allegorical scenes painted in panels all over the walls and ceiling and a carved wooden dado had lotus flowers on it and the entire floor was a mosaic of old chips of china. Literally. They were laid in a large floral design with trailing ribbons but the detail was indeed chips of old plates and cups and saucers. It was a specially good show in spite of two solid rows of Indian officers, two Indian wives and two Indian lady doctors. They sat in idol-ic trances and now and then were moved to shrill laughter. But the BORS and the sisters and the few English officers were in very receptive mood and we did an hour and forty-five minutes of tightly packed stuff.

We have now joined the Bombay mail at Khargpur and should be in Calcutta in about an hour. The town is closing in on us and I must admit I'm very sad about it. Last night's show was probably our last hospital one. We are to do isolated gun sites outside Calcutta all this week.

March 1945

Thursday, March 1, 1945   Denham White, 4 Asoka Rd.,
                                          Alipore, Calcutta

Heavenly staying here. Quiet, cool, comfortable, and
above all we approve of the D.W.s. It is hotting up. We
were forced to grope for our beds after lunch in blind hot
sleep. Worked on new monologue all morning. It
emerges, I think. 'Interview'. I've changed the ENSA girl
from a complete chorus dumb belle to the semi-solemn
kind. She's based on that girl Joan La Something I met
doing a variety charity matinée at the Phoenix about four
years ago. 'From Convent to Cabaret' she had in brackets
after her name in the programme. Very nauseating but I
hope fairly funny. Tried it out on Viola who laughed.[1]

Saturday, March 3rd, 1945. Daddy's birthday   Calcutta

Cable has come from Reggie to say he hopes I'll be back
before March 25th which I take to mean he will be going
abroad then. It really has worked out badly with me
getting back just as he moves. The reason I chose to come
away this second time was that he thought he'd be
overseas too, by last August.

It has really hotted up here. I'm wearing the minimum
and pouring pretty freely. It is 10.45, I am under the trees
in the garden.

[1] For sketch see page 377.

On Thursday I had lunch with Virginia Vernon, queen of ENSA welfare, friend of Basil Dean and known throughout the organisation as v8. She is large, dynamic, snobbish, nosey and capable. She wished to talk hospitals with me and as it is my pet pigeon I accepted the invitation at once. She wants me to join the organisation in an official capacity under Lilian Braithwaite to have a definite say in hospital entertainment. I don't want to do it because I hate ENSA, and Drury Lane fills me with dread, but if I could get something done I feel I ought to try it. If I really had authority and could say my say and be taken notice of then I'll do it, but I won't stooge for anyone.

<hr />

Letter to her mother

Sunday, March 4th, 1945   Calcutta

My darling Ma,
Probably my last letter from India. We are due to leave fairly soon. It is getting really hot here now – all day and night. I can't think how people do it during the summer. Working, I mean. Edith Evans and a full company are arriving next week to do *Christopher Bean*[1] for ten weeks. My heart goes out to them starting off in this heat. It's ninety per cent humidity here. You just sweat and sweat. At the moment I'm ashamed to say I'm covered in prickly heat which is unglamorous pinkness of unbelievable irritation. Mercifully, so far, it's only on me bod. The face is blameless. I could happily scratch all over but I've resorted to some Calamine lotion and combined with a modicum of self-control and what Virginia calls 'holding the nose' all is fine. Just a bore.

[1] *The Late Christopher Bean*, comedy by René Fauchois; Americanised by Sidney Howard, Anglicised by Emlyn Williams. Edith Evans appeared in it at the St James's.

Anyway, God willing we'll be back about the 16th. I'm to go straight to Gin's and I expect Reggie will have fixed up a room for us in a hotel for the week[1] after which I'll perch with Gin till I have got me bearings.

. . . I'm trying to write new material for the show. I've got a nauseating character ready that I do rather like. She's an ENSA girl returned home from abroad; very arch – a singer of Ave Marias and Sacred Songs for the Boys! Viola thinks it funny. So do I. It's not very easy writing out here somehow. One needs the stimulus of the theatre to sharpen one's wits.

We are staying with the darling Denham Whites again. They *are* India for us and have been so angelic to us both. He is a doctor, never stops for one minute. I never knew such an unselfed life as it calls for. He is the real saintly kind of doctor – quiet, still, devoted to his job and beloved by everyone. And she is the most attractive, vague, delicious person you ever saw. You'd love her. She *bicycles* round Calcutta, even now in the heat, wearing a white dress and a coat of ageless design and a large brown felt picture hat! She is one of the traditional sights of the city and everyone loves her. She is amusing and witty and gentle and tolerant and wise. Being here has made the whole difference to us. It's a home. It's peace. It's cool. And they are both so real and such fun and so good.

My clothes are rotting on me with heat and hard wear. One simply cannot get an elastic belt anywhere. I used to have heavenly ones from the US, called tassarettes, *very long*; no bones; that was their charm. But I can't get one anywhere. There are literally no stockings in India but thanks to your forethought three years ago I'm *still* equipped.

---

[1] At this time, as Reggie was in the Army, they were without a home.

Tuesday, March 6th, 1945   Calcutta

Mrs D.W., just off to the bank, has told us of a friend of hers who was reading a book of poems in a train out here. An Indian Babu asked her if she liked poetry and said that he himself was a poet liking poetry. Might he, he asked, tell her one of his poems? This was it:

> Oh com, my love, oh com,
> I have loved you since last Au*tom*,
> I have loved you from heart's bot*tom*,
> Com.

Sunday. Very hot. Sleep in our darkened room under the fan all afternoon and then our last show of the tour, workshops of the 20th Regiment. So saddening was it that I closed my mind against it and it was only when I saw our familiar little mini-piano and knew it was the last time we'd see it did I get a genuine sentimental lump. It's been such a lovely job and doing it with Viola has been perfect. Now she must get on with her real music and I'm to go into Noël's revue so that's that. We did the show on a verandah on the first floor of a three-sided building. Funny for sound but friendly in feeling. We'd had a cup of tea with the little Scots captain and his lieuts and after the show there was a spread of rum drinks. We saw the start of what was undoubtably quite a heavy evening's jollity. It had been a good last show – unlike the horror in Iraq last year! It has a shape and a quality and we made some good sounds. Back through the smoky evening of Calcutta. We've got used to the little shops lit by single candles; monochromes.

The streets are crowded at that hour. White figures, so alike, wandering in the dark – startled by our blacked-out lights. Stupid in the heat that doesn't change with the sunset. Sunny incense smells. Bullock carts jerking heavily by. No women about.

Wednesday, March 7th, 1945   (I now write in the train to
Delhi)

Outside Madras there is a bend in the river and crossing it
by the bridge you see our eternal wash day. Figures
standing in the shallows pounding, men and women,
and the more athletic of them get a violent swinging
rhythm going. The sheet, shirt or saree is whirled high in
the air and then flung on a rock for purification and I
suppose premature destruction. And all around, on both
sides of the river, the ground is used for drying. There are
a few lines for the hanging of European shirts but for the
most part the wash is spread out flat on the grass; acres of
it. Sarees are five yards long and they carpet the area in
reds and whites and faded blues and greens; for the dyes
are seldom fast. Sheets, towels, bedspreads and curtains
festoon bushes and the whole place is like a patchwork
quilt come to life on a grand scale. Madras was one of the
biggest I've seen but everywhere we've been in India
we've seen variations of the same thing.

Monday morning saw us in Calcutta itself again,
tidying up ends and meeting people. I got all final
instructions about the journey to Delhi; our air passage
home and who to get at about it. Then we had an
assignation with Monty Perth at Firpo's where we were
very late and couldn't stay long, but we asked him to dine
with us at Mrs D.W.'s that evening. Then I went off to
meet John Keswick at the Gt Eastern Hotel and Viola had
a session with the finance sergeant in the office and then
bought some rather lovely white material for us to give
Mrs D.W. as a parting present to make into underclothes.
John was on his way from Kandy to Chungking and had a
night and a day at Government House in transit. He is
political liaison officer between Mountbatten's HQ and
the Embassy in Chungking. At least I think that is how it
is. He's been home on his way out from Washington.
Says the anti-British feeling grows in the US and the
anti-American feeling in England flourishes. It's serious.

And depressing. He also says the V 2s come about three every twenty-four hours. Can't say I relish the thought of them. In all honesty I just plain dread bombs and sirens and there it is. I'm grateful for the lovely absence from that sort of strain and wish to goodness all my loved ones could have it, but none of these worthy sentiments in any way minimises my own feeble cowardice.

Mrs D.W. was canteening and the colonel never gets in till after 9, so we dined alone with Monty Perth. He was gay and silly and we had intensely personal talk on a safely ridiculous level. He proposed marriage to Viola, saying he wished to get a British passport. It was all nonsense but underneath I had an uncomfy feeling that he might seriously be working to that end. He is amusing and intelligent; rooted in a lot of things incompatible to me, but a pleasing companion with just the right touch for making one feel feminine and attractive without going on too long about it. Skilled, in other words, and well practised. Mrs D.W. came in about 10, after having had a bath. And then the colonel arrived and ate his late dinner. We got on to magic and the colonel told us staggering stories of Indian conjurors and fakirs but was stubbornly convinced that they couldn't do anything that Maskelyne and Devant[1] couldn't do. 'Given the time to work it out.' His account of the man who made a row of matches travel across six foot of floor space into their box from a far corner of the room ought to take some doing. And the growing mango tree that burgeons under a white cloth from a pip in an empty pot. I hold the unsubstantiated view that it's all mass hypnotism. Though why they can't heal themselves or each other of illnesses if they can control inanimate objects so skillfully is beyond me.

And yesterday was our last day with the D.W.s. Hugh

---

[1] Maskelyne and Devant: illusionists, first appearance 1904. Their most favourite sensation as the Maskelyne and Devant Mysteries was 'The Mascot Moth.' General Montgomery employed Maskelyne's talents as an illusionist before the Battle of Alamein.

Latimer, who fumbles rather than handles publicity for
ENSA in Calcutta, came to interview me in the morning,
bringing Reg Foster of SEAC with him for the same
purpose. I went on and on about hospitals and the job.
Then Viola joined us and we went on some more and
were photographed a bit. Much cooler. Too cool really;
must have dropped fifteen degrees, I'd say. Lunch. Then
packing; tea, and then off. We were both genuinely
wretched to leave the D.W.s. They are very special
people and we have grown deep roots in Asoka Road. I
think they both loved us too. He referred to us all the time
as 'the Children' which has pleased our ageing faces a
good deal. They are a unique pair. Complete opposites,
not even liking the same friends, for the most part. But
their separate lives unite in an enchanting mutual ador-
ation. It fills the house and lights the garden. He is now
sixty-five; I suppose she is twelve years younger, possibly less. Her figure and walk are completely young, so
are her enormous cloud-grey blue eyes. A fascinating
character. She is brave as a lion, fiercely loyal, unconven-
tional and free as a bird. No wonder she is so widely
loved. They are Bill and Joey to each other but their
proper names are Arthur and Evelyn. Staying in their
house has been freedom and friendliness. Even the food
is light and encouraging, and the flowers fill the rooms
with velvet colours. Lately there have been freesias to
scent the drawing room. I remember the first day we
went in to 4 Asoka Road I didn't get anything from the
house on looks. It was dark and cool and too full of
Chinese bits – lovely in themselves – and the drawing
room into which we peered looked cold and unlived in.
But I didn't then know about the porch, with its huge
white sofa and comfy chairs and her desk table, a sea of
papers and letters and clocks (all different times), and the
two gramophones and piles of books and gramophone
records. Nor had I seen the dining room with the exquisite Copenhagen china and had a meal served by
those two snowy-clothed bearers whose rhythm and

anticipation were so perfect that meals just happened like music. Never has a house had so many books in it and all books one wanted to read.

Now we are in the train to Delhi. It's the last lap and already that uncomfortable feeling of timetables and rush and all the everyday difficulties have started to creep in. These months have been free from those problems. One has had the job to do and the time to think about it properly. The right way to work. Viola, in her old red jacket, is doing a memory drawing of Mrs D.W. inspecting the new green dovecot she's had built in the garden. It has a ridiculous roof of thatch like a rakish straw hat and so far the six pigeons destined to live in it are against the idea and when we left last night they'd gone homing back to their former roost, a few houses away. Their owners are going home.

Tuesday, March 20th, 1945   32 Cambridge Square, W.2., London[1]

We got off the train at Delhi at 6.30 a.m. and were met by a character called Mrs Prendergast who has lately joined ENSA. Viola started feeling odd on the train. She kept having roaring temperatures that we didn't dare take because we felt it was better not to know and by a course of Veganin at the right moments she kept going but felt limp as cotton string, poor darling. Even so she valiantly did two fifteen-minute broadcast recordings with me at All India Radio, dined at Viceregal Lodge where we sat on either side of Lord Wavell, and lunched with Peter Fleming[2] on the edge of the viceregal swimming pool off the left-overs from a buffet supper she missed given by Peter's hostess Mrs Tweed.

---

[1] The home of Virginia and Tony Thesiger, with whom Joyce was staying.

[2] Peter Fleming had been planting misleading information on the Japanese.

Delhi was mostly Peter, who is well, handsome, a fine host, excellent company and a very nice person. Also Harold Lindo. Also in Delhi – Peter Coats, Comptroller of the Viceroy's house (350 indoor servants!)[1] and Hugh Euston, an ADC. Sightsaw the house and gardens. Lutyens better indoors than out. Can't think why I imagined Delhi was gleaming white with endless court-yards. It is in two shades of pink sandstone and will never mellow further. It is bleak, well proportioned and satisfied my eye only at great distances and in the bulk. The gardens are a pleasure. Skilful combination of for-mality and gayness. Lots of water – 'It always reflects the sky, it does, doesn't it'.[2] Round garden a little too sen-sational but thrilling in its voluptuousness. Lord Wavell talked nature to Viola and Celia to me. The menu cards were a war economy and measured about two and a half inches by three. Sightsaw the Red Fort. Very lovely, same date as Isfahan. Mogul. Instead of the flower designs being painted on the walls they were mostly mosaics, or inlay. Delicacy in the carved marble. Saw it all at sun-down with Peter Coats, Hugh Euston and Freya Stark, who was dressed in black with fine black silk stockings and incredibly small high-heeled shoes. She wore a ring rocky with topaz and big as an entire thumb joint. I liked her.

While in Delhi I bought a fur coat for Reggie to give me as a present! It is oppossum, long and silky and very lovely. 950 rs. – about £65 – nothing for a fur coat nowadays.

We flew from Delhi on Monday, 12th.[3] Viola rather weak so I got her to rest at the BOAC mess, Somerset House. Sgt Kerridge, who had looked after us in Poona

---

[1] Peter Coats: worked for Lord Wavell, the Viceroy throughout the war. Later became an admired garden historian.
[2] Ruth Draper: from her garden sketch.
[3] They flew home by flying-boat hops. From Delhi to Bahrein in a Sunderland – 'smooth going', commented Joyce. BOAC's wartime op-erations were similar in route to its predecessor Imperial Airways.

and Secunderabad, met us at the airport. He is now stationed in Karachi. After tea, Viola and I took a gentle little clip-clop drive in a tonga around the town. Viola bought a hairbrush and I got some Pears soap and a sponge bag. Washed my hair for the journey which Viola, rightly, regarded as madness. But planes are clean and my hair was still full of soap from the rather inadequate washing it had had in Calcutta. We got to Bahrein at sunset, Viola feeling all in. Bundled her to bed in the BOAC rest house. Our room had four beds but only us, thank heaven. She took castor oil – and washed it down with consommé. Off at dawn next day for Cairo and a hell of a journey. Nine hours' endless bumping and the two little boys of six and three who were flying home with their mother, Mrs Buxton, were constantly being sick into their cardboard buckets while Viola and I draped ourselves over each other with eyes tightly shut in an effort not to see anything. Seldom hated nine hours more. Poor Viola was a ghastly colour when we got out in Cairo, but Glynne [Bernard] was there to meet us and whisked us away to stay at Mena where once more I got Viola straight to bed. Cairo was a hectic visit. Did some shoe shopping for us both.

We flew away again on Tuesday and it was a smooth six and a half hours to Augusta in Sicily. Viola and I sat in the sun by the sea and were sad to know it was over and dreaded England and the difficulties ahead. There was freesia growing in a garden and the sun was deliciously warm once we got out of the wind. And then, next day, to Poole Harbour near Bournemouth, over France, mostly lost in cloud. It was a long day and it began at 6.30 when, as soon as we'd left the water, and the three men in our compartment (we'd left Mrs Buxton and the children after some RAF had disembarked at Cairo) opened a bottle of Marsala, got out the cards and were deep in a poker game by 6.45 a.m. Viola had fever and looked grey for a bit but I got her warm with six blankets and fuzzy and she survived the ordeal of customs, health officer, censor and all the business of getting home. We decided not to attempt London that night but went to stay at the BOAC hotel till the morning. Daffodils shivered in a keen wind, almond blossom danced in Bournemouth gardens and forsythia shone in the sun. BOAC did a grand job in welcoming us. Can't speak too highly of their organisation and general friendliness. It is undoubtedly a vested interest but all the same it's very warming.

And so to London next day, grey and cold.

It has been a heavenly six months. Lots of it hard going – I'm fairly dead now, I find – but all of it worth it and all of it good to do. I'm very sad to know it's over and I dread the business of coping, without Ghulam or the sun to help, for I've grown soft in those ways. Reggie was at Gin's to welcome me. ENSA had sent us a car and a welfare worker to meet the train – for which top marks. She put Viola on the train for Boston, where she still is.

I find Dick in a nursing home, Noël in Paris, so I can't get much news of the show except that it starts rehearsing in June, plays Manchester in July and opens at the *Piccadilly* in August! Cyril [Ritchard] and Madge [Elliott] are to be in it, also Kay Walsh.[1] Dick to do music, Gladys [Calthrop] clothes. I am frankly alarmed.

Pa for lunch, looking bonnie and sweet. Reggie looks a bit done up with yet another cold. Both Thesigers longing for leave which will happen on the 23rd for all of us down at Tintagel. I've seen Harry who is wonderful; Ann [Holmes] who is a saint; Laura[2] who is an angel – Celia, who looks in good shape and very pretty.

Down to Midhurst yesterday for the night to see Dick. He looks far from well but was glad to see me, I think. I was delighted to see him, bless him.

---

[1] Kay Walsh: actress who trained in revue. In 1944 had appeared in Coward's film *This Happy Breed*.
[2] Laura Grenfell: step-sister of Reggie.

AFTERWORD

Afterword

It was in 1969 when Joyce was staying alone in New York, writing home to Reggie, that we first learn about Viola's illness.

Nov. 4th, 1969: Viola has some sort of 'thing' on her spine which accounts for the bad walking, and she has gone into hospital for tests and X-rays. Gin has cabled to say Viola was in the neurological ward of the Maudsley Hospital in Denmark Hill with a suspected growth on her spine, and that tests and X-rays were being done today, and she'd had a lumbar puncture. I gather Viola's walking got worse and worse and she was really terribly lame, and Peter insisted she saw a specialist. Knowing Viola, the last thing she'd want would be fuss, and if all goes well there won't be any from me. But if I thought it necessary I'd fly home to see her.

Nov. 6th: Gin is here, she spoke to Viola. It isn't her spine. Now they are looking at her brain. Oh! Gin says she was gay and said the rest was marvellous and doing her good.

Nov. 9th: I got a call through to Victor [Stiebel] just now. He had a long talk with Peter Tunnard and the result of the brain exam is that they think Vole has muscular dystrophy. Vic stressed it isn't cancer, it isn't a killer, it's slow. But it is a paralysis. It seems Vole has fallen down quite a lot but hasn't told anyone; that she has had a weakness in a wrist. It's as bloody as can be and the picture is clouded and difficult but all I can say is thank God we've got money. She can't go on living at the top of that building with Peter. She may be able to go on *coaching* but not performing – which means she won't be able to play the piano much; or what? Anyway, it's a nightmare. *She doesn't know yet*. Peter is shattered and emotional and Vic feels it should all be allowed to settle a little before darling Vole is told. The doctor will tell her with Peter present. Isn't it bloody?

Nov. 15th: I'm longing for home, dreading all there is to do. Still no word that Viola has been told. I daren't write freely till she has. There is to be another consultation and opinion. It is difficult not to feel agonised. She is such a solitary. Very difficult to help and get close to. She has been so independent, so self-sufficient and now this. And for a pianist to be deprived of her one way of expression.

Finally Viola's complaint was diagnosed as Motor Neurone Disease – a rare degenerative disease, from which the actor David Niven died, which affects the nerve cells linking the brain to the muscles, causing loss of movement in the hands, arms and legs and also severely impeding speech and swallowing. It usually results in total physical incapacitation (only the brain remains active) and death within eighteen months to five years: above all, there is no cure.

In 1970, writing to her pen-friend Katharine Moore, Joyce remarked:

I've got a dear friend, seven years younger than me, a brilliant musician at the top of her particular world, who has become disabled in less than two years. Can't walk, can't play any more – it is such an exercise in patience to watch her move, slowly, slowly, and remembering the quicksilver of her mind and her walking and running, one can guess a *little* what this new frustration must be like. It is *so* difficult to know how best to help. She is on endless lists for a housing association with accommodation for the disabled but

no one knows *when* or *where*. Today her beloved Stein-
way grand, a beautiful one, went to a singer's house,
where she can at least go and pat it from time to time,
but this was a very hard parting.

Dear K.M., I have a feeling you can imagine what an
agony all this is for a very sensitive, creative, out-of-
this-world creature, who was once so free and mer-
curial. *Almost* a genius in some ways.

In spite of all this I do *know* that all is well; that the
Kingdom of Heaven *is* within; that God is all good.

My friend is a *sort* of believer. Her pa was a clergyman and a *dear* man. But she has a sneaking feeling
God is a punisher, and she really does, I think, believe
in evil as a power and not, as I do, as the *absence* (or
illusion of absence) of Love. Love is always present; so
the evil is the mistaken view of what life is about and
for. And it can never have the last word for Truth *is*
Good and the original, the *only*.

In 1970, Viola went to live with Jean and Christopher
Cowan in their small house on the waterfront at Aldeburgh, where they made a home for her in the tiny
cottage attached to the back, always referred to as 'the
cabin' because it had once been a fisherman's cottage.
'She came to live with us in the last years of her life,'
recalls Jean Cowan, sitting in 'the cabin', with its two
arched windows looking on to a narrow patio with tubs
of blue and mauve hydrangeas, in front of a log fire, with
pots of geraniums against white walls, shelves of books,
paintings by Mary Potter, and a small door leading to the
attic bedrooms, which Viola was not able to use. 'Gradually she began to lose all movement in her legs, hands,
eventually her head. In the end she couldn't move at all.
Yet in spite of seeing her crumble gradually, there was
about her a luminosity, a distillation of all her qualities in
those last years. She had played for Peter Pears, played
duets with Ben [Britten] – she adored Ben – but it dis-
tressed her when she began to play wrong notes without

understanding why – and he would get cross with her. It was after that she began having the tests.'

Christopher Cowan had taken early retirement from the Foreign Office and ran a bookshop in Aldeburgh. There is a moving letter written by Viola to Christopher in awkward stumbling characters on a fragile piece of paper, dated simply March 1971:

> Sitting in my cabin on a fine silver morning while you stump off to work and earn, I have time to ponder on the realisation that it is a miracle and nothing less that I am sitting in my cabin on a fine silver morning while you stump off to work!
>
> I can't write silly thank-you letters for such huge gifts, but that you and Jean should dole out such things and make someone who belongs nowhere feel they belong somewhere is a thing not to be forgotten.

Her introversion, shyness, the separateness, may also have stemmed from the fact, as Jean Cowan observes, that 'she had an absolute thing that nobody loved her and that she belonged nowhere. In actual fact she was adored by countless numbers. Everyone fell madly in love with her. She was a creature of terrific moods, that is true. She and I used to have the most flaming rows. But she said, "I think I'm happier now than I have ever been in all my life." She didn't have to struggle any more. All her life she'd had the most enormous inferiority complex. "Do people say I'm a good musician?" she'd ask. Everyone said she was brilliant, Ben Britten, Imogen Holst, and so on. In the end she couldn't hold anything, not even hold her head up.'

During these years Joyce was incredibly generous, providing essential funds, unknown to Viola, and when Joyce died it was revealed that she had left in her will £10,000 towards the Viola Tunnard Memorial Trust, which provides scholarships for young musicians. Ironically, as so often happens, Joyce's deep devotion to, and love of Viola, was not wholly reciprocated. Joyce loved her as the daughter she never had, but Viola did not want to be mothered or possessed. Joyce would telephone daily to Aldeburgh to speak with Viola and there were times that Viola would refuse to speak to her. Yet once she learned of Joyce's own illness, the loss of an eye, which led to her retirement from the stage, she became remarkably loving and attentive towards Joyce. Writing to Jean Cowan on October 18th, 1971, Joyce says, 'I love her so very dearly and have felt so inadequate and useless. Now I am aware that this situation is in hand between us all who love her.'

In a later letter to Katherine Moore:

Just now I am full of thoughts about what Life is. My darling paralysed friend is now totally immobile except for her neck, and we are told it won't be very much longer. What I find a sort of miracle is that a rather diffident and complex character has dissolved into a wholly warm, appreciative, generous and grateful woman, with all her humour and high intelligence developing all the time.

This physical dwindling is so hard for her; she was like quicksilver, moved through the world, a room, a crowd, with a deftness that matched her beautiful playing of the piano. To be totally helpless must be the final lesson in humility, and oh, my word, she is learning it well.

She doesn't want my Christian Science teaching, because she thinks it is rude to God not to believe in matter. But the concept behind the wonders of flowers, music, words, mountains, light, etc., is the reality. The rest goes to dust. Even light seen by our limited view fades.

Next week I go to a concert in aid of 'Save the Children', in the Maltings at Snape, and we'll be at Aldeburgh where she lives with *marvellous* friends and a helper to care for her, and I can spend some time with her.

The last time I was with her we spent a quiet afternoon talking about the good times we had shared. We both knew she would soon be on her way. I said, 'I wish I could set you free.' By this time she did not find it easy to speak. There was a pause – and what she then said to me is the most precious thing she ever gave me: 'Perhaps I am free already.' I knew then that she had discovered something which I, too, was beginning to understand, and that is: no matter what happens to one's material body, it does not, cannot, touch the spiritual identity that is our eternal body.

Viola Tunnard died in July 1974. After her death Joyce wrote to Jean Cowan:

She has been a part of my life for so long and so closely that her absence is difficult to accept. But Jean, I owe her so much in the way of illumination and disciplines, all she is will stay for ever. Difficult, don't we know! Naughty, oh, yes! and her own worst enemy, *but* the guts, the character, the intelligence, the humour and the talent, all stand out like stars. I love her dearly and always have and it's a tribute to her that she always came back for more slaps! She was – unique, *utterly* – an original, it's a privilege to have known her so well, to admire so much in her. She looked so beautiful the last time I saw her. As I've said before, she always felt like my child to me, and that is why I am so grateful to you and Christopher for sharing your home, your time, and your love with that darling creature. She was so widely loved.

Letters poured in from the famous and from students. One from Vivien Asquith[1] reveals one aspect of the

---

[1] Vivien Asquith: daughter of Lady Evelyn Jones; a first cousin of Reggie.

generosity of the Cowans: 'I'll never forget Viola telling me how important it was to her to remain part of a real family life, gutsy and grumbly when people felt like it, each to each, perfectly natural. So she felt free with you to be bloody minded or beastly or whatever! She didn't have to put on an act!'

Writing again to Jean Cowan after Viola's death, Joyce says:

> I could go on and on about all my gratitude for all that you and Christopher have done. It is written in heaven. Viola knew it and was very grateful. She felt safe in her cabin and in your love, and the more I think of it the more amazing I know it to be that you two gave up so much of your privacy and freedom to do this loved thing.

On November 30th, 1979, Jean Cowan was to receive the following telegram from Reggie Grenfell: 'REGRET TO TELL YOU THAT JOYCE DIED TONIGHT. STOP. SHE DIED QUIETLY AND COMPLETELY AT PEACE. LOVE. REGGIE.'

After the war Joyce and Viola had done one more tour for the troops, beginning at Benghazi on December 18th, 1952, and ending on January 22nd, 1953 in Malta. This journal lacks the urgency and vividness of the wartime journals. The final entry, however, sums up much of what both women felt about the whole experience of entertaining the troops.

January 22nd, 1953: I hate endings. This has been a well worth job. Looked at backwards the discomforts and doubts recede. Instead there is the sound of singing and laughing and sun. The sight of rows of healthy faces, poinsettias, roses, Vole's face peering over the top of the piano at the end of a good concert.

Less than forty minutes. Over the Channel. I feel very messy and know that every garment I'm wearing is loaded with dust from Egypt and cigarette smoke from in here.

Later: We flew in to Stansted in Essex and when we got out of the plane the wonderful *green* smell of England met us as the doors were opened. A piece of newly turned earth beside the runway, full of growing smells, rich and exciting. Reggie was there to meet us. It was damply cold and there was no light. Egypt – the sun diminished.

THE VIOLA TUNNARD
MEMORIAL TRUST

TRAVEL BROADENS THE MIND

The ENSA *Sketch* written 1945 and performed by Joyce in Noël Coward's revue, *Sigh No More.*

Oh, do come in. You must be the one who 'phoned from the Newspaper Office and wanted to hear how two Tulse Hill girls had done their bit in the war. This is my great friend and the girl who went overseas with me to help entertain the troops, Doreen Le Mair. We've had many good laughs together, haven't we, Doreen? I expect she'll tell you all about it later on.

Well, you'd like to hear about the tour, wouldn't you, Mr Pool? Statistics as follows: we were away for over two years, we visited fifteen countries and I sang the Ave Maria over six hundred times. I do all Deanna Durbin's numbers. Well, we started in West Africa.

It was *West* Africa, wasn't it, Doreen? Yes, and you got your tom-tom for your friend's flat – he uses it as an occasional table. And from West Africa we went over to North Africa, and I shan't forget that in a hurry. I had to keep on singing 'The Holy City' for a Major in the Tank Corps who followed our show around until they took his tank away from him, foolish fellow.

Well, from North Africa, we went over to Malta. That's an island, you know. So of course it's mainly Navy. Oh, it's quite a cheery spot.

Then from Malta we went over to Sicily, and there wasn't much in the shops there. And from Sicily we went over to Italy, and in Italy I had a big thrill in hearing *La Bohème* done in its native tongue. And while we were in Italy a Wing-Commander I got to know rather well made me sing Handel's *Largo* for him by moonlight in the Forum at Rome. Doreen played for me on the accordion.

Well, I don't know what I'd say was the most popular item on the programme, do you, Doreen? I suppose some might say my Ave, but I think I preferred Doreen's Drummerette Dance. It's a novelty number and she does it against a backcloth depicting a huge toy drum, and she wears just a little red, white and blue brassière and panties and a pillbox hat at a jaunty angle. It's very sophisticated, it's quite West End. The boys used to whistle like anything. I must admit they whistled at my Ave too, if I say it as shouldn't.

Well, from sunny Italy we went over to Egypt, and in Cairo we were very much fêted and spoiled. I saw the Sphinx seven or eight times with different friends. And while we were in Cairo we managed to get our costumes freshened. You see, I only wore white in the show – it's more suitable for my type of song, isn't it? Just a very simple, white, draped gown. Very simple, very draped.

Someone rather special said I put him in mind of a lily in it. But he was rather prejudiced. And he did have the most unusual gift of second sight. It was really very remarkable.

Well, I mustn't talk too much about myself because I know you want to hear about the tour. Well, we went across the desert and down to Basra, then over to India, Land of Magic and Mystery! Oh, and problems too. I heard all about the problems from a Brigadier I got to know up in Dacca, but I'd no idea till I read Beverley Nichols's little book just what really did go on out there. Oh, it's very worrying. I mean to say if you stop and think. I'm a terrible thinker, I can't stop thinking, I'm thinking all the time, it's awful.

Doreen, why don't you tell this nice person a bit about yourself? You know, you're not a bit like a newspaper man, Mr Pool, you're so quiet. But then I do rattle on, don't I, and neither you nor poor Doreen can get a word in edgewise. I'll tell you about Doreen. Not only does she dance but she plays the accordion as well, gipsy style, up and down the stage, or, when we're in canteens, in and out of the tables – when they've got the tables. Oh, it's a lovely gift. I wish I had it.

With me it's rather different. I think it must be the music. They seem to more or less put me on a pedestal. I don't know why . . .

No, I don't think we had any unusual incidents. Well, we did get to know a rather rich Rajah up in the hills. He called me Little Flower and gave me an electric iron. I think he'd been to Cambridge or somewhere like that.

Oh, yes, we saw our boys everywhere we went. They looked marvellous – lovely and sunburnt. I think they'd like to get back though, judging by what they said.

Oh, there's Auntie tinkling for elevenses. That's a temple bell she's tinkling. A Chindit gave it to me. Would you like some elevenses?

Good, and I can show you my Den, and I'll make Doreen talk. I'll make her tell you all about the time we were in Greece and she had to do a tap dance on the Parthenon.

INDEX